# A WANDERING STUDENT

SIR BERNARD PARES

# *A* WANDERING STUDENT

## THE STORY OF A PURPOSE

SYRACUSE UNIVERSITY PRESS

IN COOPERATION WITH HOWELL, SOSKIN, PUBLISHERS

58366
920-P228w

*To my Darling Dochka*

ANNIE

*with love and gratitude*

Routs and discomfitures, rushes and rallies,
Bases attempted, and rescued, and won

—E. E. BOWEN: *Harrow School Song*

# Contents

# Preface

THE STUDENT wandered about the world much like his prototype of the middle ages, looking everywhere for what he wanted; but his wanderings were more and more concentrated on a single purpose, of which this book is the record. When his wanderings began, the English attitude toward Russia was a mixture of complete ignorance and an unreasoning fear, not at all unlike that of many Americans of the present time. Only, then the word to describe it was Russophobia and now it is Communism.

I grew up in this atmosphere in the fortress city of Portsmouth among half-pay Colonels retired from service in India, who were all certain that Russia was our natural enemy. I set myself to find out whether this was so, and the further I went, the more clear it became that the question was still in the balance. There was no provision whatever in our educational system for the study of Russia; and as time went on, I also set myself to fill this gap, without which we should be quite unarmed for any crisis where the question might become vital.

I saw very early the extent to which our information about Russia was permeated with German influences, and I understood well that, from Bismarck onwards, it was a settled policy of Germany to keep England and Russia in permanent misunderstanding. Before the great work of Mackenzie Wallace, this domination was almost absolute. The Poles among us and the Russian revolutionary refugees also ranked among our chief informants and they were heavily biased. Why should we not have our own knowledge at first hand?

The Germans planted in Russia very well understood the reasons for the presence of an English inquirer; and though their relations with me were always quite correct, the inherent antagonism in our purposes was fully realized. Here was someone trying to break the ring of their vested interest. They claimed the right to manage our relations with Russia as well as their own. It was taken as almost an offense if we were to shake hands with Russia over the head of Germany. Besides, the Germans had deep roots in the Russian system of government and shared fully in its unpopularity as agents of authority; this was true even of the German stewards on the estates of absentee Russian landlords. They were against all changes, and above all against any reform which would bring the Russian people into the management of its own affairs. On the other hand, nearly all Russians welcomed any British initiative as an alternative to Germany, which gave them at least some measure of free choice in their foreign friendship.

I was at first almost alone in my venture and always followed my own course, with no regard for British policy. In the course of time I came upon various colleagues working also almost alone towards the same end; and this in itself formed us into a brotherhood. These were scholars, who left the initiative of any organized efforts to me. For instance, I founded university schools of Russian study in Liverpool and later in London; I brought the leaders of the Russian Duma to London, and took a return party of distinguished Englishmen to Russia; and I lived for over two years in the front line of the Russian Army in the First World War. In war time, I was sometimes in government service. Twice I was dismissed from it; in each case, I believe, because I saw something which it was not thought desirable to see. In each case, amends were made to me later. In the period which led to the second World War, when the factor of Russian help was almost completely disregarded in England, I must have been almost the only representative of average non-party English opinion with whom that fine Ambassador, Ivan Maisky, had frequent contact.

Well! the thing which I hoped for has happened twice. In both World Wars Russia was with us; and in the second she contributed most perhaps the greatest sacrifice to the common victory; and now no durable peace is thinkable without her friendship. So that it is two up for our side, but each time only by German mistakes; and now, as we shall see, we have come around again to just the same problem, perhaps in a more baffling form than ever, and there has been no crisis more serious than that which we now face.

I am grateful to my friend and publisher, Jonathan Cape, for allowing me to make free use of materials contained in *My Russian Memoirs,* published by him in 1931. I have also sometimes returned to matters covered in greater detail in my earlier books on Russia—*Russia and Reform* (Constable, 1907) *Day by Day with the Russian Army* (Constable, 1915) and *Moscow Admits a Critic* (Thos. Nelson, 1936).

I am grateful to my friend and student, Hans Rogger for the index and for much other skilled help in connection with this book.

# CHAPTER I

## Early Days
## (To 1894)

### JOHN PARES AND HIS FLOCK

THE MOST profound influence in my life has been my Father. I think of him as a great fountain of life, and he has grown upon me through the years. I don't think his heart was ever older than 25. There was a contagious warmth about everything he said or did, and I can never think of him as dead.

He was a big, strong-bearded man, normal and healthy in all his instincts, which he always expressed with a boyish vigor. For instance, one day at breakfast, on opening a circular from a money lender, he hurled it fiercely to the floor. "Faugh!" he muttered (I've never heard anyone else say 'Faugh'), "he'll ruin you body and soul!" I was a small boy then, and the effect on me was lasting. "Ruin you body and soul?" I thought, "I'll have nothing to do with that gentleman," and I never have. That was the way that Father taught us many a lesson.

He was very naive, sometimes with a suggestion of Pickwick. I was strongly reminded of the respect that we had for him in all his amusing little ways and sayings, when long afterwards I saw and read Mr. Clarence Day's "Life With

1

Father." There was something conquering about both of them. When he was moving from some summer resort, you might see a little crowd instinctively gathering around him to see how "the old gentleman" got off successfully; it had the interest of a campaign.

"Very thick on the ground today!" he would say, gazing round the table: he had ten children, but who had been responsible for that? Or else it was, "I'm always either mobbed or deserted." "Ten children, and not one black sheep!" he would say; and some one of us would mutter, "Ah! how do you know that?" When he was asked to stand as candidate in the Liberal interest for Portsmouth, he would answer: "I've got ten reasons against it." Or sometimes, in special confidence, he would say, "I don't want the whole family in full cry over this!"

He would drive triumphantly through the gates of Portsmouth Dockyard with protesting policemen gesticulating on either side; he carried us through too, and we felt a certain pride in being with him. At Lords Cricket Ground, where he was a constant and enthusiastic visitor, he would entertain his friends freely; we all had a proud confidence in what we used to call "the fat purse." Once, at the Oxford and Cambridge match, he noticed a new rule saying that only Members of the famous MCC might lunch in the Member's dining room. Father had four healthy sons in waiting. This was always the country parson's day, and a hungry old clergyman hoped to attach himself to the party. "None but Members today," warned the old ex-professional on duty (all the "pros" loved Father). "Yes," said Father, as if agreeing, "Members and members' sons," and strode through, followed by all of us, but conveniently shedding on the way the hungry old clergyman, who couldn't have passed under that arbitrary classification. "Members' sons" became a catchword meaning that with Father we could get in anywhere.

Father could recite long stretches of Latin verse which he had not seen since he was at school, and always with spirit. He was full of excellent stories, which he told with the greatest heartiness, often illustrated by gestures and always in the same words. We boys were very naughty, and would say them in a whisper just in front of him, to see if we had got them right. We thought we knew most of them, and we had already a good fund to repeat to others; but in his old age he started producing a new lot, just as good and, as far as we knew, just as true. Many of these related to his boyhood on Grandfather's estate in Derbyshire; and the "plain man," with all his little simplicities usually had a big place in them. For instance, there was the huntsman of the Quorn hounds, who on passing Grace Dieu Monastery, generally murmured "the Oly of Olies" which according to Father, was an expression of native and sincere reverence. Or there was the more critical farmer who, after a lengthy sermon, said, "I notice with the parsons it's the same as with the cows: when they give down much, it's mostly wishy-washy stuff."

Grandfather, if I'm not wrong, was Liberal Member for Leicester at the passing of the first great Reform Bill in 1832, about the time Father was born, and he himself was a devoted follower of Mr. Gladstone for the whole of his life. For all these early Liberals, the world was young and they went out to conquer it, which they did with zest and to absolute victory, till as far as liberty and justice were concerned, there was nothing left to fight for. Interwoven with the Gladstone tradition was the memory of the colony of distinguished exiled Liberal patriots from Italy, driven out by Austrian persecution. One of the most distinguished of them, Santa Rosa, was, I believe, public librarian hard by in Nottingham, another was received in Grandfather's house to teach a brilliant daughter. One, Sir Antonio Panizzi, became Director of the British Museum.

Father was the third son of a big family—the third son
to whom Grandfather gave the name John. The first two
died in infancy, and Grandfather wrote a little poem about
them, but he stuck to this name, and the third John had
a long and full life, to over eighty.

Father's Liberalism, when we younger boys got to know
him best, was by then of a strongly conservative brand; he
would not allow a Tory paper in the house. It got mixed up
with his memories of scholarship and his strong High Church
views. Disraeli, for him, was an uneducated man, and he
was really annoyed when we produced, with the aid of a
circulating library, a number of his Latin quotations in the
House of Commons, some of them extraordinarily apt. I always detested "party," and when I was about 20, I told Father
I couldn't agree with all his views. "You seem to think," I
said, "that anyone is morally worse for being a Conservative." "Yes," he said boldly, "Jesus Christ was a Liberal,"
which was undoubtedly true. He was a little hurt at my
protest, but he always respected it afterwards and would say
affectionately, "Now here, old boy, is something I expect we
agree about." As time went on, and when I witnessed in
Russia just the same movement for justice and freedom which
he and so many others had seen through to complete success
in England, I rallied more and more to those early memories.

Father got his Liberalism largely from Frederick Denison
Maurice and Charles Kingsley and was always loyal to it.
Kingsley, it may be remembered, advised anyone to make
friends with a working man, which at that time sounded
rather original, but with Father it was a habit. He was a
county magistrate for Gosport, at that time really almost a
slum of Portsmouth, and he was very constant to his duties.
Once when he was absent, a colleague on the Bench came
down on purpose to acquit a young naval officer who when
drunk had knocked down a policeman. Father was furious.

The next session he was in the Chair, and a "down-and-out" was brought up for much the same offense. "The Bench acquits you," said Father, "to show that there is one law in England for the rich and the poor."

Father had an amazing memory of the liveliest kind and an inexhaustible store of real and useful knowledge, with practical resource for meeting any difficulty. In his early days he had made a number of driving tours, and it was almost impossible to catch him as to the whereabouts of any small market town in England. "Oh yes," he would say, giving the locality, and would add a whole lot of local details as to the neighboring country seats, hounds, and historical connections. On his early marriage he settled at first in a second son's estate (he was really a seventh child, and I his seventh); but he soon disposed of it to live in London and to take up any inconspicuous task of public service. He read law and found this invaluable afterwards. He used to speak emphatically of the value of the Charity Organization Society, which took the greatest pains to identify swindlers and warn charitable persons against them.

As the family increased, Father leased a succession of country houses. The last of these, where I was born, was in the vale of Albury in Surrey. I constantly return to it, for I know no country of more satisfying beauty. There ran the old Pilgrim's Road of Chaucer. Travellers making for Becket's Shrine at Canterbury from Normandy and Southampton could use the level, natural causeway of the Hog's Back, with a commanding view of any approaching danger. They would halt at Guildford at the crossing of the Wey, which at this point breaks through the North Downs to the Thames; here were two little chapels, one at the foot of the Hog, the other St. Martha's, a little lady perched on a northward wooded outpost of the lovely Surrey hills. Legend—but it was only legend—said that Bunyan came this way and took from the Pilgrim's Road his title

for the Pilgrim's Progress. Shalford Fair, on the flats around
the winding river, was Vanity Fair; St. Martha's, with its
steep southern scarp, was the Hill Difficulty; and Newland's
Corner on the bare skyline of the North Downs, with a
reputed view of eleven counties, was the Delectable Mountains. An explorer of this legend, asking the name of a
farm in a wooded cleft on the slope, was answered: "Doubt-
ing Castle."

Martin Tupper, that poet of painful platitudes whom
Queen Victoria so much admired, lived in Albury; and here
too in those days there were twelve "Apostles," quiet country gentlemen who had delved too deeply into the Book of
Revelations and believed they were appointed to hand over
the kingdom of Christ at the Last Day, as the first twelve
had received it from the hands of their Master. Mr. Cardale,
who was St. Peter, wore a short Petrine beard and was prepared to seal the limited number of 144,000 elect. "They
don't keep us out of heaven," said our robust-minded Rector, "they only say we are to black their boots when we get
there." According to their followers, the so-called Irving-
ites, the twelve were not to die; but after the last had gone
the way of nature, the sect remained and still continues
"waiting for a new revelation," in which, I suppose, they
don't differ from anyone else. All round our house there
were little wooded knolls; and on one or another of these
Father would read to us of a Sunday some tale of Christian
faith and triumph. Sometimes, great clouds of smoke would
cover the sky. That, we were told, was the smoke of
London.

The family of ten had a curious order: boy, four girls,
three boys, girl, boy. Later, on Christmas day we would march
into dinner in six couples, father and mother coming last.
The big Father was very happy among his four eldest girls,
who called him "the Gentlemanly Bear." His authority met
no testing till the advent of three riotous boys, and then,

in my opinion, Father joined the rebels and became one of them. I can remember how his excitement attracted members of the crowd, as he sat in his coach watching a football cup-tie. "That old gentleman," said someone, "has got a lot of money on this match." What he had really had was four sons, two on each side.

Lance was the eldest of us three and he was the natural leader to me and Basil in all our incessant escapades. To me, indeed, he was my big brother at each of my schools, at Cambridge, and ever after. On our birthdays he and I always exchanged taunting verses. Long and powerful, he was a glorious center forward for his County: the old kind, not lying off for chances, but thrusting his way through his foes with the ball at his toes and scoring with a cannon ball shot from 30 yards out or more. "The deadly side-stepping and shooting of G.L."–so wrote of him William Pickford, President of the English Football Association. Pickford tells how one long shot of his knocked over a boy standing behind the goal. I can remember his winning a cup-tie against a tempestuous headwind by twice running the whole length of the ground and scoring each time. Basil was like a twin to me; he was a splendid half-back, master of the old amateur shoulder charge, now abolished, and would always dispose of anyone who interfered with me. Between us we could make a good nucleus for a whole team.

Of my sisters the eldest, Alie, was a natural leader, and took the place of my mother after her death as the head of the rest of us till her own death at 80. I saw her the day before, as I was starting for Russia, and looking at her fine clear features, apparently still quite youthful, and her hair which had not turned, I said, "Alie, you are 26." The next day she was gone. My second sister, Elfie, with wonderful sweetness, wisdom and humor, handled Father in his last years as if he were a big boy, which indeed he was. She was herself one of the first of us to go. She had always asked me to be with her through her last night. I was back from the Russian front, and lay on the floor by her bed, holding her hand through the long hours as she battled with the fierce pain. Later I was to see nearly all the rest out. There was not a break or chink in the closeness of our family unity. Basil sent me in America a letter which I got, together with the telegram announcing his death, "To a beloved brother, the last of a glorious band."

When the ten children had all arrived, Father, with the keen backing of my Mother, who did far more to guide him than we ever realized in her lifetime, moved down to Portsmouth, to see what he could do there for others. He was well off, with no actual profession, and put his heart into anything that was worth doing and was waiting for someone to do it. Besides his work on the Gosport Bench, he was Chairman of the town hospital and a governor of the big Grammar School; he was one of the Bishop's Commissioners for Portsmouth; but most of his work had no particular name to it and was done entirely on the quiet. He himself ran a little Convalescent Home for men and boys which he visited every day. He also supported a home for children taken from evil houses by legislation which he himself had helped to promote. He was able to send them there as a magistrate. He was the fearless and outspoken backer of every good cause and every brave man. Archbishop Lang, when he left his parish at Portsmouth, introduced Father to his successor with the words, "Here's the man who's behind everything good that is being done in Portsmouth." He saw through their troubles those bereaved in the submarine and other accidents of the experiments of that time. He was a personal friend, on a footing of equality, with every engine driver in Portsmouth. He called on them on Sundays, always taking a son with him, not to tell them any views of his own, political or religious, but to enjoy their company.

Father belonged in full to that great period of hope and endeavor which bred him. He gave to all of us a wonderful zest for life. "It's a P.A. day today," he would say, which meant "It's a pleasure to be alive." It was a great and wonderful world, and every one in it had something good, presented some special kind of human interest. I don't think that there was one of us ten who did not get from him a natural instinct and habit of talking on terms of perfect equality and mutual interest with anyone of any age or of any calling. I have sometimes seen how others envied us and instinctively set about seeing if they could do the same.

Almost to the end, he made about a thousand miles a year on his tricycle, followed by a pet bull terrier, and many were the affectionate eyes that followed him as he went by. In the first year of the First World War, he would stand on his balcony waving to the troops as they passed. The guns of the fortress kept silence as he lay dying.

## Two Peculiar "Prep" Schools
### Ancient and Modern

In a former royal residence, with the Victorian tradition written all over it, old Dr. Gates conducted a well-established school of a rigorous but healthy type, to which I followed my brother Lance and two cousins at nine. Old Tom was a kindly gentleman with healthy red cheeks and white hair. Mrs. Gates, with Victorian trimmings, was his trusty helpmate. Once a boy named Rivers with a very wide mouth, whom we used to call "Crocodile," came into breakfast straight from a flogging with much too challenging a smile. He caught the loyal attention of old Mrs. Gates. "Rivers," she said, "it seems the Doctor hasn't given you enough. Go back and ask him *with my love* to give you five more!"

Old Tom was assisted by Old Bill, who taught the smallest boys and was believed by us to be his elder brother. Schoolboy legend explained this. Old Bill had been a "rich merchant," and was captured by Brigands in the Black Forest. The Brigands were apparently misinformed as to the limits of Old Bill's wealth and demanded an impossibly high ransom. The difference was paid by Old Tom, who exacted in return an agreement that Old Bill should teach the lowest form in his school for the rest of his life.

Old Bill was up to the conventional tricks of silly little boys. His chair was on a narrow raised platform, and Old Bill would habitually raise it before sitting down, to see that it had not been tilted over the edge of the platform. It was here that took place what in the circumstances I consider the bravest deed that I have seen in my life. A fresh-faced boy named Fairbairn rushed into the room and shouted, "Old Bill, you're a fool!" We all stood aghast at such reckless courage. There was no escape, only to the walled playground and no further. He was promptly pursued and appropriately administered.

There was a terrible black book, three entries in which automatically brought a flogging. "Old Harry," a fierce bearded man, son of Old Tom, had a fancy for entering you five times at once, which took you through one flogging and two-thirds of the way towards another.

We lived under Spartan rule. Boys who failed to finish their portions of the "resurrection" pie served on Saturdays were called up about tea time and made to eat the rest, which by that time was cold and greasy. In summer a stimulus was provided in the shape of a pottle of strawberries, which remained unapproachable till this was done. In this school to ask for a glass of water was to ask a favor. This discipline taught us realization of the world as we found it and patience in finding our own way. For all that, the school was thoroughly healthy; we never knew of evil there. The teaching too was stern but thoroughly sound, and the grounding which we got served us faithfully later. No one did more to prove that than Walter Headlam who was my schoolmate there.

From this school I was transferred in my twelfth year to a crammer who had a high reputation for successes in scholarships at Harrow. His methods were original. His scholarship class he called his "prize pigs" or his "favorites." They were encouraged in every way to work hard. Money prizes were offered for the best Latin prose of the week and later charged in the bill as "rewards." The winner could invite his particular friends to a party at the best tea-shop downtown. Lance was very much our prize pig, having been *"proxime accessit"* at the last Harrow examination. He got his scholarship all right, and so later on, did I, as second to Walter Headlam; and though we all saw through the headmaster's quaint methods, I still have a kindly thought of the sporting crammer who was the first and last person to "tip" me two whole golden sovereigns at once.

## H.M.B. of Harrow

### A Great Headmaster

At the first roll-call in Dr. Montagu Butler's house at Harrow, I felt as if I were in the presence of Socrates. He had a mild, firm, bearded face, rather tired but with a natural authority. Dr. Butler belonged to Harrow. His father, like him, had been Headmaster there, from 1805 to 1839; indeed he was headmaster to Lord Byron and was the subject of one of Byron's lampoons. Our Dr. Butler had taken over the duties of Headmaster from him at 27, and had already held Harrow high in honor for twenty-one years. He was

now beginning his last five years and his hold over the School
was absolute.

It was equally so in the House. There were over sixty
of us, and the boys themselves recognized a natural authority
of their own. It had long stabilized itself by tradition, resting on two bases, place in the School and–still more
important–seniority in the House. The Sixth Form were
a body apart, whose authority was corporate, in no way
dictatorial. The Fifth Form was "republic"–free lances, neither under authority nor holding it. Below that came the
Fags, organized with system and order. If you were asked
to look after a small newcomer, you took him as your Fag,
and so guaranteed him against any oppression from other
sides. He brought up your breakfast, and answered your call
to take it away. Every boy knew what was expected of him,
and for how long.

A Scholar travelled up the school very fast; and of my
five years, nearly the last three were spent in the Upper Sixth,
under this most inspiring teacher. In a word, he breathed
public spirit into generations of Harrow boys. The curriculum for classical scholars was sternly and inescapably classical. The French lessons were a riotous entertainment, the
mathematical perfunctory, the scientific an unmeaning drill.
Even the classics included no archaeology and hardly any
history, the subject to which I already knew that I was gravi-
tating. I have often thought since, that this dreary routine
had a good deal to do with the distance between masters
and boys, especially in the lower forms of the school (all this
is completely altered now). It was the masters' duty to make
us do the work, and at that time many were schoolmasters
because they themselves had been trained in the classics and
didn't see what else they could do. We on our side evaded
in any way we could, not with direct lying, but any other way
that offered.

Dr. Butler made some wonderful translations of passages of the Bible into Homeric verse. There was another side on which he was almost unique, and it was here that he found his best opportunity to instill public spirit into us. He knew by heart the quotations in Latin made in the House of Commons and the occasions for them. With an air of mystery he would send for a book, read out the whole passage and then explain the occasion. This was about all we got of English History, but it certainly left its mark on us.

Looking back, I feel that Dr. Butler was always teaching and forming us, and in a way, even forming himself too. He was accused of affectation, but his son Jem, who wrote his life later, produced from his father's own diary much harsher criticism of himself than anyone else would have made of him, almost as if anticipating and silencing in advance the worst that the hardest critic would say. Sometimes it seemed as if this kindliest and most generous of men had encased himself in a kind of armor which none of his pupils would be able to penetrate. He could annihilate our feeble excuses with mordant comments; he was our master not merely by his office but by intellect. One of his acutest critics, a former Head-Boy, invented a whole series of the wittiest imaginary dialogues, illustrating how impossible it was "to score off Butler." To do so you would have to arrange a packed chorus, for instance in a railway carriage, who would persist in failing to see the point of any of his crushing repartees. The last of these imaginary dialogues was a monologue. It was a masterpiece. Butler drowning: "Strange! it appears that I am going to the bottom!" Duller boys, completely foiled, came out furious from his presence. All this defensive armor he laid aside completely when he resigned as Headmaster. And from that time on, he passed more and more into a timeless and absolute simplicity, in which his kindness had its full and natural play.

Dr. Butler, though not a wealthy man, was nothing less than munificent to any cause associated with the School. Harrow had no endowment, and for all the school needs the Headmaster, himself giving a shining example, had to address himself to the generosity of the Old Boys, which never failed him. This, after he had himself left Harrow, was the occasion of one of his wittiest speeches. At a Harrow Dinner of Old Boys, his successor had to warn the company that our treasured cricket fields were not really ours and might be bought for building. Speakers were few and distinguished at these meetings, but someone jumped up to inveigh against the Governors of the School and himself offered "to head the list of subscriptions." There was a general sense of offense. The only remaining speaker, as always, was Dr. Butler. He said: "Someone whose name I did not quite catch said that he would head the list of subscriptions with— I'm getting rather deaf now—was it a thousand pounds?" It was felt that justice had been done.

Several of his speeches lived in the memory. He adorned his tribute to a former British Minister to China by delicately recalling his schoolboy excursion with fireworks on the night of Guy Fawkes' Day (November 5) "with the result that as the 6th of November dawned, he exchanged the Upper Shelf for the Lower." At a dinner given him on reaching 80, he looked round at the thatchless skulls of contemporaries who were still left, to exclaim, "It is a sight for bears!" Once he was honoring the achievement by the famous Indian cricketer, Prince Ranjitsinhji of his "40th century." He quoted Napoleon's speech to his men in Egypt, "From yonder pyramids forty centuries look down upon you!"; he continued, "You Sir, if I am rightly informed, look down on forty centuries." He was equally neat in his delicate phrasing when dismissing a troublesome visitor. Someone came down to Harrow to arrange for a railway to pass through the cricket field. "You had better," said the

Headmaster, "go and see the Senior Trustee, the Honorable Robert Grinstom (a famous figure of Harrow cricket renowned for his roughness), and if I were you," said Dr. B., as the visitor was closing the door, "I should see that the interview took place on the *ground* floor."

With silvery voice and faultless tone and gesture, he seemed able to say things which no one else would have dared, but in his farewell to the School in his last sermon, which I shall never forget, he could not trust himself to finish in his own words, and in a voice breaking with devotion to Harrow he repeated the last verses of the 122nd Psalm: "Oh pray for the peace of Jerusalem; they shall prosper that love thee. Peace be within thy walls, and plenteousness within thy palaces. For my brethren and companions' sakes I will wish thee prosperity. Yea, because of the House of the Lord our God, I will seek to do thee good."

I feel sure that most of us who came directly under this powerful influence asked themselves earnestly how they could best serve their community. One question, instinctive enough to me living among so many Anglo-Indian families in Portsmouth, was whether the call was not to India. I thought often of it, but never seriously accepted it; my feeling was that our whole position there was a false one, to which one would not succeed in giving any real durability. Another field, natural enough to any pupil of Dr. Butler, was the House of Commons. I never considered it, except to dismiss it. One would sit on a back bench for endless futile hours, having to vote as one was expected, till perhaps one might get a moment's fleeting attention for the cause that he cared for. It would be far more effective and far more fun to go and look after it outside. Least of all did I admire the politician who was ready to take any post if it gave him increased consequence.

Later one of my school fellows, not at Harrow but at my first "prep" school, reminded me that even there I had said

I meant to study Russia. I can recall, amid the sporting memories of the Crimean War, a feeling of exhilaration over the visit of a Russian battleship to Portsmouth, and especially the vigor of the comradely challenge, which the ship's band brought into the playing of our national anthem. Life in a fortress constantly suggested the possibility of war.

I had eight years under Dr. Butler, his five last at Harrow and three of his first years as Master of Trinity College, Cambridge. He was a magnificent host and entertainer—once, according to "Punch," for a goodly section of the army, and never was the prestige of the College higher than in his reign. It was a long and golden autumn to his life. I saw him several times in his last days. He took me into his garden during the First World War. "Here is where I parted with my three soldier sons," he said, and speaking of the second —there must have been fifty years between them, for they were children of his second marriage—he added with an amazing simplicity, "I reverence Gordon. He has something pastoral about him." Gordon was lost to him very soon after. The old father collected his son's school books and put them round him in his bedroom. At our last meeting—he was well over 80—he said to me, "They tell me I shall simply break up, but till then, friend, we go on."

## E.E.B. AND HARROW SONGS

In my first week at Harrow there was, as usual, house-singing, for we had community singing once a week in every House about forty years before the nation again took to it; and there was the inimitable John Farmer, this time to teach us another new song which he had composed to words of E.E.B. Those words have stayed with me all my life. Long afterwards, in a single year, three old Harrow boys —Harrovians all their lives are boys, not men—wrote three different books, and each book took its motto from a different verse of this song. I was one of them, and my verse was this. The song pictures a rather lonely small boy doing his "prep" and looking over, as he could do from our House or from E.E.B.'s, at the twinkling lights of Hampstead across the vale.

> Good night! Sleep and so may ever
> Lights half seen across a murky lea,
> Child of hope and courage and endeavor,
> Gleam a voiceless benison on thee.

Later when I pored for two years over Plato at Cambridge, I got to know better the meaning of the "lights half seen across a murky lea"—the true forms that stood behind their imperfect earthly presentations. And later still, this verse was the key to my whole study of Russia, where so often the real thing remains unseen. "The things that are seen are temporal, and the things that are not seen are eternal"; and the whole of life should be a constant effort to see them.

E.E.B. was Edward E. Bowen, the first founder, I believe, of a Modern Side in a great Public School. He had a slim form and wore a short beard. He was a tireless walker; he liked someone from Harrow to walk each year in 24 hours the 55 miles between Cambridge and London. He himself once attempted Cambridge to Oxford, which was more like 85, in the same time limit, and he is said to have collapsed just outside Magdalen Bridge, Oxford.

His sphinx-like face with the quizzical eyes, inscrutable but all-seeing, was like one sculptured out of stone. He was always on the alert, and no one could foresee his quaint and various ways. He was said to have sat in the bay-window of our beautiful Vaughan Library at the top of the Hill, with a powerful telescope, writing down, as they passed through a hole in a distant hedge, the names of the boys who had gone over to a forbidden race meeting. He was the inventor of a lightning-like roll-call which only he could take to perfection, where the School was ranged in fives, each five with a "shepherd" who was trusted to report all absentees; they don't try it now.

Bowen was a poet of the first order. The best known of his songs is of course "Forty Years On" (1872), but many of the best came out year by year while I was a boy in the school (1880 to 1885). They were real poetry; and over and over again a given line would come back to one just when he was in a tight place as almost proverbial wisdom. "For what you must you can!"–that of itself would carry one through an emergency. Or take the line in "Underneath the Briny Sea" where Bowen imagines us all as fishes in an ideal Harrow.

> "Learning unworked for is just as well forgot"

One might not notice it as he sang it, but how much of wisdom there is in those few words!

Once a daring and ungifted imitator wrote a foolish song about the boy who united all the talents of work and play. Bowen, who had been dormant for some time, came out of his shell and showed what the absolutely mediocre boy got from Harrow.

> They glide, the months of worry and work,
>   Of desk and floor and grass,
> *And till you trust them, fright the soul,*
>   *And as you trust them, pass.*

There must have been in all something like fifty of these songs. Anyhow, we had, each term, an hour for the school to sing nothing else. This hour was simply called "Songs," and there was always plenty of choice. They illustrate every tradition of the Hill, from its foundation by Queen Elizabeth through Rodney, Peel, Byron, etc., or again any phase of study, sometimes with extravagant fancies—such as "She was a Shepherdess Oh So Fair" who will only marry "the boy who gets the Gregory Prize." But the substance of Bowen's message is contained in the last lines of "Forty Years On," which is recognized as *the* school song and is sung in many other schools. A base is a goal at Harrow football.

> God give us bases to guard or beleaguer,
> Games to play out whether earnest or fun
> Fights for the fearless and goals for the eager
> Twenty and thirty and forty years on.

E.E.B.'s irreplaceable partner was J.F.–John Farmer, who set all his songs to music. He was a bit of a pirate and raided the *Kommersbuch,* the rich treasury of German students' songs, which are unquestionably the best in the world. On occasion he even took without acknowledgment. His great art was to set us distances which we could cover if we tried–"For what you must you can." At Harrow it was bad form not to sing, and bad form to shout; every one just put out his full voice, and hence the rousing effect of the chapel services. House singing with John Farmer was the liveliest entertainment. He exuded humor and heartiness, with his sallies and impromptu nicknames, which seemed to stick.

Bowen had a wonderful House at the very top of the Hill, for which he also wrote special songs. I think the boy who best repaid him in his later career was the outstanding historian, George Trevelyan, who many years afterwards went on to fill the same post which Dr. Butler took on leaving Harrow, as Master of Trinity College, Cambridge. I wrote him at the time some lines which are printed in the Appendix.

I saw most of Bowen after I left. He had walked over most of the more famous modern battlefields in Europe with maps which he sometimes lent me. At the northern channel at Lobau Island on the Danube, which was so critical for Napoleon's fortunes after his defeat at Aspern in 1809, I found in pencil the note, "Only three feet when I bathed here"; that was how Bowen explored battlefields. He still played school football, a very muddy and rough-and-tumble game, in his fifties and even sixties. And he died riding his bicycle up a steep hill in France. "Poor Bowen," said someone on hearing the news. "Poor Bowen, indeed!" said an old Head-Boy of the School indignantly. "Hit hard, all round the wicket and got clean bowled!"

## WALTER HEADLAM

Among my close friends in Dr. Butler's House were two, among others, who later won distinction. Walter Headlam had also been at my first private school with me. He was a classical scholar such as only comes to a given school in ten years. The curriculum seemed to have been made for him; but he had a complete and conquering contempt for it, which always seemed to me its condemnation, as it was at that time. Instead of preparing his Latin lessons he would spend his time writing Greek Alchaics. He was even "turned down" in the Upper Sixth time after time; once when it happened to be a piece he liked and he had put it into delicate verse, for he was a graceful minor poet. In maturity of criticism he stood without question higher than the headmaster himself and he subjected him to a form of intellectual teasing which must have been an almost unique experience for Dr. Butler. Headlam was one of the first persons who ever taught me to think clearly.

The example of Walter Headlam started me on a rebellion against the system of classical studies of my time. Another Harrovian, Lord Byron, had long since written:

"Who scarcely skilled an English line to pen,
Scans Attic metres with a critic's ken.

Yet prizing Bentley's Brunck's or Porson's note
More than the verse on which the critic wrote!"

(Byron: *Thoughts Suggested by a College Examination*)

Evidently, the system had remained since his time when
boys from wealthy families could complete their education
by a Grand Tour of Europe. It is hard to understand how
it had continued, if it were not that the teachers had got
into a groove and could not get out. And indeed it was a
groove. If, like Headlam or myself, you had won a scholarship in the Classics, that was how you had to go on; and
it was the same at the University, so that in all I had nine
years of it. Also, though it was a contradiction to common
sense, seniority and therefore authority in the School depended largely on your ingenuity in Latin verse, and there
were always a number of small undersized monitors like
him and me.

At King's College, Cambridge, which only receives
Honors students, Headlam was a practical certainty for the
Regius Professorship of Greek. At one time he blossomed
out into a horseman, but later he went into complete reclu-
sion. His floor was covered with various English turns for
phrases of Aeschylus, between which I am sure he would
never have made his final selection. His meals were brought
in from the college kitchen. I was one of the very few who
could invade his sanctuary. We had some walks together,
and he discussed many things with me, even his own affairs. I remember that I suggested to him to adopt a little
girl, and he liked the idea. His comments were unusually
apt on subjects which lay in my field and not in his. I could
not persuade him to come out of his seclusion, and he died
tragically alone in his college rooms, remote from any possible help, the night before brilliant successes of his pupils
were announced in the Classical Tripos.

## STANLEY BALDWIN

Stanley Baldwin won no school prize and achieved no special distinction. If we had been told we had a future Prime Minister among us, we might have thought of a number of names before his. Yet to one who knew him as closely as I did–at one time we had a joint menage for our meals–there was no one better worth listening to. All his thoughts were his own, never just quoted, and there was deep in them that gracious High Church culture which one finds in some of the most elect English families, for instance the Cecils. Though he was never prominent in examination results, I don't suppose there was anyone who carried away more of the instinct and tradition of the classics. Myself brought up in the Gladstonian tradition, which had then reached its highest peak, I would say to him that the future belonged to home interests and liberal principles. Baldwin denied this, and told me that he was then studying the speeches of Disraeli.

In his later political career, when he guided the country through the most entangled domestic problems, I realized that all the qualities of his success were inherent in him even then. Baldwin was a leader, never a dictator; in that period of his great responsibility a dictator would have been fatal. He had the instinct of all those imponderables, reticences and reservations, which so often get left out of our reckoning. The question of those days was whether England would yield to the unrest which was passing over the world–whether the country might flounder in civil strife– and he was three times raised to our highest post, because he was at home with other views than his own, was one with whom it was too difficult to quarrel and who had inside him the instinct of internal peace. That was why he carried the vote of the plain non-party man, an enormous value to the party which he loyally served. I doubt if the

two great settlements of his time–the General Strike and
the Abdication crisis–could have been achieved by any other
Englishman, or if they could have passed without grave
social wounds in any other country than England. He did
these things for us, and he did them by character and wisdom. He has told me he had never given enough attention
to foreign policy, and here I do not defend him, though it
was he who gave us Anthony Eden. He also told me too that
he always felt sure that the one man who could carry us
through such an ordeal as the Second World War was another Harrovian, Winston Churchill, than whom no one
could have been more unlike himself. But even here I will
say that Baldwin's peace work in England, the transformation of Lenin's prescription for us of a "heavy civil war"
into the comedy of the General Strike of 1926 was exactly
that turning point which gave Stalin, with his sensible
national policy of construction, the victory over Trotsky's
fantastic "Permanent Revolution," and so set the stage for
our alliance in the war.

## THE GREAT HOUSE ROW

We had during Baldwin's time in the House, though
he played no part in it, a highly educative struggle. We had
our own House traditions. There was the corporate authority
of the Sixth Form (12 out of our 60 boys were in it); the
head of the house was rather a chairman than a monarch.
But there was another more formidable authority, also
corporate, recognized only by the boys: it rested with those
who had been three years in the House. That term, there
had been a great exodus, which left no obvious candidate
for head of the House. K., a home boy from outside (he was
later a model bishop) was imported to fill the post. To
strengthen his authority, we elected him to three years'
privileges. K. was extremely conscientious and, I think,
over-estimated his responsibilities.

Some of us boys near the top ran a crude little musical society. Returning one night from dining with one of the Masters, I learned that K. had peremptorily ordered its suppression. Taking one of the instruments, I blew a loud blast in the passage. K. was on the spot at once and demanded its surrender before roll-call. I refused point blank; and K., hissed by most of the House, who by now knew the whole story, bravely went up to the Headmaster. I, and a friend named B., were summoned and deprived of our house privileges as Sixth Form boys; B. and I were close to K. in the school order.

K. had a very bad time after this, especially at House football, but he stuck it out nobly. When the hissing was repeated, B. and I were threatened with expulsion, and that brought it to a stop. Generally, we all had a very poor term of it.

We had a strange House ceremony for one night in the year only, the first in examination week before Christmas. The Sixth Form took no part in it. The next senior boy in the House invited three or four other senior "three years" boys to go round with him for "turning up." We had beds that went up into cupboards during the day; "turning up" consisted in lifting them up with the tenant in them about five A.M. and letting them drop with a bump. This made an awful noise, as the "turners" passed from room to room. On the authority of the Matron it had gone on for over 17 years, and it was a wonder it had never been interfered with. It was regarded as a yearly event–tradition said, in order to wake up the sluggard to work, for we were a very hard-working House; and we had never heard that anyone was the worse for it. B. and I, as far as the House was concerned, now stood outside the Sixth Form, and the leader T., a boy of unimpeachable character, invited us to join in, and in the same spirit of challenge, B. and I consented. Three years' boys were not turned up, but as K. had, in our opinion, abused his privileges, we proposed to include him. K., however, sprang from his bed with a cane; and as there were five of us, it seemed ridiculous to go further, and we retired in some shame.

Now it happened that on that particular night a new young policeman was on duty outside. Alarmed by the heavy thumps and the flashing lights of the candle as we passed from room to room, he rang the bell and informed the House butler, Mr. Ellis, that murder was going on. Mr. Ellis was a seasoned friend of all of us; "Go away," he said, "it's 'turning up' night." But this naturally failed to reassure the young policeman, and next morning he waylaid Dr. Butler on his way down from school and told the same story. Dr. B. summoned the matron, who of course knew of everything that went on. She gave only two names of the party, T. and H. She omitted B. and myself, for she knew that the next speck on our character would mean expulsion. T. and H. were in the next form to the Sixth, which was supposed to mean exemption from corporal punishment, but they were very vigorously flogged, as we could see when they showed their wounds to the House.

Dr. B. then set himself to trace the remaining members of the "turning up" party; but he was never told the number, and from T. and H. he could learn nothing. K. too was questioned but would not breathe a word. Dr. B. began sending for others on chance and asking them; to tell a direct lie, especially when so much was known, was not in our code.

Dr. B. had an imperfect knowledge of the rules of the ceremony. He began by sending for the lowest boy in the Sixth. This was a stout fellow named Grogan, the Father of the House, who had drifted into the Sixth in his last year, but had led the party the year before. If this went on, the Headmaster would inevitably come to B. and myself, as our names still stood high up in the Upper Sixth. Grogan was asked the question, and was able to say no. As he came down from the Headmaster's study he met, coming up, the next boy above him, also in the Sixth. This was a sturdy Yorkshireman named Bromet. "Bromet," said Grogan, "the Head is going to ask you if you turned up last night. Say very indignantly, 'No sir, I'm Sixth Form.' " Bromet did his job admirably. The Headmaster's inquiries now travelled down into the Fifth, and B. and I were saved.

The next event was a visit of protest from the fathers of T. and H. One was a Peer, and the other a Railway Director. According to their sons, they demanded an apology for the flogging; the boys, they said, were only carrying out an old tradition. I don't think they got an apology. Dr. B. assembled the House and mentioned the visit. He only disclaimed any reflection on the characters of the two boys whom he had flogged. He then solemnly called for an impressive volume, the House Book, and there he entered in front of us his decision abolishing three-year privileges. I saw that entry some fifty years later. The abolished privileges were again in full working order; in fact, they were just the same as those which B. and I had defended in our time.

However, it was certainly Dr. B. who took the last trick. Just before the end of term, some foolish boys twisted and distorted a number of forks and spoons. This time the matron was of course inexorable. She laid the mutilated things on the Headmaster's desk, with the name of each offender attached. The Headmaster's tactics were masterly. Everyone who visited his study came back saying: "I say, Drummer (or whoever it was), I saw your fork lying there." Otherwise nothing at all was done, and the criminals waited with an awful anticipation of judgment.

Then came the end-of-term supper; the next morning we should all be off. Dr. Butler rose to make his usual speech —the best, I think, of any I heard from him. He said we had had a very turbulent term, and it would be a good

thing for us to part company for a while. We should all
be going in different directions. For instance Mr. Howson
(his assistant in the House and future son-in-law) was off
to Troy, while he with his family would go to Tunbridge
Wells. He continued with a smile–

> Observe the contrast! How the bosom swells!
> He goes to Troy and we to Tunbridge Wells.

"Mr. Howson," he went on, "goes to Troy in pursuit of the
study of archaeology, a subject which just now very much
hangs in the air. In fact, an important discovery was recently made no farther off than Harrow. Mr. Ellis (to the
smiling old house butler), bring me my text!" Mr. Ellis
advanced carrying an awkward-looking package, that bulged
at every corner. From this Dr. B. took out, one after another, the wounded little forks and spoons, making an
appropriate artistic comment on each of them. I remember
a twisted little salt spoon. "This," he said, "is touching!"
Then suddenly, changing his tone, "All these things serve
to prove that barbarians *once* lived at Harrow." Drummer
and his friends were red with confusion. K.'s voice rang out,
"Three cheers for Dr. and Miss Butler," and the stormy
term ended in peace and amity.

## CAMBRIDGE MUSINGS

I am sure that the chief differences between Oxford
and Cambridge lies in the contrast in the curriculum, and
it goes into everything else. Oxford aims at proficiency and,
if possible, brilliance in several subjects; Cambridge demands
real attainment in one. Cambridge life, both for teachers
and for students, is therefore much narrower and more broken
up. On the other hand the Cambridge man is more serious
–probably too much so. He has more leg-drive—not only on
the river, where it is proverbial; he is more intent and more

sure to get somewhere, not only in his studies but in his other purposes. That seems to me the principal difference. It is a debatable question whether it would not be right to send a Cambridge-minded boy to Oxford and *vice versa,* but this would not promote his success in either place, and the natural trend is the opposite.

My own time at Cambridge, as with so many of my fellows, was one of confused thinking. I was terribly cramped. As a classical scholar of Trinity–I had been taught nothing else–I had to go on with the classics, though I well knew that I could never do any good with them. I was thinking at that time of being ordained; in a vague way that seemed the ordinary course, if one wanted to be of use to others; and as none of us had any real experience of life, there was no question on which there might be so much confusion as religion. We had an extraordinary society–it was called The Trinity Sunday Essay Society–founded by a very live "Don" (or lecturer), Dr. Cunningham. It had a good deal of prestige and lasted much longer than most of the ephemeral student organizations. To be elected (apart from the founders, who enjoyed being critical) you had to be regarded as one with original views on religion; you read a paper on yours, and the others rubbed off your edges for you. My own paper was rather sarcastic and aggressive: it was on the Society itself and was called "Gnostics Ancient and Modern." Count Bologna Strickland of Malfa read a paper on "The Church": there was only one, Rome. A few weeks later an Orthodox Russian, Mr. Pashkov, read another paper on "The Church and the Western Schism" (i. e. Rome); the title alone seemed to rob Count Strickland of all weapons of defense. We included a Baptist, a Mohammedan and, I think, a Salvationist–the claims of an Agapemonist were rejected. One member was elected on the ground of his conviction that the cloak left at Troas by St. Paul must certainly have been his chasuble.

I think my time at Cambridge defined my attitude to the average modern intellectual. We had those long walks, when we fixed everything in heaven and earth by our rules of logic, with leakages of all kinds in them which we did not stop to suspect. The man who argued best must be right. After my slow wrestling with Plato, I wanted some subject that was more concrete, one in which experience could show me my own misjudgments—above all, something that was human and alive; and I certainly found it later in the Russian peasant, spoon-fed by all his imaginary superiors, but at long range so often proving wiser than his would-be teachers.

At one period I was also much in the company of the Cambridge Evangelicals, disciples of Charles Simeon: so far I had followed my father, who was a healthy high churchman, but he always spoke of them with respect. What I most admired in them was their honesty; they were often long distance runners; they had no sense of humor. They would go to the backs of the colleges on a Sunday and ask any parading townsman whether he was saved, and they were quite normal enough to feel very uncomfortable in doing so. The best answer I know to this question, quite approved by the best theologians, is to say (preferably in a whisper), "Well, to tell you the truth, I am! But it was such a near squeak that I don't care to talk of it." What I objected to most in these good friends was a kind of convention, by which an emotional confession of "conversion" was expected in their families, and even artificially forced at an early age.

Like many others, I practiced what was called "district visiting" in a poverty-stricken village near Cambridge. I didn't feel that I was really doing any good; but it was something to get a sight of that barren world. The one great piece of civilization for these benighted minds was the Bible —that is, for those who read it. It is, of course, a whole culture in itself. I remember how an old laborer told me how he saw the Last Judgment come over the little hill outside his village. It was an awe-inspiring picture, full of color and poetry. But some of their reactions were very quaint. Another rustic, who had put his crude mind onto the Bible, pronounced judgment as follows: "You know, sir, I believe in the Old Testament, but not in the New." "Oh, why is that?" I asked. "Well you see, sir, the New Testament was written to sell the Old!"

Just then, it was for the first time made possible to take the examination in "pure classics" at the end of the second year. I welcomed this means of escape, and I must have been one of the first to do so. But still, one could only escape from the classics into the classics. The second part of the examination, which many did not take, was still all in the ancient field, and I was a modern. At least it was a broader syllabus with options, and I chose ancient philosophy. This meant Plato and Aristotle.

I was listening at this time to two of the greatest teachers I had ever had, Dr. Henry Jackson on Plato and, at the same time, Dr. Westcott, Regius Professor of Theology. The audience at Westcott's lectures were a public scandal. These students had to take this course to qualify for their ordination, but only the front two or three rows were worthy of their magnificent teacher, one of the greatest theologians the Church of England has ever had. The middle rows openly took in another book to read—sometimes on their work, sometimes not. The back rows used to stamp continuously for the last minutes of the lecture. Dr. Jackson's class was naturally small and select, but it included lady students (one could hardly have said "girls" then) who arrived in cabs from the women's colleges with their chaperons and passed quickly to the front row, evading our nearer scrutiny.

In spite of the difference in their subjects, Jackson and Westcott were both great enough to have common ground, and what I got from them was practically the same from both. Both were idealists, like all the best Russian philosophers and writers–say Tolstoy, Dostoyevsky, Turgenev, and Lopatin. I made a terrible muddle of my reading. For all those two years I was refusing to pass on till I had fought a kind of rear-guard action on each sentence. I was so unwilling to surrender any of the existing prejudices in which I had been moving and thinking, and I would not abandon my position till I reached conviction. I read Plato at a snail's pace, and never got to Aristotle at all. Sometimes my wrestlings mingled with the anthems practised by the wonderful college choir in the neighboring chapel. Many a Russian thinker has gone through such wrestling–and with all the great ones, such as Belinsky, the founder of Russian literary criticism, they maintained throughout an uncompromising honesty in thought. Russians have far more of this intellectual honesty than have either the English or the Americans.

Of course, this was a deplorable way of preparing for an examination. I had not read my set books, and only just got into the Third Class, a miserable fate for a Foundation Scholar of the College. I remember how after supper I went and sat on the secluded side of the great steps from the Hall and regarded the world as lost. There was one person who understood my trouble perfectly with the fewest words, my old Headmaster, Dr. Butler, now Master of my College. But those two grim years are perhaps the ones that did most for me. In my own very limited philosophy, I was on firm ground for the rest of my life. Plato's metaphysics as expressed in the *Timaeus* lay at my foundation, and its teaching blended perfectly with what I learned elsewhere; for instance from Westcott: the reality of the ideas behind their imperfect presentation in phenomena, the constant effort called for by Christianity, as I understood it, to visualize "the lights half seen across a murky lea."

ARTHUR HENRY FISH
## Who Taught Me Too

I had always wanted to study history, and if I had been under Bowen's direction, I should have had a splendid start. As it was, I had had the most expensive education, considered the best at its time, and had made nothing of it. The only post I had been trained for was a classical mastership. I was not going to my Father for anything more; so now I would somehow scrape up the funds for myself and go into foreign study.

One day at my Portsmouth home there were two letters for me on the silver salver in the hall. One was from a Countess who invited me to be tutor to her son; the other was from the Rev. A. H. Fish, headmaster of a small "prep" school at Chester. Instinct–which I nearly always followed– told me to choose the second.

Mr. Fish came of humble origin and had earned his own education; this included a Degree of B.Sc. at Victoria University, Manchester; but, he had started schoolmastering at 17. Here he had a colleague, a Mr. D., who was paid only five pounds a year and was tyrannically fagged by his chief. "Mr. D., will you pick up that piece of paper on the floor?" his headmaster would say in front of the boys. Young Fish spurred Mr. D. on to rebellion, himself audaciously wrote him a testimonial, primed him up with whisky and kept him up to the mark to give notice. There were numbers of private schools at that time which might be described as "submerged." Any totally unqualified person could set one up.

Mr. Fish–I always like to call him Mr. Fish–came to the very conservative cathedral city of Chester with a few pounds in his pocket. He started a rival school to the old-established one, put his fees higher, never advertised and, by the time I joined him, had most of the best boys in the city.

He limited himself to 6o: "I can't know more than that," he would say. And indeed he did know them better than they could know themselves. "Always be prepared to go to the end with a boy," he said. "They'll never do that, if they see you are going to." I taught my few boys mostly in the same big room; and I was constantly distracted from my own work by the fascination of listening to Mr. Fish. He never took any two boys the same way; he seemed to go to the bottom of each of them. "We have no school rules," he would say, "I don't believe in them." A boy who protested, "I didn't know there was a rule about that," was told that there wasn't, but he would be punished because what he had done was a silly thing to do. He really did compel all these little fellows to think for themselves.

He had an intimate respect for a boy's inner sanctuary. He always said the most grateful were those for whom one had done least. He asked me what I thought of such a boy, big and clumsy, but perfectly well-meaning. "I have made nothing at all of him," I said. "He is perfectly indifferent to everything I'm doing with him." And then Mr. Fish said the wisest thing, I think, that I have ever heard said on the subject of education, and it was of infinite service to me later with the peasants of Russia: "You mustn't expect to rob the poor boy of the only weapon (indifference) that he has, to meet all the *attacks* you and I are making on him." As he also could hear me at my work, he came along once and suggested a different method to mine. I told him I preferred my own. "Then go on with it!" he said. "If you try mine without believing in it, you'll probably make a mess of it." In a few weeks, I had adopted Mr. Fish's way from conviction.

Most headmasters, especially of a day school, are in considerable awe of the parents of their boys. Mr. Fish had the grand quality of absolute loyalty to those who served him. There was a small mischievous boy, Guy, who was out to give me all the trouble he could. On Saturday mornings the boys had to copy out the corrections of their mistakes of the week, after which they could go home. Guy was not particularly anxious to go home, and put me to such trouble that in the end I wrote out all his corrections myself and simply asked him to copy them out. This he did as incorrectly as possible. I was so annoyed that I gave him a slap on the face. At once he started bleeding at the nose —you might have known he would. I thought no more of the matter and did not report it; but a week or two later Mr. Fish sent a message to me: "Will you please send me Guy's exercise book?" That was all he asked. The boy's mother, who was a widow, had come and complained with tears. Mr. Fish said no more to me, but at the end of term I told him myself of the slapping. "Yes," he said quickly, "I know all about that. That's why I sent for his exercise book, and I saw at once that this was a case of sheer impertinence. I don't believe in hitting the boys, but this sort of thing is quite different; your authority was directly challenged." He went on, "I think we'll clear this up now," and came down with me to the boys. "Guy," he said, "stand up! What you did to Mr. Pares was sheer impudence. Now you boys, when you come to this school, take what you get here and don't go back home whining about it. And Mr. Pares, if Guy does this kind of thing again, you send him to me, and I'll *really* give him something to take home."

The head of the School, Osbert Francis, was a particularly fine boy. When I went out with the team to outmatches, there was never any trouble if Osbert was there. I mentioned that to Mr. Fish, and he told me this story. Osbert never had any evil in him; but when he first came, he set himself to see how often he could defy discipline. "Osbert," Mr. Fish told him, "I'm here to run this School, and you're trying to see how you can get in the way. I've nothing against you, but if you come here, you've got to help me. Now I'm sending you home for a week to think it over." And this was the result.

But we sometimes had to deal with more difficult questions than these, where an acute understanding was required. Young L. was the son of a mean parent who would not even pay for his lunch with the other day boys. L. had spirit. He gave his father's name, which was well-known, and ordered a first-class lunch at the most fashionable confectioner's, one of the best in England. His father cut off his niggardly pocket money till the lunch was paid for. L. then broke bounds and sold evening papers outside the station. He was now an enemy of society, not a mean thief, but a bold robber, taking great pride in his loot.

He was wary and very successful, but at last he was caught out, being detected through a mirror, and was brought to Mr. Fish. As it was a day school, Mr. Fish had no responsibility for what the boys did outside, but of that he made no account. "Will you take a licking from me or from your father?" he asked. L. gave the preference to Mr. Fish. When that ceremony had been duly performed, Mr. Fish said, "That puts things straight between you and me. Now I'm your friend, and I'm going to help you all I can. Bring me all the things you've taken!" L. had kept nearly all of them, and produced a fairly satisfactory list of those which he had given away. Mr. Fish, who was not only a schoolmaster but a clergyman, spent most of the next fortnight going round in the twilight and himself taking them back to their rightful owners, who sometimes hadn't even noticed their loss. Nothing else was said, and L. later did excellently in the army.

There was another case of stealing. This was of the ordinary sneaking kind. The theft was in a public place, and every one heard of it before Mr. Fish, who did not ordinarily go out into the city except on business. The boys were all talking about it at their games. This was the only place outside school where I was "on duty," and they used freely to tell me everything. To keep this confidence, I got the chief ones together and asked them to commission me to tell Mr. Fish, who clearly had to know.

Mr. Fish had always told me he would have nothing to do with expulsion. That would be a simple confession of his own failure with the boy. In this case the publicity left him no choice. The boy had to go, but there was no exposure, no denunciation. Next day, before school prayers, the little boys were all commenting on the thief's absence. Mr. Fish went in his usual quiet way to his desk and began reading the day's portion from the Bible; he was an excellent reader, avoiding all undue emphasis. In a minute I realized that he had specially chosen this passage, and directly afterwards, from the close attention in the room, one felt that the whole school realized it too. It was about the woman taken in adultery. "Neither do I condemn thee. Go and sin no more!" That was all that was said about the culprit's departure; but Mr. Fish called together the chief boys who had commissioned me. "We're all ashamed of this," he said in his strong northern accent. "He was one of us, and we don't talk of it–and if you hear any of the little fellows doing that, I give you free leave to punch their heads."

My time with Mr. Fish was one of profound rest and refreshment and a progress much faster than I could have known at the time. This was the true Intellectual, not an imitation but intellect itself, following no hard and fast rules. He was opening my mind all the time by the strength and breadth of his own. It was a superiority in which I bathed and rejoiced. A clever young Frenchman who came to stay with me, said of him: "Il serait libéral, même en France." (He would be Liberal, even in France) and that, at the time, was high praise. It was afterwards that I realized how well, in that seeming by-water, I was gathering strength for fresh labors.

I never knew anyone who could see further through a difficult problem than Mr. Fish (we call it "seeing through a brick wall"); and it was many times in later life that I sought his advice. Pretty well always, he would say something perfectly simple which at first sight might hardly seem connected with the question; and when one thought it out, it contained the whole point of everything. One time I went to him and told him that I had heart trouble. "That's splendid," he said. "Now you'll live all your time." And later, "Don't leave your heart without some work to do; it wants some."

Here is a story which Mr. Fish told me only near the end of his life. I had sometimes wondered why he had not married. He had a dear friend, but he remained single as long as his old mother was alive, and that meant very late. When she was over eighty, she broke her hip, but made a complete recovery. At long last she died. Then, as he told me, he thought he would go and find out whether Mary would marry him. He took a hansom to Waterloo Station, and it broke down under him. He took a cab, and it broke down too. A third conveyance failed him, but he simply went straight on. Mary said "Yes"; and this late marriage, much of which I witnessed, was long and peculiarly happy.

## Father Dolling
### A People's Parson

Robert Radcliffe Dolling was a full-blooded and full-fleshed Irishman. I remember his saying to me, "You ought to eat plenty of bloody meat." Another Old Boy from Harrow, he was for some time in business, I believe as a land agent, and then he became a clergyman. He did a lot of rough-and-tumble parish work in the poorer part of London. He had a way with him, which generally worked well. Once he was tied by rowdies into his chair; he said this wasn't fair, as he was ready to fight any one of them. His offer was accepted, and he won in more ways than one. In his later work in Portsmouth, he served as his own "chucker-out."

Dolling was put in charge of the Mission of Winchester College, the oldest of our best-known Public Schools, dating six centuries back. The Mission had been set up in perhaps the worst slum of Portsmouth, near one of the Dockyard gates. This was a part which practically knew nothing of God except for purposes of cursing. On Saturday night, when it was full of gas flares and cheap stalls, the sailor boys of the training ship H.M.S. St. Vincent would be turned loose here for the week-end. Dolling built a fine gymnasium and provided them with hammocks to sleep there, and it was often full. He had a number of plain, spare rooms; and he would sally forth into the street, take a drunken man firmly by the arm and bring him in to spend the night here. He had also a large, comfortable, semi-public sitting room with a good grate and fire, the door on the latch, where anyone could come and sit. One found here the most variegated company. "I like going and staying with Dolling and his thieves," said his superior, the wise and kindly Bishop Thorold of Winchester. There were also cripples, particularly a boy in a wheel chair bought for him by Dolling, who practically lived in this room. Then, on a Sunday, there would be two nice, bright school prefects from Winchester, who loved these visits.

It was always intended to turn this district into a new permanent parish, and Dolling set his heart on building a great church. Not the less heart-warming were the services in the temporary mission hall, where the atmosphere was still one of effort and adventure and not yet of attainment; but gradually the great church of St. Agatha was built. It was a magnificent building, in the nature of a basilica. The services were also magnificent. There was extreme ornamentation, almost Roman, and beautiful music; but the sermon was quite different, for it was only regarded as an expression of human opinions, and Dolling's brilliant curate, Charles Osborne, another Irishman and one of the finest products of Trinity College, Dublin, gave intellectual fare of a standard higher than anything else to be found in Portsmouth. I used to delight as he vigorously stripped himself of his stole at the start, to take sole responsibility for what he was going to say, for I knew I was in for a real treat. It seemed somehow dimly reminiscent of an athlete stripping himself of his sweater for a race.

Dolling's motto was really that of St. Paul: "If by any means I can save some!" He was quite eclectic in his methods, and on a week day he would give his plain talk in a black gown. Two dissenters from the Church of England, who strayed in one day, were so attracted that they repeated their visit on a Sunday and came in for the full, ornate service; but to their credit, that did not divert them from realizing the true evangelical character of everything that was done at St. Agatha's, and they kept on coming. One found there on a Sunday evening people whom one would never have expected to see at all in a church–the agnostically inclined secretary of a left-wing political party, or some of the "fastest" girls from fashionable Southsea.

I was often up at St. Agatha's; I ran a week-day group for reading Shakespeare, and also took part in a working men's debating society, where we tried to follow parliamentary procedure and pretended to be Cabinet Ministers. These were very superior men, mostly holding responsible posts, a color sergeant, expert of gunnery, a dockyard foreman, etc., and I remember the distaste with which they received a socialist orator with a red tie, who preached absolute equality. Each speaker who followed seemed to begin: "I'm a radical, but–" This was really the same England as that of the General Strike of so many years later.

What attracted me most in Dolling was his blunt plainness of speech. I never took him for a theologian or indeed for a representative of any particular view. One Sunday there blew in a peculiarly vain cleric who offered to teach us all theology of the extremist Anglo-Catholic kind, such as Dolling was supposed to favor. "Do teach me some!" said Dolling, "I don't know any." "Well," said the volunteer professor, "we must begin with Trichotomy." "Does that mean hair-splitting?" said a bright school-prefect from Winchester; it was a clever Greek pun, and it was quite too much for our would-be teacher.

The time came when St. Agatha's was completed and a regular parish would be established. Up to this time Dolling had been merely Missioner in Charge. Now he would be a parish priest, and as such, by our church law, he would be irremovable. Among his clerical colleagues in the town there were some who were jealous of his success. Bishop Thorold, though a convinced Evangelical or Low Churchman (as it was called), had been deaf to their complaints. "I'm not going to throw Dolling to the wolves!" he had said. He could always have kept him in hand. As Dolling told me himself, whenever the Bishop had any question to raise, he would say, "Now Dolling, you and I are not going to agree about this, so let's have a word of prayer together first!" But Thorold was now dead; and his successor, though of the more ordinary High Church variety, proceeded differently. "Can't we compromise about this?" he said to Dolling; and from that moment the game was up.

In the new church a special "third altar" had been provided for prayers for the dead. For myself, I think there is a great deal of humbug about this question; I don't expect that many of us strike our dearest out of our prayers as soon as they are gone; but here was one of those wretched subjects of theological conflict, and there are always the famous "Thirty Nine Articles" of the Church of England— "the forty stripes save one," as someone has wittily described them, parodying the flogging of St. Paul. Anyhow, there appeared in the local press a letter from the new bishop prohibiting the third altar, with at least a suggestion of Dolling's resignation. I was teaching then at the great Grammar School in Portsmouth. I got on my bike and rode straight up to Dolling. I found him in a very lay-looking coat, comfortably reading a thriller of Wilkie Collins, the contemporary and friend of Dickens. "What *does* this mean?" I asked anxiously. "It means," said Dolling, "that they want me to join the Church of Rome, and I'm not going to do it."

For Dolling's parishioners, the whole question was non-sense; all they knew of God they knew from him, and here his chiefs were throwing him out of his own accomplished work. But there was very much the same reaction all over Portsmouth. Dissenting Ministers rallied to the High Churchman Dolling, and even said from their pulpits that the town was threatened with a blow to all that was good in it. Very unfortunately, Osborne had been appointed by the Crown to a parish in the North. He knew much more of theology than Dolling; in fact, Dolling once charmingly described his own efforts in that field as "Undigested Osborne." Osborne could have held his own, and kept Dolling straight too. A public petition for Dolling to stay was being widely signed when the Bishop made it known that his decision could not be affected by it. In the middle of the discussion, he himself conducted what must have been a memorial service for one of the great of the land. He later admitted frankly that of every ten friends he had, nine thought he had mishandled this matter. Dolling himself was everywhere telling his parishioners to submit to authority and welcome his successor. Many were the times that I was to be brought face to face in Russia with this conflict between true religion and the official version of it.

My Father, as I have mentioned, had been one of the commissioners for Portsmouth of a former Bishop. Though in no way sharing Dolling's various vagaries, he had always been firmly behind him. I asked him if he would not come up and try to get Dolling to give up the third altar, which was the bone of contention. Dolling agreed at once, and my Father wrote this to the Bishop. The Bishop replied that the matter had now gone too far, and that the services at St. Agatha's must undergo a general revision.

Dolling came and stayed with us for some time before leaving the town. Other Bishops, from whose dioceses he had received invitations, refused to admit him. The successor who was appointed to St. Agatha's, a very worthy man, was much more definitely "High Church" than Dolling; the chief difference was that he was not one who could shoulder the all-round social work of the parish. The wonderful community sitting room, opening on the street, was now locked, with the words "servant's bell" outside. There was one man who stood up for Dolling. This was probably the youngest of all the Bishops, Lang of Stepney, who had himself formerly been in charge of a great parish in Portsmouth and had then told me that he would rather have been a curate with Dolling. He invited Dolling to the parish of Poplar in East London, but Dolling soon died, worn out with all his worries. His funeral was taken by Bishop Lang, who later became the well-known Archbishop of Canterbury.

## William Pickford and Hampshire Football

My eldest brother, Norman, who had won the gold medal of the English Football Association as a Cup winner with the Old Etonians, was the first to introduce "soccer" at Portsmouth. Later he was called the Father of "Pompey," the famous professional Portsmouth Club who won the English Cup in 1939. Four brothers were a good start toward a football eleven, especially as they were a kind of inner group that knew everything about each other's ideas and tactics.

Dr. Conan Doyle, the author of Sherlock Holmes, sometimes played full-back to my goal-keeping. He was a big, slow, heavy man, easily evaded; but if left alone, he could kick almost the length of the ground. I had a grisly time against the Royal Engineers in a Hampshire Cup Final, when our other full-back had been knocked out, with a nightmare of five striped forwards on me at once and Doyle toiling along hopelessly outpaced behind them. In those days they were allowed to charge the goal-keeper through his own goal.

I used to go and smoke and drink bottled stout with Doyle, when he was writing his Sherlock Holmes. He regarded these sketches as by-play; his ambition lay in the direction of historical novels after the manner of Walter Scott, and he did sound work of that kind. His *Brigadier Gerard,* which is first-rate stuff, as well as most amusing, is fully grounded in the original materials. Once he asked me to jot down a few words in Russian, which I next saw in one of these stories. I think his "Professor Challenger" is quite as good as Sherlock or any other character that he created. Doyle bore himself much more as if he were Watson than Sherlock. From certain indications, I am pretty certain that I knew the original of his arch-villain, Professor Moriarty—this was the only man of whom I knew a great deal but nothing that was not definitely bad.

We had a little club of our own called the Sunflowers, actually the first in Portsmouth and almost a family affair. We only played in the four weeks of the Christmas holidays, but then nearly every day of the week, and we were very nearly invincible. At Bournemouth, at the other end of the straggling county of Hampshire, there was a wonderful little missionary of clean football, William Pickford; he had belonged to one of the great northern clubs, the Bolton Wanderers who thrice won the English Cup. He had built up a Football Association of two counties, Hants and Dorset, centered around Bournemouth. He asked us to join. After some discussion we told him we would, on condition that as soon as possible, we should break up this unwieldy organization and create two separate Associations–for Hants and for Dorset. This was in no way in Pickford's interest, but it was clearly in the common interest and he agreed at once, and faithfully kept bond by telling us when to move. The decisive meeting was to be held in Dorset, which was opposed to the separation. Four of us got on bicycles, and we out-voted the Dorset men in their own county. But they later showed their chivalry by asking for me as referee in the first match between the two separated counties. And my brother Lance was playing for Hants, and indeed won the match with a thundering surprise shot from far out which left the Dorset goal-keeper bewildered.

The great question of that time was the legalization of professionalism. Anyhow it was there, and entirely uncontrolled. The amateurs from the great "Public Schools" refused to recognize its existence, and broke with the Football Association when it decided to put the matter in order. The Pickfords and their like–he was a small newspaper man– were left to fight the battle alone. They grappled firmly with the question and established an absolute discipline with clearly defined rules. For instance, instead of our having to prove that a rival club was playing an unqualified man, which was practically impossible to establish, the rival club had itself to prove that its players were all in order. When a big Manchester club had broken the rules, they were ordered by the Football Association to pay a fine of hundreds of pounds to Manchester charities, and their ground was closed to all visiting clubs till it was paid–as it was. This was how the

most popular sport of the time, which even drew crowds
of over a hundred thousand, remained clean; and that was
the reason why the English Cup Final became one of the
favorite recreations of our good King George V. He always
came, when he could, to give away the medals to the winners,
who were invariably professionals.

Pickford rose to be Vice-president of the English Football Association. At a dinner given in his honor at Southampton all the magnates of "soccer" were present to celebrate the
jubilee of the Hampshire Association. Pickford and the Chairman had whistles in their hands, with which they proposed
to "call time" to any speech over five minutes. To be sure
against transgressing this order, I put my own tribute into
verse as follows:

> A Bolton Wanderer came down
>     To wake our sleepy South
> And taught the science of his town
>     To Bourne-and-Portès-mouth.
>
> We were benighted savages
>     And little knew that art;
> But he was full of friendliness
>     And worked with all his heart.
>
> By courage and integrity
>     He rose to heights of fame;
> First Hampshire honored William P.;
>     Then England did the same.
>
> And now that Hampshire football climbs
>     To glory in the land,
> I think with joy of those old times
>     And grasp that friendly hand.

This was in April 1937. Very soon afterwards the President of the Football Association, Sir Charles Clegg, died and
Pickford was elected to this, the highest post in the game. He
gave an impressive radio address on the control of the game,
the subject to which he and a whole group of comradely fel-

low-workers had devoted the best of their lives. Pickford
had the keenest eye for anything that endangered fair play.
He was himself a tough little fellow, perfectly ready, if necessary to lead the biggest man on the home side off the field
for foul play. The rules of the game, which are a model of
clearness, are largely his work. He had systematized the study
of refereeing and built up a great corps of trained referees. On
October 26, 1938, replying to the toast of the Association at its
75th anniversary, he ended his speech by quoting the following four lines:

> For when the one great Scorer
> Comes to write against your name,
> He writes not that you lost or won,
> But how you played the Game.

These were the last words that he ever spoke in public. A
few days later he passed away in his sleep.

# CHAPTER II

## 𝖘𝖙𝖚𝖉𝖎𝖊𝖘 𝖎𝖓 𝕰𝖚𝖗𝖔𝖕𝖊
## (1894–1899)

### QUARTIER LATIN AND SORBONNE

AT LAST, in January, 1894, I had saved money enough to set out on my own enterprise. This time I should be my own paymaster and my own tutor. I may say that in all my studies I followed my own nose, that is, my instinct. I knew roughly enough what came first, and what had to be done at some time or another; and later, when my choice came to be tested pretty sharply, I found that where I did not stand the test, my instinct had told me what to do but I had not done it.

I was to enter a new great field. We had not been taught even the history of our own country, to which I devoted some time later. As to other countries, we knew practically nothing. I once wrote to Mr. Joseph Chamberlain, asking whether if we were to study our own empire it was not absolutely necessary to study our rivals too, to which he agreed. It was a long range task—no matter of "kick and run"—that I had set myself if I was later to concentrate on Russia; and no perspective was possible if one could not place not only England but Russia in her right setting among the great powers. So, what follows in my story is an essential part of my apprenticeship, as it will be for others who attempt the same task.

I would first get a background, not only of study but of actual experience in the chief countries of Europe, living always among their own people and visiting the places where great historical events had happened. In particular, I found it useful to get familiar in each country with their own people's ideas about themselves, their own prejudices and especially their *clichés* or catch phrases, by reading the textbooks of history which they provided for the lower and middle schools. For France, Victor Duruy, Minister of Education for Napoleon III, had produced a whole barrage of such textbooks; I believe he once boasted that the school boys in Lille and in Bordeaux would all be diligently studying the same pages at the same hour. He always added "Europe" as a kind of appendix to the same period of French History. France was the leader of thought, the source of light for all.

It was with France that I began and, though I spent a lot of time on the back numbers, I started my serious studies from the French Encyclopaedists. This period, continued into contemporary history, served me well later. It was full of revolutions and of wars, and I was to see plenty of both; but the one subject which I could not get myself to study, was the history of modern socialism. It seemed to me too abstract and theoretical, and after my two years of Plato, I wanted something concrete. I would have given a lot later to have covered this ground.

I had a method which may seem curious. I would start the day with an hour's work on a school textbook devoted to national history. After each sentence I would stop and guess at the next before I read it. At first all my guesses were hopelessly wrong. With time I seemed to reach some kind of a sequence—I mean some sense of what would follow what in French history. I think this helped a good deal later. Anyhow I found that when I had to bring a historical work up to date, what had come before fitted on fairly well to what was to come next.

France, of course, is essentially a part of Europe, which England is not, and generally has had a far more consecutive influence on European thought. I have immense respect for that influence and for many lessons which France has taught, for she is clear-cut and could always teach with lucidity. But in my opinion, formed at close quarters with them, the French are the last people to take as a standard for other nations. Logical as they are, they seem to me inaccessible to logic in so very many of their own conventions. The perfect phrase passes without examination; and so may a convention, if it is accepted with the same confidence.

They have put their best thoughts into other subjects than those on which the English especially concentrate. I never felt that they were born politicians–anything but! But I have found in all services of theirs which relate to instruction and knowledge such a seriousness and conscientiousness as the Englishman is more likely to apply to politics. As was explained to me by M. Victor Bérard at the Ecole Normale Superieure, the highest training college for professors, a workman's son with real talent can arrive there by the admirable ladder system of selected scholars without any expense to his parents. The University of Paris was open to all without pay, and such French as I have was mostly learned there. They had an excellent custom of holding courses for students which were also open to the public without charge; and if Petit de Julleville was lecturing on French Literature, you would see in the audience a number of fashionable ladies from the West End. After Cambridge, the standard of exposition in Paris seemed above perfection; it made everything almost too easy. On the other hand, at the Collège de France were scholars of the highest order who were not tested by their gifts of exposition and were there to be hunted up by researchers in their sometimes out-of-the-way subjects. I was kindly admitted to the Agregation class (M.A.) of Professor Marion, who would in England have been simply called Professor of Education but was in Paris "Professeur de Pédagogie, Morale et Psychologie." He once said "En Angleterre peu d'instruction, en France point d'éducation!"

I got leave to visit a number of secondary schools of various types, and though Marion's phrase was too sweeping I was inclined to agree with him. In all that concerned Public Instruction–and that was how their Ministry of Education was named–the French were far away ahead of us. The chief criticism would be that they were too serious. The experience of the student in the Classe de Philosophie–their "Sixth Form"–was overwhelming and exhausting. I lived later in Germany with four young Frenchmen of the Ecole de Monge, who told me they were all worn out by the end of the school year. Yet on our country walks they were infinitely better informed than I was, on any chance subject that might come up–botany, architecture, history, or anything else–and all their knowledge was simple and fresh. One might smile at the textbooks of "philosophy" which had passed the State scrutiny, for instance the chapter on "God," but the French had a most sensible way of solving the problem of religious teaching. It was simply a question of supply and demand. Parents might claim instruction in any form of religious belief in the hour set apart for this subject, if there were enough of them to pay for the teacher.

In my first real visit to Paris, I found a comfortable and homely hotel in the Quartier Latin (the University Quarter) –the Hotel Corneille. Since then I have always returned to it. It has changed a good deal in the years; now one meets more foreigners there, but it always was and is a superior student's hotel. In those early days, when there was far more life in the Quartier than there is now, the rapid play of it was a constant source of entertainment, only with a sense of strain. One hardly ever saw a drunken man, but, generally speaking, everyone seemed to be enjoying himself. There were little tragedies in the break-up of the temporary sex friendships but I always thought the Quartier the cleanest part of Paris. Above all it was the intellect that was satisfied; for instance, the hunt for strange books, especially along the lengthy quays of the Seine, was always a diversion. What was lacking was a sense of permanence. There was a break somewhere, which had never been really bridged and left in the present a constant restlessness and a sense of fatigue.

I think France was well on her way down from her greatness when I first really got to know her. The things which I respected most in her were those which were most traditional, especially the work of public instruction. There was still some kick in her in those days, especially in the Latin Quarter, but less and less as I came again, till in the period between the two world wars there seemed hardly more in the Quartier than in the provinces. It looked as if the first of these wars had bled her white, and this prepared me for the collapse of 1940.

## GERMAN STUDENT LIFE AND SONGS

I had a feeling of the relaxation of a strain when in 1894 I landed from France in the middle of the beautiful hills and woods of Heidelberg. Here were people whom it was quite easy for an Englishman to understand, only there was much less to take account of, and much less to respect. Even when they were trying to do the same thing as the French, they did it so much more grossly. The spoken language, too, came so much more easily to an Englishman; but by no means the written language–a slovenly piling up of phrases, artifice being only successful in the concealment of meaning. Once, when I was applying for a post in the British Museum, the then Director, Sir Edward Maunde Thompson, a scholar in philosophy, asked if I could read German easily. I replied that I didn't think the Germans could. He agreed; he said he had written to a German scholar to ask him the meaning of a certain sentence in his own book; the German scholar replied that he had forgotten. In a little impromptu German play which a party of us Englishmen put on in Heidelberg my witty old Harrow friend, Wilfrid Meek, filled a theatrical gap by searching for the second half of a separable verb and finally laid down his newspaper in despair, saying, "It must be in the supplement!"

It was the same in the university lectures. Exposition was at a lower standard even then with us. There was no arrangement. Here was a reputed high authority on "Das Revolutions und Napoleons Zeitalter" (The Revolution and Napoleon period). He only covered half his subject, and that the half in which Germany almost remained out of the picture. With one more lecture in store, he arrived at the eve of the battle of Jena in 1806, which does at least really bring in Germany. I expected a good account of that vital battle, and next time a sketchy summary of the rest of the period. No, he turned aside to a Viennese pamphlet written on the eve of the battle, which he had recently been reading, and we never got to the battle at all. I could not find an intelligent short textbook of German history. I was offered a perfectly enormous volume, with the words "But you know, it's only popular." That was true; for if you looked at the account of a famous battle, among an array of sounding phrases the whole point of the issue was left out.

One of the chief sights in Heidelberg was the "Mensur" (measuring), the name given to the students' fencing matches, which has been sympathetically described by Mark Twain. Though the main object seemed to be blood-letting and disfigurement, there was a good deal more point in it than might appear. Ordinarily, it was only friendly clubs that fought each other. The "measurement" was not necessarily by victory or defeat, but by how one stood up to punishment. Vulnerable parts, like eyes and throat, were effectively protected. Timing of rounds was scrupulously observed. The umpire was the surgeon; for it was for him to judge the extent of damage which he could repair. In a match between Alemania and Franconia, our nearest German friend, Hugo Müller, had been roughly handled; his opponent, finding himself the master, inflicted a whole number of flat blows on the top of the head which were very painful. A freshman who joined the club was always given a protector, and as Müller was very popular, he later became protector of a most promising young freshman named Schneider (or Cutter), who later came to be about the most skilful fighter in Heidelberg. When Schneider became Captain of the club, he chose for his opponent in a coming match the man who had mishandled Müller. Watching through a broad window and knowing that something was coming, we saw Schneider adroitly parry the nervous attacks of his victim and then with a neat stroke detach his nose. "Take him off!" (*Abfuhr*) called the surgeon umpire, but it was not many weeks before the nose was there in its place again, apparently none the worse for wear.

But far and away the best thing in the student life was the club singing, on which John Farmer had based our community singing at Harrow. I joined a student club and sat through interminable hours of pedantic talk for the sake of those glorious songs, which intervened about every quarter of an hour. There were many peculiar little rules of the club. On two boards were chalked up the names of those who were temporarily debarred from joining in songs or toasts. BV meant "beer infamy" or disgrace. BK meant too sick to drink beer; I put my name up when wanting to avoid heavy drinking, and I think it was taken as a credit to have got "beer sick" so soon.

As far as I know, there is no student song-book to touch the "Kommersbuch." There are some six hundred songs, some from medieval times, printed out on end as if in prose, with the melody only; they fall into categories–patriotic, countryside, and especially songs relating to every field of study and every event of student life. A first-class song might receive as many as three different accompaniments, all also first class; this was a favorite field of competition for the best composers. Admission of songs to the Kommersbuch was regulated by a national committee. All singing was in unison, generally slow and weighty, which gave a tremendous volume. Each student's copy would carry the arms of his club, and also four little nails to raise it above the beer on the table.

The only really first-rate humor that I have found in Germany is in these songs, especially those of student life, and more especially the so-called "beer humor." They used to say we English drank our beer too fast (and certainly too strong), and so on the way missed all the poetry of drinking. The best of all were those of Viktor von Scheffel of Heidelberg whose statue in student's cap stands outside the great red sandstone castle high up on the wood-clad Königsstuhl. The best of Scheffel's are, I think, the saga of the Rodenstein, a ghost who has never drunk his fill in life, and with his host of rioters similarly frustrated, raids the local publicans at night to make them open their bars again.

> Then serve me right and come what will
> Till all the world go bursting;
> Men talk of too much drinking still,
> But ne'er of too much thirsting.

Or again the Rodenstein, dying:

> The finest thirst the Rhine has seen
> Will soon be stilled in slumber;
> I have no strength to drink it clean—
> That last domain I number.

One daring song "Der Sang ist verschollen" is never sung but last of all in the evening, and held almost sacred. It is a vision full of this "poetry of drinking." [1]

At the end of session there was a Fackelzug or torchlight procession. That lovely embosomed valley, with the red sandstone Castle and Bridge and the laughing river Neckar, was all lit up. In their old medieval uniforms the leaders led the students of their clubs through the city, stopping to do honor to this or that popular professor. All the processions would unite on the university square, and throw their torches on the common pile. As the pile slowly burned out, all in unison sang the great final student song: "Gaudeamus Igitur." There were three vigorous brass bands, but you could not hear them—only the clash, clash of the swords of the leaders as they met, setting the time for the singing.

> Vita nostra brevis est,
> Brevi finietur.
> Venit mors velociter,
> Venit mors atrociter,
> Nemini parcetur.[2]

## WITH VETERANS OF THE FRANCO-GERMAN WAR

One of my favorite interests in Germany was to walk over old battlefields with military maps of the time as Bowen had done. He always got someone to follow up any fashion that he set, and though I could not know it, I was getting ready for the years which I was to spend with the Russian Army in the First World War.

Among other things, these wanderings took me off all the ordinary beaten tracks, over plowed fields and through woods. This kind of wandering was very much developed

---

[1] I will give some of my translations in the appendix. We made great use of them when we were making the Liverpool University Songbook.

[2] "Short is our life; soon will it finish; death comes swiftly; death comes cruelly; none will be spared."

among the students at Heidelberg, where they had what might be called beer picnics *en masse,* but here I was alone, I liked the honest Bauer, or peasant, and enjoyed my chats with him. I liked the simple country inn keepers, with their clean quarters and their kindly hospitality. At Jena I got drenched through, and my host put me to bed while he dried my clothes, brought me a lamp and all his illustrated newspapers, and asked me to write to him when I was gone. I did not like the Prussian officer, who was now more and more forcing himself into the lives of these good simple folk.

I have always felt that the Prussian "swagger" was essentially founded on an inferiority complex. I have often put this question to any Englishman who has lived in Germany and always found agreement. If they really were so sure they were such fine people, why did they have to take so much trouble to show it? I was sitting in a clean white-washed room in a country inn, drinking my beer. I was alone. A typical gentleman of this type came in and obviously felt that it was due to him to impress the stray civilian. He strutted about, stuck out his moustaches, and generally made himself ridiculous. I began to smile; in a moment I shouldn't be able to help laughing. He saw the demonstration was not coming off, turned quite red and went out of the room.

I once saw the Kaiser drive in an open carriage down Unter Der Linden on an afternoon inspection of his docile flock, and somehow his expression as he looked round seemed like a direct challenge and affront. It was the look of an absolute Master, making sure that his subjects were all doing as they were told. Exactly this look was later repeated on all the portraits of Hitler.

I was beginning to become very conscious of our own isolation and unpreparedness, and I felt a respect for Lord Salisbury, who successfully steered us without damage through that dangerous period. I also felt I was getting closer to my study of Russia, and I sorely wanted to get in a train at Berlin and go straight there, but my background studies were indispensable, and I had to be patient and see Austria and Italy first.

The battlefields of Europe were then mostly in three clusters–Belgium, Thuringia and the Italian quadrilateral near the Po. I have been over most of Napoleon's biggest battlefields. Usually there was one place where everything could be seen, and that was where Napoleon was to be found on that day. As the numbers of men increased–from 30,000 in 1796 to 300,000 in 1813–this became less possible; at Borodino outside Moscow in 1812, there was no point where more than a third of the field was visible; and Napoleon, without our modern appliances, himself owned that no one could keep a grip on the direction of more than 100,000 men, though he had an uncanny eye for guessing the strength of a detachment at sight. He divided fighting into the "terrestial" and the "celestial." The celestial consists of achieving decisive results with the least possible expenditure of men.

Of this, the outstanding example, the very queen of battles, is Austerlitz, which I have visited twice. It has the beauty of a perfect picture, or of any other great work of art. Lord Acton, the renowned scholar, who was believed to consume a book a day, when testing my knowledge, feigned ignorance of the position of some village and made me draw a map of the field.

Germany, in 1895, was in a period of transition. One felt Prussia creeping over western Germany, and western Germany did not like it. Walking over the battlefield of Hohenlinden–a very interesting one, Moreau's greatest victory–I stayed at an inn where Bavarians were discussing a recent speech of the new young Kaiser. "Unbelievable!" said the man who was reading it out, and threw the newspaper on the floor. They saw I was English, but insisted on bringing me into the conversation. "You don't like our Kaiser?" they asked. He had recently sent a celebrated telegram to Paul Krüger, President of the Transvaal, which implied a challenge to England. "Well, perhaps we don't," I said; and they, "We don't like him either!"

I got an unique opportunity of visiting the battlefields of the war of 1870-1871 with veteran rank and file Saxon soldiers. It was 25 years since they had lived through the most vital moments of their lives on those fields. I was able, as if through a telescope, to get a good look at the Germany of that earlier time, and it was a complete contradiction to those who read Prussia into all the history of Germany.

I had with me Moltke's small staff history, with the German military maps. Moltke himself wrote that simple and noble German which one finds in the poems of Uhland. He only twice mentions "the Chief of Staff" (himself), and each time to say that he had made a mistake, which was rectified by someone else. There are two passages of classical beauty, one of them describing the gallant charges of the French cavalry at Sedan.

My comrades would come to "the Englishman with the maps" (I was "Kamerad Pares") to identify the spots where they had stood in action a quarter of a century before. If one knew the territorial divisions of the German army, one could identify the homeland of anyone who stood gazing and thinking of those far off days, and he would carry you back to them and tell you his whole story. These memories were full of a simple modesty; never anything about himself, but much, perhaps, about the gallantry of his captain. Walking up the steep slope of Weissenberg, I asked the man next to me how he had felt the last time he had climbed that hill. "I was terribly afraid," he said simply, "but I looked at my neighbor and saw his face was quite as white as mine, so I thought it must be all right."

The memory of the whole atmosphere of this trip is enough to prevent me from ever sharing the bitterly hostile view of all German history which has been presented, to my surprise, by that highly cultured diplomat, Lord Vansittart. My comrades on this trip were Saxons, and what I saw "backward" through this "telescope" shows how mistaken it would be to identify their manners and conduct with those of the modern Prussians.

At Metz I hurried ahead to make sure of my quarters and found that far too many had been billeted on my French hosts. They asked me to help them, and I had no difficulty in getting all who couldn't be accommodated to go away without complaint.

Next morning, decked with green and white favors, the Saxon colors, our party marched through the village of Saint Privat, which they had stormed exactly 25 years before. The French housewives looked out at us with challenging faces as we passed. This village, high on the outer ridge which defends Metz to the west, had been the anchor of the French line in the battle of Gravelotte. The Saxons, who had not been in action till then, had begged the honor of making the final out-flanking movement; for this, they had to exchange places with the Guards. They passed them drawn up near a side road, listening to a short and simple sermon from a gray-haired pastor on horseback. After the exchange, the Guards went first into action up the deadly "poplar alley" and lost heavily without reaching the top of the ridge. In the evening the Saxons, now at the end of the line, went forward; they had had nothing to eat since dawn. The 107th regiment was held up for a time just where we were standing, short of Saint Privat, and seven men fell in turn carrying the colors.

Here was the monument to the regiment, to which we were bringing fresh wreaths. We held a simple little ceremony. It seemed to me that the only thing not full of reality was the presence of the chaplain and myself, who had not been there in the battle. "We were young," said the speaker, "and didn't think we could die; but my greatest friend died here just covering me." Then they said the Lord's Prayer; the deep hushed voices sounded like a rumble of thunder, and next they sang Uhland's lovely lyric, "Ich hatt' ein'n Kamaraden" unsurpassed in its noble simplicity. I'll give it in John Sampson's [1] and my translation (the lines are almost alternately his or mine)—

> I had once a trusty comrade;
>    A better could not be,
> The drums beat up for battle;
> Amid the cannon's rattle,
>    My friend kept step with me.
>
> A bullet comes a flying;
>    For me or is't for thee?
> A bullet comes a flying,
> And at my feet he's lying,
>    As 'twere a part of me.
>
> His hand he reaches toward me,
>    But to my gun must I.
> My hand I may not give thee;
> May God in Heaven receive thee!
>    Goodbye, old friend, goodbye!

These Germans were out to show every possible consideration for the French inhabitants. To me they were almost apologetic in their modest claim for their justification in the great duel. The next village had escaped annexation, and the French Government had given leave to cross the new frontier to those who wished to lay wreaths on the graves of their comrades. We took a char-a-banc, and I was asked to sit by the driver and explain what he said. I am afraid his remarks in French were very much less friendly than their replies in German. At Gravelotte I found an old

[1] The Romany Scholastic Librarian of Liverpool University.

veteran named Pohle, now a shopkeeper in Berlin, standing close to the border and hesitatingly discussing with a young nephew whether they could go across the frontier together. The nephew was a soldier now stationed in the garrison at Metz. They appealed to me, and I advised against it, so Pohle asked me to come with him, and he could not have behaved with more deference and courtesy to every French officer whom we met.

The French were full of resentment, for all their wounds were opened afresh. In Servigny, which had changed hands five times, a Bavarian military band was thundering out Körner's "Sword Song" and the other German war music. A courtly old French peasant, moving away, said to me as he passed, "Nous avons la gaité, monsieur, aujourd'hui, dans notre village." (We have gaiety today, sir, in our village.) I had a long talk with one villager, who had served first in the French army and, after annexation, in the German. "Our children will never forget," he said. "Their mothers see to that! We were offered land in French Algeria, but we French are like cats, we can't leave our home country. But never another war here! Not for those who saw the typhus which came with it last time!" and then, with a gesture toward the new frontier, "D'ailleurs ils sont mal gouvernés là-bas" (Besides they are ill-governed over there.)

It was an open sore—the first situation which I had seen that seemed to cry insistently for change. The French cared so much more than the Germans. "Are you French, Sir?" "No, I'm a German—annexed" and that 25 years after. The Germans seemed mostly indifferent. "Sky and soldiers"—that was the name for Alsace-Lorraine with the German troops quartered there. Everything seemed wrong. In Metz, on the east side, was the statue of Marshal Ney, a fine Lorrainer, on foot, pointing towards Germany; on the west, with his back to Ney, was Kaiser Wilhelm I on horseback, pointing towards France. Each shop in the city seemed to be either for the French only or for the Germans. When I started back from Servigny, at night, my French host asked with alarm, "Wherever are you going? The Germans are about everywhere." As I entered Metz, the German sentry, on learning where I belonged, said, "Be careful! The French are all about!"

On my way to the station I was struggling along alone, overburdened with my luggage. I called in German to a man with a truck, but he went past me unheeding. A few yards on, he stopped and waited for me; "Monsieur, était à Servigny hier soir," he said. "Montez vos baggages!"

Certainly the French cared most. At the other end of France, off the far-western coast, when spending a night on the castle rock of Mont Saint Michel, I passed outside a little café. The homely customers were all singing in unison a song with a lovely tune and all their hearts were in it. I came again the next morning and learned from the inn keepers both the tune and the words. It was about Alsace-Lorraine—

> Oh Alsace Lorraine
>   Hapless sisters too
> Crushed and bruised with pain,
>   German race, by you!
>
> Ah! But France can see;
>   France will not despair;
> She shall set you free
>   For a life more fair.

## ITALY: AND "RISORGIMENTO"

In 1897, I spent a hot summer in Italy travelling over the country and learning the language in the Apennines, right above the city of Florence. As to the language, the beginnings were amazingly easy. If one knew Latin and French, one could almost make up the words for oneself, and I was soon reading with ease a hundred pages a day.

It was a totally different story when I tried to get on to idiom–it was quite beyond my reach.

This was a "villeggiatura," or regular summer gathering of several families who all knew each other and came here every year. Our high terrace commanded a view of beautiful Florence far below. Across a great ravine, rose Fiesole; the Apennine road to Bologna passed our door.

One day there was a tremendous noise, though I never found noise offensive in Italy. This was the arrival of the Palmerini family, who all talked at the same time. Usually it began with something very provocative from a roguish boy named Ugo, addressed to his aunt; then came the protests of the aunt. At that point Father Palmerino joined in, as emotionally as the others–but with no success. Finally, when all voices were exhausted, someone suggested: "Listen to Grannie" and a few wise and weighty words from her, heard in a respectful silence, ended that little scene till Ugo started again with a fresh provocation.

Every Sunday there was an informal dance; and in the early dawn we would stand still, listening long to the guitar and mandolins as they passed through the ghostly olive trees on their way down the mountain to the city. Every sound vibrated in the air, and the voices of the "contadini" or peasants distracted me pleasantly from my reading. Nature in Italy seemed to me something which one had to recognize as more beautiful than anything else that he knew of her elsewhere, but somehow not as belonging to himself. The masculine figure is, I think, comeliest in Italy. No nation has had a larger share in civilization, and it goes right down into the courtesy of the peasants. I used to feel this later when comparing the captured letters of the various nationalities opposed to us on the Russian Front. "It doesn't matter whether you write," so says Angelina to Edwin, "because, if we're going to get married, it's all right anyhow, and if we aren't, nothing matters." Or again, "We hope peace will come in time for the baby Jesus"–that is, by Christmas. Civilization is packed into the "hundred cities" of Italy (*Le cento città*) each of which has had its turn in history at one time or another.

By far the finest school textbook of a nation's history that I know is the "Sommario" of Cesare Balbo. Think how much history it has to cover! It starts with the Pelasgians and comes down to his own time, the 1840's, when he was Prime Minister of little Piedmont before Cavour. It seemed an impossible task to give unity to this story, but Balbo does it with short compressed sentences which leave you thinking and understanding. Take this on Rome's road to the leadership of Italy! Vaei, her neighbor and enemy, is threatened by the overwhelming invasion of the Gauls. Rome at once goes to the help of the nearer enemy and faces the major menace, and she is routed. After that, says Balbo, every other city looked to Rome as the natural leader; and he sums up: "Potenza ammirabilmente iniziata e meritate!" (Power admirably initiated and deserved!)

As a kind of commentary on his *Sommario*, Balbo wrote a companion volume of his Thoughts (*Pensieri*) on this story, and these essays are full of suggestion on the major issues which he treats. Naturally, I enjoyed reading him. He is a kindly old gentleman, especially towards England. What Englishman, after our break with America, when most people thought we were finished, would have dared to write this: (I quote from memory, but it is not a passage that one could forget) "What does it matter how there are detached or reattached or combined in any way you please elements which are anyhow English! No, England is beyond doubt both Rome and Carthage of the present time, and as any imitation would be hopeless, so any envy would be stupid." It is my comfort again now (1947), and for the same reason that it gives.

Madame de Stael in her brilliant novel *Corinne, ou L'Italie,* which is better described as a glorified guidebook, says that Italy is so crowded with her past that it seems almost an impertinence to claim existence for the present. I felt this in my study of the "Risorgimento" or Resurrection of Italy as a State in the nineteenth century. Yet, as compared with other national movements of liberation of that time, I think this is the purest. To start with, look at the name always used "Resurrection." But in general this movement has almost a character of sanctity, often expressed in words. For instance, Atto Vannucci's big book on the precursors of Italian unity is entitled "The Martyrs." Daniel Manin, the great Italian Jew who defended besieged Venice in 1849, ends his appeal to the besieged, "With faith one always wins!" The same quality runs through the autobiography of the Unitarian socialist, Mazzini; he is much more truly religious than his official religious opponents. Take the striking passage in his memoirs on his "storm of doubt!" Sitting enveloped in a London fog, he learns that he has sent a number of young men to their death in a futile and ill-improvised rising, and he is deeply questioning how he can justify his own purposes till he finds satisfaction in the formula: "Life is a mission, and its first law is duty." The same spirit is to be found in Garibaldi, and also in Victor Emmanuel. The young King retorts to papal excommunication, "Can't they see that if they would make their subjects happy in the next world, they should make them happy in this?"–a biting criticism on the misgovernment of the Papal State. The dying Cavour, certainly the greatest of modern liberal statesmen who has also been excommunicated, asks that his door should be thrown open –"I want the good people of Turin to know that I die a good Christian," and his last words are themselves a summary of his liberal faith, "Monk, monk, a free Church in a free State!" There is a peculiar appeal to us English in the common sense that refuses to be driven from its moorings by a misuse of official authority. In the most important historical study which I read in Italy, Oriani's survey of her whole history, I was most impressed by his triumphant explanation of how Christianity won out in the three or four centuries between Jesus Christ and Constantine, the period when–thank God!–religion was not yet official, and which he regards as the finest and purest in its whole story.

Two writers especially attracted me. The first was that great fore-runner of Italian liberation, Vittorio Alfieri, with his remarkable life story "written by himself." He is the typical young noble of Piedmont, for whom his first "ten years of vegetation" are followed by ten more of "uneducation." His budding vigor is sapped when he falls into the lap of a luscious "Omphale"; he rides away from her in shame to Novara, but comes back and surrenders. Having failed in an easy task, he tries a harder one. "Omphale" lives next door, but he gets his trusty man-servant, a kind of Italian "Sam Weller," to cut off all his bright red hair and tie him in his chair; and so he does not succumb to the calls of his siren, and celebrates his moral victory by his first sonnet, beginning "I have won!" He becomes the greatest Italian dramatist of his time, with lovers sometimes on the stage "but never as loving," preaching old Rome of the Republic to the degraded Italy of his generation; and all his plays, *Brutus the First, Brutus the Second, Virginius,* are moral victories like his own. Alfieri is the precursor of Garibaldi.

The second was the poet Giuseppe Giusti. He was one of the charming group of Liberal Catholics, like Balbo and Manzoni, author of the delightful tale of *The Betrothed* (*I Promessi Sposi*). Giusti had their peculiar delicacy and distinction, but he also corresponds to the French Bèranger, as the poet of his people. He wrote the famous "Jack Book" (*Lo Stivale*), a spirited record of all Italian history, which circulated in manuscript and stirred the future leaders of the liberation. He died of lung trouble in early middle age, content to have added a few more stones to the majestic monument of Italian history.

But the Italy that I knew in 1897, was certainly sound asleep, and her lessons were again those of the past. The country seemed to be generally in charge of the "impiegati" or government officials, and they were very limp. I was prepared for Italy's attitude and conduct in the First World War; and that, in spite of Mussolini's attempt at galvanization, fixed my expectation of her in the Second.

Italy has had a share in my friendship with the historian, George Trevelyan. At his marriage I gave him Garibaldi's autobiography, and he has told me and others that that was the starting point of his own far more important Italian studies. In these he made a fine use of a method which I also practiced extensively in Russia, namely, collecting evidence from survivors of great events. When I quoted to him a sentence of Vittorio Alfieri, "The plant man grows strong in Italy," I can remember G.M.T.'s vigorous "By God it does!" as he strode about the room. To me Italy is something apart and essential. I do not think a liberal education can be complete without her.

In my rambling in country parts all over Europe I had met units of all the big continental armies on the march. In Italy it was like a very disorderly picnic, but my hosts said to me, "You should see the way they march through a big city!" The Austrian Army seemed to me to straggle along not much better. Stopping one of the stragglers to verify the name of a local village, I found he could not pronounce it and had to make a crude attempt to write it down. He was in a foreign country, as most Austrians were in many parts of their own State. In Germany one would perhaps see a squad of a few men pushing along mechanically but persistently through the dust with the same uniformity as if they were a whole regiment. The boys for me were the French, always born soldiers, full of individual spirit and enterprise, and probably singing on their way.

### RUSSIA IN THE TWILIGHT

By 1898 I was ready for Russia. Military England, what there was of it, was still for the Turks; some wit, who was asked the whereabouts of Russophobia, said, "Next to Turcomania, I suppose." Russophobia dated back before Napoleon, and had still lasted on till now. However, the verdict of British traders who had lived in Russia and even of British prisoners from the Crimean war was just the opposite.

Now that I was more or less equipped for my main study, I decided to go direct from England by ship. Certainly this was the way to plunge straight into mystery, which was then, as by many now, considered the only proper atmosphere for a study of Russia–the country where everyone was supposed to be either a nihilist or a police spy. Mystery was the atmosphere in which I passed down the Humber from Hull under fog and rain. The ship had hardly any other passengers. In the cabin was a photograph of "Queen Victoria, Queen of British Israel," and the captain firmly believed that we British were the "lost tribes." "They have 47 marks," he said, one of which to my surprise was national drunkenness. "Ye drunkards of Ephraim." They were destined to possess "the gates of the earth," i.e., the world's ports. Their gates were to be "open day and night," and an English port was the only one that could be entered after sundown without waiting for the custom-house officials. They were to go into Egypt in 1880, because there were that number of steps in

the Great Pyramid–four short, by the way, as Christ is
reputed to have been born in B.C. 4. There was to be a
great battle on the plain of Magiddo (and so there was),
and the other nations were to be crushed by huge hailstones
"the size of that bulkhead, sir." Queen Victoria was then
to be crowned Queen of all the earth in Jerusalem, and
reign a hundred years. To my plea that she might object,
the captain replied shortly, "The original order has been
given." I asked him whether, if he had been a Russian, he
would not have argued the Russian claim to be "the lost
tribes"; perhaps they would have done equally well as "the
drunkards of Ephraim." He replied that they might set up
a claim to be "Moab," in which case "a remnant will be
left." He seemed to me to challenge defeat when he insisted
that all human events had been foretold in the Bible, but
he was too good for me. To my inquiry where the Treaty
of Berlin had been foretold, he replied: "Seven men shall
take hold of the skirts of a Jew (of course Disraeli) and say
we will go with thee!"[1]

The mystery was well kept up in the customs examination, which the captain asked me to handle. Every imaginable question was put to me as to my knowledge and my
plans, and I supposed that all my answers would be recorded. "How will you learn the language?" "By entering
a Russian family." "Do you think you will find a family
to take you in?" "If not, I shall ask the police to find one
for me." "La Police n'est pas si polie, monsieur." By later
experience, I was convinced that these people had nothing
else to do that day but waste their time and mine in childish curiosity.

I found a family which knew no English, and there I
set about learning the language. Conversation was for a
time rather strained. "Potolok" (ceiling), my old host would
say, sympathetically pointing upward, or "pol" (floor),

[1] Zachariah 8.23.

pointing downward. But Russian is not anything like as difficult as it is represented to be by those who should have learned it and have not, for instance diplomatic attachés. To escape a foreign accent, one must do what the Russians did at that time with English—that is, learn it at seven; but it is a fine language for the adult, for it can be learned by understanding; it has a reason for everything that it does, and if you learn the reason, it will not let you down. I wished the inhabitants of Russia were equally consistent.

With a son of the house, I went up country to a farm more than fifty miles from any railway, and there buried myself with no books but Russian. My principal reading was in the dictionary (there was only a poor one in those days). Personally, I think that our ordinary language teaching is on a wrong basis. We take as our unit of study—the measure of a lesson—so many pages of a book; and even the most conscientious student is encouraged to think that he has done his duty when he has discovered the meaning of a given sentence. He will never need to see that page again, or even that sentence. The pages are really there to send him to the dictionary; there is his real field. I went back to the smallest unit, the most commonly to be encountered, and that is the stem. I hunted up all the correlatives and all the compounds, and was most satisfied when my search brought me on to another family of words which I had already mastered. This was by far the quickest way to acquire a vocabulary, or to put words together for oneself. One then tried them out in conversation, at first mostly in the nominative case, for it was imperative to hear as much talk as possible. For instance, I would jerk out: "Men, dogs, Germans —Women, cats, French," and then see what the rest of the company made of that. It is a peasant language, sonorous and full of color. It is a wonder what the peasants can make of their small stock of words, and they always pronounce the whole of each. Russian, unlike French or Italian, gets progressively easier; for the main obstacles, including the alphabet, are at the start.

I lived in a little log house, wore top boots to go through the long wet grass, and in some nine months was thinking as well as speaking in Russian. I travelled back alone by post horses. I carried my own sheets and a rubber tub, both of which were most necessary. When I asked for a bucket of cold water for my bath, the postmaster asked why I could not stand out in the rain. To a friend who followed me on the road, he said, "Who is that man who pours cold water over himself in the morning?" "Oh, he's an Englishman, they do that." "Is he dead?" asked the postmaster.

I can well remember that passing through a forest glade, I realized that I was having the same opportunity as the scientific farmer, Arthur Young, who travelled France in the year preceding the French Revolution and then saw it happen there; for there was every sign that what I saw around me could not last. Only Young had but two years to see the old system before it passed away, and I, as it turned out, had nineteen.

There was the same atmosphere of mystery in Russian life at that time, especially in St. Petersburg; it was a barrack city of officialdom, separated from the real life of the country in a far corner of the empire, where even transport and food supply were an unnatural strain. The Russians of that time were living in a fog. Even their own social contacts were made difficult; as late as 1902, the house porter, who was a direct agent of the police, had to be informed in advance of any proposed gathering or entertainment. It was an odd experience for a Victorian Englishman to be plunged into the Russia of Chekhov, who has often been called "the poet of the twilight" and has given us a wonderfully true picture of his period. Great masses of people, but with no common life except the chief church feasts and

other official landmarks; initiative a privilege of the officials
alone; all the real life underground and sundered. Government fundamentally suspect, as typified by the proverb,
"Crown property can't spoil"–it is too bad to! When would
all this world become vocal?

I had an entirely fresh experience. On the one hand,
everything that was said or done seemed to me so peculiar
that it stamped itself on my memory. On the other hand,
I could not trace any kind of sequence. It was indeed a new
alphabet which I had to learn.


## BASIL

In this process of unravelling, I soon had a dear and
invaluable ally. Basil was just then leaving the University
of St. Petersburg, and I only met him when I got back from
my country sojourn. He was then a lissome young fellow,
good-looking with a gentle face and peculiarly kind eyes.
We made great friends at once and have remained so, in
spite of long separations, all through the years. Basil and I
liked to take a given situation in England and try to translate it into the corresponding one in Russia, or vice versa,
to see what the difference would be. We imagined two
brothers, very close friends sitting at breakfast when one of
them gets a letter from his girl to tell him she is jilting him.
The Englisman hands it over to his brother without a
word. The brother simply says "Hard luck, old chap!" and
the subject is never referred to again. Basil's Russian brother
began just the same way, as far as the "Hard Luck!" Then,
after a pause, the other brother bursts in: "Come to the
gypsies!" which in Russia means an exaggerated "Café
Chantant"—"and after that," he ended dramatically, "there's
a break in his life forever." The gypsies served as the break. I
guessed that, in the England of that time, 80 per cent at least
of our people knew what was their work and purpose in life.

Basil was sure that in Russia this proportion was the opposite. I would say at once that, as in the statistics of literacy, the Russian figures have been practically reversed under Soviet rule, and this is really the most significant change made by the revolution.

Basil came to live with me in England for a while. He was correspondent of the best-known Russian newspaper. He was very clever and versatile. When I saw his articles, I was astounded at the variety of personalities for which he made me responsible as his informant–at one time, a "comely Englishwoman with shapely legs." Basil fitted in everywhere, as Russians are so good at doing abroad, and had always some neat and entirely appropriate remark to make when called upon for an opinion on the institutions which we visited. He also fitted into all my own plans better than any Englishman could have done. The Russian word for "friend" means "alter ego," your second self. Once when we were starting for the Lakes from Sunderland, I got a disturbing message from London which called for my presence and which I would not have wished to explain. With Basil it was quite right to say "Don't let's go to the Lakes! Let's go to London!" And to London we went, and had plenty of amusement on the way.

He was greatly fascinated with the smoky features of a big industrial town. He was amazed when he saw a miner working alone in a far out cutting under the sea. "In Russia," he said, "he would have seen devils and gone away." I asked him who he liked best of all the people he had seen in the north with me, which included a bishop and other notables. He replied, "That man who shouted 'Good old Notts!'" That was the lonely supporter of a visiting side in a league football match.

I stayed with him at his Russian home, and we went on together to St. Petersburg. At the last stop before the terminus he bought a large bouquet, and on our arrival presented it to a young lady with a child who met him there. Shortly afterwards he came round to my hotel to say he was ashamed at not telling me before that she was his mistress, though the child was hers by another connection. He wanted to know what I thought of such relations. I said I thought they were unsound, not fair to the girl, either the one thing or the other. He asked me to go and see her and talk it over. She was very anxious for marriage. I couldn't put it that way to Basil; that was something which he would have to settle for himself. She had told him that she was going to present him with a child of his own.

As we talked in my hotel, he turned over the leaves of a little Greek New Testament which I had with me, as if looking for a chance guidance. He found it in the words "He that honoreth the Father, honoreth the Son; ye cannot honor the Father without ye honor the Son." [1] Certainly the application of the text was a very novel one, but he decided at once to go off and offer her marriage. He found that she had flown. He felt convinced that she would have taken a certain train to Central Asia, where he had first met her. He took me with him, and we were in time to search the train right through between us from the two ends to the middle. She was not in it. She had gone straight to his Mother, who as far as I know, thus got her first information on the affair, and Basil received from her a wonderful telegram which I have always remembered. "The X's have arrived. Never mind, don't worry. We'll settle it, Mama." Some Mama!

Basil was always having new ideas and always asking me to share in his new enterprises. I was to come with him on a raft with the lumbermen down the broad Dnieper. I was to join him when he served as an attaché in Central Asia. I opened an envelope and found a card certifying that Bernard Pares was correspondent of a Volga newspaper

1 John 5.23.

"The Voice of Samara." This meant that Basil was the editor.

During the civil war of 1918 and 1919, after a long separation, I found Basil running a little military newspaper at Omsk in Siberia. It was called "Forwards!"; but as we were always retreating, he thought this should be changed to "Forwards Backwards!" He was living, like all of us at that time, in a railway carriage, and he offered me a bed if I ever had need of one. As it happened, one night soon afterwards, my own carriage was sent rambling down to the junction, and I took Basil at his word about two o'clock in the morning. He quickly installed me in what I think must have been his own cot, and when I awoke I saw by my side a photograph of myself which I had given him at the beginning of our friendship and which had apparently accompanied him on all his strange journeyings.

Basil's resource was never more striking than in the whirlwind of revolution. At different times he served as a night watchman, as a sportsman hired to shoot game, as a writer of plays for co-operative theaters or of tales for children, founded on ancient history.

Basil and I do not depend on meeting. Each of us knows well that the other has not forgotten him.

## Moscow University–Klyuchevsky

I arrived in Moscow with an introduction from Bishop Creighton of London to Professor Vinogradov, the famous historical scholar, who was later Corpus Professor of Jurisprudence at Oxford. Vinogradov was a big man, suggestive of Teutonic mold, bearded and spectacled; he was in every way formidable to the student, still more so to the aspirant to academic honors–say, a candidate for the doctorate–with imperfect knowledge of his subject; he would firmly push such a man into a paralysis of apology for his own insufficiency. Once when he was visiting his partner of study, Maitland at Cambridge, a well-known academic snob who used to affect acquaintance with any notability, hearing that a professor from Moscow was at Cambridge, went up to him and said, "You must know my old friend Professor Vinogradov." I should have liked to have seen the little snob as the big Russian in his metallic voice answered, "I *am* the man!"

Vinogradov found me a host and teacher, fixed me up as a "free listener" at the University and invited me to a dinner party. Everyone there seemed to know English literature better than I did, with the single exception of our lovely children's books, and they were all keenly interested in these too. They all seemed to be talking of education, and I constantly caught the expression "strength of will." I asked the lady next to me why they were all talking of "strength of will." She replied, "Because they haven't got any!"

Moscow University was on a military footing. The students wore uniforms; they were not allowed to have any student organizations. The Ministry of Public Instruction (the Russians used the French title, not the English) was not inaccurately described by an eminent academic critic as "the Ministry for the prevention of public instruction." The Minister at that time had probably been appointed because, as a Moscow professor, he had been the most reactionary of all his colleagues; he was assassinated not long afterwards.

There was a far greater number of students from the peasantry in Moscow than there could have been in Oxford or Cambridge; but I used to think that this section of the Intelligentsia had travelled further from its original moorings than any other. Only a sprinkling of the population got any higher education, but the standard of attainment was certainly much stricter than with us; it must have been much harder to become a professor then in Russia than it is now in England. Learning was sacred; for many it was almost the only thing that was. Learning, at least, had nothing to do with Tsars and police. Moscow University had a long and noble tradition of academic independence. It was indeed a light in a dark place. Nowhere in any country were there closer ties between the students and the "narod," the people, which meant the underdog population.

The students detested the program imposed on them; not the professors, but the government made the curriculum. That was the time of the close compartment system, as opposed to the happy ladder system of France, which helped an efficient student to pass up into a higher class. In Russia, Latin and Greek were literally used to bar the way to poorer scholars who had not been able to get access to those subjects. Later, in 1907, I met in the Second Duma a bearded peasant member who had triumphantly made his way past this obstacle; he sold his labor to a priest, who in return taught him Greek, and in that year he passed his final examination, though not, I am sure, in Greek. Left to themselves, the students would generally choose natural science, which is the favorite subject of all Russian children; and the Soviets had firm ground to go on when they put biology at the center of their teaching. For this and for other reasons Russian University students were strongly tinged with materialism, though it in no way extinguished the instinctive idealism of all Russians and only produced an irreligion which itself wore a religious character.

Student converse was direct and instinctively comradely. When they passed out and joined the ranks of the obedient officialdom—for nearly all posts were official—they no longer carried the flag of freedom. I had my share of the interminable talks which Russian students so much sought and enjoyed. They were the chief recreation in life, as they were also the chief business; for they had no chance of putting their ideas into practice, and a good speech was regarded as in itself a big achievement. They therefore treated these talks very seriously. They would begin with a word which I learned to fear, "printeipialno" (in principle), which meant you were in for several hours of it. I would sometimes ask, "Can't we get on to 'konkretno'" (which meant "to sum up"), but they would never agree, because that would spoil the whole game. Then would follow a whole string of general principles, and the means for their attainment had only secondary importance. If one was following this kind of logic, political assassination became a secondary detail. The claim they made on your sympathy was one of emotion, because the system which they were fighting had so much greater opportunities of violence than they had. The Russians recognized a certain "heroism" which was based solely on resistance and sacrifice.

The leaders of student strikes could claim respect not only for their courage, but for the very real damage they did to their enemy, the government. The universities were indispensable to the government in order to equip the State with public servants. Even in times of reaction the work of technical education went forward. A university degree was as good as a guarantee of paid employment, and the student who was thrown out of the university for his part in a strike was automatically thrown out of the state service.

I had the great privilege of attending the lectures of the best of Russian historians, Klyuchevsky. He succeeded his teacher, Solovyev, who had done more through digging into the archives than anyone before him, and Klyuchevsky presented the conclusions based on the spade-work of Solovyev and himself. The son of a priest and at first designed for the priesthood, he was unlike the Intelligentsia, though he inevitably belonged to it, in giving full value to the old traditions of the people, its patriotism and religion; but his patriotism and religion had nothing whatever in common with the official parodies of them current at the time. He received the direction of his studies from the great reforms which he had witnessed in his youth, the emancipation of the peasants from serfdom, the introduction of trial by jury, the establishment of local self-government based on election and responsibility to the public. His first studies traced those institutions of Old Russia which moved toward constitutional government; and later, when Nicholas II was setting up the Duma, Klyuchevsky was one of the very few scholars consulted. He delighted me by his always sound and discriminating objectivity. For instance, in the eternal controversy between the idolizers of the West and the idolizers of Old Russia, he went his own way with firm step, doing justice alike to all that was reasonable in the views of either School.

Klyuchevsky was rather slight in stature, with keen, clever, kindly eyes. He talked rather than lectured, with simplicity and freedom of inflection, every word being carefully chosen. It is known that he spent infinite time on preparation, but the result was a perfect lucidity, like that of Robert Louis Stevenson or again of Pushkin. It was an intellectual treat to listen to him, and he was a sure guide through all the complexities of Russian domestic history and all the tangles of Russian public thought. That is why his pre-eminence was and is still recognized by all. He did not live to see the revolution; he gave up his Chair in 1911, when the government put spies in the classrooms to watch the students, and he died directly afterwards; but his work has been claimed by the Soviet government as a national possession. Though Klyuchevsky dealt principally with the economic history of Russia, it won him election to the Imperial Academy of Science in right of literature, and it is a thousand pities that so far the only English translation of this cardinal work entirely obscures its literary charm.

Klyuchevsky set me a standard which I have always followed in my own study of Russian history; he bound one fast to the Russian people. He carried his survey of its story only down to Catherine the Great, and one had to fill in the rest as he would have taught it. It is significant of the darkness of that period that the work of this loyal and faithful interpreter of his people could only circulate in the notes of his students till 1906, the year of the First Duma; the succeeding volumes showed an increasing freedom. The last appeared after his death.

One day in the spring term of 1899, going to listen to Professor Vinogradov, I found all the lecture halls in commotion. The Rector of the sister university of St. Petersburg, appointed by the government, had utilized a public occasion to give a sharp rebuke to the students for their political activities. He was publicly hissed, and in the demonstrations which followed, the Cossacks used their loaded whips. Now, Moscow University was going on strike in sympathy with St. Petersburg. No lecturer except Vinogradov got a hearing that day. He spoke a few wise words of understanding and sympathy; he realized what they felt, he said, and he realized too the broken lives that were the price of disorder; but work was work, and he was going to give his lecture. The Tsar appointed a more liberal-minded Minister of Public Instruction who, on learning that Vinogradov had got a hearing from the students, invited him to confer with their leaders. The government policy was then sharply changed back, and those who had met Vinogradov and put their views to him, being identified by these conferences, were arrested. Vinogradov resigned his Chair in protest and left the country. He was escorted to the station by a great mass of the student body and made a short, wise, and brave speech to them there. When later established at Oxford, he was appointed to a visiting professorship in Moscow; but this coincided with another sharp period of repression, and

Vinogradov, with Kluchevsky and some forty other professors, again resigned, this time finally.

I did not come to Russia again for five years–until 1904. My year of study had given me more than enough to digest. For some time, everything seemed to me so strange that I asked whether in Russian thought there was some unknown extra dimension which was to us inaccessible. Why did *this* lead to *that?* My puzzling ended in the opposite conclusion. It was we that were complicated. They were much closer to nature; they were big children swayed by the moods of men; they were to be reached most easily by simple friendliness, to which they would never fail to respond.

# CHAPTER III

## 𝕮𝖊𝖆𝖈𝖍𝖎𝖓𝖌 𝖎𝖓 𝕰𝖓𝖌𝖑𝖆𝖓𝖉
## (1895–1914)

### THE UNIVERSITY EXTENSION MOVEMENT

I HAVE mentioned in the preface that I had a second task beside my own studies. So far, Russia, as a subject, was almost entirely outside our program of education. The very little that was done was haphazard and almost exclusively concerned with the language and not the history. The one instrument which I could myself utilize was not directly inside the universities, but in the missionary enterprise of public lectures outside, which was known as University Extension.

Almost up to 1900, England had really little more than two teaching Universities, Oxford and Cambridge, and these, I am afraid, were largely luxurious clubs for the favorites of fortune. A needy student who arrived at one of them by a scholarship, with all the subscriptions to clubs and other expenses, was compelled at every step to feel his lack of means. As to study, the universities were the most difficult places in which to do much, except in the long vacation. There were constant social interruptions–often, it is true, connected with intellectual interests; and the only thing to do was to close one's oaken double doors, and pretend to

82

be out. Meanwhile little Scotland, which, in the continental sense, was always truly a "university country," had four higher institutions, France had seventeen, and Germany twenty-two. I will not hesitate to say that the educational movement in England and Wales, which, since then, has brought up the number of our teaching universities to 12, with most of the students hard at work, has been powerfully reflected back on the habits of Oxford and Cambridge. It has been equivalent to a peaceful revolution, which already makes its effects very visible in parliament and profoundly changes its atmosphere and traditions.

This peaceful revolution was in the first place largely due to conscience-stricken scholars of Oxford and Cambridge, who by means of the University Extension movement threw out feelers into all the big centers of population, by regular lecture courses on any subject chosen by the audience. These audiences were called centers. The lecturer was sure of his pay, for the necessary sum had to be collected in advance; this was done by vigorous citizens; but the continuity of the work entirely depended on the success of the lecturers. Though these came to be a very competent and sometimes gifted personnel, I think there is hardly one of us who has not at one time or another ruined a center. This created a new condition for university teachers; namely, a tolerably competent standard of exposition became a first essential. This has most certainly reacted on the standard of teaching inside the universities themselves, where the students hardly had the choice of attending or not.

The enterprising pioneers of Oxford and Cambridge found many existing solid centers of culture. In the north of England, which apart from Scotland was the finest field, there were Literary and Philosophical Societies, with good lecture halls and sometimes with good libraries. These were invaluable as nurseries for the growth of new local universities or university colleges (the latter had not the right of granting degrees), which in many places the work of Oxford and Cambridge University Extension helped to foster. Correspondingly, the advent of these new colleges replaced the old extension lectures.

In other ways than exposition the work supplied training for the lecturers. At the time-honored "Lit & Phil" of Newcastle-on-Tyne, when I lectured there on the unification of Italy in the nineteenth century, I think there were as many as seven persons in the audience who probably knew the subject more intimately than I did. One was Dr. Thomas Hodgkin, author of "Italy and her Invaders," and he kindly allowed me to hand over some awkward questions from the audience for him to answer.

While I was carrying on my study abroad, I found university extension work, apart from its stimulus, an ideal instrument for putting out the results of my own studies. I never had to lecture on any subject which I did not like, for each engagement was a separate offer. Also, as compared with regular university work, I was free to spend as many lectures as I wanted on a given subject; for instance, I covered the Napoleonic period in 24. The lecture season stopped in early spring, and I had the rest of my year for continuing my work abroad. The social spade work, practically begun by my Father's generation, had developed into organized movements of many kinds for cultural activities. With the one difference that in Russia they were widely repressed by the government, which only gave them an extra stimulus, I was to find the same atmosphere and the same movements in that country, where good citizenship was at this time an ideal; and our English experiments were always appreciated there for their spirit of freedom and for their practical good sense.

At that time I was reading five hours a day and travelling and speaking at various mining centers in the evening. I did not have to present any course until I was ready to. I began with the French Revolution; then, Napoleon, then the national movements which brought unity to Italy and Germany; but I continued to evade the history of theoretical socialism. At least, in these industrial centers I had the substance of that problem all round me.

I had a course consisting of six lectures on "Patriotism on the Defensive," in which I took each of the great states, of Europe at a moment when it had its back to the wall, to repel an invader. Each nation had its own type of patriotism and even its own type of contemporary lyrics, but it seemed to me that there was a generic difference between the last moments of successful defense and the first moments of aggression.

We got a great deal of education from our audiences, and one came into close contact with many fine leaders of culture; not, of course, with our colleagues in the movement, for we were like commercial travellers and always on different roads, though we passed each other every now and then with an augur's wink, for we all had common experiences. But we met social workers of all kinds, of whom the north of England was full. One stayed with the organizers of the lecture courses, of whom I found a goodly proportion were doctors; that is a profession which is always "in action," always at grips with real life. I gained a firm impression that the northern working man was the best asker of wise questions and the best educational material with which I have had to deal. At the bottom of all his instincts lay a determination not to be swayed by any propaganda, but to rigorously reserve the right of forming his own convictions for himself.

## ROBERT SPENCE WATSON
### Quaker and Fighting Radical

No one among those whom I met interested me more or was more formidable a critic than Dr. Robert Spence

Watson. Like Hodgkin and many other supporters in the north, he was a Quaker; for the Quakers almost formed the nucleus of the "Lit & Phil," as of so much cultural and social work in the district; but Spence Watson, whom I knew only in his old age, was the most militant Quaker whom I have ever met.

As a young Radical of the vigorous north, he had first attracted general notice by a hardy and successful attack on the then Prime Minister, Benjamin Disraeli, of which he told me the story. Disraeli issued a circular to captains of the British merchant navy instructing them that if a slave from a Spanish-speaking State in South America escaped to a British ship, he was to be sent back. Spence Watson was of our bold English crop of Hampdens, whose individual civic courage is speckled all over our history. He wrote to the papers to say that if any captain obeyed this order, he, Spence Watson, would prosecute him under the law of England, and also one Benjamin Disraeli "as an accessory before the fact." "Who is this fire-eating fellow, Spence Watson?" asked Disraeli. "Well," he was told, "he's a man who will do what he says." Disraeli was far too good a humorist to risk a prosecution on this count, and the circular was withdrawn.

Spence Watson had been a personal friend both of Garibaldi and of Mazzini, and had dearly longed to break his Quaker bonds and join Garibaldi's "Thousand," who conquered Sicily and Naples for Italy. In those days Joseph Cowan, a big business man in Newcastle, used to smuggle Mazzini's propagandist literature into Italy in the innocent disguise of "Cowan's bricks."

After the Italian cause was won, Spence Watson took the same keen interest in Russian liberty; I am afraid he did not quite see the profound difference between the methods of the two movements. He was President of the Friends of Russian Freedom, who, among other things, financed the escape of political prisoners from Siberia; he told me it could be done, on an average, for £12. His house, Bensham Grove, just outside Gateshead, was a nest in which the Russian emigrant conspirators often gathered—Kropotkin, Volkhovskoy, Stepniak, who had killed his man in St. Petersburg and was later run over by a train in England; and letters with the Gateshead postmark were an object of special interest to the Russian police. The Society worked separately in two sections—the Quakers and others who found the money, and the Russian revolutionaries, who used it. Once, as Spence Watson told me, the Russians were equally divided on a question of the first importance; so they came to Spence Watson, as President of the whole Society, and asked him to give judgment. "All right," he said. "What's the question?" "It's whether to assassinate the Minister of the Interior." "No! no! no!" ruled Spence Watson who, Radical as he was, was also one of the best types of John Bull that we have ever had.

Spence Watson was typically British; but his mind and temperament were an excellent introduction to those stout Russian radicals, with whom he worked so closely. Before the Revolution they were called the S.R.'s, or Social Revolutionaries—*par excellence* the party of the peasants, among whom their work lay and from whom they drew their chief characteristics. Though they were all social workers, they were sturdily independent and could never have accepted the cramping discipline of the Russian Marxists. They were in fact fearless individualists, many of them in the best sense patriotic and religious. I was to see a great deal of them, and greatly enjoyed them. Nearly all the acts of individual daring before the Revolution were their work.

The Spence Watsons' table was supposed to be teetotal. "What will you drink?" asked my host, when I stayed with him to address the Sunday Tyneside Lecture Society. "I

would like some beer," I said. "I'm sorry, my wife won't
have it in the house; have some champagne!" After the lecture he said, "You'll want something after an effort like
that, have some more champagne!" We settled down into
a conversation on the condition of the Liberal Party at the
turn of the century; he had been one of its early pioneers.
He found that now the Liberals had no energy, and went back
to a comparison with his earliest days. "Then," he said, "we
Radicals were very few, but quite determined to turn our
small minority into a majority, and quite prepared for it
to be a long and strenuous job. Say we would bring a Bill
into Parliament to introduce the Ballot in elections. No one
would know what it meant, and we should be routed. Next
year we would try again; we should have improved our Bill
and would get a few more votes. Next year the enemy would
mock at us: 'Aren't you going to propose your ballot again?'
'Certainly!' we said. At last people would begin to ask themselves, 'What *is* the ballot?' and then its advantages would be
obvious. But there would still," he said, "be several more
years' work required to beat the vested interests arrayed
against it." He ended, "Of course, we had plenty of other
proposals too, but we wouldn't think sixteen years too long
to get through some really good reform. Nowadays the
Liberals are quite different. They meet at their yearly conferences and discuss, say, woman's suffrage. Someone asks,
'Didn't we pass that last year? Very well, we'll pass it again.'
And not one of them puts a hand to the spade work."

During the Boer War, Spence Watson went through a
period of public hostility as a "pro-Boer," and a wild doctor led a mob to an attack on his house. The visiting book,
for a few perilous days, bore the words: Siege of Bensham
Grove. This brought a reaction, and the wild doctor was
generally condemned; but Spence Watson wrote a letter to
the paper to say that this was quite wrong. He and the doctor were good friends, and he understood his motives.

The Liberals of those days were fighters, for liberty had to be fought for. By now it was taken for granted. "I must own," he said to me, "I'm usually agin' the government, even if it's my own side."

## Bishop Westcott

It was in these same northern counties that I again came upon Bishop Westcott. The north was rather slipping from under the influence of the Church of England when one of our two greatest theologians and bishops, Lightfoot, came to revive it. He was followed to Durham by the other. West-cott was a little thin nimble man, quick of movement, with a wonderful, peering, almost illuminated face, framed in its gray whiskers. He was entirely selfless, absolutely simple and alight with intellect. I think his was perhaps the best mind that I have ever met, and he was then 80; all the other prelates of the north looked up to him as something more spiritual, something above them. His eyes, half asleep under his thick lashes, would suddenly flash out with a childlike brightness at some new interest.

I lived in his castle lodge while I worked over his area, and I had a standing invitation to Sunday supper. He lived only in a portion of the vast palace of the old Prince Bishops of Durham; but he housed a number of keen young men, training for ordination. One of his most sincere admirers was an old agnostic, Mr. Nicholas Kilburn; he was an iron-master, but he had also built up three first-rate musical societies, which sometimes rendered music as yet hardly known outside Germany. At one of his rehearsals, in the stormy weather common in those parts, the little bishop peered in one evening; he had heard the music from out-side. One of Westcott's favorite subjects was co-operation, and Mr. Kilburn explained to him that originally the differ-

ent parts were written as separate tunes, and only later were
they brought into complete harmony.

The bishop was always asking me questions about the
Russians. "Are they collectivist or individualist?" he once
asked. I thought it would be hard to give an answer to so
general a question for a whole people. "It's worth trying,"
he said very quietly. This, from him, made me think; and
when I thought, I saw something which I had never noticed
before. "Well," I answered, "they all say they are collectivist;
but I think they are the most rampant individualists I have
ever met!" I was thinking especially of the Russian "S. R.'s"
who in 1917 proved much the most numerous party in the
country, and were the most typically Russian. "They'll have
to change it," said Westcott quietly–and surely that is just
what, long after Westcott's death, they have actually
done.

One of his answers bowled me over completely. He was
sharply critical of professional football, which was the most
popular sport in that district. Like many others, he called
the professionals "paid gladiators." I asked if he would like
to hear what my Russian friend Basil, who had lived with
me in this district, had said about an English League football match. "I should very much like to hear it," said Westcott. "Well," my Russian friend said to me, "you English
combine the Greek ideal of the joy of life with the Christian ideal of self sacrifice." "The second! The second!" said
the Bishop quickly, his witty eyes sparkling with mirth.
"The Greek ideal is confined to amateur football."

The young men trained by Lightfoot and Westcott
achieved a real recovery for the Church of England in this
area; it was the agnostic Mr. Kilburn who emphasized this
to me. Clerical salaries were low in these parts; and that
helped the Bishop to place the best of these young men at
key points in the growing population, where the first require-
ments were zeal and vitality.

The vastest room in this huge palace was very difficult to heat and was called the drawing room; it was really more like an ecclesiastical concert hall, adorned with portraits of bishops in their full canonicals. There was a great strike of miners in this district, which only Westcott was able to settle to everyone's satisfaction. He invited the miners' deputation to stay to tea in this huge room. Glancing round at the ecclesiastical portraits, one of the miners made the delicious remark: "I suppose, sir, that this is something like what Heaven will be!" The Bishop told me this story with a malicious relish.

## ALBERT MANSBRIDGE
### Founder of the Workers' Educational Association

In the early years of this century Albert Mansbridge, a young married working man, sacrificed his own interests to create a new organization which by now covers all England. It is called the Workers' Educational Association. I have been proud to hear him tell how he and his little wife went out to sit among the trees on Clapham Common and read the first letter from a university, that of Liverpool, which gave him any encouragement, and which came from me.

Mansbridge made no attempt to set up a new educational authority or a class propagandist organization. He assumed that standardized teaching was to be obtained from the universities. But he insisted on the right of the students, who in this case were all workers, to choose their own subjects. They might be quite ready to take a dive even into such a subject as Dante under a well-known scholar such as Mr. Philip Wicksteed; but more ordinarily they chose subjects which in the end turned out to be a most valuable addition to the existing university curriculum—the history of the In-

dustrial Revolution in England, the history of the Trade
Union and Co-operative Movements, or the rights and duties
of citizenship. To satisfy these demands, the universities had
to train lecturers who were later very useful to the teaching
inside. The W.E.A. never dictated any particular views; on
the contrary it insisted that all views must be presented to it
—"whether Marx or Marshall"—as they used to say.

I have spoken of the working man's insistence on forming his own convictions. The first time that I addressed the
Tyneside Sunday Lecture Society, an exclusively working
men's organization with an audience of two thousand at two-
pence each, the secretary, himself a working man, with entire
sincerity, said to me as I went onto the stage, "Don't forget
that if they applaud, it's a failure!" No better thing has ever
been said to me about public lecturing. I could see at once
what he meant. On that forest of faces, as thick together as
blackberries, the common expression was one of the keenest
interest and the most alert caution. It was as if they were saying, "This man has been in Moscow, and we haven't; and
we must watch him carefully, to see whether his account
hangs together." Applause would thus be a politeness, a sign
of interest relaxed.

Suppose that Albert Mansbridge had been a Russian and
free to do what he did in England! But of course, he would
have been swept away into Siberia, by the idiotic suspicions
of the Tsar's police! I think the Russian revolution might
then have followed a much more temperate course. He was
not setting up a new kind of knowledge, but going to the recognized sources of learning and insisting on getting what he
wanted from them, and above all reserving the rights of his
fellow students to be told every side of a question and to form
their own conclusions. It is precisely in this instinct of intellectual caution in our working population that I have always
seen our best safeguard against ill-considered change. Mansbridge's work has been recognized by an honorary Doctorate
of Oxford University.

## The Great Days of Liverpool University

In the movement which raised the number of universities in England and Wales to twelve, the most brilliant part was played by Liverpool, and there I was invited in 1902 to work as staff lecturer of University Extension. The design of those who invited me was, that in this way we might hope to introduce the study of Russia for the first time into the full curriculum of a university.

In their extension work one might say that Oxford and Cambridge had "gone wide" and had practically divided England and Wales between them. The new universities, on the other hand, had to try to "go deep," that is to get in contact with all educational activities within a much more limited area and give them an intelligent and consistent direction, as has sometimes been done by foreign universities.[1] We had, for instance, in the Liverpool area, a number of isolated little groups conducting their studies entirely on their own. Such an organization was the Home Reading Union, and it was very valuable; it had been founded by a great social worker of the northern counties, Rev. J. H. Paton of Nottingham, and it circulated good programs of coordinated study in print. Dr. Paton at one time invited me to be its organizing secretary.

The work of University Extension in Liverpool had been entrusted to an exceptionally interesting man. Norman Wyld remained all his life an eternal child, a child of intellect; he was full of quick and stimulating ideas; he took little account of conventions, and not too much of the demands of tact. He carried the better minds with him by his inspiration and his keenness; the trouble was that he was not a good finisher. Later, he won considerable initial success in getting really important spokesmen of capital and of labor to join in pro-

[1] Particularly by the Polish universities towards the end of the eighteenth century on the eve of the final partition of Poland. It was an heroic attempt to save the country by moral resources.

moting the study of problems which were not controversial
but were of equal importance to both parties. Norman Wyld
was the first university organizer to give real support to Albert
Mansbridge. We invited him up, got his ideas and set about
applying them. Norman Wyld, again, was the first to do something for that poor lost class called "Acting Teachers," that
is, uncertificated, and arranged special classes to help them
to complete their own studies.

Only one new university was founded in Russia in this
period; but the air there was full of everything that Liverpool stood for, with its courageous attack on new or neglected
fields of study and in particular it was full of all those activities which came under the heading of University Extension
and in Liverpool were fostered by the University.

All this Extension work was only an outcrop from a
peculiarly brilliant group of men, who were out to give new
life to the university idea in England. The first of the new
British universities was called "Victoria." It was a league of
three colleges—at Manchester, Liverpool, and Leeds. The last-
named was still backward till it fell under the inspiration of
that great educationist Sir Michael Sadler. But both Liverpool and Manchester felt confident that either of them could
do much more alone than the two or the three could do
together, and this confidence was certainly proved right by
the event.

Liverpool, still only a university college, set up a "University Club" to help to make it a full university; the club
had a fine motto: "Expectate, veni!" (Come, expected one!)
You could not obtain from the government a full University
Charter with the right to grant degrees unless you could prove
to it that you commanded the necessary local finances; and
either Liverpool or Manchester would of course do far more
to build up its own university than both of them together
would do for a mixed institution. The Club existed to foster
this idea, and it caught the imagination of the best minds in

the city. It became the right thing to belong to it, and several of the most enlightened and important business men made a habit of lunching there, say, once a week, to keep in touch with all the new and often brilliant ideas which were floating there. I think the average business firm in Manchester was a much more solid affair than in Liverpool; but we certainly had an exceptional galaxy of great captains of business at the top. In particular the great shipping firms had, I think, a wider outlook of business statesmanship, which framed us squarely in the general pattern of national needs in education. Such were the Holts, Rankin Gilmore and Co.; and above all perhaps, Sir Alfred Jones, who combined the Elder Dempster steamships with many other responsibilities. Then, in chemistry, there were the two great names of Brunner and Mond; and Liverpool too was the center from which radiated far and wide the activity of Lever, later Lord Leverhulme. All of these were munificent benefactors of the university idea in Liverpool.

There was a little upstairs room at the Club, in which would meet the conspirators in a new enterprise. "Who's the coming man in Classical Archaeology?" someone would ask. "John Linton Myres." "Does anyone know him?" "Yes, I do." "Ask him up for a few days!" "All right." At the next meeting John Linton Myres would be present. "Myres, supposing you had an absolutely free hand, how would you run your department?" John Linton was peculiarly prolific of ideas, and we got a fine flow of them. "Now, let's see! What would that mean in the shape of regulations?" The detail of this question would be thoroughly canvassed and criticized, and we should get an agreed program. "Yes, I think we can put that through quite easily."

One of the big merchants would be there; they did not throw their money at us; they came in, and helped settle how to spend it. "Now what would that mean in staff and equipment?" he would ask, "Oh, yes, I'll do that." On one single day Liverpool founded four Chairs of Archaeology! There was a rush to found professorships, and the matter would be almost one of routine. "Mr. Vice-Chancellor" (the equivalent of an American College President) "I would like to found a Chair of Spanish." "Well that, at present reckoning, would mean £10,000!" The expected one came. And imagine the satisfaction of the newcomer at finding everything so easy. "Congratulate me!" said Myres. "I've got my regulations through in a month. At Oxford it would have taken me three years!"

This last detail will help to explain Liverpool's most remarkable success. A stable progressive majority had been built up in long years on the Faculty of the old College and was able, if it was united, to write any new word that it wanted on the slate. We had a little genius of a legislator in Alexander Mair, later Professor of Philosophy, who had a practical and important part to play. "Look at page 150 of Regulations"—this might come from the Vice-Chancellor, always objective and circumspect, but not obstructive, "You find there that this is something we can't do." "Ah yes, but turn to page 457," said Mair "and there you'll find that this is just what we are ordered to do." We had a much more powerful pillar of progress—there can be pillars of progress—in the greatest Celtic scholar, Kuno Meyer; his brother Eduard was, I believe, favored by the attendance of the Kaiser at his lectures, when Wilhelm felt inclined to display his patronage of learning, Kuno had first come to Liverpool as a very young man, and by now was professor both of German and of Celtic. In our faculty battles, which were well worth fighting, Kuno would come out, backed by the general prestige of German learning at that time, as a kind of conservative spokesman of progress. He would explain that what seemed new in England, had long been practised as a matter of course in any self-respecting German University.

Kuno was recommended to any young professor who came to Liverpool as the ideal "father confessor" on academic construction, but he had a very sad end. A year before the first great war he was invited to a new Celtic Chair in Berlin, and we even allowed him, though absent, also to retain the Celtic Chair in Liverpool; but it came out that in his activities in England and more particularly in Ireland, he had all through been acting as a German agent against us. In the war I had evidence that he visited the German prison camps where Irish soldiers had been segregated from the rest, to collect men for Sir Roger Casement who, as we know, landed in Ireland to promote a rising and was captured and hanged as a traitor. Kuno wrote abusive postcards, not to his academic opponents in Liverpool, but to those who had worked so intimately with him. For him the crash of the Hohenzollern monarchy was the bitterest of tragedies, and he died soon afterwards.

I very much admired the attitude of our Vice-Chancellor, Sir Alfred Dale, toward our sharp academic controversies. I think he struck exactly the right mean between latitude and firmness. I was at that time engaged in founding a School of Russian Studies. Dale let me go ahead on my own, but made me feel, without saying so, that he liked me to come in to see him in the evening before any proposal of mine was ventilated on Faculty, and therefore became official; and he invariably improved it and then supported it. This was, I think, an ideal attitude for any head of a free university.

By the excellent procedure which I have described earlier, Liverpool got its great men while they were still on their way to greatness. We had already a number of famous names—Charles Sherington, the physiologist, Ronald Ross, Nobel prizeman for the discovery of the malarial mosquito, Walter Raleigh, later professor of English Literature at Oxford, and his successor, Oliver Elton. I met Elton first when he read a

paper of a very critical kind on mysticism. I'm afraid I came
to the conclusion that he was always to be approached as a
mystic, and in our long and intimate friendship this approach
always worked out very well. Elton had already published a
first class textbook on the Romantics. After what had ludi-
crously been called his "retirement," he published an even
better textbook on the great Augustans of English Literature,
and later his survey of English poetry *("The English Muse")*
which was regarded as the best of the three. He learned Russian when in the fifties, and at 78 he produced the best verse
translation of Pushkin's major work, *Eugene Onegin.* He
next did even better with that masterpiece, the *Epilogue* of
the magnificent Polish poet, Mickiewicz. When well on in
the eighties, he seemed to learn a new Slavic language every
year, translating their lyrics into refined and scholarly English verse.

I could add a whole roll of names to these great ones;
and on the administrative side, I was not surprised later,
when the reformed and reconstituted University of London
took four of its Heads of Colleges from among the teachers
of Liverpool University which had only been founded as
late as 1902. A conservative in Liverpool was a liberal in
London.

We had a number of half-time professorships at half
salary, and our skirmishers were constantly coming in fresh
from excavation in Egypt, like John Garstang, or exploration
such as my own in Russia. I was thick with the reformers in
Russia while I was taking part in new ventures of university
construction in Liverpool, and I'm bound to say that it was
my friends in Liverpool who were really cutting most ice.

## THE LIVERPOOL SCHOOL OF RUSSIAN STUDIES

It was in this brilliant company, with the advantage of
all its wisdom, vision, and enterprise, that I, as a younger

man and a late arrival, set about building up the first school
of Russian Studies in a British university. There were few
antecedents; the somewhat eclectic work of Professor Morrill,
once professor at Oxford, a few very modest beginnings in
Cambridge and in London. We aimed from the start at a
whole department, on the principle now known in England
as "regional studies" or "nation study" and in America as
"area and language." I could not have founded the School
without my continued visits to Russia, to which I shall return
later, nor without the existing presence in Liverpool of a
number of what we called rather casually "side-shows–such
as the School of Tropical Medicine of Boyce and Ross, handsomely endowed by Sir Alfred Jones and others, the School of
Archaeology, already mentioned, with its very able organizer
John Garstang, the School of Architecture of the brilliant
Charles Reilly, and the School of Town Planning of Ads-
head; all these Schools were growing up in my time in Liverpool University and the organizers had a fellowship of
purpose.                                              58366

Our own School was inaugurated in 1907 in the City
Hall by the Lord Mayor, and had an independent committee
of its own, strongly entrenched in the Chamber of Commerce
and other centers of city activity. It collected money for definite objects and offered it to the University on the sole condition that it be applied to them. It could thus have a con-
structive policy of its own and made it unnecessary for us to
ask a share in the distribution of common funds. We began,
of course, with a teacher of Russian; and we had at different
times, apart from my own teaching of Russian History, posts
in Russian laws and institutions, Russian economics, and
Polish language and history; I was myself appointed Reader
in 1906 and Professor in 1908.

We issued a quarterly *Russian Review,* in which most
of the articles were by Russian scholars or public men; latterly, if any important bill was introduced into the Duma, its

author wrote an account of it for us. We had a tremendous strength in Russia in Harold Williams, who knew everyone worth knowing and could get them to do things for us. Vyacheslav Ivanov, leader of the School of Symbolist poets and friend of Alexander Blok, took the responsibility for our literary criticism. When the Russian monarchy fell in 1917, seven out of the twelve Ministers in the first Cabinet of the Revolution were among our regular correspondents.

There were some Russian contributors who, so far as I know, never published their views elsewhere. The President of the Third Duma, Nicholas Homyakov, who led the visit to England in 1909 and was my wisest counsellor in Russia, wrote to an extensive list of the most important Russians in scholarship, literature, and public life asking them to write for us. He himself gave us one of our best articles. We never paid any contributor except, curiously enough, the exiled revolutionary, Khrustalev, President of the Soviet of 1905, and that was because we heard he was starving in Paris, and we sent through his views to lie on the table of high dignitaries in Russia.

One thing that we did, was to send in by invitation, to the Foreign Office a memorandum advocating the establishment of a special branch of our Consular Service for Slavic countries. I wrote the memorandum, but the notes, which were more extensive and much more valuable, were by my colleague in Russian economics, Vladimir Höffding, perhaps the ablest pupil of the famous Russian professor, Peter Struve. We appended a map, showing that Russia was probably the part of the world most neglected by us. We had already a very distinguished corps of specially trained agents for the Far East, and India was looked after by our India office; the School of Oriental studies later also took care of Africa. Our "memo" received official consideration, but the general direction of policy at that time was to blend all Consular Services in one.

Sir Alfred Jones

## Shipping Magnate

No one became more active in the support of our School of Russian Studies than the shipping magnate, Sir Alfred Jones, the prime mover for the institution of Chamber of Commerce in Great Britain. He was, I think, the quickest thinker of all the men I've met; the second was Mr. Lloyd George; the third was Lord Northcliffe. When I first went to him–and you had to get everything you wanted to say into one sentence–he said, "I've no time for this; I've no money for it, but it's a good thing; would you like to address the Liverpool Chamber of Commerce?" I replied, "Yes, if you'll take the chair," and he did, but as time went on he became more and more fascinated with the idea. I sometimes received from him two letters in one day, but each always only of one sentence; I had two from him on the day he died, and one the day after. Once he threw in a third letter to say: "This is a fine thing you're trying to do, and I wish you good luck with it."

I saw him write such letters. He would touch a bell, the moment some idea came to him in a conversation, and dictate the one sentence which over and over again made all the difference in getting things done. Only once did he ever put to me any question which could have an interest for him in his own business. He asked "Is there a shipping line in St. Petersburg that takes emigrants directly to America?" I said I thought not, they seemed all to come through Hull and Liverpool. He never said anything more, but I learned after his death that he sent someone to St. Petersburg to make further inquiries.

Sir Alfred Jones spent three days every week in London and three in Liverpool. He was still only in middle age when his health was greatly damaged by his active rescue work during an earthquake in Jamaica. At a certain crisis in our Russian organization it became imperative for me to see him. He was at Africa House, dealing with a whole host of employees and others, and it was only by insistence that I could get through to see him. He said, "Come and lunch with me at the North Western Hotel," and then turning to one of his sea captains, "What was the depth of this rock?" At the hotel there was waiting quite as large a gathering, and Sir Alfred arrived very late surrounded by a third crowd. "Go in to lunch, all of you!" he said, "I haven't got time." "Sir Alfred," I said, "I must see you." "All right," he said "Come out onto the platform. Now what do you want me to do?" While he ate a bun at the refreshment bar, I asked him, "Will you go to the London Chamber of Commerce and say so and so, and will you go to the Foreign Office and say so and so?" He telegraphed me that night that he had done both. A week afterwards he was dead. After his death his secretary sent to me a copy of a letter: "Why didn't you give that little fellow Pares a better chance of seeing me? He was looking dreadfully ill; we must give him a voyage to Madeira."

I will record an incident which filled me with special respect for him. Once when we were discussing our next moves, he proposed something which seemed to me very dangerous, and I said "Sir Alfred, I think that's the biggest mistake we could make." He simply replied, "Don't let me make a mistake!" and I wondered how many other big men would have taken it like that. After his death I was going to see a successor of his, a man of only moderate ability, at his old place of work at Africa House, and I felt that somehow I was instinctively bracing myself up to be at my very best and quickest. It was simply because whenever I had gone there before, it was to see Sir Alfred Jones.

## John Macdonald Mackay

### Highland Chieftain

The man among our colleagues whom all progressives hailed as our leader by right of genius and spirit was John Macdonald Mackay, one of my own dearest friends and teachers. Mackay came to Liverpool University College as a young professor of history and grew with it till the time of his rather early retirement in 1914. He, if anyone, could be called the maker of the university. When he left Liverpool, Oliver Elton collected from his colleagues and ex-students, articles on what they owed to Mackay; and even in subjects far removed from his own studies, it came out that what they owed to him was vision. In my own case, this sometimes seemed to me uncanny. This great Highlander had second sight. He had had no relations with Russia or Russians. All he had to go on, in my problems of building up my School, was what I had told him; yet he would tell me back things about Russians whom I knew and he didn't, things which were undoubtedly true.

One of the most constant benefactors of the University, Mr. John Rankin, a man whose name stood for honor, had had a ship sunk by the Russians in the Japanese War; they accused it of carrying contraband, which it certainly did not. I made the matter a test case in Russia as to whether they really wished to promote better relations with England, and I ultimately secured for the firm, after full examination of the case, a sum of £17,000 in compensation. In the course of this, I got the help of a great international scholar, who, on the other hand, had by no means a fine reputation in Russian domestic politics. "He has the soul of a slave!" said Mackay, as if talking to me of someone he knew very well, "but you can get him on his international reputation," and

I'm afraid he was exactly right. One night when I was discussing with him some difficulties in my organization of a
representative visit of Englishmen to Russia, which in the end
came off with great success in 1912, Mackay, with prophetic
eye suddenly said, "Pares, write!" and dictated a telegram to
the Russian Minister of Commerce, which solved the problem
in question.

You always had to listen to Mackay. Sometimes his talks
would be long and rambling. At such a time Kuno Meyer,
just for the fun of the thing, discharged a pistol at a picture
just over Mackay's head and shattered it, without producing
the slightest interruption in Mackay's discourse. Yet you never
knew when there would come suddenly a flash of genius, cutting a bright vista through all the clouds of talk. Mackay
definitely taught me everything that I ever knew about university construction, and his ideas are at the bottom of all my
later work at the School of Slavonic Studies at London University. But he was also the architect of genius who charted
the streets of the heavenly university.

In academic debate Mackay was sometimes impossible.
The magnificent portrait of him by Augustus John, perhaps
this artist's finest work, which hangs over the dining-room
fireplace of the University Club, shows Mackay in doctor's
red gown, boldly probing the unknown. He might have been
not a professor but a highland colonel scanning the vision
of his coming attack. Sometimes he could only say things with
the rude vigor with which he thought them. I have even had
to pull him back into his seat on the Senate when it passed
all limits. In an academic duel with another great scholar, we
could only induce his opponent to visit Mackay with a guarantee of safe conduct, and two of us were there to keep the
peace. At one point, I was pulling Mackay back by his coat-
tails. "If that's what you think," said the visitor, "I shall
resign." Mackay, this time, went back to a perfection of con-

tented calm with the reply: "A very proper step for you to take." Yet the issues for which Mackay fought, were great ones. He had in him the full spirit of the great medieval universities, especially of his own country. He had truly charted our course, and he had no patience with timidity or convention.

I remember so well Mackay's exit from the University. With Highland secretiveness he had made all his arrangements for going; I knew of them, but no one was to be told. He had many opponents, and he wanted to remain in action until the end. His last meeting of the Senate appropriately, like the end of Napoleon, took place in a storm. Mackay was fighting point by point all through it. Suddenly, about a quarter of an hour from the end, he said very quietly, "This question, I think, should be settled by my successor." So he was really going! The secret was out at last, and the ranks of Tuscany breathed a deep sigh of relief! But they still asked "Where is Mackay going next?"

## THE TRAGIC STORY OF MACKAY AND MUIR

As it was the progressive majority which had started the new course and brought in the new colleagues, it strengthened itself with each fresh newcomer till it was vulnerable only to our own dissensions. We had a rather offensive name for our group, "The New Testament"; and N.T. was the cypher on our summons to a caucus. A witty opponent, when criticizing our too overwhelming emphasis on research, translated it "No teaching." And indeed our greatest weakness was the mediocre material of our student body. A poor pedestal to bear on it all these high ambitions.

The ordinary spokesman of our group was a younger man of singular ability as an expositor, and much better known to the city world than Mackay. This was Ramsey

Muir, later Chairman of the British Liberal Party. Muir's life was also identified with Liverpool–not only with the University but with the city. He had been Mackay's pupil, and glimpses of his teacher's greatness never entirely left him in the tragic conflict which followed. After further study at Balliol, Mackay's old college at Oxford, where he made a great impression, particularly on the Master, A. L. Smith, Muir came back to Liverpool as Mackay's assistant. Ultimately the Department of History was divided between them, Mackay taking the Ancient, and Muir the Modern and Medieval.

Of my affection for Mackay I have already spoken; but Muir was also a good and true friend, and though he well knew of my part in what followed, he gives me an especially generous word in his autobiography. Muir was a real good fellow and a fine colleague. He helped generously in the work of others; on his own impulse, he subscribed five pounds a year to the guarantee fund of my School; he supported more than one student out of his own pocket. He was obviously very gifted, particularly as a speaker. He was once brought over to the United States as the best lecturer of his day in England. The honesty and sincerity of the man were above all question.

There were radical differences between these two men. Mackay was reprehensibly idle in writing, and left hardly anything behind him; Muir wrote profusely on much too many subjects. Muir was, I think, the most fluent man I've ever heard; and "fluent" was just the right word. He had a big booming voice with great rounded phrases, which simply demanded attention, but quite often there was very little behind it, and I had a naughty feeling that sometimes Muir himself didn't know how he was going to finish a sentence, and the end was settled by the sound and rhythm. Once when he was to address a student group of mine, he asked me to suggest a subject, and straight off talked on it for 45 minutes without a break. Mackay was no orator at all. It would have been easy to say that Muir was always speaking, and Mackay was always thinking. Generally the N.T. caucus left the interpretation of its proposals to Muir.

A sharp issue devoloped between the two. It was of the first importance, a question well worth quarreling about–the respective emphasis to be placed on lecturing and on tutorial teaching. The tutorial was the new thing, and Mackay stood for it. By the way, he was not a good example for his own cause. His dreaming was altogether above the heads of the kind of local student that we had. The lecture I have always myself regarded as a *pis aller* or second best. If we could only converse with each of our students, instead of just haranguing them, we should certainly be able to do far more real teaching. Lecturing was Muir's forte. In particular, he gave a general course of history covering Mackay's period as well as his own, and he had no particular research behind him outside English history, and there it was chiefly a study of local records. The medieval period was one stumbling block; for Muir, with even less scholarship, covered that period as well as the modern.

It was a most pathetic quarrel. I acted as a kind of friend of Mackay and did my very best to moderate his attitude. In this way I saw all the correspondence. It varied with all the different moods of the moment. At one time it would be "I can't possibly quarrel with you," and at another "I can't possibly agree to *that*."

The decision was entrusted by the two men to three of their colleagues, another of us acting as a kind of friend to Muir. The three judges, almost inevitably, were closer in view to Mackay than to Muir. But their chief aim was to make an acceptable compromise, and they allowed Muir to continue his general course of lectures. They sought to remove friction by introducing a medievalist to separate Ancient from Modern History. Neither contender was satisfied, and a deep split was carved in the staff. Both men left Liverpool not long afterwards, and this was really the end of the greatness of the University. Anyhow, we were bound to be dispersed in part by the Great War, which followed directly. After that, the era of great visions was finished, for little money was left anywhere; and the University settled down to an unexciting life of routine work.

To poor Ramsay the disappointment was profound and permanent. All his roots were in Liverpool where he was an important figure, and he had rendered the most devoted and effective service to the University. I can remember so well the delight which he had felt in it, his sense of privilege at living at such a time, and the reverence which I have even heard him express for Mackay as our leader. His whole heart was in the place, as one must feel from the rousing university song which he wrote for us to the tune of "The Low Backed Car."

> For Liverpool's a city
> That makes your pulses leap!
> Enthroned beside
> The racing tide
> Of her river, broad and deep;
> Where ships from all the nations bring
> Rich freights across the seas
>
> And the harbor lights
> Glitter out of nights
> And the flag flies in the breeze
> O'er the Liverpool Varsitee!
> Oh that is the place for me!
> Be you poor, be you rich,
> For it matters not which
> At the Liverpool Varsitee!

Disappointment awaited him too in his later political career. He was quite exceptionally qualified as a public speaker, an excellent candidate for parliament, and would, I believe, have made a good Under-Secretary in a Liberal

Government. But there was now no possibility of a Liberal majority. The Great War had put an end to a long liberal period of European history. Muir did get into Parliament but was only there for a year. He became Chairman of the Liberal Party. He did see better than others that it ought long ago to have passed on from the attainment of political democracy to that of economic security, without which political democracy alone can almost remain a fiction. One of the saddest books I have ever read, is Muir's account of his own career, which he frankly regards as a failure. The book contains an extravagantly distorted portrait of Mackay, which I think Muir himself would have modified if he had been alive to issue it. I could allow for and dismiss this feature; and I was struck almost poignantly by a most impressive section under the head of "Confessional," in which Ramsay showed that he had fully and honestly recognized his own inner weaknesses.

Ramsay Muir did himself to death with an impossible program of public speaking, to hold up our morale during the war, a task for which he was splendidly equipped. I came on his traces, among other parts, in a remote corner of Lancashire; and from what I learned of his work there, I could not be surprised that with its endless motor journeys day and night through storm and snow, it had proved fatal to him. Before this, Mackay had also died, though, with that secretiveness which he shared with so many Scotsmen, the only record of the place given to the public reads, "Somewhere in the Highlands."

And it was in the atmosphere of storm and stress of this great quarrel that my own married life came to an end. For several years radical differences had proved insurmountable. I went off to the War; and as there was no breach on either side of the only conjugal obligation of which the laws of England then took cognizance, a legal separation by agreement was reached in December, 1918.

# CHAPTER IV

## Russia Awakes
## (1904–1907)

### ON THE CROSSROADS

IN 1904 it was evident that in Russia the long reaction and the long sleep were over. I had had five years to puzzle out the strange materials of my first long visit. In general, I had come to two conclusions: First, that Russians were not the enigma that everyone seemed to suppose, that it was not that they had some extra "dimension" which was lacking in us, but that, if anything, they were short of a dimension. Second, that the right way to regard them and treat them was as very clever and delightful grown-up children, with the mutability of children but with the passions of men, which is just what very often made the trouble. I have ever since felt that in Russia the first requisite was character, and the first need education.

I went to Russia for some three months in 1904 with a thought-out program of country travel and study. My special task was now somehow to get through to the Russian people and find out what we had in common, both in ideas and interests. The government was always to me entirely secondary, except that it was the only window through which Russia was allowed to look out on the world and the only door by which we could come in; and once inside, I always got as far away from it as was possible. This was not very hard, and if you got lost perhaps they forgot all about you.

I carried a letter from that fine soldier-churchman, Archbishop Maclagan of York to the Metropolitan Antonius of St. Petersburg and Finland. The two had been photographed hand in hand like two nice children. The Metropolitan was a firm Liberal; he died, after an unsuccessful attempt to enlighten the Tsar on the real character of Rasputin.

My talk with him was very instructive to me. He said my plan of country study was a "nice" one ("dobry," which means both good and kind), but he warned me against any comparison between Russia and my own country. I had much better try to compare Russia of today with some earlier picture of her. "If you do that," he said, "I think you will find there is a little less *laziness*." He put his finger on just the weakest feature of the Russian character, and it is the one that is most radically improved since the Revolution, which he was not to live to see.

I followed his advice systematically in all my travels. If I visited the out-patient department in a rural hospital and found it well filled, I would ask what sort of attendance there was five years before, and it would be clear that the staff were quickly capturing the confidence of the peasantry.

In bidding good-bye and Godspeed, he very kindly asked if I would like to have his blessing. I made a bad mistake in my Russian. Welcoming his kind offer, I added "though I am not of the Orthodox faith." He gave me a kind rebuke which I have always remembered—"Christian faith," he said. I have often thought of these wise words. This was the whole attitude of the Russian Church, so very different to the Roman Catholic. It was right for an Englishman to belong to an English confession, but that was only another part of the Christian Church throughout the world.

The sky was heavy with a coming thunder storm. Between the clouds it was lit up with great patches of bright
red, as is common in the northeast near the Urals. I had
unwisely given part payment to my peasant driver at half-
way, and he had promptly got drunk. I had to bundle him
into the cart and drive in his stead. As we hurried on to
escape the storm, there came from behind me his mutterings,
"Woe! woe! to them who live to the great world war." This
was in 1904! The Russian peasant is full of poetry, especially
when drunk.

Just escaping the downfall, we stopped at the nearest peasant court-house, the home of the local elective peasant
administration, where I had been authorized to pass the
night. The Elder was away; so was the Clerk; there was only
the little ragged care-taker, perhaps the lame duck of the
village. We spent the evening together, and he was excellent
company.

His questions about everything English were endless.
This was not long after the time of a sharp conflict in England over the House of Lords. He wanted to learn in detail
how we passed a law. This, I explained, began in the House
of Commons; then it went on to the House of Lords. "But
what happens," he asked, "if the House of Commons passes
the law, and the House of Lords won't?" "Oh, then we elect
a new House of Commons." "Oh, yes, I understand *that*,"
he said with a touch of impatience. "But what happens if
the new House of Commons passes the law and the House
of Lords still won't?" That was exactly the question to which
we had been seeking an answer in England.

"What sort of parish priest have you got?" I asked.
"The little father is no good, but the little mother is; and
then, you see, he's only the priest." I don't think this distinction between religion and its representatives is so readily
made in England.

At night he carefully planted a line of five chairs against
the stove for my bed; that would be how a peasant would

sleep, but for me it was far too hot. Next morning at my request, puzzled but obliging, he brought me a bucket of water; and while I poured it over myself into my rubber tub, my little host stood shivering in active sympathy. He saw me off like an equal and an old friend.

Ivan Kostrov was the most well-to-do man in his village in a district which was often held up as a model of a self-respecting peasantry. His cottage had something of a towny look, with stuffy windows, decorated with flowers and even with books.

Kostrov had been chosen as member of a government commission to study the causes of peasant drunkenness. As the only peasant member, he felt a natural nervousness; would he succeed in worthily representing his class? There was nothing stronger in the instinct of the peasant than his loyalty to his class. It was not for nothing that the peasantry alone had had for many centuries its own social history and an administration founded on election. And the whole class was a submerged or under-dog class. The Minister of Education encouraged him not to be afraid and speak up. He thought it wisest to ask to give his opinion in writing, and sought the help of a small lawyer.

His titled colleagues on the commission said confidently that the peasants would always be drunkards; in fact, that the emancipation from serfdom had come too soon. Kostrov asked what steps the squires in their time had taken to improve things, and in particular to give their serfs any education. The peasants had had to set up their schools for themselves, and they regarded it as a "holy work." They very well knew how to discipline their community. If serfdom had continued, none of this would ever have happened. And weren't they ashamed as they had so long been masters of the peasantry, to speak ill of their own people. "Good lad!" said the Minister to him afterwards, "I thought you'd speak up. You'll see, they won't slander the Russian peasant."

The peasants had been told, in the Tsar's summons to the first Duma, to send "their best men," and they sent Kostrov and many others like him. I saw him again after the Duma had been forcibly dissolved. He was very dejected. Said another such ex-member, "It went past like a dream."

I got word of Kostrov again after the Revolution. It appeared he had been classed as a "kulak," and dispossessed of all his property. That was what was likely to happen.

I was going to visit a country factory. These were much praised at the time (1904) as helping the peasant to combine something like town wages with country conditions of health. France and Belgium were given as good examples, and there were several in the province of Vladimir, not far from Moscow. This one was owned by a Belgian family which was very proud of its interest in the peasants, and also of the good which it believed it was doing them.

On the road lived a peasant elder, whom I had been especially advised to visit. Often these men were of a fine type. He was a tall, upright, bearded man, probably in the early fifties, neatly dressed, with good top boots, and with a simple and sound intelligence and a perfect poise and simplicity of manner. There was an easy independence about him, not aggressive but quite ready to hold his own. A good peasant never cringed and never encroached; he was content to be what he was, and his approach was that of an equal. When he knew I was going to the factory, he thought I should save time, if he stood on the step of my cart and came with me, so that we could have our talk on the way.

All Russians who had to deal with the peasantry would preach to them, whether it was the Governor, the Colonel, the priest, the doctor, the schoolmistress, or the revolutionary propagandist. It would have been worse than senseless for me to do the same; and once they saw that it was their opinions that were wanted, they responded with a simple vigor of thought which often delighted me. I had no better or more enlightening conversations, and they took a conscientious trouble in expressing their views which one would hardly have found with an Intellectual, but might in England have expected from a Northumbrian miner.

The pompous little Belgian manager of the factory spoke at great length of the little patriarchal paradise which his family had created for the local peasants. As he showed us around, he saluted each passer-by cordially by Christian name–sometimes wrong, it appeared. Then came the usual samovar and tea and further explanations. The peasant elder sat quietly listening. "And what do *you* say to this?" I asked him. "Do you feel the factory is a blessing to the village?" "Disinfectors!" he said pleasantly. "What do you mean?" I asked. "Well," he said, "they draw off all our scum, and we are very grateful to them. A good peasant doesn't need to come here." The manager was on his mettle and broke in with a great flow of words. "Well," said the peasant elder after a time, "I must be going—to the Disinfectors!"

I arrived by train in pouring rain at an unearthly hour of the night at Borisov on the river Berezina, the Birch Tree River. It was a little wooden Jewish town, very squalid. It was here that Napoleon on his retreat from Moscow, found his road cut, and only by brilliant strategy made his way across the river, which runs here through half a mile of black peat bog in various currents, like a bunch of silver snakes. This was the time of the Japanese War. I was making my way on foot, which was always thought suspect for a strange traveller. I had sent on all my luggage and carried only a knapsack and two large cannon balls wrapped up in paper, which I had acquired on the battlefield of Borodino.

I arrived in a torrential rain and took a cab to a small shabby inn, where I was given a room with a door with no lock. I told the inn keeper to have a pair of horses ready for me next morning to drive to Studyanka about six or seven miles out, where Napoleon made his crossing.

Next morning, while I was having my breakfast and was studying my maps, I felt the inn keeper looking over my shoulder. He informed me that I was summoned to the local police station. The police captain clearly did not believe my explanations. He wanted to know why I should wish to study "a fortress"; this was a simple village, and had been mostly taken to pieces by Napoleon to make his bridges. I produced the visiting card of the Governor of a neighboring province, but he evidently suspected me of having stolen it. At this, it was necessary to play my last cards. "I have had special permission for my travels," I said, "from the Minister of the Interior, and I was asked to report any instance of incivility. It seems to me that this is a case in point." He was rather baffled at this, and sought a way out. 'You will have to get special leave from the police colonel," he said. "All right, where does he live? Let's go and see him." So we formed a little train, the inn keeper still following, curious to see the outcome.

With the police colonel, I began at the right end with the Governor's card, and said I was sure I should have the same courtesy as I had had everywhere else. He replied in the same vein: "What can I do for you?" "I want to go to Studyanka." "Then why not go?" "Your police captain says I have to get your permission." "What nonsense!" he said, and turning to the police captain: "You will be in attendance on this gentleman during his visit here." And I followed up, "Won't you come with me to Studyanka?"

He was very gloomy during the long drive in the rain. Fortunately we had a hooded carriage, and I left him in it for five hours while I tramped the battlefield on both sides of the river. "You've pretty well tortured me," he said, not unamiably when I came back to the carriage. "Well, what could I do? You tried to stop me from coming here." "Is it necessary," he said thoughtfully, "for history to be so accurate?" I asked him to dinner, and we parted good friends.

One word which I was constantly coming across in my country travels was *Nachalstvo*. It meant "initiative," but it was used as a name for the government, to whom all initiative was presumed to belong. The corresponding phrase for leave to proceed with anything ran: "There will be no hindrances." On the fields near Smolensk where I was studying the local administration during the Japanese War, an old peasant woman asked my escorting police officer why, if I was an Englishman, I was allowed to go about like this. No explanation was given her, but the one magic word "It's allowed." If anyone questioned the official view which my escort had given me, he would be shied off with the words "Where are you climbing to?" Consequently there was no intervention of the public where there would have been in another country. For instance, for a drunkard walking in Moscow and brandishing a large saw–the treatment was left to the "Nachalstvo." The government was not challenged; it was a foreign body, with which it was better not to interfere. Here again was one of the most significant changes to be produced by the Revolution.

## Two Fine Liberal Leaders

In the twenty-three years of black reaction, after the senseless murder of Alexander II (1881-1904), the faint hopes of lovers of freedom had rallied round two close personal friends, both sturdy paladins of Liberalism–Petrunkévich and Ródichev.

John Petrunkevich, as I always called him throughout his long political struggle, resolutely abjured all weapons but those of reason; in consequence, he was more suspect to the reactionary government than the revolutionaries themselves. In 1878, on the County Council of Chernígov, when the Tsar appealed to the loyalty of his people, Petrunkevich tried to obtain a truce from the revolutionaries in their hunt

for the sovereign's life, and came out boldly with a speech
of pure liberalism; he pointed out that while the opinion
of the country was suppressed, there could be no real answer
to the appeal for loyalty. Soldiers entered the hall, and he
was sent away into exile, where he was kept longer than
the revolutionary leaders themselves. Nicholas II had once
said that Petrunkevich should never enter his palace. On his
return from exile Petrunkevich moved north to the Province
of Tver, which was the heart of Russian country Liberalism,
and was also the home of Rodichev.

Fedor Rodichev three times in his long life spoke up
boldly to the Tsar himself. He had asked Alexander II to
give to his loyal subjects "what he had given to Bulgaria"
(by liberating it from the Turks), that is, a constitution!
When Nicholas II came to the throne he had framed the
address of the Tver County Council; he asked that the voice
of the people should be listened to and not only the people
but the officials also should keep the law. Nicholas dismissed
this appeal, describing it as "senseless dreams," and Rodichev, who was one of the most brilliant barristers in Russia,
was forbidden to live in St. Petersburg.

I was to get to know both men intimately, and they
became two of my most honored friends. Of John Petrunkevich I would say that he was the only Russian I have ever
met whom I would have wished to see as Prime Minister of
England. His daring was matched by his sound political
wisdom, and he was quite capable of recognizing points of
contact with the best of his opponents. He used to discuss
with me English conservatism with a restraint and respect
which sometimes proved exasperating to his devoted wife,
who followed him through all the buffetings from right and
left of his political career. The liberalism of Petrunkevich
was something broad, strong and general, which could have
rested on the instinctive support of the more enlightened
of the peasantry and on the whole mass of Russian non-

official opinion. It was, I think, a great misfortune that just at this time the leadership should have passed to a much narrower man, Milyukov, who turned liberalism into a kind of party formula, with a party discipline and curious but often most unfortunate tactics.

Rodichev, in his old age, was to become one of the four greatest orators produced by Russian parliamentary life, which in oratory, if in nothing else, certainly set a higher standard than we had in England. His was a natural eloquence, and his speeches read as first-class literature. They would rise and rise in height until at the critical word—always the peak of boldness—they would scatter like a rocket into a shower of sparks. It was he who stamped the field court-martials of Stolypin with a phrase that stuck—"the Stolypin necktie"—which cost him a temporary exclusion from the debates. Both of these two men were the truest types of Russian liberalism before it became the creed of a given Party.

### "ENGLAND IN RUSSIA"

## The Moscow Congress of Town and County Councils, July 19, 1905

The movement for freedom, as the word is understood in England or America, took public shape in Russia in November 1904. It was the County Councils that led. They, like the town councils, were legal institutions on an elective basis created by the sovereign, and they were really the only bodies which could rightfully claim to be the chosen spokesmen of the public opinion of the country.

In November 1904 the county councils, at a meeting of their chairmen, had called for freedom of conscience, speech, meeting, association, and press, with freedom from arbitrary arrest (*Habeas Corpus*) and for an elected national assembly.

The Tsar had replied with a feeble promise that he would himself make reforms and with a rebuke to the county councils, after the manner of the one he had given to Rodichev, for interfering with what was not their concern. But the movement had received the backing of the professional class as a whole through vocational unions of all professions, the first "trade unions" in Russia. The Tsar was himself abashed by the national indignation at the failures of the Japanese war; and on June 19th of this same year, 1905, he had been compelled to receive at his palace a deputation in which the most illustrious figure was Petrunkevich. He had even unexpectedly replied to the deputation, "Lay aside your doubts! My will, the Tsar's will, to summon a national assembly is unchangeable; I am thinking about it day and night. Go and tell those near you, both in town and in country, and ask them to help me in this task!" This was taken as a direct invitation to the county and town councils; and on July 19th representatives from all of them gathered in the magnificent house of a great noble in Moscow. It was Petrunkevich who secured me admission.

The chairman, Count Heyden, was a reverend figure; he had been reader of petitions to the reforming Tsar, Alexander II, and he set the highest example of the constitutional instinct in Russia. The first great act of the congress was the proposal of a Grand Remonstrance, carrying the name of a great English precedent of the Long Parliament in November, 1641, in which were exposed• all the illegal acts of the government itself. This proposal was rightly entrusted to Rodichev, whose knowledge of law and at the same time his fearlessness pointed him out as the right spokesman. It was debated with intense interest, but without any real difference of opinion, and was adopted unanimously.

The government had published its scheme for the establishment of the promised National Assembly. This was considered next. It contained absurd limitations of the franchise, and restrictions on procedure and competence; most of the meetings would not be accessible to the public. This so-called "Bulygin scheme" was unanimously repudiated; but it was decided not to abstain from making use of it, if necessary, to obtain something better.

At this point came the highlight of the congress. What was "the something better"? The gentle Count Heyden, with a glint in his wise old eye, had recommended us to buy, before the next day's sitting, copies of *"The Russian Gazette"* (*Russkia Vedomosti*), the unofficial organ of the liberal professors of Moscow University. This number we found to contain the whole draft of a constitution for Russia to be discussed that day. It was a neat piece of journalism, for in no other way could it have been printed. The introducer and also the principal author of the draft constitution was Professor Muromtsev, a figure combining the highest scholarship with the greatest dignity. Murontsev was professor of Roman Law in Moscow University, a subject on which so many constitutions have been based. In his youth a gypsy had foretold to him that he would be the president or "Speaker" of the first Russian Parliament, but the whole of his life and public work had made the choice inevitable.

Muromtsev explained to the congress that it would not have been proper to propose to fix a constitution except by representatives chosen for the purpose from the whole country. He therefore turned to a precedent in British parliamentary procedure. In the House of Commons a bill is presented "for the first reading" only to show the general principles at which it aims, and discussion and voting are deferred till later. What Muromtsev and his fellow-authors wished to offer to Russia, was a document showing the public the kind of thing that was meant by the word "constitution." The provisions in the suggested draft were as wise as the way in which it was presented to the congress. It did not propose to abolish all existing laws at the outset and to start out of nothing. On the contrary it took the form of amendments, of course of the most sweeping kind, to the existing regime. There was no need to fight over controversial points, and the draft was adopted almost unanimously on the general understanding on which it was presented.

The *Russian Gazette* was at once suspended by the local authorities, but its work had already been done. Toward the end of the congress, the police made an attempt to disperse it, but this only resulted in a fiasco. The courtly chairman politely quoted the words of the Tsar's answer to the recent deputation, explaining that all present were "near to them in town and in country." The police found no answer to this. There was a little explosion which some of us took for a bomb, but it was only the snap of a photograph of the discomfited police as they walked out.

The congress finished with an appeal for the support of the country, worded by the veteran leader Petrunkevich. I have never forgotten certain words of that appeal, for in the light of history they had later to be taken as the noble epitaph of Russian Liberalism. "The path which we point out to you is a path of peace. It is to lead the country to a new order of things, without convulsions, without bloodshed, without thousands of unnecessary victims."

## Harold Williams
### Linguist, Saint, and Scholar

Through the discussions of the congress, I sat on the floor by the side of Harold Williams, the greatest scholar whom we have ever sent to Russia. He was well known to me by reputation. The year before Mr. C. P. Scott, the famous and fearless editor of the *Manchester Guardian*, had invited me to become his correspondent in Russia. This would have broken up my work in founding the School of

Russian Studies in Liverpool. Very soon it became clear that the *Guardian* had found a better man.

Harold was the son of a Non-Conformist Minister in New Zealand of Cornish origin. Very early he developed a quite uncanny gift for languages. At 12 he had written a glossary of the dialect of an obscure island in the Pacific. His parents thought of making him a missionary preacher, but this went against his nature and gave him a stutter which never quite left him. Continuing his interest in languages, he made his way for further study to Europe; at that time, if I'm not wrong, the number of languages which he had so far acquired was two less than his age, but he learned two more on the voyage.

Arrived in Europe, Williams took the degree of Ph. D. at Munich. At that time in the neighborhood of Stuttgart a group of Russian Liberals were gathered around one of the most striking of all Russian political thinkers. This was Peter Struve, at once perhaps the most brilliant and most erudite of Russian economists. Struve began his public career as an exponent of what was called "legal Marxism" and supplied books for Lenin to study during his imprisonment. But Struve could not go the way of Lenin, of whom he became perhaps the most formidable opponent, and gravitated toward Russian Liberalism. During the Liberal period in Russia, Struve was really the flag-bearer, though he was always evolving further and further, sometimes for the time, leaving his followers bewildered, but carrying them on in the end to some new advance. Williams regarded him as the best intellect he had met.

Williams was already the best interpreter to the British public of the liberal movement in Russia. So much I knew; but at the time not very much more. We came out of the Great House in which the Congress had met, full of exhilaration and perhaps almost of exaltation; yet I could not help feeling much more than doubtful, as we passed the lines of churches with beggars stretching out distorted arms to us, whether English constitutionalism could really find a firm footing in Russia. We passed on into the Kremlin. There, on the low platform, with the Old Russia all around us, we talked on through the whole night till the dawn again lighted up that galaxy of churches and monasteries and the crenelated walls. We discussed Russian terrorism. In my view, it led nowhere. Williams had a better understanding of the Russian Intelligentsia and a greater sympathy with it. When we separated, we were close friends and partners for life.

I have known no such linguist as Harold. Before he was 40, we counted up together 40 languages of which he confessed a knowledge. But the extraordinary thing was that a change directly from one to another did not seem to be any kind of strain to him, and—more than that—natives of the language did not notice any particular accent. I used to think his mind must be something like a plasm, taking immediate and accurate photographic impressions. When he left me on the Polish front in the war, a Pole said to me, "Has your Polish friend gone?" In a field hospital he started straight off in Hungarian with a big wounded Magyar sergeant, who had had no one to talk to for months. It was as if a switch in Williams was turned, and he became unintelligible to me and entirely fluent with someone else. When Edward VII visited Reval in 1908, the Esthonian Press gave a banquet with speeches in French, German, and English. Harold replied in good Esthonian, and they carried him round the room. His objective was never philology, though he could not help being a philologist. It was the riches of these unknown literatures that fascinated him; hardly anyone else seemed to have the key to them. Yet there was no place for him in our system of education; he had to make his way by newspaper work; and at times he was even without that, or perhaps drudging at some spadework for a sensational American correspondent. But he ended his life as foreign editor of the *London Times*.

There was something saintly about Harold Williams. He was very gentle. He carried a kind of culture in himself which charmed all the best minds. I was twice with him under fire; and his particular kind of courage was something that rose above the danger of his surroundings, as if they had nothing to do with him.

On the day after his memorial service in London, his friend Maurice Baring published in the *Times* these four beautiful lines:

> Upon the bread and salt of Russia fed,
> His soul in her high sorrow soared and bled.
> He kept the bitter bread, and gave away
> The shining salt to all who came his way.

## PAUL MILYUKOV
### The Professor in Politics

It was at the Congress that I first met Milyukov, who in a political sense was the chief organizer behind the whole movement. He had been arrested by the tyrannical Minister of the Interior, Plehve, in connection with some hazardous work of University Extension. Plehve had visited him when under arrest and asked if he would like to become Minister of Public Instruction. Milukov replied with spirit that he would prefer Plehve's own job at the Interior, which included the control of the police.

At the point which we have reached, Milyukov was, in my opinion, at the highest peak of his career. It was he who had organized the professional class as a whole, in support of the movement initiated by the county and town councils. This was a very briliant piece of work; for one can imagine the difficulties of getting for any single political expression the support of all the members of a given profession. I think Milyukov had even then clearly in his mind the purpose of organizing a single Liberal Party in Russia, practically on exactly the same lines as would have been followed in England. Milyukov was a first-class historical scholar and a life-long friend both of England and more especially of English Liberalism. His views never seemed to me to diverge much from what one could hear at any time at the National Liberal Club in London.

I had no idea at the time how important he was, and he very courteously allowed me, even during the Congress, to detain him with a long conversation; but I noticed even then a certain impatience which he showed at the suggestion that to go too fast now might mean to go very much slower later on. "We can't," he said, "go the way of your four Georges," which would certainly have been the last thing for anyone to ask of him. I think I gauged his position correctly when I reckoned him to be trying to hurry on the Congress while at the same time wanting to hold the support of the much more theoretically minded professional class, who were more to the Left. I couldn't help thinking that I saw too much here of political maneuver, and that not of a very able tactician. In fact, when I later saw him at work with the Zemstvo Liberals I could see that he was not "putting it over." He was particularly interested in all I could tell him of how in England Labor politicians had always to be anxious of losing the confidence of their supporters, who suspected them of passing up into a higher class where they would no longer belong to the "people."

To follow his career farther here, would be to tell the whole story of Russian Liberalism, with all its successes and all its failures. But whatever I may think of Mulyukov as a leader and tactician, I have a profound admiration of him as a man, for his invariable coolness and courage, sticking bravely to his course, which disclaimed any violence,

and indeed for a wonderful personal gentleness under every
kind of harassing from left and right. Nothing could shake
his fiber, and he remained deeply true to his Liberal principles.

## A Peasant Meeting for Reform

Petrunkevich's appeal for the support of the country was
circulated, and I heard of an impending meeting of peasants
in his own Province of Tver. This was at a distance of over
ten miles from any railway station; yet of these peasants
forty per cent had worked either in St. Petersburg or in
Moscow. It was, in form, a legal meeting, under the existing
system, of chosen representatives of the seventeen villages of
a given canton; but the promoters had determined to turn
it into one of support for Petrunkevich's appeal.

When I arrived by cart with no one else but peasants
there, I was taken for an official come to forbid the meeting. When they knew I was an Englishman, they entertained
me handsomely in the local court-house, killing a chicken
for me.

The meeting was intensely interesting. The first demand
in the program was in itself a surprise. "We want," they said,
"to read real books," evidently with a well justified suspicion
of the kind of literary fare which the censorship allowed to
reach them. As a matter of course, they passed unanimously
the demand of the Peasants' Revolutionary Party—commonly
called the Social Revolutionaries or S.R.'s—that all the land
should belong to those that labor on it. The common demand of the factory workers for an eight-hour day went
through with the same unanimity, as was natural with so
many present who were partially factory workers.

Then came an interesting moment. The organizers proposed a demand to stop at once the war then going on against
Japan. This almost broke up the meeting. The last thing
that these peasants meant to do, was to vote for the humilia-

tion of Russia when she was already being soundly beaten. There were angry protests, with a shaking of fists, and the speaker could not continue.

In Slav communities there has always been an ideal of unanimous decisions. When this is apparently unobtainable, the meeting stops of itself and there will be a heated discussion. To put the procedure into English terms, it might be said that "the House went into committee." At last a speaker again mounted the table and tried his luck with an amendment. It showed in a high degree the common sense which one so often met in peasant discussions. His "demand" was that the promised national assembly should be summoned as soon as possible and consulted on whether to go on with the war. At once there were shouts, "That's right! That's right!" One man added, "And if the national Assembly says the war is to go on, you'll see we shall be sure to win it." The amendment went through triumphantly.

The last "demand" appealed to me strongly. It claimed "an amnesty for all who had suffered for the just cause of the people." "People," in Russia, meant before all things the peasantry, and their demand was for the liberation of their political champions.

Torches, flares, and even lamps were brought out onto the muddy street, while every one present signed his name to the resolutions which had been adopted. A doubt then arose as to what should be done with this document. To send it in to the government authorities, would simply mean to ask for the imprisonment of all those who had signed. On thinking it over, they allowed me to take it away with me; and I published the resolutions with a description of the meeting in the English *Contemporary Review*.

## COUNT WITTE'S SPIT

In October of the same year, followed the great "General Strike" which hung up all public life and service in the country. This brought the famous Manifesto of October 30, which granted in principle all the demands put forward a year earlier by the county councils–that is, the so-called "freedoms" which I have enumerated earlier. The Tsar was finally driven to this step by Count Sergius Witte, much the ablest statesman of this period who more than anyone else had been responsible for the great economic development of the country during his eleven years at the Ministry of Finance. Witte had strongly opposed the disastrous Far Eastern policy which had led to the war with Japan, and had been dismissed for doing so; but when the Tsar had to cut his losses as best he could, it was Witte whom he sent to America to negotiate with Japan, and Witte made a far better job of it than anyone had a right to expect.

He had now returned with his laurels, and during the General Strike he had insisted to the Tsar that there was no way out of his home troubles except by granting a constitution, and he was himself made Prime Minister to bring this about.

I will not go into Witte's difficulties and his failure; I am here only concerned with his convictions. Witte was an enlightened but a convinced supporter of the Russian autocracy; he only asked that the principle should be intelligently applied, and that could not happen if the Tsar himself had no resolution and no will. Witte was in a false position when he tried to inaugurate a new system which was in contradiction with his own convictions.

I met later nearly all the party leaders whose support he had tried to enlist, and not one of them trusted him a yard. It seemed only right, then, to get a talk with Count Witte himself. By the time that I got it, Russia had again passed ino reaction, and Witte himself, to judge by all his acts, had changed his course again.

I asked him first about his chief success at the Ministry of Finance. Was he the sole author of the gold standard and the gold reserve? This he claimed, and with justice. And the liquor monopoly? That he claimed too, and justly. Was there any compensation to previous license holders? "None," he answered. Was there not an exception (for the German Barons) in the Baltic provinces? "Don't go into detail," he said, "or we shall be sitting here all day."

I saw that I was going to get very little out of him, and passed on to the constitution. 'Are we right in regarding you as author of the October Manifesto?" "Certainly!" he said. "Then we may regard you as author of the Constitution?" "Certainly!" he said. "And what do you think of the Constitution now?" "I have a constitution in my head," he said, "but as to my heart, I spit on it!" and he spat on the floor in front of me. Was there any wonder that he was generally mistrusted?

## AT THE FIRST RUSSIAN DUMA

The first Russian Duma of 1906 was a peculiarly picturesque assembly. It had the atmosphere of a big naive schoolboy conspiracy, which exactly suited that big schoolboy Rodichev. Everyone was wanting to find out, by experimenting, how much audacity you could get away with, and he was the boldest and best at it. One form of challenge was for the peasant members from various parts, especially the Poles, to come attired in their national costumes, with every variety of color. Everywhere one felt the Russian warmth of social converse; leave these people alone, and they will quite soon become one big family. But at present it was all new to everyone, and full of hopes and delights. In Russia there was always far less of a barrier of class distinctions than elsewhere, and at this time less than ever.

As there had never yet been a Duma, no one knew what it was going to be like, and the Russians–all of them, government included–were terribly anxious that Europe should admire and like them when they were playing at this new game. This was cleverly utilized by David McGowan, the elected head of the Foreign Press Association, in which British and Americans co-operated and dominated. He succeeded in making the authorities entrust the distribution of press tickets to the correspondents themselves, who would certainly know how to get the best publicity for their new Duma.

Several of these correspondents were notable men. To start with, McGowan himself, our natural leader whom we all loved, was our "Abraham Lincoln," rugged and fearless in his old, worn frockcoat. A police agent had taken convenient cover in the Foreign Press as correspondent for a Chicago newspaper. He used this "cover" to glide into groups of talkative peasant Members and try to get them to commit themselves. We called him alternately "Black Mike" or "The Hound of the Baskervilles." I saw McGowan fetch him roughly out of such a group with the threat of taking away his ticket. Once, when McGowan was sending off his telegram, Black Mike entered the office. McGowan finished his cable in haste and strode into the street. Black Mike followed him, whining, "Why do you run away from me?" "Because I don't like you!" said McGowan. "Try to like me! Try to like me!" said the sickly creature, and he was in a position to threaten, for he combined with journalism the role of police spy and blackmailer.

Then there was Frederick Rennet with a face like Punch, once Foreign editor of the *Daily Mail*, who scintillated with journalistic flair. He once made a bet that you could knock any Russian down with impunity. This he tried out after too good a dinner on the waiter, but with the result that he found himself in prison. That only went into the stock of his journalistic experiences; but what made him positively furious was that he was amnestied at the tercentenary celebration of the Romanov dynasty in 1913. So

far he had been friendly to the government, but from now
on he was its dangerous enemy.

Harold Williams acted for the *Manchester Guardian*
and he was much the most effective of all, though the
humblest. There was another of the elect from England in
Maurice Baring, brother of a Peer, former diplomat with
the appropriate monocle, but with more acute understanding of Russian nature and character than any foreigner I
have known and almost than any Russian. Baring's simple
and clear vision had made the discovery that the greatest
gentleman in Russia is the underdog soldier or peasant, and
that was where he found his natural mates. "Little Brother,"
they would say to him, "you are very bald," but they would
speak out their hearts to him as perhaps to no one else. He
discussed with them *Paradise Lost,* which was circulated in
prose as peasant literature, or he would even talk to them
about Herbert Spencer. Baring's Russia is gone; but there is
no book that will tell more of Russian character than his
"What I Saw in Russia," for he saw deep beneath the sur-
face.

There was one other great and distinguished figure, of
whom it is difficult to write. Dr. E. J. Dillon ought by right
to have been the leader of all of us. Gray-haired, delicate-
featured, and with a fine delicacy of mind and speech, he
had been longer in Russia than any of us and had been in
intimate touch with the Russian Liberals. But he suddenly
and unexpectedly became the mouthpiece of the opportunist
Count Witte, who as we have seen, spat on constitutions.
Already posessed of a Panhard, he suddenly appeared in a
Rolls Royce. This aroused searchings of heart among the
correspondents, and one of them quoted an outstanding
piece of misrepresentation of what was happening in Russia in Dillon's British newspaper. Frederick Rennet brilliantly short-circuited the debate as to whether this was
evidence of bribery, by saying, "The man has no right to

write that, unless he's paid for it!" That was the only possible palliation!

As a student and not a telegraphing correspondent, I could not claim a ticket. My press friends were kind, but the most that they could offer was a place in their little hencoop during the less exciting debates. But it happened that in Moscow University I had met, in former days, the elected President, Muromtsev, so I went to him for help. In his view, a student of Russian history was even more important than a correspondent. He called the "Black Rod," or head of the Duma staff; this was a bald old gentleman who was as new to his job as anyone else. Murontsev asked him to give me the best possible facilities. The "Black Rod's" way was terribly simple; he put me on his own staff. When I went through the rules, I found that I had broken every one of them; but anyhow now I was a gentleman usher of the Duma, and I still have the precious little ticket.

The next thing was to see how much fun I could get out of it. I sauntered into the hall with the Members and stood under the Tribune. My press friends in their hencoop were amazed—"Look at that fellow's cheek! Watch and see him chucked out!" A portentous young official with a silver chain round his neck came up and asked rather aggressively, "What ticket have you got?" "The same as you, I fancy," I said. Yes, he was a colleague, and the "chucking out" failed to materialize.

I remember how another of my "colleagues" asked me, "When is the evening *performance?*" And this was not a bad sample of the general attitude to the Duma, both of the Members and of the public.

## NABOKOV AND THE "ADDRESS TO THE THRONE"
### More "England in Russia"

The beginnings of the first Duma were brilliant, and this was not surprising as it included the cream of educated

Russia. Muromtsev, as President, was mostly responsible for the rules of procedure–a fitting task for a Professor of Roman Law. These rules were a mirror of absolute justice; and if the government itself had risen to the same level, Russia might already have claimed to be a constitutional country.

The Tsar's regulations had insisted that a great deal of the debating should be done behind closed doors, in commissions set up to deal with different subjects corresponding to the Ministries–the budget, agriculture, trade, etc. Muromtsev's rules turned each of these commissions into a little microcosm of the whole Duma. In the multiplicity of parties, it was laid down that each should be entitled to exactly the number of members on each commission which corresponded to its proportion of the whole House; and each party, of course, sent its best experts. The commissions had the right to catechize the Ministers or their representatives and obtain all information on the subject in question.

Through the whole of its existence, the Duma was persistently following the model of the British Parliament, while the Tsar wanted to limit it at most to the functions of a German Reichstag. In England, the session begins with the reading of the King's speech. The nearest substitute in Russia had been the almost colorless remarks which Nicholas II had addressed to the Duma in its formal meeting at the Winter Palace. But in England there is an answer to the King's speech–namely the House of Commons' Address to the Throne; it can include those suggestions which the House wishes to insert in the government program. Under this actual title ("Address to the Throne") the first Duma put forward its own program of reform.

This would inevitably be a very arduous task. The most obvious reforms had been so long delayed; and so many views were represented in the many groups of the Duma. But the whole future of this new institution was at present so dubious, that it was essential that there should be as much unanimity as possible. The task was brilliantly handled by one of the ablest of Russia's new parliamentary statesmen, a young Liberal named Vladimir Nabokov.[1] His father had been Liberal Minister to Alexander II. The family was anything but unanimous in its politics, but Vladimir, who had a rather striking personal resemblance to the British Liberal premier, Lord Rosebery, had gone in the same direction as his father. I watched him carefully as he moved about the House in anxious consultation, first with one party leader, then with another, and I noticed that when he mounted the tribune and proposed a short but practical formula, it always went through. The "Address to the Throne" was passed *nem. con,* that is, with no opposition. The very few who disagreed, stepped out of the House to avoid breaking the unanimity. Yet this long and detailed document dealt with every aspect of Russian life, and on each put forward practical proposals of reform. The whole was then microscopically reduced and circulated on a postcard all over the country.

The government had no idea what to do next. It even made difficulties about forwarding the Address to the Sovereign. The aged Prime Minister, Goremykin, led his colleagues down to the House (by the Constitution, they were not ordinarily members of it). This old gentleman with side whiskers, who reminded one forcibly of a picture of Dickens's Dr. Squeers with ferule in hand, gave a scolding to the House in general. This, that, and the other of its proposals were declared to be "inadmissible." English precedent suggested the answer, a vote of censure on the government, and Nabokov mounted the tribune and proposed it. Never had the Ministers had to face such open contradiction.

---

[1] His son, sometimes writing under the pen name, Syria, has won a place in the world of present-day American letters.

Great gaps showed in the prestige of the government. Abuses of administration were laid bare in every detail, and one Minister was frankly apologetic in his reply. Only one of them was firm; and that was the future Premier Peter Stolypin. The vote of censure was passed *nem. con,* but before that, Goremykin had led his battered colleagues in confusion from the House, and only Stolypin stayed on.

This was a very promising beginning; but how much further would English precedents count? The government had been censured almost unanimously, but it did not resign; and from that moment both sides were looking to the country to decide the issue.

## Samuel N. Harper
### My Comrade of Travel and Study

Among the foreign visitors to the Duma was one who, like myself, had come not as a newspaper man but as a student of Russian history. Samuel N. Harper was the son of President William R. Harper, the famous builder of the University of Chicago. While Russia was still in the twilight, one of her firmest and truest friends, Charles R. Crame, had taken President Harper there with him. When he got home, the President said to his young son, "Samuel, I want you to be the first authority in the United States on Russia."

Samuel had just completed his preparation in time for the First Duma. Neither he nor I were bound to the telegraph office, but were students of contemporary history. I suggested that we should live and work together for a week, and this developed into a life-partnership, whether direct or indirect. We worked out a procedure of our own. We visited anyone who took a prominent part in the hectic public life of that time–but never as interviewers; and as all confidences were respected, he would tell us his whole story–how he started, his views, his aims and the part that he had played. Usually we went together; one of us handled the conversation, and the other committed it to memory; and the results we always recorded before we went to bed. Usually the work of each of us is recorded in the handwriting of the other. Suppose we were seeing, say, the fifth person present at some historical meeting; we could ourselves suggest corrections in his account, so that it was almost as if we were helping him to revise his memoirs before they appeared in print. To take an outstanding example, Milyukov gave us no less than ten "sittings," to cover his whole career. Our friends were mostly among the liberals, who at that time held the center of the stage; but we had intimate friends in all parties and kept ourselves rigorously out of all of them.

We took far more interest in the Russian people than in Russian politics; and in the vacations of the Duma we travelled systematically over great areas of the country, always with a prepared program and never leaving a place until we had done all that we wanted to do in it. Samuel was at all times a delightful comrade, with the zest and spirit of a great boy. The Russians loved him–perhaps most of all, the children–for he carried the pleasure of living with him wherever we went; and the whole of our work was like an enthralling adventure. But he was also more practical than I, particularly in the tracing and capturing of out-of-the way materials of political history, which we hunted up over the country.

For a time we worked together in the University of Liverpool, but his own university claimed him as professor of Russian language and institutions. Samuel always limited himself to those subjects in which he was a first-class scholar, but he certainly carried out in full the assignment he had received from his father—to become the first authority in the

United States on things Russian. As such, he was recognized by the State Department, which frequently sought his opinion and at one time absorbed him in its work.

Harper rendered a great service to many others besides Americans when, in spite of obstacles, he returned to the new Russia after the break caused by the Revolution. He was the first expert of his standing to do so, and personally I consider that his study of the Soviet period is even more valuable than the work which we did together earlier. I gained enormously from his short crisp letters, which always told me far more than they expressed in words. In 1939, I witnessed in London a part of his last great journey of study; this time I was a spectator and rejoiced in his mastery and success.

## The Viborg Appeal

Government and Duma sat for two months glaring at each other, waiting to see which had the support of the country, and meanwhile all legislation was perfunctory and futile. It was the silent voice of the immense Russian peasantry for which both sides were waiting. Most of the peasant members had organized themselves separately from all parties under the title of "Non-Party." Harper and I spent most of our time with them. They were visiting all party meetings in turn, looking at all of them as representing only "the masters," and in their reports home, which were diligent and regular, they gave their views as to which was likely to do most for the "people."

"Which party do you think will win?" Harper asked one of them. The reply may seem cryptic, but it was very sound: "Every party has its secret, and that party which keeps its secret longest, will win. And I think it will be the non-party." The Duma raised the land question and so did the government. Each side made its own bid, and the government even advised the peasants not to listen to the Duma. There were all sorts of comings and goings in the official world. At one moment anything might have happened, even a surrender to the Liberal party of Milyukov.

On July 21, 1906, members of the Duma, on their way to their work, found the streets full of soldiers. On the door of the Tauris Palace, where the Duma was housed, they read a blunt notice saying that it was dissolved. The President, Muromtsev, as he told me later, had not been informed. We all hurried about, trying to find out what was to happen next. I was luckiest. I learned that the majority–Liberals and Labor–were off to Viborg in Finland, to decide on their action; I always thought this was rather a shame, because it endangered the liberties of Finland, such as they were.

I caught an evening train and found myself in company with Milyukov and Lednicki.[1] The last named, who was a member from Moscow, was of Polish origin, and he had been invaluable, as the chief intermediary of his country with the Russian Liberals. We reached Viborg late at night and slept side by side on the floor of the Hotel Belvedere. Lednicki woke up in the middle of the night and said something which I didn't catch about rats. It was these two men, Milyukov and Lednicki, who later in 1917 after the fall of the Tsar, drew up the treaty between Russia and Poland, guaranteeing Polish independence.

Milyukov had been excluded by a police maneuver from the Duma, but he had more or less led it from outside; and it was he who drew up for discussion at Viborg a protest against the dissolution. The Viborg Appeal demanded the recall of the dissolved assembly; as the sovereign incontestably retained the right of dissolution, this demand clearly went outside the new constitution. Till the Duma was restored, it appealed to the country to refuse to the government recruits, taxes, and the recognition of foreign loans, which Witte had

[1] Father of Professor W. Lednicki of the University of California.

successfully obtained in order to make the government independent of the Duma. It was only this last item that had any
sense as no village could be expected offhand to refuse taxes
or recruits. The Appeal was debated all day. Nabokov was
against it, and only withdrew his opposition to leave his party
unanimous; of course, he was right in his view, and for his
party loyalty he paid with his political career. The Moderates
paid a visit to Viborg but took no part. I never saw a man
age more in a night than the President, Muromtsev; he must
have realized that the protest was outside the law; he died not
very long afterwards.

I left when the decision was reached. On the train I
found myself alone in a carriage, except for one companion.
As we approached St. Petersburg, he asked me to take over a
document and hand it back to him when we had passed
through the station. It was the original of the famous Viborg
Appeal, with all the signatures.

From the station I took a cab straight to the British Embassy. It was here and now that I first met the great pioneer
of Russian Study in England, Sir Donald Mackenzie Wallace.
He was an equerry of King Edward VII, and he had come out,
apparently with some mysterious commission, to get an idea
of what was happening in Russia. The Ambassador, Sir
Arthur Nicolson, was one of the brainest that we had. He set
Wallace and me to argue out the rights and wrongs of the
Duma's protest. He seemed to be taking quite an active part
in our conversation; but when I tried afterwards to remember
what he had said, it amounted to exactly nothing.

Stolypin had been appointed Prime Minister, in place
of the helpless Goremykin, to carry through the dissolution.
He took no steps to arrest the members, and they justified his
inaction by doing nothing whatever to organize resistance
in the country. The protest fell absolutely flat. Maurice Baring had turned for his information to his friend, the under-
dog. He travelled twice in a fourth-class carriage to Moscow

and back, and on his return simply said "There will be nothing." He proved entirely right.

It was at this time that I first came into contact with the British Foreign Office, and the relationship was a curious one. Hardly any of the attachés in our Embassy could talk freely in Russian. Young Russian officials with fluent English were at hand to give them the most superficial and misleading ideas on all the subjects in which we ought to have been most interested. We were at the mercy not only of the Russians but also of the Germans, who had of course taken the trouble to learn Russian; and the Germans were against all reform. Yet here was a lawfully elected National Assembly, established by the Tsar himself, the voice of a new Russia. This was no subject for the methods of secret service. If an outsider from England, "a university man"–which was a very popular title in Russia–chose to study it closely, he was free to do so. From time to time I would write to Mr. Herman Norman in London or to Viscount Cranley in Petersburg, and these letters came to be printed and filed in the F.O. The one on the Second Duma, of which I attended all but two sittings, was a very detailed study. On the other hand, the "outsider" was quite free to act of himself. This position gave me at the same time a footing on which I could later ask for support, whenever I might be taking an initiative of my own.

## STOLYPIN

## "A Superhuman Task"

Sir Arthur Nicolson said to me: "You know the Duma people. I should like you to know Stolypin. I will arrange it for you." In evening dress, I sallied out one morning to cover the immense distance to the famous Islands at the mouth of the Neva. Stolypin was living in a very pleasant little summer house. There was no ceremony. He was a big man with a

dark beard, rather like a big and kindly bear. He invited me
to ask him questions.

"Why did you dissolve the Duma?" I asked. I did not
then know that he had, but I proved right. "There were only
two alternatives," he explained, "Either to dissolve or to call
the leaders to power. The Liberals were far too dependent
on Labor; and this would have meant that in a month or two
the government would have irreparably lost all authority."
But he had summoned a new Duma on the same franchise.

I inquired into his program. "I am a constitutionalist,"
he said, "but I am not a parliamentarist. What would you
think in England," he asked, "if all proposals of reform came
from the Opposition?" He was himself going to take the initiative in reform. "I am facing on two fronts," he said. "I am
for reform, and I am against revolution. You may say that
that is a superhuman position, and very likely you would be
right." He would start with land reform. That was indeed
taking the bull by the horns, for it was the thorniest question
of all. The event proved that he did just what he had said—
with very little support for his quite sensible views, but with
drastic proposals and with fearless courage.

"And could you tell me," I asked, "whether any of the
higher officials are to blame for the armed attacks upon
Jews?" (of which one of the worst had just taken place at
Bialystok). "No doubt," he said, "some of the soldiers or
police may be to blame." "Excuse me, Your Excellency," I
said, "That is not quite my question. I was asking about the
responsibility of the higher officials." "Are you a journalist?"
asked Stolypin. "Only an occasional writer," I said, "and
if I write anything on this interview, I will send it to you
first." "Thank you!" he said, and then the big man naively
added, "When I am talking to a journalist, I feel something
at the back of my head, warning me to be careful." Then he
continued thoughtfully, "Well, there's a word that is in
fashion just now—*liberalnichat*, playing at liberalism—there

ought to be another word–playing at conservatism. There are some who know that that kind of thing is approved of high up, and I don't say that they didn't use their posts in that way. I have just dismissed the Vice-Governor of Suvalki (Bialystok), and I have sent out a circular to officials to say that they above all others are expected to obey the law.' And then Stolypin added the best thing he is known to have ever said: "I want to show the country that we have parted company forever with the old police order of things." Oh, if he could only have done that! But with such weak backing as he could count on from his sovereign, it was impossible.

Very considerably impressed, still in the inappropriate evening costume, I made my long and broiling journey by tram back to the middle of the city. Being very hungry, I made straight for our usual rendezvous, the Hotel de France, kept by a Frenchman with Tartar waiters, who looked like amiable little devils in their tailcoats. This was the best quick lunch in the city, and here gathered foreign office officials, Duma members, revolutionaries, journalists, spies, dubious ladies, all talking themselves out as if no one else was there to hear them; that was the way that Russians then made a revolution. Three American socialists from Chicago had come to help through a socialist revolution in Russia. They had lots of money and were giving a great luncheon party. "Hello!" said someone, "here's Pares. Why are you in dress clothes?" "Oh, I've just been to see Stolypin." "Bring him into lunch!" After a while they came to the subject for discussion–it was whether to kill Stolypin! "No! no!" I protested. "The biggest mistake you could make." One was always hearing this kind of talk, and one did not take it very seriously. But in the evening, when Harper and I, following our regular practice, were writing up our notes, I looked on it differently. I was dictating to Harper. "Is that all your talk with Stolypin?" he asked. "Have you had anything else today?" "Oh, yes, a proposal to kill Stolypin." And then one realized how absurd it was that I should have passed straight from the one place to the other.

They did try to get him some weeks later in the little house where I had seen him, and the bomb which they threw crippled his daughter for life. Stolypin showed splendid nerve. With his face spattered with ink, he was the first to see to the wounded. He himself escaped that time, and by the Tsar's wish, lived for a while in the Winter Palace; but five years later, in 1911, he was shot at a gala performance in the presence of the Tsar in Kiev by one of those strange and slimy creatures who played the double role of police spy and terrorist. He had always thought that it would be from such a quarter that he would meet his end. As he fell, he crossed himself toward the Master whom he had done his best to serve.

## PEASANT REFLECTIONS: AT BAKUNIN'S HOME

Harper and I went straight down to Mashúk, the home of the Petrunkéviches, and from that center we drove round to village after village. In each we found the peasants quite puzzled by what had happened. In his summons to the Duma, the Tsar had asked them to choose "the best man who had the confidence of the population." That is exactly what they had done; and now the Tsar had sent their men flying.

We were invited to sit down on the elder's bench on the village green, and they began by asking us to advise them what to do. This was, of course outside our province, as they quite understood. "Then will you tell us what has happened in Petersburg?" they asked, and that we readily did. "And now, do you think you would tell us how these matters are managed in your countries?"–(that is, in England and America). "What matters do you mean?" "What control has your Duma over your budget?" Of course, that was the whole point of everything, and the First Duma in trying to carry the central fortress by moral pressure, had never waited to use its budget powers. The procedures in our two countries were heard with approval. "And then, what control has your Duma over your army?" Again a radical question. I explained that in England the army depended on an annual vote by parliament for its upkeep, which is called the Mutiny Act. If there is no parliament, there is no Mutiny Act, and therefore no army. This way of doing things they greeted with hearty approval. "And one other thing, please. Are your taxes direct or indirect?" Again the whole point of the matter! Where was the use of starting a movement to refuse taxes, which were deducted at source?

The Petrunkéviches were closely allied by marriage with the family of Bakunin. Michael Bakunin, a leading figure in two earlier reigns, is known all over the world as the prophet of revolutionary anarchism. He believed in a minimum of State control; he thought the *mir*, the historical village community in Russia, was in itself a sufficient bond of society. His brother Alexander did not share his views. He was a bold liberal, and had played a worthy part in the emancipation of the peasants in 1861. He was now an old man, but still the squire of the Bakunin estate.

We heard that he was allowing the neighboring peasants to meet for a political discussion on his grounds, so we drove over and attended the meeting. It proved very interesting. The peasants, among other things, discussed the official church schools. These sometimes only existed on paper and were always very inefficient; for the priest, who often himself came from the ranks of the peasantry, was but a poor teacher. One of the peasant speakers said, "They tell us we shall have a very fine dinner in the next world; but we should really like to stand up now and get a first bite here!"—an allusion to the abundant display of *hors d'oeuvres* which usually precedes a Russian dinner. Evidently these peasants were a good field for the Marxist propaganda, which describes religion as simply "dope for the masses" ("opium for the people").

They also discussed what to do when punitive troops were quartered on them, an experience which they described as being "as good as going to a university." "Bring the fellow into the family," said one speaker, "and just make him one of us!"

After the meeting, we stayed the night with the old gentleman. He had a natural dignity; he was magnificently built, on the same scale as Leo Tolstoy, and had a great head, a fine broad forehead, and a noble beard. Great dogs fondled him as he sat there in his gray lounge suit. He had not come to the peasant's meeting himself, he explained, because he did not wish to embarrass them, but he gladly allowed them to meet on his grounds.

Of course we talked politics. "What do you think will come of all this?" I asked. "Before I answer your question," said our grand old man, "let me put you one of mine. 'Is religion to go on or not?'" I replied, "I say it is going on." "Why?" he asked. "Because I'm going on with it." "That's the answer I wanted," he said. "Nowadays, everywhere there seem to be herds. There is the herd of the barracks, your imperialism, your Joseph Chamberlain. And there is the herd of the factory, all quoting Karl Marx. Both herds are all the while watching to see how people will vote and asking where will be the majority. If there are enough people in Russia who are really thinking for themselves, and will answer your question as you answered mine, then what's happening here now will come to something. If not, not." Certainly he was right; it was a Russian version of the question of the old English radical, Robert Spence Watson.

## THE PEASANTS AND THE SECOND ELECTIONS

When he had got rid of the first Duma and boldly summoned another on the same franchise, Stolypin at once set himself to make a great bid for peasant support. What he did was unfortunately done without the proper legal sanction, that is, without the Duma which, as the Constitution had promised, was to discuss and pass all new laws. But if they could have been judged on their merits, Stolypin's reforms of 1906 were not only bold and radical but dictated by common sense. This is all the more remarkable because he had no party behind him, neither the reactionaries nor the revolutionaries, nor yet even the Liberals, who by Milyukov's tactics were playing down to the revolutionaries. He completed the work of those who had emancipated the peasants from serfdom in 1861, by equalizing them before the law with all other classes, opening to them access to all posts, allowing them to move freely from their communes, and even by his famous edict of November 19th, to claim as heritable property their just portion of the common land of the village.

What would the peasant say to all this when he was called upon to elect, under the same franchise, successors to the men whom he had chosen and who had now been chased away? How would he meet Stolypin's bid, which under ordinary circumstances he would have been bound to welcome? To us British, to whom constitutional history is a matter of the deepest interest, the answer to this question was a vital test of the capacity of the peasant masses for political judgments. This was seen by an intelligent Russian liberal named Smirnov, who went to the length of organizing a service of information on the course of the second elections.

"Have you chosen your men yet?" says one of his representatives, entering a given village. "Yes, yes, we've *doomed* them." This meant of course, that they had chosen persons suitable for the rôle which they would be expected to play—namely, to represent faithfully the wishes of their constituents and not to be surprised if they were at once punished for doing so. That, of itself, indicated a choice of the revolutionary agitators, who were better used to sitting in prison than

anyone else. But ingenuity did not stop here. Many of
these agitators had already been sent to prison without trial.
Now, a member of the Duma could only be imprisoned after
being tried. Consequently, if the peasants elected revolutionaries who were still untried, the government by its own law
would have to set them free. They would be given a nice little
holiday, which no doubt they would appreciate, during
which, clothed with the inviolability of a Member, and the
freedom from the censorship which pertained to the Duma
debates, they would be able to say exactly what they wanted
to a public which consisted of the whole nation. On the
other hand, the peasants ardently wished the Duma to continue in session as long as possible. They welcomed it as a
forum of free debate, and numbers of them were for the first
time learning the alphabet from its discussions. Therefore,
after electing revolutionaries, they instructed them to be as
careful as they could to make the Duma last as long as possible. The government had excluded all who had signed the
Viborg appeal, that is, the majority of the First Duma, consisting of Liberals and Labor. Whatever the defects of that
appeal, this was a very foolish thing to do. It was not surprising then that the Second Duma, though painfully lowered
in quality and experience, was much more revolutionary than
the First.

## THE SECOND DISSOLUTION

We all knew the Second Duma might be dissolved at any
moment. It was a poor ill-fated thing. There had been no
challenge from the country at the first Dissolution; the reactionaries were cock-a-hoop, and were now out to get the
Duma abolished altogether. Police maneuvers had brought
about the election of a group of them, and they boldly
marched the spacious lobby, saying "Nonsense! Bedlam!" (the
English word).

Two bogus plots were deliberately manufactured by the police, as was fully established by records of Cabinet debates after the revolution of 1917. The two main revolutionary parties were now in force in the Duma. The S.R.'s (Social Revolutionaries), the party that carried the most support among the peasants, was accused of plotting against the lives of the Tsar, Stolypin and the Grand Duke Nicholas. There was no evidence except that a Cossack Raitirov, acting as a provocative agent, had offered information to the S.R.'s and that they had taken no action on it. As a matter of fact, both the main revolutionary parties had decided that all terrorist action was to be suspended while the Duma lasted; nevertheless some S.R.'s were hanged on this charge! A country priest, who was a member, was unfrocked for making a speech against the application of the death sentence for political offenses. On May 30, the Duma was badly caught out by a provocative raising of the question of political terrorism, and the nine groups in the House could not agree on any formula on the subject.

About this time Maurice Baring told me he was going home, which meant a resignation of his post of foreign correspondent. "Why do you go now," I asked, "just at the most important moment?" "It has all become entirely uninteresting," he said. "And when will you come back?" I asked, as I saw him to the station. "Never to St. Petersburg," he said, "but perhaps to the country." A fortnight later he had proved absolutely right; the reform movement was over, and Russia had gone down to a dog-trot; but when he got home he wrote that this was not the end, adding the words, "In ten years we shall know." 1907-1917. Exactly ten years were to run before the Great Revolution.

Shortly afterwards, going one morning as usual to the Duma, I found the doors closed and outsiders refused admission; however, Williams was inside and telephoned the news to us. The government claimed to have discovered a second

plot, this time of the S.D.'s (Social Democrats, or Marxists).
The chief alleged offense was an appeal for mutiny in the
army, which at that time was more than ever unlikely. As
we know in full, the appeal had been prepared in the Police
Department. A young girl, whom the police had managed to
introduce into the Secretariat of the S.D. Party, was to plant
a copy on one of the members named Ozol, and the police
were to come in by collusion directly afterwards and find
it on him. This failed, as Ozol claimed the personal inviolability of a Member and refused to be searched; but that
did not matter, as there was a duplicate already in the Police
Department. Even at the time, the customary "Act of Accu-
sation," which Harper and I studied at once, was evidently no
more than a hotch-potch of charges, without dates, taken
from the time of unrest before the Duma period. We invited all our friends among the correspondents to our flat
and pooled our knowledge with them. Thus, the only dispatch to an important British or American paper that gave
the version of the Government was from Dillon, correspondent of the *Daily Telegraph*.

By our house telephone the hall porter had been ordered to arrange for some forty cabs to take away the accused members. Their spies were waiting outside, to identify
them as they came out. When the correspondents were told
to go away, David McGowan replied, "We will go when those
gentlemen do!" and to this the police found no answer. I
tried to get into the Duma garden from outside, but was
faced by a soldier poking his bayonet at me.

By the law which guarded the inviolability of Members, the Duma had to examine the charges and agree to
the arrest. It set up a committee; but before it could complete its work, the House was dissolved. The President,
Golovin, had gone back late from the committee, which was
still in session, and next morning, a foreign correspondent
called on him at breakfast to ask where he was going to live

now. He replied, "Of course in St. Petersburg, as long as the Duma lasts." The correspondent had to tell the President of the Duma that the Duma was dissolved!

Each party had had its headquarters in the apartment of one of its members. Harper and I knew that all these apartments would be raided by the police as soon as the Members' inviolability had expired. So we put on our frock-coats and visited them in advance of the police, in search of interesting documents. We found the members in a great flurry destroying papers, and they were only too glad to give them to us. "We accept them," we said with a formal bow, "as historical materials."

The collapse of the first two Dumas, with the violent withdrawal of universal suffrage, was a bitter disappointment to Sam and me, but also a heavy personal blow. We had made friends with some seventy key members of the first Duma and most of them were struck out of public life for their part in the Viborg appeal. The same thing happened with the second Duma, and we then had to begin building up our connections again with the Third; but this time the results lasted for the ten years up to the revolution.

## "THE RED COCK"

As in the previous year, Harper and I went straight down to the Petrunkéviches at Mashuk, to see the reaction of the peasants to this second Dissolution. Here in the summer gathered a number of other faithful and fearless liberals. We could always go there without giving notice, and in that fresh and free life one lost all account of the days till one decided to go. There was no lack of entertainment–plenty of young people, keenness for every kind of sport and equal keenness for spirited night conversations on every subject under the sun. Michael Petrunkévich, the son of John, managed the estate and was chairman of the local Zemstva, or

County Council, and also Marshal of the Gentry for the district.

One day we improvised a game of "soccer" with two bearded goal-keepers; Michael was at one end and his brother-in-law, Alexis Bakunin, member of the Duma, at the other. The game was interrupted by the intrusion of a band of sturdy peasants, carrying knobby sticks; the local schoolmaster, who was a Marxist, had told them they ought to come and claim the land. Michael invited them to tea on the balcony, and the subject was debated with good temper. The peasants departed and we resumed our game.

Some time later, the neighboring village came wholesale by night with a much more definite purpose. This time it was to be "the Red Cock"; it had for centuries been a traditional peasant practice sometimes to burn down the squire's house, which made it less likely that he would come back. Michael had two large wooden houses at about a quarter of a mile from each other. The schoolmaster had argued, on the same lines as Lenin, that "a good squire" was even more dangerous than a bad one; but the Petrunkéviches were very popular among the peasants. When John was sent into exile a second time, numbers of them had accompanied him as an escort of honor to the station ten or fifteen miles off. They had therefore adopted a typical peasant compromise; they would only burn the empty house, not occupied by the family. Michael too had his own reservations. Any appeal to the police was at that time hopeless; the nearest squire was far off, and was probably busy enough facing the same problem. Michael equipped himself with an armory of small-arms —if necessary, to defend his family; but he refused to fire in defense of property.

While he sat at home, I went by his wish to the scene and lay down on the grass among the peasants. On my way I met the most archaic little fire-engine that I've ever seen.

It came from the same village. This seemed derisive, and I asked sharply, "Why do *you* come?" "To save my reputation!" said the local fireman. He squirted ineffective spits of water at the burning building, and the crowd cheered him.

My presence was in no way resented. They had hoisted the red flag of the old revolutionaries of the 1870's, with its inscription "Land and Liberty," and they asked me what I thought of it. "To my mind," I said, "you're spoiling both." Later on, Michael called to his brave wife, by birth a Bakunin, "Liza, come and have a look!" and they walked unchallenged through the crowd. Some peasants had brought their carts with them to carry away the loot. In the early dawn, the rioters were off *en masse* singing the Marseillaise in Russian–a pretty crude and raucous performance.

On the next day, Michael was due to examine the school of the very village that had raided him; it appeared that this was one of the multifarious duties of the Chairman of the Zemstvo. We accompanied him; there was no demonstration beyond a stone thrown which passed near the carriage. We boldly entered the enemy territory of the Marxist schoolmaster. Michael examined a peculiarly stupid-looking little boy. "This gentleman," he said pointing at me, "is an Englishman. When did we fight the English?" Silence! "Why, the Crimean war! Who was Tsar at that time?" Silence! "Why, Nicholas the First. And who is Tsar now?" "Nicholas the Last!" said the little boy. That seemed to be all that he had been taught!

After the revolution of 1917, Michael, a liberal like his father, was also exiled without trial, and to the same place, Kostromä–this time by the Bolsheviks! While the family was in Moscow, some of their peasants, hearing of their poverty, came all that distance to bring them food. Mashuk was turned into a State farm; and, curiously enough, a cousin of Michael's, who like him was Liberal, was put in charge. The peasants bore no malice; only while they were entertaining members of the family, they explained, "Now we are masters here."

Starting from Mashuk, Harper and I made a rather extensive tour through about a third of European Russia. The whole country was in chaos. These months were prophetic of what was to follow after the fall of the Tsar ten years later, but with the difference that his police were still there and were in full reaction.

At the Second Duma, Harper and I had collected all the peasant members from the province of Vyatka near the Urals, where there had never been many squires. Its elected local Zemstvo was regarded by all as a model of good sense, progress and efficiency. In the comparative security of the Duma, these peasants vied with each other in invitations to come and see them in the country. After the dissolution, they let us know that this might be dangerous to them. However, they sent us the names of the more prominent of those who had elected them.

We had difficulty in evading the attention of the police. One of them insisted on accompanying us, but we managed to shake him off. In this province there was a great band of robbers under a kind of Robin Hood, who raided government convoys and dispersed charity among the peasants; he even entered the railway carriage of the Governor of the province *incognito* and, after a chat with him, left his card as he departed.

In the autumn of 1905 during the time of confusion, some peasant districts had set up their own administrations which they called "republics," but we were too late in our search for their materials. There were police spies in the villages. "Why do you go into the town?" they would be asked—for the peasant, "town" and "police" were practically synonymous. "My wife and children," would be the answer, which meant he was poorly off. "Then you've not kept up your character" (that is, of loyalty to the peasantry). With a repetition of the offense, the spy might disappear on a dark night.

## THEOLOGOV

Theologov, as his name suggests, was the son of a priest. Like many other such, he became a revolutionary. He was a great believer in the virtues of the old peasant community, and, like all S.R.'s, he thought it might serve as a direct bridge to modern socialism, making it unnecessary for Russia to pass through the stage of capitalism. He managed to enter the peasant class. This was done by marrying a peasant girl, which made him legally a member of the rural working unit known as the peasant joint family–very like the terms on which Jacob worked for Laban. He was elected to the important post of clerk to the village community of Ivanovka Vtoraya, and set himself to make this village a working example of modern Co-operation. In this, as he confessed to Harper and me, he failed; but we could certainly bear witness that he left a profound moral impress on the peasants of this village.

When we visited him, he was an old man with a fine flowing beard and something of a patriarchal look. He brought some of his peasant pupils to talk with us in his little orchard. The word "conscious" which it was the fashion to apply to revolutionized peasants, was in this case a reality. We discussed with one of them the question of religion and its future. The village discriminated in this matter. In settling when to work, which they did in common, they observed all the few "great feast days" of the year and disregarded the innumerable others that clogged up the calendar. As to the future, he said one of the wisest things that I ever heard in Russia. I have often quoted his verdict, for it was a most exact analysis of Russian history.

I had asked him, "When you have all the reforms that you want, will you have a Church?" This was his answer— "There is a community; that's why there is a State, and that's why there is a Church. The State has got wrong with the community, and it has carried the Church with it. We are going to put the State back right with the Community, and when we do that, we shall put the Church back too, and then, you'll see, we'll all be Orthodox." Orthodox to what? Of course, orthodox to the community.

Another peasant gave us the shrewdest account of all the troubled years, which were just finished, of the so-called first revolution of 1904-1907. At that time, everyone had been waiting to see how the cat was going to jump in Petersburg. This was like a barometer of their various and changing attitudes—the priest, the local policeman, the doctor, the schoolmistress. I only wished I could have committed his lively account straight off to paper. "And now," I asked, "could you say what is the difference between the peasant's attitude toward the government five years ago and now?" Peasants were never ready with formulas. "I could hardly tell you a thing like that," he said. "Well, have a try!" Thus challenged, he thought for a moment, and then gave us far the best summary we ever heard of this subject. "Five years ago there was belief and fear; now the belief has gone, and only the fear is left."

Saràtov was known as "the unquiet province." It was here that Stolypin first made his reputation as Governor. To Theologov he said, "Where you are, there the government has no power." Yet it was from Theologov that we also heard the most sincere tribute to Stolypin. He was fair, and he was very brave. He travelled his restless province with a small military escort, dealing with all troubles on the spot. Making his way into a crowd of reactionary hooligans of the city, who were throwing bricks at Liberals and Jews, he cried: "Is this the way you show your loyalty to your

Sovereign?" In another part, surrounding a revolted village with his men, he advanced alone under fire and called out, "Don't compel me to use my power!" A revolutionary clutched him by the arm. Stolypin silenced him with the words, "Hold my coat!" And he was obeyed.

I paid a second visit to Theologov after the great success of Stolypin's land settlement. It was entirely based on individual farming–the opposite pole to Theologov's most cherished conviction. "Think of it!" said Theologov. "My Ivanovka Vtoraya has gone the way of all the rest!"

## Count Leo Tolstoy

In our country travel of 1908, Harper and I found ourselves in that district where lived the famous Russian writer, Leo Tolstoy. We called at the door and were told that he was laid up, as he had sprained an ankle. We wished not to disturb him, but we were heartily asked in, and we stayed with him for nearly an hour. When we from time to time suggested going, he asked us to stay on.

He was fully dressed but lying out at length. It was a magnificent figure. So too were the great head with the high forehead, the heavy eyelashes, and the big blue eyes and the noble beard. He was very fatherly and inquired into our families and counseled us not to write too much. But he was wholly contemptuous of the Duma and all its works, which by that time (1908) gave a much better promise of achievement. "If it were not ridiculous," he said, "it would be disgusting!" He said he was wholly concentrated on the writings of Henry George. All the land should belong to the peasants. It was a great iniquity that there should still be large estates and great landlords. "My wife is one," he added naively, and naturally enough because he had given her his land, still living on there. I don't think we brought away anything to compare with the wisdom of Theologov's peasants. And after all, why shouldn't he have an off-day sometimes? But all the while, I was contrasting the shallowness of what he was saying with that magnificent figure before me and the lively remembrance of his glorious works.

# CHAPTER V

## Russia and England
### (1907–1914)

### ALEXANDER GUCHKOV

## The Churchill Type in Russia

THERE was no more fascinating figure in the life of Russia of that time than Guchkov, and on him largely depended the enthusiasm for the understanding and later the alliance with England. In spite of the difference in origin, Guchkov might be called the Winston Churchill of Russia, and the two men met and respected each other.

Guchkov's grandfather came to Moscow as a serf. His father became a business man and a magistrate. Alexander made brilliant studies both in Moscow and in Germany, where he already acquired a taste for fighting duels. He was always in the limelight. With the Boers, he fought England in South Africa and was wounded and taken prisoner: Winston Churchill had the same fate on the other side. He travelled through both Armenia and Bulgaria in times of violence and drama. He fought more duels in Manchuria. In the Japanese war, he was captured while in charge of the Civil Red Cross, which had been organized, in spite of opposition from the government, by the Russian County Councils. On his return, he took up the position of a kind of tribune of the people, loyal to the monarchy if it would

159

only be true to its own responsibilities and commitments. As such, he was received and amiably entertained by the Tsar and his consort. That was as yet far off from the time when she wrote to her husband, "Could not a railway accident be arranged in which only Guchkov would suffer?" After the Constitutional Manifesto of October 30, 1905, which followed immediately on the General Strike of that year, he became the leader of a new party known as Octobrists, who simply asked that the Tsar should keep his own promises, which unfortunately he never did. The first revolution of 1904-1907 saw the failure of Milyukov and his party of Cadets or Liberals, who now passed into constitutional opposition.

After the dissolution of the Second Duma, radical restrictions of the franchise, which had long since been prepared, became law, and from this time it could not possibly be claimed that the Duma was really representative of the country. But its competence was not touched; above all, its powers over the budget remained intact. The chaos and prostration of the country which followed the second Dissolution soon began to give way to a soberer mood, of which Guchkov became the best spokesman. In the progressive decay of the monarchy it was practically certain that any national assembly, even if composed of former servants of the government, would be bound to be keenly critical. Guchkov was to lead this criticism. After all, in the Third and crippled Duma, which lasted out its full five years and was followed by another not unlike it, the standard of education and, still more, of practical or even of administrative experience was much higher than in its predecessors. These men knew how and when to criticize.

Guchkov's use of these conditions was masterly. He found himself leader of a Party which constituted one third of the House and, sitting between the other two sections, it could generally govern the decisions. He made the ablest use of the commissions set up under the procedure of Muromtsev. The law obliged the Ministers, on the demand of the Duma, to supply all information on the administration of the Empire. Guchkov made it worth while for Ministers, if they wished to get their budgets approved, to come down in person and give this information. This was a mutual education both of Ministers and of Duma, and a considerable number of the Members came at least to get, at second hand, some experience of the real state of things. Ministers who were ready to act on criticisms of the Duma saw their estimates not only approved but sometimes enlarged. The Sovereign himself could not be too well satisfied with a Minister who reported a failure to pass his budget.

Becoming familiar with most of the leading men in the Third Duma, I recognized that the time had come when Russia could be brought into closer contact with England. The Cadets, now in the minority, already took their models from us. The Octobrists had a natural affinity with intelligent British conservatives of the type of Mr. Balfour. As clouds began to gather over the skies of Europe, such a contact could be of real service to both countries, and it could also be a valuable factor in the advance of constitutional practice in Russia.

Guchkov had at first been an admirer of the German Constitution; but at this time, in view of constant disappointments in the attitude of the Monarchy, he was coming over more and more to our British ideas. This was invaluable to us in our prosecution of Russian friendship. As with Milyukov, so with Guchkov, to tell the rest of his career, throughout which I was in close intimacy with him, would be to tell the story of his country. He was for a year President of the Duma; and his work as chairman of its Military Commission was productive of real reforms, which greatly improved both army and navy before the First World War.

He had many friends in both, and secured their hearty co-operation.

He adroitly made the Duma appear more truly patriotic than the government, and even drove Grand Dukes from their irresponsible posts. He had the habits of an English rather than a Russian politician; he said the most outright things in a quiet voice. Entering the Third Duma one morning in the spring of 1908, I saw him reading from the tribune a balanced but very plain speech, in which he pointed out that the sinecure posts of members of the imperial family were a direct obstacle to army reform. Just because of the quietness of his tone, the vigor of his words was all the more telling. He called upon the Grand Dukes to resign "certain terrestrial benefits" for the good of their country, and the speech actually achieved its purpose. The public began to see that even a crippled Duma could do something, and possibly more than its better-grounded but ill-fated predecessors.

Guchkov saw how much could be done by independent co-operation with Stolypin, to whom the only possible alternative at that time was a reactionary Prime Minister. There was no deal; but the two sides could be very useful to each other, and were so. It may be added that Stolypin was as much in favor of friendship with England as Guchkov and the Duma were throughout this period.

Here is a pretty little story, told me by Guchkov himself, of the inter-relations between three very different men. A certain Count was anxious to break Stolypin's co-operation with the Duma. He came, therefore, to Guchkov and reported some offensive expressions as having been used by Stolypin about him, Guchkov. Guchkov quietly asked Stolypin whether this was true, which it was not, and Stolypin replied, "You can tell him from me that it is a direct lie!"

Now Guchkov understood very well that the Count would then challenge Stolypin to a duel. He might even kill him; but he would anyhow compromise him seriously, as dueling was illegal, especially for a Prime Minister!

With his natural taste for duels, Guchkov decided to draw the Count's fire himself. He tackled him publicly in the Duma; and when the Count didn't move, he said in his quiet voice, "How long, Count, are you going to let me go on insulting you?" The Count was bound to challenge, and the duel took place, but with Guchkov, not Stolypin, and without result.

As President of the Duma, Guchkov had from time to time to report to the Sovereign. Nicholas II had the same general sneaking respect for duels, but was particular on points of law of this kind. Guchkov himself reported his duel; and then, seeing a friendly look on the face of the Tsar, he said, "Your Majesty, if I may say so, I'm afraid you mean to pardon me. I hope you won't. I've broken the law and I ought to serve my sentence!" This was just the kind of situation that the kindly and sensitive Tsar understood. Guchkov, of himself, went off to the prison and asked to be taken in; but within a fortnight or so the Tsar sent one of his most important Ministers to amnesty him and fetch him out.

## THE DUMA VISITS ENGLAND

In 1909, I decided to make a move of my own. In my memorandum to the British Foreign Office on the dissolution of the Second Duma and the crippling of the franchise, I had confidently predicted that *any* Duma, however elected, would be bound to be very critical of the government, and this was fully borne out in the Third Duma. The revolution had died down. The Third Duma was trying to establish itself and to win constitutional rule for Russia, and the time had come when, without the need of any challenge, parliamentary relations with England could be of real service to Russia. I knew very well that all German influence

was being thrown on the other side against reform, and of
this we have since had the most convincing confirmation
in the letters of Kaiser Wilhelm to the Tsar full of arrogant advice and incitements to absolutism.

I had seen for myself in the great lobby of the Duma
the daily comradeship of members of various parties and
surprising friendships between men of opposite views, and
I knew it was possible to show my country a Russia united
in friendship for us.

An impertinent Englishman, who has specially put on
frock-coat and top hat for the occasion, enters the President's cabinet at the Duma to attend a formal meeting of
the leaders of parties, and invite them to come to England.
He has letters from the Foreign Secretary, Sir Edward Grey,
and the Opposition leader, Mr. Balfour, just to say it would
be very nice if they did. He has also invitations to dinner
from the Lord Mayor of Liverpool, and from Sir Alfred
Jones and the Liverpool Chamber of Commerce; that's all!
The impertinent Englishman, who has been left to run this
business on his own, suggests the acceptance of two conditions
—no party discussions in public while in England, and
nothing to be said against Germany. Anything else would
certainly embarrass Grey in his persistence in avoiding all
provocation of Germany in the interest of world peace. We
were simply insisting on our friendship with Russia, whether
Germany approved or not. In our return visit to Russia in
1912 we had of course to travel through Germany; and the
*Hamburger Nachrichten,* which had been Bismarck's old
newspaper, showed its annoyance by insisting that such an
exchange of Anglo-Russian visits "should never have been
allowed to happen." The impertinent Englishman will only
begin the full arrangements for the entertainment of the
Duma when he has received a telegram to say that the President, the Leader of the House, and the Leader of the Opposition are actually coming. He receives that telegram when

he gets home: START THE THING—HOMYAKOV, GUCHKOV, MILYUKOV.

Sir William Tyrrell, brilliant private secretary to Sir E. Grey at the Foreign Office, casually suggests to the impertinent Englishman that he might get valuable advice from old Lord Sanderson, now retired but once permanent head of the F.O. as far back as Lord Salisbury and Lord Rosebery. A delightful series of confabulations follows. Russia has only had a parliament for three years, so it is agreed to make the invitation not simply parliamentary but representative of all the best of British public life; that will do much more to raise the prestige of the Duma in Russia. So Lord Sanderson–this time almost as audacious as myself –concocts with me a list of seventy of the greatest celebrities in England to sign the invitation.

"Let us go on," says Lord S., "with our curious and interesting list." Among other things, it is to include possible hosts for the visitors. "Deans are very presentable people. Yes, it is a good idea to stress the part of the Universities." (We were avoiding too obvious political implications.) "Who have you got for Cambridge?" "The Master of Trinity," I said, "has promised to do the whole thing." This by the way was that same famous host, Dr. Montagu Butler; Trinity is far the largest college at Cambridge, and the Master is appointed by the Crown. "Was it right?" asks Lord S., "to go to one of the *secondary* men?" Secondary man, indeed! The Master might have a fit; one of his predecessors once said, "There are many Bishops, but there is only one Master of Trinity!" But Lord Sanderson is quite right. If the King wants to know how his loyal University of Cambridge is thriving he would send, not for the Master of Trinity, nor for the Vice-Chancellor (President) but for the Chancellor–an honorary post usually held by some Statesman.

"Who shall we get for music?" asked Lord S. "I've no

idea," I said, "I'll ask a musical critic." "Who is the best English composer?" I asked the critic. "What a ridiculous question!" he said. "Yes, I know it is. But suppose there was a great dinner of musicians and the King was in the Chair and proposed the toast of music. Who would reply?" "Oh, Sir Hubert Parry, of course." No other musician would be jealous of this choice. That was all I wanted to know, and down went the name of Sir Hubert Parry.

And now the list was ready, only just in time for the arrival of the guests, and the various invitations, public and private, were filling in. Near the end, King Edward VII himself sent for the program and put in four. This had to be careful going, of which he was such a master; for the Tsar had never yet visited his own Duma! King Edward talked to his guests about the weather. The Foreign Office also stood aside; but a dinner was arranged with half the Cabinet, and another at which Sir E. Grey sat apart, like a big dragon, in the next room, and I took each party leader for a few minutes' chat. The House of Commons could be much more demonstrative, and there was a great lunch on the terrace, with the Duma President, Homyakov, ensconced between the leaders of our two great Parties, Asquith and Balfour. Michael Stakhovich, a giant with forked beard like the statue of Moses by Michaelangelo and one of the most eloquent orators in Russia, ended his toast to the British Parliament by crashing his glass with a will on the stone floor of the terrace. My dear Alexander Zvegintsev, who followed him, avoided the usual platitudes of international friendship and raised his glass to "the glorious traditions of the Parliament of Great Britain." I could see a smile of approval on the face of Mr. Balfour.

The Duma party, throughout, was like a great band of schoolboys on holiday, always perfectly at home among us and sometimes rollicking. I had known beforehand that the party differences were of themselves subsiding in Russia in

the warmth of the common work of the Duma for the good
of the country as a whole; that was sure to happen in Russia. "Their weak suit," as with all Russians before the
Revolution, was speed. We used to have breakfast parades
in the hotel. At Edinburgh we were confronted with a precise and early time-table of reception, and my only chance
was to tell them that the program started an hour earlier
than it·really did. But once they were launched, as is usual
with Russians in England, everything went swimmingly of
itself. Everyone enjoyed these nice guests. They had asked
me to introduce them into our home life, and we quartered
them on different hosts. I had insisted on top hats, which
they said they would throw into the Channel on the way
back; but they wore them, to the general entertainment at
Henley regatta, which is a straw-hat affair, and everyone
cheered the Duma in its special boat, which could so easily
be identified.

Several among them spoke excellent English and carried the speech-making. At Edinburgh where we had haggis,
pipers and "Will ye no' come back again?"–Count Bobrinsky,[1] speaking the English of a British guardsman, began:
"Gentlemen, I am one of those who have come back again,"
for he had been on the Student's Representative Council of
Edinburgh University. It was difficult to keep at bay the
Russian newspaper men who tried their hardest to travel
everywhere with the party–it would have been fatal to let
its private chat and gossip be the prey of inaccurate articles.
One of these, getting in front of the party, actually forced
his way as one of its members into Windsor Castle!

Just as we were starting for Liverpool, Stakhovich, who
was very typical of the "broad nature" of Russia, came back
from an expansive dinner, furious at the news that British
Labor was going to demonstrate against an approaching
visit of the Tsar to our Regatta at Cowes. This protest was

[1] Father of Professor Bobrinskoy of the University of Chicago.

timed absurdly. No revolution was going on in Russia in 1909, and how could we entertain the Duma and refuse the Tsar permission to visit his uncle? Stakhovich was all his life a fearless liberal; but he said they were all insulted and should go back at once to Russia. To interfere with the stormy eloquence of Stakhovich was rather ˙like trying to check Boreas in his wrath; but I had to try. I cut in quietly, "I beg you to give up any such idea; the consequences would be deplorable." The matter was taken in hand by the wise and tactful president, Homyakov, and the question was settled in a way that was typically Russian. Bobrinsky, the Tory, proposed that his great personal friend, Basil Maklakov, the brilliant Liberal, should write a statement for the press, and that Homyakov, as President, should sign it on behalf of all, and this was immediately agreed. The statement said that had the Labor attitude been shared by the numerous persons who had entertained the party, they would have gone; but as it had not, they would stay.

The climax of the visit was a luncheon at the Mansion House. It was agreed in advance that each of the three sections of the visiting party—right, left, and center—should give its own reasons for wanting friendship with England. This was carried out with the charming chivalry of which I had seen many examples in Russian politics. The Tory Bobrinsky, quoting the famous story of the Seven Bishops, who were put on trial by James II, insisted that there could be no order without freedom. The Liberal, Milyukov, using a traditional English expression, declared that his party was the Opposition not "to His Majesty" but "of His Majesty." Such was the influence of a visit to England—but he got into plenty of trouble with his Party on his return to Russia.

## THE SPEAKER'S BEAR

We had a great deal of difficulty over our own return visit to Russia. In 1910, Stolypin was forced away from his co-operation with Guchkov and the Octobrists, and he brought in a bill taking away the long-established and guaranteed liberties of Finland, which country was always a kind of barometer in Russian politics. At that time, there was such estrangement between the parties whom we had entertained in England that they told me the English friendship was the only subject which they could all meet to discuss. The British leftists who had been cool toward the Duma visit to England and were responsible for the British Labor protest against the visit of the Tsar, butted in again, and wrote to every member of the Duma in order to put their own price on our friendship with Russia, which was that the Members should vote as directed from England on the Finnish question. I had to write to the Russian press to explain that these letters came exactly from that minority who had not entertained the Duma in England, in other words that they were "stealing our show." But I did make it clear that all my sympathies were with Finland. I remember how next day, when I appeared in the Duma, the charming Rodichev took my arm almost demonstratively and walked me up and down the lobby, especially among the reactionaries, to show that he understood me and knew that my views on Finland were like his.

In 1912, the centenary of our alliance against Napoleon, we did get going with our reply to the standing invitation from the Duma. It was Lord Sanderson who picked our party. I couldn't at first understand some of his selections, but I did, when we all got into the train. They were known in Russia as the party that never quarreled. Only one of them ever suggested that he wanted to be among the speakers, and there were two who specially asked me to assign them to any group which I had any difficulty in making up. We had about sixteen members of both Houses of Parliament—four Bishops (who were in the House of Lords), three generals (one from each arm of the service and picked by the War Office), Admiral Lord Charlie Berresford for the Navy, and a number of others distinguished in the arts or in trade. Mr. James Lowthar, then Speaker of the House of Commons, was to have headed the party and lead us all into the Duma attired in his wig and gown and preceded by the famous mace, but his father died when he had only got as far as Berlin.

The Speaker had to give me a little lesson on the order of precedence. It is a very complicated affair. It appears that there is actually an "Upper Ten Thousand" in England. Younger sons of Marquesses take precedence of Barons in their own right. The Speaker had to consult his "dictionary"; for between Lord Hugh Cecil and Lord Charles Berresford there were only eight places. But the custom is a sensible one, for once we knew our places we never straggled, and we had to see the Russian sovereign.

I had had to send in to the Tsar short biographical notes on the party, and for an hour and a half I watched him as he made the most adroit use of my notes. The Sovereign, of course, has in each case to speak first, and he was ready and apt with each of his guests. He spoke perfect English with complete simplicity. Personally, he was the most charming little man, with delightful manners, who wanted to make everyone feel comfortable. When he got to old Sir William Mather, a grand type of the Manchester Liberal, who had spent much of his life in Russia, the Tsar asked him if it was his first visit; and Mather showed the liberal flag. "My first visit, Sir," he said, "was when your grandfather liberated the serfs" (that was 48 years before), "and I felt I didn't want to die before I saw the legislative institutions which *you,* Sir, have given to Russia." I was last but one, and of course here there was no note of mine, but Nicholas had apparently been told that I was constantly visiting the Duma. So he began, "The Duma is doing better now; it started too fast, now it is slower and better."

In an excess of audacity I asked, "And more lasting?" And he graciously repeated my words, "And more lasting," but he didn't say any more about Dumas. I told him of our great appreciation of the lavish hospitality of our Russian hosts, and he said almost apologetically, "It's East, but it's good East." At the end he said to us, "Would you like to see my children?"–the surest sign that he was well pleased with us, for this, we were told, was the greatest treat he could offer us.

The Tsar had put at our disposal three of his own special trains, so that each of us had an apartment to himself. He also gave us two more treats. One was the imperial ballet, "The Sleeping Beauty," in which, to the lovely music of Chaikovsky, miles of stage forest moved past us till the Prince with his boat reached his destination. The other was the Imperial choir of religious music–only vocal, for an Orthodox Church contains no instrument, but in many parts. This music was mysteriously and enthrallingly beautiful, like that of another world. Many a first-class reputation, unknown to outsiders, has been made in this field.

As Secretary of the Delegation, I was bombarded with all sorts of strange applications–one even asking me for an "audience!" Letters arrived for all our party, each addressed as "Lord." Any kind of queer inventor took the opportunity to advertise his wares. I could seldom attend the evening festivities, as I had generally to work half through the night on the next day's program. The culmination was an Inter-Parliamentary Dinner of the two Houses of each Parliament, British and Russian; no such thing could have happened earlier in Russia. The chief host was the burly President of the Duma, Rodzyanko, who was an old friend. When we discussed the speakers the night before, he was in despair. Bitter enemies, who would ordinarily never have sat down together, wanted to come and speak up for friendship with England. At my suggestion we arranged them all in compartments, our extreme Tory to be answered by theirs, the same with the Liberals, and so on.

But at the dinner, Rodzyanko suddenly called on an aged general who had stood as one of the targets of the famous Charge of the Light Brigade at Balak Klava. Everyone crowded round the old chap to catch his words; at the end he raised his glass with spirit "To the glorious British Cavalry!" He had certainly passed outside the limits of an Inter-Parliamentary Dinner! But we had with us General Bethune of the British Cavalry, and he had to reply impromptu. He said, "We soldiers have nothing to do with politics; we fight when we are ordered to. But the Scripture tells us that wars will never cease, and we hope that if there is another war, we shall be fighting heart to heart and side to side with Russia against the common enemy!" The whole audience rose in an uproar of the utmost enthusiasm. The word had been spoken, but next day the newspapers, especially those in German, were wanting to know who was "the common enemy." Two years later Bethune was quoted as the prophet of the alliance.

In the pressing warmth of Moscow hospitality, the party sailed on to further successes. I had to divide them into groups, so that every invitation should be honored. At the University, Mackenzie Wallace, who was a pretty big bundle, was carried down the stairs to shouts of "Hurrah for the representatives of free England!" At the wonderful Tretyakov Picture Gallery, Lord Hugh Cecil made a speech in perfect tune with the old Slavophil culture: "The heavenly choir," he said, "is a harmony and not a unison," which by the way was the whole spirit of our visit.

We were now in the home of the elective local self-government of Russia, and the opportunity was fully used. Coming out from a sumptuous dinner in the City Hall into the beauty of a frozen starry night, one of the party, who was especially religious, excitedly said, "I can't go to bed!

I can't go to bed!" "You're not going to bed," they told him, "we're taking you up to Yar," which was one of the most daring entertainments in Russia. Next day I asked with interest how he got on there. "Oh," they said, "he was perfectly happy; he was talking of the union of the Churches!" That presumably was his particular form of intoxication.

The last day was like an orgy of friendship. Two of our party were being driven through the big wooded park of Sokolniki. French writers were reported to have written that bears ran wild in the streets of Moscow, which served as an occasion for a little practical joke. Suddenly, as the guests approached a shady corner, three shots were heard to ring out, and lo! there lay three bears, a mother and two cubs. "Your bears!" said their hosts. "We've just shot them for you." Amidst the preparations for the return journey I had to go round the party asking, "Would you take a bear? Do take a bear!" I managed to dispose of the two cubs. As to the big one, everyone fought shy; but as the Speaker was not there to say nay, we all agreed that it should be his, and if I am not wrong, it still stands in the hall of the Speaker's House at Westminster as a reminder that there was once a Russian Duma.

## "WIGGINS"

During the Duma visit to England in 1909, there were set up two committees, one on each side, for spade work of various kinds to deepen the friendship between the two countries. The choice of the Duma men of a colleague to myself in Russia was a member of the leading party, Alexander Zvegintsev. He became one of my nearest and dearest friends, and for frequent use I simplified his difficult name into "Wiggins." He was a big bearded baby with the most alert of minds and masses of valuable knowledge. He was most appropriate for the imaginary post of Member for

England in the Duma. He was a keen student of that period of English history when constitutionalism was merging into parliamentarism, a very important study for the Duma. He was a diligent visitor of the Distinguished Strangers' Gallery in the House of Commons and the author of a little summary of British parliamentary procedure. He had an intimate knowledge of the history of the Church of England, and was reporter to the Duma for its committee on religions. He reported also for the military committee. He knew a lot about English shorthorns. He took his duties very seriously, and turned up frequently in London. He would sit with a childlike and conspirative awe in an ABC Teashop, talking of British statesmen with Russian names which he had fitted to them. He studied cricket with me, and adapted its terms, for instance the complicated leg-before rule, to Russian politics. "You must know everything," he said, and he told me so much of the inner gossip of the Duma that I thought it no longer fair to make a record of it.

The spade work which Wiggins did at his end 'was unlimited. Any distinguished Englishman who visited Russia, fell–he would not know how–into exactly the company that was most congenial to him, whether ecclesiastical, military, parliamentary, academic, or commercial. Wiggins was a genius in matters of detail. When our visiting party reached Russia in 1912, we found him at the frontier; he had given orders that all our baggage was to be transferred, just as it was lying about, from the German carriages to our compartments in the Russian train; each door had a visiting card in English, and he had put me next the veteran liberal, Sir William Mather, whose wife–though Wiggins did not know it–had specially asked me to look after him. About a hundred miles short of Petersburg he flooded the train with a band of young people, sons of leading public men in Russia, to fetch and carry for us throughout the tour, so that they might have the English friendship as one of their earliest memories in Russian public life. Later, when I was working for an Anglo-Russian Exhibition at the White City in London, he piloted me everywhere, coaching me all the time with live knowledge of persons and things. Through him, any house was open to me and any service at my disposal.

The great charm of Wiggins was that he was essentially a good man, good and kind. All his quick cleverness went into helping others, and working for a great cause. He used to say to me, "When they all see it, then others who are thought more important will come in and supersede us"— but that he would never have minded and it would only have pleased him. He used to write me long letters in childish English, sometimes with little verses, adaptations of the English rhymes taught him by his old governess. As he lightly chatted away cleverly on anything, one forgot that there was an encyclopedic knowledge, easily mobilized, behind it all. He was sometimes as naive as my dear Father, of whom he had so many of the characteristics, and most people did not take him too seriously. Yet his was one of the best judgments. A devoted Liberal, he was one of my only two Russian friends who told me I should not wish for a Russian revolution. "It will be far more savage than the French!" he said. I am thankful that he never saw it.

When the war came, I made my way up to him on the Front as soon as possible. He was second man in the Intelligence Department of the Third Army, his Chief being Dukhonin, later Commander-in-Chief. He introduced me at mess as "Expert of the Foreign Office in East European affairs." I begged him to put it more modestly, but he said it was worth while to do it well once for all. The result was a sweet little pass which would be the dream of any war correspondent: "The Englishman, Pares, attached to the Russian Red Cross, has the right to be with any fighting unit and in any fighting position." I could and did simply walk up and join in as I pleased. Wiggins was always nursing me from the rear; it was he who sent up the news of Father's death, which I received in front of the front line; he had translated into beautiful English, from my Russian over the telephone, my last message of love. His staff loved him and teased him, and so did I. I once presented him with a reconnaissance report on the Reconnaissance Department, where on a visit to him, I had found every door open. When I sprained my ankle, he put up a bed for me in this department and fed me with all the reports.

Zvegintsev had charge of one of the very few giant airplanes called Ilya Muromets, the name of an old peasant hero of popular legend. The Tsar was coming to the Third Army, and Zvegintsev was planning an aerial escort. He was to make his first flight on this plane, and sent his car for me to come and accompany him. When I entered his department and asked where he was to be found, the answer was, "The colonel has been smashed to death." They made so many jokes about him, that I thought they were joking now, but it was only too true. He had gone up a day earlier without me to make a trial trip. The giant plane had four cylinders, two on each side, and carried a crew of eight. The two cylinders on one side were hit by one of our own guns some thirty or forty miles behind our front. I visited the spot to see that the cross was in order and carried away some pieces of the plane. The peasants spoke of it as if it were a great bird. "It hovered on its wing, and then came straight down." At the memorial service in Petrograd, the British Ambassador, Sir George Buchanan, who was very fond of Zvegintsev, knelt with lighted candle side by side with Rodzyanko, president of the Duma. I put on my wreath: "To one of the best friends England has ever had."

Wiggins' boy was educated free of all charges at Winchester, where I had entered his name at his father's request before the war, for Wiggins had wanted to turn his big country house into a kind of "Winchester" for Russia. They took him, as they said, "in recognition of the noble work of his father for England." The boy raced up the school with exceptional ability and served England in a responsible post in the Second World War.

## Roman Dmowski and the Poles

In 1907, in the tea room of the Second Duma, to which I had been given the right of access, I found myself sitting opposite Roman Dmowski. After the exclusion of all who had signed the Viborg Appeal, the Duma was sadly impoverished in political ability. Dmowski, leader of the Poles, stood out as the ablest man in it. Son, I believe, of a Vistula fisherman, he had a good square face with a powerful jaw and a manner full of confidence and decision, and his hold on his colleagues seemed absolute; he reminded me of the great leader of the Irish, Charles Parnell.

He was playing a most difficult game; in this predominantly revolutionary Duma he was balancing his support between it and the Russian government, and trying to get what little could be got for Poland. Witte, in his memoirs, without naming Dmowski but speaking only of "a Polish lawyer," mentions with respect the novel plea which this able man had put up to him—that the Poles were really an element of order and even of conservatism and could be of use to the stability of the Russian empire, if it were not the Russian policy to demoralize the whole culture of the country.

Dmowski asked me straight out if I would try to help the Polish cause. I answered at once exactly as I would answer now. Poland was then partitioned between Russia, Germany and Austria. England could not plant an army in Poland to fight both Germany and Russia. If so, an Englishman

could only help Poland through one or the other. I would
gladly try to help in England and through my ties with
Russia, which were many and useful. This understanding
was at once accepted, and it led to a close co-operation between us for ten years, 1907 to 1917.

Dmowski wanted to make a pronouncement to British
and American correspondents, and we arranged that he
should give a lunch to Williams, Baring, Harper, and myself. He asked me afterwards how his statement had gone.
It was straightforward and effective, and I only made one
criticism. I hoped he would not talk of Russia to the Russians with the same contempt for them which he had shown
with us. We then drove together to the Duma (this was on
May 30, 1907), and there stood one of his colleagues at the
door with the news that the House was discussing political
terrorism, a theoretical question which should never have
been brought before it. There were nine parties, and they
proposed the most contradictory formulas. Far and away the
best was Dmowski's; "Terrorism is incompatible with
parliamentary institutions"; in other words, if the government dissolved the Duma, which it was evidently thinking
of doing, this formula would cancel out of itself. But in his
short and plain speech, under the ten minutes rule restricting speeches, he used the expression "An Asiatic Government"
–the very thing against which I had just ventured to warn
him. Russians knew very well that Poles regarded them all
as Asiatics, and the revolutionaries were as much incensed as
anyone else.

There were a number of things which Dmowski and I
did together. He asked me to find a young Englishman, to
be trained in Warsaw in the study of Poland. I chose a
young Scot, Bruce Boswell, who worked for five years in
Warsaw with great success, and later succeeded me in the
Chair of Russian at Liverpool. In 1909, I got the Russians
to include a strong representation from Poland in the Duma

visit to England. I reported on the Polish question both
to the British Embassy in Petersburg, which would have
found it very difficult to touch this question, and to Sir
Edward Grey, who at once took the same view as many
Liberal friends in Russia. In 1913, knowing that war was
inevitable, I raised the Polish question as a sharp European issue in my *Russian Review,* which had many influen-
tial contributors and subscribers in Russia. Dmowski got
the most distinguished Poles to write, and himself contributed four articles. When I stopped in Warsaw to complete
the arrangements, Boswell, who had prepared all the detail,
informed me that I was very popular, for the curious reason
that I avoided talking German or Russian and spoke particularly bad French, occasionally taking refuge in a word of
Russian, which language they knew as well as I did. "The
worse French you talked," he said, "the better they liked
you." Such was their hate of everything Russian. My preface
to the Polish articles was meant to leave no doubt at all that
average British opinion regarded the Russian treatment of
Poland as intolerable. One of the nicest of the Polish members, young Goscicki, once asked me why we could not do
more to get the Russians to be reasonable. I replied that we
were trying to act as a good conscience to them. "You must
be very tired!" he said.

At the beginning of the war Dmowski gave me a lunch
with his chief friends in Warsaw and declared that he cared
more for Polish access to the Baltic than even for the Polish
province of Poznan, then under Prussia. After the crash of
the Russian armies in Galicia, which I had witnessed in the
front line, I hurried to Warsaw to tell him the city was
sure to fall to the Germans and asked what preparations he
had made for neutrality under a German occupation. He
brought in several friends to discuss the matter. Dmowski
and those who depended on Russia would go there. Those
who stayed on, would remain correctly but firmly aloof to

German bids. I later heard that this policy was working out very well; and of this fact, Ludendorf in his memoirs gives the strongest confirmation.

As the approach of revolution became self-evident, I advised Dmowski to go to London and plead the Polish cause there. All Poland was now in German or Austrian hands and could be reconquered only by a joint effort of all the allies. Dmowski had shown me a map, I think by Spett of Leipzig, which though German, gave accurate details on the limits of Polish population; it practically coincided with the Curzon line, later on so famous. I recommended him to take this map with him, but when I joined him in London, I found he had left it behind. The revolution had now arrived; Russia was down and out, and Dmowski, like his Polish rival, Pilsudski, from the Austrian part of Poland, though with much less extravagance, was trying to get back as much as possible of the so-called "lost provinces" of the medieval feudal empire of Poland, where Polish landlords dominated a Russian peasant population. From that time we did not meet again.

I went to report to Mr. Balfour, then our Foreign Secretary, who described the Polish claims as "preposterous." This was also the view of his successor, Lord Curzon, whose name is associated with the Curzon line. The State Department in Washington was equally plain-spoken in begging the Poles to go no further, as it well foresaw the complications which have given so much trouble throughout the Second World War. But, in May, 1920, Pilsudski marched on Kiev, the mother of Russian cities. The Red Army, still in its infancy, marched on Warsaw but was driven right back to the so-called Riga line of the Russo-Polish Treaty of 1921, which stood up to the Second World War. A year and a half after this treaty Pilsudski himself told me, in a long conversation which we had in Warsaw, that he had just come back from a part of the Polish State where the population was 80 per cent Orthodox, that is, of course, non-Polish.

## "Political Unreliability of a British Subject!"

After the British visit of 1912, I escorted the party to the frontier and then returned at once to Petersburg. Harold Williams was in trouble and it was a matter of showing whether the prestige of the exchange of visits was really of any practical value. The Tsar's police were always against Williams, especially those elements in it, and they were many, which were strongly associated with German influence. At the instance, it appears, of a police agent named Kürz, Williams' flat was searched. The police found very little; there was the diary of a sailor who had taken part in the naval battle of Tusushima seven years before, which had been given to Williams by the well-known Russian novelist, Remizov, and had lain unused by him in his desk. On the strength of this the police founded a charge of military espionage!– of course, dear Williams would have been the worst spy in the world. They also found a letter from the famous revolutionary exile, Vera Figner, arranging for a meeting when the Williamses were in Switzerland. On these grounds Williams was forbidden to live in Russia. He was then correspondent of the highly respectable and conservative English newspaper, *The Morning Post,* which had temporarily sent him to Constantinople because of his knowledge of Turkish.

Our new Ambassador, Sir George Buchanan, gave me all possible help and sent me to Makarov, the Minister of the Interior, who was in control of the Police Department. I represented to the Minister that we might think it quite serious enough to expel the correspondent of *"The Morning Post"* immediately after the exchange of visits, but that it was really a much more serious matter to exclude the greatest scholar we had ever sent to Russia; this, I put it, was the sharpest rebuff we could have to our attempts to promote the study of Russia in England. The Minister listened courteously to me, but seemed very unwilling to give any details. However, when I asked whether the charge was one of military espionage, he said, "Yes," and added, no doubt with the letter of Vera Figner in mind, "He is also acquainted with undesirable persons." Having a good deal of knowledge of the morale of the Police Department, I felt sorely tempted to reply, "So are you!" but that would not have helped. I asked simply that Williams should be allowed to return to Russia to answer all charges against him. "But he can't do that," said Makarov, "because we have closed the frontier to him." "Then can't you open the frontier and let him come?" I asked. "Oh, but he won't," said the Minister. "I assure you," said I, "that the moment he hears from me, he will get into a train and come back." "Very well," said Makarov, very reluctantly. "We'll give him till the 15th to answer the charges." "New style or old?" I asked, for the Russian calendar was 13 days behind ours. "Very well, old style!" said the Minister graciously.

Williams, of course, returned at once. He was ordered to go and see General Zuyev, head of the political police, who was later to be dismissed from his post with none too savory details. Williams was very gentle, and Zuyev tried his best to browbeat him. At the end he said, "You'll send in a report to me, including all the answers which you have given me here."

Williams' Russian wife, who was a well-known member of Milyukov's Liberal Party, was a great deal more combative than Williams. We at once saw that Zuyev had played straight into our hands. We drew up Williams' reply with him in three copies which were destined one for Zuyev, one for the British Ambassador, and one for the *London Times*.

It was quite easy to tell this stupid story in such terms as could have been no use to the Russian Police Department. At the end of the afternoon, Mrs. Williams said, "Three journalists have worked the whole day without remuneration."

Several members of the Duma were only too anxious to speak up for Harold. Sir George Buchanan, lunching with his friend the Russian Foreign Minister, Sazonov, remarked very happily, "What's all this rubbish about Williams? Mackenzie Wallace has got a far better collection of papers;" and Wallace had just been perhaps the leading hero of our return visit to Russia. It was finally Guchkov who hit the mark. He called me up on the telephone and said, "Mr. Pares, it is all right. Mr. Williams can remain in Russia." The outcome was a literary curiosity, or rather two. The Williams case had been labeled in the Police Department "Case of the Political Unreliability of the British Subject, Harold Williams"; it is not quite clear what claim the Tsar's government had on the political reliability of a British subject; but still more striking was the document which Williams now received and which I think he ought to have framed, as no one else ever had anything like it— "The British subject, Harold Williams, may cross the frontier whenever he wishes."

In the latter phase of the First World War, not long before the Revolution, the Secret Police got to work again on Williams; Kürz by now was apparently in German employ. Harold was refused his ordinary ticket at the Duma. This time short work was made of the matter. Sir George wrote to Sazonov: "Please get these people to stop worrying Williams; he's very necessary to me," and indeed Williams at this most critical time was the chief source of information for the British Embassy. Sazonov, who himself was quite near dismissal, said to me, "I shall show my flag"; and he replied to Sir George, "Williams shall not be worried any more."

### THE PEASANTS "DIVIDE UP"

The large, square room was a rural office of the local self-government (Zemstvo). The peasants of a certain village were all gathered here–for the first time in history to divide up their communal land permanently into personal holdings. This was a process which originally came about slowly, but historically all over Europe; and it was at this time passing into Russia.

The old communal joint ownership was a great drag upon all private initiative. It is true that the Russian peasantry had derived from it a strong corporate instinct and a keen sense of equity; in fact, precisely through the village community, this under-dog class had a more real system of self-government than any other in Russia. But in the past, they had no access to expert land surveyors and so generally decided questions in the gross. When they divided the village holding–only for temporary use–in order to be fair all-round, they would draw long strips through the whole length of it; and a single peasant often had 150 such strips scattered, it might be, over several square miles, with perhaps only one horse, or not even that, to work them. As the population grew, in order to preserve this same rough and ready equity, these strips would only be divided in width and not in length, so that they might even reach to a mile, but were now so narrow that I had myself several times stood astride of one. This involved even the manufacture by the county councils of a very complicated plow, which could turn round without going on to the next neighbor's strip. With this multiplicity of strips, a substantial amount of land was wasted on boundaries. These were just ditches –one never saw any hedges–and when your neighbor let out his cattle, they might naturally wander all over your strip.

In November, 1906, Stolypin, who aimed at producing a new class of yeomen or independent peasant farmers, had

ordained by decree that any peasant might demand his share
of the common holding in perpetuity as personal property.
This led to intolerable confusion. The village did not care
to lose one of its best tax-payers; the outgoing peasant might
have to face persecution of every kind, or even be "burnt
out." He probably did a bit of thinking and found that it
would be in his best interest to persuade all the rest to do
the same. This distinction was described by the words
"dividing out" and "dividing up." It was "dividing up" that
was the occasion of the present meeting.

But there would have been no success for a reform
of this kind without the support of the peasants themselves.
In the past, two-thirds of the house-holders could legally
demand a re-division, though only again for temporary
occupation; and this good rule was wisely retained for the
final division. Land was a subject on which the peasant
had his own first-hand knowledge and his own self-interest.
To "divide up," a village would choose a kind of jury of
elders, those best acquainted with the varying qualities of
the holding. Assisted by expert land-surveyors, they would
then go round the village holding and divide it into categories representing different values, A., B., C., D. and E.
An inter-relation was then established between the different categories; so much of A. was reckoned as worth so
much of B., and so on. Thus there was set up a number of
lots of approximately equal value. These were now put up
for bidding. By a plan which the peasants themselves had
invented, no money changed hands. Each bidder, to get the
lot which he wanted, said how many square yards he would
give up to be pooled, as common stock which went to in-
crease the less fertile or more distant lots. The older ones
would try to stay near the village, while the younger would
go out to pioneer in the remote and neglected parts.

There was a quiet tension, and the business went on
with a slow deliberation. It seemed to me that women hold-

ers, such as were involved, were more businesslike than the males. Woe to that family which was on this day represented by a drunkard, for this was the last deal.

I spent in all about ten weeks studying the effects of this vital phase in the history of the peasantry, traveling day and night in many different parts of the country. It certainly seemed to me the most important reform since the Emancipation. The peasants were inspired by it and threw themselves into it, with their most intelligent and progressive elements leading the way. There was the same spirit in the numerous extra land-surveyors who took service with the Ministry of Agriculture especially for this reform, and I came to feel something like an affection for the green cap of this Ministry, as I associated it with the first instance that I had seen of real co-operation between government and public. The new young farmers were, visibly to the eye, more alert and efficient. The cattle everywhere looked more plump and well tended. The rate at which the movement was going gave great hope for the future. I may say here that, when the war came, the German invaders were instructed to destroy the new Stolypin farms wherever they found them; for the new vigorous farming initiative was already a foreboding of escape from German economic exploitation.

## Among the Moscow Merchants

Homyakov, in his article on the Russian visit of 1909, in our *Russian Review* had described it happily as an "overture," sounding the various "motifs" of all the different lines of co-operation which were now opening up between the two countries.

Never so far had Russia advanced faster in economic prosperity than in this period. Meanwhile, by 1913, the skies of Europe were fast darkening and the competition for Russia's friendship was never sharper. It seemed that the strongest of all the German roots in Russia were in the growing domination in the field of trade. On the other hand, British and French money was coming into Russia faster than ever; for there was now publicity of finance and the Duma was making excellent use of its power over the budget. In 1907, the Russian government had set up the first Chamber of Commerce in the country, the Anglo-Russian, known as Russ-Brit, and it was by the Tsar's personal wish that the Minister of Commerce, Timiryazev, was its first chairman. The moment was ripe for a challenge of the German claim to trade monopoly.

The secretaries of the Anglo-Russian Committees in both countries were Zvegintsev in Petersburg, and myself in London. Among other projects to deepen the good understanding was one for an Anglo-Russian exhibition to be held at the White City in London, of which Imre Kiralfy had been the brilliant organizer. He was to be held to firm conditions –the exhibition was not even primarily to be commercial, but to show Russia in all its picturesque variety.

I was entrusted–not, of course, with the financial or commercial–but with the political work, to bring the project into being. This was in 1913-1914. On reaching Petersburg, I sought first the advice of the wisest friend I had in Russia, Nicholas Homyakov, who had been President of the Duma during its visit to England. "You will have to go first to the Minister of Commerce," he said. "I'm afraid he does not think with his own brains but with those of Krestovnikov, Chairman of the Moscow Stock Exchange, which are very poor ones." I went to the Minister. I asked him first to let me outline the details of our plan before he gave an opinion, and in my outline I was careful to answer in advance the objections I knew were likely to come from Krestovnikov. "Well," said the Minister, when I had done, "if you have an exhibition at all, that's just the way it should be planned. But you'll find that in our commercial world there's a positive horror of exhibitions." I said, "I'm going straight from you, Sir, to Gregory Alexandrovich Krestovni-kov." "That's just the point!" said the Minister quickly. I was amused to see my adviser's forecast so immediately verified.

To Krestovnikov I went. I was very carefully coached by my Moscow friends including Guchkov, whose brother was Mayor of Moscow. Krestovnikov was a hidebound conservative. He had a fine market for his tallow as far as the Pacific, comparatively free of competition, and he feared all change or progress. I went about the business in the same way as with the Minister. At the end Krestovnikov said, "I am not at all against it, but you'll find all our Moscow merchants are." "I'm going round to see them all," I replied, "and I'll come back in a month with the results." At the end of the month I was able to bring him a list of nearly all of them, as prepared to join in a Moscow Exhibition Committee "under the chairmanship of Gregory Alexandro-vich Krestovnikov." "No, no!" he said, "I'm too official."

My friends, as I could see, were using me to serve a purpose of their own. They were not yet ready to get Krestovnikov out of the chairmanship of the Stock Exchange, but they wanted to put him in an evident minority. England was very popular at that time; a counterpoise to German exploitation was desirable; and there was a growing liberal movement among many of the larger firms against protection-ism. While I was away, Krestovnikov induced several of those who had consented, to withdraw their names. I went round again and got about half of them back. Then I went into a hospital for the poor. I was quite worn out.

Never in Russia was I faced with anything so sticky as the Moscow merchant world. It was far more conserva-tive than the Russian government, and that was saying a good deal. The Chairman of the Stock Exchange was much firmer

in his seat than any Minister of Finance. One of Krestovnikov's predecessors, when the Minister of Finance appealed
to his authority, replied, "I have known many Ministers of
Finance." Another peculiarity was that like Krestovnikov,
the Moscow merchants never liked to say "No." One young
merchant prince, liberal and enlightened, kept me talking
for an hour. "Well, I'm going now," I said. "Why?" he asked.
"You have said 'No,'" I explained. "Not quite!" he said.

My next experience was to go round to each of the
Ministers in Petersburg and ask his support. This was a
much easier job; for several who were not specially well
disposed to England, in particular the Minister of Religion
who was really a puppet of Rasputin, were at least anxious
to make a great show of their Ministries. The Cabinet was
divided between those who were afraid to displease Germany
and those who were glad to have the alternative of a different friend. On our side the leader was Sazonov, the Foreign
Minister. As he once told me, his decision to enter the diplomatic service was taken while he was in the Isle of Wight
in England, definitely to work for an understanding between the two countries. The project was presented by him
to the Tsar, who typically enough came to the decision, "It is
to be (the usual official wording) but not this year."

The reason why the Exhibition never took place, was
that the Great War came directly afterwards and was followed by the Revolution. But the same Cabinet whose
members I had had to visit continued in office unchanged
by the war, and it was very useful to me to get this glimpse
of the divergencies in its political sympathies. Something like
nearly half of the Cabinet entrusted with carrying on the
war against Germany was really pro-German, and we might
count in this half, the War Minister, Sukhomlínov.

# CHAPTER VI

## On the Russian Front
## (1914–1917)

### WANDERINGS ALONG THE FRONT

IT CAN be imagined with what intense interest I had followed every move on the international chessboard that
led up to the German declaration of war on Russia. Would
they make this enormous mistake? They knew far more about
Russia than we did. They had far more numerous real ties,
far more agents and workers inside the country. For any of
us few Englishmen who followed closely events in Russia,
the magnitude of the issue was almost like a personal secret.
It was only they who could win the game for our side, but
they did it twice, and the second time with far less excuse.

I was in England when Germany declared war. I was
quite convinced that England would be involved in the war.
I had been going to Russia every year for a few months, and
the conditions of my professorship in Liverpool University
left me free to choose my own times; in fact, I was just
preparing to start now. I had said in my inaugural lecture
as Reader in 1906 that I could not make a real mark in my
field without forty Honour Students, and it was we in Liverpool who had now more than half of the University posts
in it in the British Empire (four out of seven). But the stu-

dents were not there, for so far there were no openings for them. Clearly I had to go myself.

I wrote to the Foreign Office offering to start at once. All these journeys were made on my own resources. This particular one reminded me of the way in which two casual acquaintances might arrange that one should undertake a service for the other. By the time I started, England was already in the war; I should have to cross the North Sea and travel through neutral Scandinavia, which was sure to be packed with German spies; but how to get to Russia at all I had to find out from the tourist agency of Messrs. Thomas Cook and Son.

I was asked if I would mind taking out with me some uniforms of a military attaché at our British Embassy at Petersburg, with his name and rank prominently published on the familiar tin cases. Would I also take out some official dispatches? I had little time to catch my train, and my cab was drawn up in the inside court of the Foreign Office. The neat little cream-colored dispatch bags, with their pink ribbons, were tossed into it, while the cabman said huskily to the small group of casual by-standers "King's service." "And what shall I do," I asked, "if we meet a submarine in the North Sea?" "Take a large stone!" said my official friend dreamily. I caught the train in the last few seconds. There was no berth for me on the boat, and I slept in the passage with the dispatch bags for a pillow; there was nowhere else to put them. Of course, I couldn't get up, and kind friends brought me relays of refreshments.

In Petersburg the Russian Foreign Minister, Sazonov, described to me in his room at the Russian Foreign Office the scene of the delivery of the German ultimatum by their extraordinarily futile ambassador, Count Pourtalès. He had reckoned confidently on Russia's submission. When Sazonov quietly repeated his "No," Pourtalès said "What has become of my mission?" and leaning against the window almost fainted, and Sazonov had to help him out of the room. He even left behind him the piece of paper on which his Embassy had decoded his instructions to declare war. Better than that–the instructions had contained two alternative wordings –always with a declaration of war–for the event that Russia might ask for more time; and both had been decoded on to the same bit of paper, and this was the paper, which Pourtalès in his confusion left behind in the Russian Foreign Office. It is almost too good to be true, but it forms the last document in the Russian *Orange Book*.

After many weeks of pottering about in St. Petersburg among disgruntled foreign correspondents who could not get to the front, I received from that very able diplomatist, O'Beirne, Councillor of our Embassy, a commission which he described as one of the most curious he had seen. Sir Edward Grey, the British Foreign Secretary, requested me to go and live with the Russian Army. The point was that the Russian War Minister, Sukhomlínov, who was among the pro-German members of the Russian cabinet, had no enthusiasm for the war and obstructed access to the front to our first-class military attaché, Alfred Knox, and his very capable assistants—and Grey apparently thought that I had enough Russian friends to get there somehow.

So I had, and the most useful of them was Sazonov, the Foreign Minister. The commander of the Third Russian Army was a Bulgarian, General Radko Dmitriev, who had won a high reputation in the recent war of his own country against Turkey. Radko had a Russian wife, and all his sympathies were with Russia. So when he saw his country going in another direction, he transferred to Russia. Now it was a standing rule in the Russian Army that if once you were the guest of the General in command, you could not very well be dragged out.

The Third Army, which was to have a glorious record, was regarded as playing the part of liberator for the smaller

Slav peoples under Austrian rule. In that vast and cumbrous military machine which the Russians put into the field, things were so fluid that it was not too difficult to get where you wanted; and, not only in the military command on the southwest front, but also in the Red Cross and its subordinate organization, there foregathered a goodly company of Russian liberals and especially Members of the Duma. To get the necessary official standing, I became a stretcher-bearer in the Civil Red Cross. Homyakov, Stakhóvich, and Guchkov had all offered me front line service in it. Above all, Wiggins was with the Third Army, having resumed his military service as second in command in its Intelligence Department. That was how I obtained from Radko direct the lovely little pass which authorized me to be anywhere in the front line.

My position was a very peculiar one. At the officers' mess I was the only "white crow," the only one in uniform without shoulder straps. My simple friends in the ranks sometimes asked "Why is that 'countryman' standing among the officers?" The Red Cross was in itself sufficient cover and carried me anywhere for nothing; but I also had in my pocket the delightful fables of Krylov which very slowly–only in twenty years–I was translating into English verse, always seeking the idioms which would match the original. I used the soldiers as dictionary. They would tell me little stories to show the shade of difference between one idiom and another. Once I heard one of them say to a comrade, "I can't come with you just now. I am working with my friend the professor. We are translating Krylov." I might find myself at the saluting point, or I might be followed as a spy. Then I would produce my little pass and ask that I should not be worried. As to outfit, besides the sheets and the rubber tub, more than ever necessary, I enjoyed a variety of overcoats for all weathers, which would also serve as bed. Everything was carried for me. As to conveyances I used all kinds–trains, which near the front, sometimes made only one mile an hour (once I got out and walking and carrying my kit, I beat the train by an hour and a half), then closer up I was on horseback, and finally on foot. At one point I used a bicycle which fortunately broke down before taking me in a wrong direction straight to the enemy; at another there was a rail machine worked by hand to cover our part of the line to the next station; the enemy had the rest. The enemy was always "He." You would ask what is that hill, and they would say, "He."

After the Revolution there was printed in the *Red Archives* a very insulting letter about my presence from Sazonov's own representative at headquarters, Prince Kudashev, complaining that the English had sent there not an ordinary military attaché, but a man who knew quite a bit about Russia to see whether the Russians were really trying to do their best. Fortunately this letter was addressed to his Chief, Sazonov, who had himself put me there; and that is why I heard nothing of it at the time.

The Russian Red Cross represented in full at the front the broad generosity of the Russian public. In the Japanese war the Russian government had done everything to cramp its work; now it couldn't do without it. The government's own services at the front were always short of personnel and of equipment; every regiment (of 4,000 men) ought to have had five surgeons, which, God knows, was little enough in the actual conditions of fighting, and seldom had more than three. The road transport supply was so unsuitable that it had to be largely scrapped and replaced by the Civil Red Cross; and there were at first practically no points for the distribution of food.

No one could suggest that the Red Cross was itself perfect. It is true that in little over a month it had set up hospital beds for a possible two million wounded, but there was no crispness and promptness in the organization, nor was the equipment at all adequate; at first, for instance, there was an almost entire lack of iodine. I can remember how I have been called in to try and distract a wounded soldier by my conversation while, without any anesthetics, the surgeon was poking about in his head, and this more than once. One wounded man, Ivan, who was trying to tell me all about his family, at last interrupted the surgeons with a mild protest, "Gentlemen, that's enough!" Once Ivan was incautiously left on the operating table and rolled off onto the stone floor, but from that time his recovery was rapid. But what was abundant in the Russian Red Cross was the broad and warm humanity of its whole atmosphere. Never did I find in a Russian field hospital any trace of a distinction between the enemy's wounded and our own. And this instinct was equally triumphant with our own wounded soldiers. They regarded a wounded enemy as one who had a right to special care and kindness because he had no friends. I used sometimes to write for wounded war prisoners their letters to their homelands which the Red Cross was able to send through for them, and I remember how one of these asked me to write "I am lovingly tended" which, in the given case, I knew to be no more than the truth.

I was sometimes requested by the Red Cross to tell a front line general that if only he would ask for it; this or that was waiting for him close up to the front line—say a dental chair which red tape had blocked from coming through. At first I was among very few who could get to the front, but the complete inadequacy of the military ambulance gradually led to a merging of front and rear, and this had a marked influence on both.

My talks with the wounded prisoners were for me almost a kind of map of the Austrian Empire, with its medley of races. I sometimes compared the picture which I got from them with Colonel Dukhonin, head of the Third Army Intelligence.

Very similar were the relations between our people and the surrounding Austrian population, for we were in conquered territory. The Red Cross helped the civil hospitals of the district, equipping them both with money and with extra personnel. It was very much the same with the lower ranks of the army. The Ruthenians, who are the same as the Ukrainians or Little Russians, were on our side, though they were Austrian subjects; and here troops and populations got on together quite naturally. But we had also conquered quite a bit of Western Galicia where the people are Polish, and here too I could notice the simple familiarity with which Russian soldiers played with the children of the Polish peasants on whom they had been quartered. One incident in particular remains in my memory. In an army motor, I was carrying wounded Russians from the front; I had to go about fifteen miles before I could find a first-aid station and there I took my wounded into a roomy, Polish hut. The old peasant housewife had the features of a Duchess. One of my wounded was a Russian yokel with his face all crushed in; she pointed to him to lie down on a beautiful bed with lace trimmings, and he wouldn't do it for fear of spoiling the bed.

It was very much the same in the matter of religion. Whatever trouble there was, was at the top. The Ruthenians are Uniats, the product of a peculiar medieval political deal by which Russian Orthodox Christians under Polish rule were relieved from persecution by their Catholic masters if they would only say that the Pope was Head of the Church, and could keep their belief and worship unchanged. The Austrian priests had all fled at our approach. When we asked members of their flocks what religion they were, they said quite simply "Orthodox"; in fact, one of them is known to have explained the situation by saying that the Pope had become Orthodox! We had no difficulty at all on either side. It was agreed to say the Lord's Prayer together and leave it at that.

One day I was returning, mostly on foot, from the front line to Army Headquarters. As I approached, I heard the strains of a familiar melody that was prohibited in Russia. It was the national anthem of oppressed and partitioned Poland. Obviously, it came from Radko's own military band; and as I came onto the Square I saw him holding a review of adventurous Czechs from the Austrian army, who were constantly making their way over to us in great numbers because we were the side where all their sympathies lay. In fact, we had received instructions never to ask a Czech war prisoner "where he had surrendered" but "where he had come across," and this was often done under fire from his own side. Here, in front of Radko, was parading the first of the famous Czech legions, originally composed of Czechs living in Russia but reinforced by those other Czechs who made the dangerous passage to us. As they marched round with military alertness, they were singing to the strains of the old Polish anthem the common war song of all Slavs, which begins "Slavs, come along!" They had already carried out the most dangerous tasks on our side, and were receiving decorations from our "Bulgarian" General Radko. Then he turned to a number of other Czechs who had just come over and were still in Austrian uniform. He asked them to take note how their fellow countrymen were being honored. They could, if they wished, go to the Russian interior, or they might join the Czech legion. He ended "And when you get back to your own country, I hope you will find that it has been freed!" He turned to his interpreter and said "Tell them that again!" Radko, who was a thorough-going republican, was shot as a hostage by the Bolsheviks after the revolution; but his dream came true.

## IN THE GALICIAN SMASH

I began my visits to the actual front line as soon as I got near it. The little pass worked wonders; I only had to walk up and join in, whatever they were doing. My nearest First

Aid point, that of the Duma, served as my base, and from there I could forward my dispatches by anyone who happened to be going back to Petrograd. I can't count how many people did this service for me, but not one of my dispatches went astray and I recovered them all when I got back to the capital. One of the censors was most conveniently a kinsman of Wiggins; he said to me, "As you represent an allied government, I think you ought to be your own censor." So each dispatch, without going through any formalities, was simply dropped in the letter-box of the British Embassy.

I was taken in, on equal terms by each regiment that I visited. I had my camp bed; and it was simply put up among the rest. The colonel would then turn to any soldier who was in the room. "This," he would say, "is our friend and ally" *(soyuznik)*, which came to be the name by which I went. "You're going to go with him and help him. He's very near to us, and you must be sure to bring him back safe."

These excursions were a great delight to me; they were generally at night or still better, in the twilight, when you could see the enemy's lines but he couldn't pick you out on your background. I know that my guides enjoyed them fully as much as I did; it was a novelty for a simple peasant soldier to find himself roaming all night with a strange creature called an Englishman, who came from a free and friendly country and, having no official rank, was simply a new friend. There was one thing which I objected to; they took far too seriously the instruction to be careful of me. More than once, my guide would actually mount the trench and walk on top of it, as if that would make me safer. I had only to say, "If you don't come down, I come up," and that was always enough. They were most respectful, in fact too much so. I was visiting with one of them at a place called "the Secrets"; these "Secrets" were man-holes close up to the actual dividing line. We were discovered, and there was a volley of machine-gun fire. My guide, who had been discussing with me in a whisper what our army was doing on the other side, called out "Lie down, your high nobility!" and I would have gladly dispensed with the title.

These men ordinarily talked their hearts out; and often I only wished that I could have written down at once the actual lively words which they used, so as not to lose all the color which they put into them. They certainly hoped that the war would lead to greater freedom in their own country. I can remember a Cossack riding back just in front of me in a morning mist to the regiment. "Russia is night," he said, "We must have light." They never boasted, not even of their obvious superiority over the Austrians, who hardly ever faced them fair and square with the bayonet, but they were perturbed by the barbarism of German army orders. One of these, it seemed, prescribed that if a captured Russian scout was chary of information his ears should be slit, and several of those who escaped back to us bore the marks on them. My improvised batman would say to me, "Sir, aren't they more cultured than we are? Do cultured people slit your ears?" or again "Won't they be punished, Sir, for the things they have done contrary to the law?"—a Russian expression which meant the law of God.

The officers, like the men, were great big children. They would always be wanting to show me something which I hadn't seen elsewhere. "We must show him the places which are 'interesting'" they would say; "interesting," of course, really meant "dangerous." "Have you seen this?" "Have you seen that?" "Have you seen the Secrets?" "Yes, I have seen the Secrets." "Then, it seems that he has seen everything except a bayonet attack; we must arrange one for him!" Fortunately someone else cut in, "But he won't see anything unless he's in the middle of it," so I was relieved to find that this hospitable idea was abandoned.

The Polish peasants insisted on remaining in their huts, even when these came to be in the actual front line. There was one such hut which made the Russians very anxious for its inhabitants. You see, they had around them their turnips and cabbages, and nothing else in the world, and they were loth to leave. One day a near hit damaged the house, and there came out a middle-aged whiskered man with his wife and children and some sheep. "Thank God, they've gone at last," said the Russians. But a day or two later this hut came in for a direct hit, and then out of its door emerged an old grandfather, smoking a pipe, and a cow! Once my batman told me I had got to be very careful in climbing a slope in front of us because we were under fire; but as, with almost cowardly caution, we sneaked out on to the top, we saw just in front of us two hefty housewives vigorously airing their laundry right in front of the enemy.

One interesting feature was the mortal fear that the Germans had of the Cossacks. The first night that I actually dined at the Front, a Cossack came in to report to the Colonel, in these words, "Arrested eleven Germans"–presumably for being Germans. One trench was even taken by a little Russian boy of 12 to 13, in uniform; he jumped into it with a terrible shout, and that proved enough.

It was the Austrians who were in front of us, and through the early months of 1915 they followed a routine which we thought very gentlemanly. At fixed hours and with intervals for refreshments, they would pour shell-fire on a given patch of our front. "Francis Joseph," said one officer, "seems to have a lot of extra shell." All we had to do in reply, was to withdraw our men from that patch for the day and put them back at night. We knew that the Austrians practically never came up to attack, and always depended on their guns. What we didn't realize was that all this was range-finding, in preparation for the day when all the patches would be plastered with shell at once, making human life almost impossible.

In those months, the Russians were slowly and at great cost fighting their way by infantry alone, through the broad belt of the Carpathian Mountains, full of separate sharp heights in which the slope was often one foot in six. In November, 1914, the incompetent War Office had informed the Generals that munitions had run out, and were not to be expected till the spring. "Why, no science has taught this method of waging war," wrote the Chief of Staff of the whole Army, Yanushkevich, "without cartridges, without rifles."

Yet the advance through the mountains continued; in April, 1915, I even passed the country house of the Hungarian Premier Count Tisza, on the Hungarian side, which we had conquered. One couldn't help seeing the absolute poverty of the Russian front line, but it was still advancing. Radko had been very kind to me and asked me more than once to dine alone with him. He liked me to pass a greeting to the front from the British Army. At one point this resulted in the Russian troops being drawn up outside their line and shouting a loud "Hurrah!" which was at once followed by a burst from the enemy machine guns. And then came a belated order from the Colonel "Leave out the 'Hurrah.'" Rather an anticlimax! In one place where I slept, with practically not even any wire entanglement in front of us, there was written over the door of our hut an unconscious invitation to the enemy with the word "Willkommen."

In the pretty little Polish town of Jaslo, which was Radko's headquarters, I met him in the street walking with his two young aides. "Where are you going next?" he asked. "To the Orlov regiment," I replied; "they've invited me." "No," he said, "Go to the Tenth Corps." I don't think he could have possibly said that, if he could have known what was going to happen to the Tenth Corps next day. That was the actual point at which on May 2, 1915, Mackensen broke the Russian Line and started the movement by which we were all swept out of Galicia.

I had a very capable army chauffeur who had driven me in previous trips. At headquarters of the Tenth Corps I found everything in confusion, but they gave me a Cossack to take me up to the Front. I left the car under the cover of a low slope and went on to the staff of the Tambov Regiment. We halted for a while in an empty hut at the top of the hill. We had a glorious view for five miles on either side. It was a continuous deluge of enemy fire without any reply at all from us. Then, as we descended the slope towards the front line and I left the hut, I took away with me a horse shoe which was hanging over the fireplace. We hadn't gone on a hundred yards when the whole hut burst out into a blaze of fire. As one shell burst near us, my big Cossack turned round with a sweet smile and said "That's for us!"

The regimental staff was sheltering behind another hut. "A guard for the flag!" said the Colonel, pointing to the men around the Colors. He took my arm and we went forward into the open. He showed me that the regiment was turned on both flanks. He himself telephoned to the Divisional HQ. "I am surrounded." It was no business of mine to stay, he told me; so I went off with one of the wounded, turning back after a few yards to salute these brave men. That regiment, in this and the following engagements during the retreat, was reduced from a potential 4,000 to 41; and 40 men and one officer, for the Russian officers stood during battle while ordering their men to crawl.

I passed on to other divisions, where I saw the same picture of courage facing overwhelming odds. From the diary of a captured Austrian officer, I learned that he did not order an advance till he was sure the gunfire had extinguished all possible resistance. I often saw the Russian troops sitting helpless all day in their trenches under shell-fire, while their own artillery, which was very effective when it had any material, was unable to give them any protection. In this time of general retreat, even our own people in some vague way,

half suspected that I might be a spy. The enemy tactics consisted in massing a great concentration of artillery, which we
sometimes called "the circus," boring a hole through our
line at a given point and then passing on to another to do
the same until the whole front collapsed.

The Russian infantry, in its frequent counter-attacks,
unlike the Germans, always advanced in open order, led by
those soldiers who had received the George Cross. The Order
of St. George, founded by Catherine the Great, did not lay
its emphasis on personal gallantry or adventure but on the
performance, under the most trying conditions, of just what
ought to be done. Every soldier received a number on his
Cross, and I think the idea is that they are the cream of
the Russian Army of all times, who will stand in their appointed places in the last great review. Of the twelve ranks
of the Order, the second can be won only by the conquest of
a province, and the first by entering the enemy's capital as
Commander-in-Chief. We know that that will be Suvórov, the
greatest Russian general of all time, and I shall be privileged
to stand a private in his ranks.

The Civil Red Cross showed the same courage. As no
regimental surgeon could be spared to go into the Front Line,
several detachments were brought up, and sometimes they had
even a first-aid point under the actual trenches. The most
impossible conditions of work did not disturb their serenity,
and I think that the women were the least distracted of all.
At a moment when shell was falling all round, I could not see
even a trace of recognition on the faces of the nursing sisters.

## THE HAPPY WARRIOR

General Irmánov was a nimble little man with kind eyes
and a short gray beard, but he was reckoned by friend and
foe one of the most formidable fighters in the Russian Army.
Though over 70, he was one of the hardest riders; when he

invited me to come along the trenches with him, his staff
said, "You'll never keep up with him!" He had a little high
voice in which he barked out his morning greeting to his
men. He was dearly loved. No matter how often his corps
was renewed, and that was constantly, no one lived in it long
without taking its tone from him. He was the happy warrior,
simple and unclouded.

I came on him first when he was feasting a triumph in
the captured Polish town of Kelce. His corps, The Third Caucasian, contained many Moslems, and they were singing their
song of triumph, "Allah Verdi"–God has given Victory.

The next time that I joined them was during Mackensen's
smashing attack in the Carpathians. Radko, the army commander, had himself led them out to the counter-attack; they
were to get, if they could, to the enemy's heavy guns–Radko
himself had hardly any–and Prussian guardsmen whom we
captured told me later that they nearly got there.

I found them sheltering in a hollow, preparing to start.
I asked to go with them. "Will you come with me or with the
men?" said the Colonel. I thought it more polite to go with
him, but I had not yet appreciated that that meant standing
up while the men crawled.

It was a still summer evening. When we got to the starting point, the little Colonel halted them. "Well, boys, what
shall I say to you?" he asked, and then added "With God!"
the words with which you say goodbye to a friend who is
going on a long journey. We went forward under heavy shell-
fire which broke away branches from the trees above us; he
looked back at me with a gentle smile. At the top he ranged
us in line. The Austrians came up at us and I shall not forget
the look of sheer indignation as our machine-gunner wiped
out the little group that we saw coming on us. We were being
out-flanked and in the end we had to retreat; but as the sun
set, the officer with me shook his fist at the enemy saying,

"It's getting dark, brother!"–for the night fighting was always ours.

The Third Caucasians covered the rear of Radko's army as it went back. These operations brought them down from a full strength of 40,000 to 6,000. When they reached that figure, at a place called Seniawa, they went out one night with the bayonet which was practically the only weapon that they had, and captured 7,000 prisoners and a battery of heavy guns!

It was soon after this that I came again to them, this time to stay. "What would you like to see?" said the General in his little high voice. This was perhaps disarming, but it was rather delusive. Certain pressmen had begged to go to the point of greatest danger, and he had put them under a triple cross-fire, so I asked him to say. "Would you like to go with this Colonel?" said Irmánov. "He's a very interesting man." The Cossack Colonel took me into the regimental lunch and inquired as to my wishes on the subject of saddles; I had only just learned to ride and was the worst rider in the army. I carried no weapon but only the armlet of the Red Cross. We galloped off, turning in and out among trees; a bough swept off my fur helmet, but a Cossack behind me just climbed under his horse and handed it back to me. We passed one of my Red Cross colleagues, and he simply roared with laughter. "Where are we going?" I asked my next neighbor. "To fill a gap." "How do we do that?" "If they're there, we charge them. If there's time, we dig in." I wondered how much of the gap I was going to fill. Soon we reached a small wood and were ordered to take cover in it, and I even had a bit of a sleep. Then we saw a General coming hurriedly to us with new orders. It turned out that the gap had already been filled, so we rode slowly back, and as we went, the men sang their beautiful Cossack songs.

I took it that this was a kind of examination; and next day, Irmánov took me with him to both his flanks, on one

of which I was to pass the night. He had been turned on
both of them, for his neighbors had retreated. "The proper
answer to this," he said to me later, "is a counter-attack, but
I've no cartridges." In the trench, he picked up any that had
been dropped and told his men to take special care of them.
"Where can I get a look?" he asked. The only place was a tree
in front of the line. He was up in it in a twinkling and called
to me, "Come and have a look!" He told me afterwards we
were only about 80 yards from the enemy.

The next day there was a lull. Irmánov had no cartridges,
and the enemy did not venture to attack him. I remember so
well how I lay with my face in the grass in the garden of
the little priest's house in which we lived, asking myself
how long the Russians could stand these conditions. I had
no fears for the front, not for those who had to face them
there. But what of the rear? These Russians were great children with changing moods, and it was the mood of the alliance that had held them so high for so long. My field had always been there in the rear, and now here was I, playing the
amateur military attaché, because the real ones couldn't get
up here. Not even the most passive country in the world
could be counted on to remain passive when it was covered
with cripples, some of whom had never had a rifle in their
hands because of the general shortage. I wandered into the
little church, where the Polish priest was comforting his
flock while the guns echoed in the near distance. I ought
to go straight home and tell the story, and see if I could not
get these splendid fellows something to fight with.

There was nothing more to do but retreat, and that we
did in good order, riding rather shame-faced back over the
Russian frontier. Irmánov entirely shared my view. He told
me it was my absolute duty to go home and try to get them
munitions, "And then you shall come and finish the war
with us and see what we can do with them!" He loaned me
his own car, and I was driven to Army Headquarters. There I

found Wiggins, who tried to convince me that we were winning all the way. Thence, to Warsaw, Moscow, Petrograd, and England.

I got back to the Third Caucasians in the autumn during a lull, far back in the Pinsk marshes. They had never retreated more than a mile and a half a day; one night, one of their divisions went out with the bayonet and knocked out two Austrian ones, which didn't move again for a fortnight.

A terrible thing had lately happened in the corps. Owing to the utter inadequacy of the military ambulance staff, a Red Cross detachment had been brought up, with a doctor and his wife. One of Irmánov's officers seduced the wife, and when she returned to her husband, the officer shot both of them. This was an incident of the progressive mixing of front and rear which I have mentioned and of the changing atmosphere of the Front in consequence. By this time the temperance edict of the Tsar, which had made the Front almost austere, had now ceased to function.

It must be realized that as far back as the Empress Elizabeth, in 1744, the death penalty had been abolished in Russia for all ordinary murders, but this one had happened at the front, where there was martial law. Irmánov was a man of the kindliest humanity. He could have no possible sympathy with the crime. He came in late to lunch–I was sitting next to him–and couldn't begin till he knew the result of the trial. The military judges entered with bowed heads. "What is the sentence?" asked Irmánov. "Death, Sir, it couldn't be any thing else." "Can't I pardon?" asked Irmánov. "No, Sir, only the Commander of a Front can do that." Still Irmánov wouldn't begin his lunch. Then he jerked out: "Send a telegram to say it has no military significance!" He could not have made a wiser plea for a reprieve. Still a delay, and then: "Send the telegram before you send the sentence!" Then at last he settled down to his lunch.

One day Irmánov called me into his bedroom. His maps were on the table. He wanted to show me which way he thought the war could be won. "The Japs are the right people to fight the Prussians," he said, "and I've fought them both." (He had distinguished himself greatly in the defense of Port Arthur.) "We ought to bring them up into the Mediterranean. You and they are the only people who understand a mixed land and sea operation. Send them in here!" (and he pointed to Salonika). "Meanwhile, we Russians will go forward here!" (and he traced a line of advance north of the Carpathians). "We shall be cutting in on Austria, and we shall be taking the enemy at his weakest link. I have twice been to General Headquarters to recommend this. It seems the opposition comes from the French and British. Won't you write all this out and send it to your people? And won't you date it from this house?" (the pleasant Polish manor house in which we were staying). The Japs were not brought into Europe; but later I heard from Irmánov that he was now on the line which he had showed me on the map, to the north of the Carpathians. And later still, it was from Salonika that the rout of the Central Powers began.

## THREE FINE BRITISH STATESMEN

### Kitchener, Grey, and Lloyd George

My journey from Irmánov to England was full of excitement. At Army Headquarters I was taken round, notebook in hand, and given the full particulars on casualties and lack of equipment. The Chief of Staff, even before this, had summoned me to write with his help a telegram to our government which, to elude the blocking tactics of Sukhomlinov, he engaged to get through to England past the Russian War Office. In Warsaw, as already related, I saw Dmowski; it seemed strange as one looked out on a perfectly peaceful city, to realize that we had to lose it so soon. On my way on to Moscow, I stayed a day with wise old Homyakov and we drew up a preliminary list of requests to the British government for action on Russian munitions. In Moscow, the first national munitions committee had been set up and I revised this list with three old friends who were now its executives—the Mayor, Chelnokov, the new Chairman of the Stock Exchange, Ryabushinsky, and the head of the Civil Red Cross, Prince George Lvov, who was to be the first Prime Minister after the Revolution. Then I was hurried off to hear the fearless Guchkov denounce the incompetent War Minister, and we learned of Sukhomlinov's dismissal by telegraph as we came out of that meeting. With Guchkov, I travelled all night to Petrograd. He was one of those who had invited me to join his Red Cross staff, and he had wandered about, along and in front of the Russian line. We compared notes on the dreadful position of the troops on our two different fronts.

Guchkov took charge of my movements in Petrograd, but he entrusted them to Protopópov, who, though a vice-president of the Duma, was later to turn traitor and join Rasputin and the Empress to the ruin óf the monarchy. I noticed that this man was very nervous and excitable, and that it was difficult to catch him at any fixed address. Guchkov had also directed me to General Manikovsky, head of the Army Engineering and Artillery Departments, who, after the Revolution, was to become one of Guchkov's Assistant Ministers at the War Office. Manikovsky was poignantly moved by the situation of the Army. "Get us anything! Anything!" he said, stretching out his arms, "and we'll pay for it." "If you were going to make any definite request," I answered, "you would of course make it officially through our senior military attaché, Colonel Knox." (Knox and I were good comrades.) "But if you'd like to go further than that and let me know all the details of your shortage, I will take them straight to Lord Kitchener." "Guchkov tells me you are a good friend

of Russia," said the General, "and I'll give them to you," and
he produced two not lengthy tables of statistics. "I'll show
them to Knox and no one else," I said. "He'll understand
them, and write an accompanying memorandum." At the
War Office another good friend of Guchkov, who was highly
placed there, General Lukomsky, gave me the official estimate
of losses for the first ten months of the war. It was 3,800,000!
And this has been fully confirmed in later records. At the
Admiralty they said to me "If you're going to ask for anything for us, you might as well ask for what you promised
and never sent." A great British munition firm had entirely
failed them.

I was not going to entrust these precious materials to any
diplomatic bag. They remained in my breast-pocket. Our
Ambassador, Sir George Buchanan, readily granted my request to go to England without asking me for details. When
crossing the North Sea on a Norwegian boat there would
have been nothing to do, but to jump over if a German submarine had come to search us, and I was very relieved when
we reached Newcastle. Scottish troops, on passage at the station, were all singing "On the bonny, bonny banks of Loch
Lomond." It was warm comfort after the dangerous crossing.

Reaching London in the early morning, I went as soon as
possible to the Foreign Office. I asked Sir Arthur Nicolson to
send me to three men, Kitchener, Grey, and Lloyd George,
all three so different but all of them men whom I deeply
admired. In spite of my somewhat irregular position, I had
the immense advantage of knowing myself the disastrous news
which I was carrying; and it was fascinating to compare the
different ways in which these three different men received it.
As we had expected, the Russian Ambassador in London had
given no real idea of the catastrophe.

In the War Office, I recognized the atmosphere of the
Front. Kitchener, saluted as "Sir" and not as "My Lord" was
big, impressive, and contained. He asked me for an account

of the Russian smash in Galicia. He was interested in the "four pockets," as the Russian soldiers called them, four shells from a battery which annihilated anything between them. He murmured to himself, "They might do that on our Front," by which I understood that Mackensen's artillery concentration in Galicia was so far the biggest in the war. Kitchener then asked about the casualties. On hearing the Russian War Office figure of 3,800,000 in ten months, which if anything was an understatement, he whistled! "But I can't get any details out of them," he went on. This was the moment to produce the secret tables from my breast-pocket. He sent them out for analysis. "And now," I said, "you will want to know what they are saying against you!" There was a snort like that of a resentful lion. This was the story of the default of the British munition firm; of course, he knew all about it and spoke of it in the strongest language. Then he brought in some of his assistants and sent me out with them for further study.

Sir Edward Gray I already knew well. Gray was always one of my great heroes. To a foreign country he represented something stable that was England, like the outline of a distant mountain range, firm and clear on the horizon, that would not change. It was many times that I reported to him on Russia; he would always say at once something quite simple, something that was understanding and discriminating —what he could do and what he could not—from which he would not depart. From the start he'd said that a liberal policy towards Poland was the only one that could be any use to Russia—that he never assumed that India would not some day be approached from the land side by rail. He even told Russia in a dispatch that we hoped for a government which would work with the Duma, when the Russian government put it just the other way round. These were not speeches; they were simple and friendly conversation. I am sure the Russians thought that is England, that's what they think there, and it's not likely to change. I wish to goodness he had been in office during the Russian Revolution which came so soon after he went out. He would have supported his splendid deputy Sir George Buchanan. He might have saved us the friendship of Russia.

One of my greatest treasures is a letter which he wrote to me in his own hand after the Duma visit to England in 1909, crediting me with those qualities which were his and not mine. After the revolution, he showed me out by a side door in the House of Commons and stood there for a moment saying, "I sympathize with you." He sent me a friendly message just before his death.

Grey sat there in his big corner room at the Foreign Office which somehow, during his tenure of it, seemed to take on some of the aspects of a country house; I half expected to see a fishing rod in the corner. Grey had always a fine simplicity and composure. He offered me some tea, and when he had heard me out, he said, "Write me a memorandum for the War Cabinet and put the British default first"— that was Grey all over. In my memo, of which I destroyed the shorthand, I wrote plainly that the most momentous internal developments were to be expected if this situation continued. This was a year and a half before the March Revolution of 1917, of which the colossal casualties were undoubtedly the first cause.

Mr. Lloyd George, whom I had never yet met, was at this time Minister of Munitions. He invited me by telegram to breakfast. Seeing that the breakfast room was full of people, including his family, I waylaid him before going in. "I've got some very bad things to tell you, Sir," I said. "Am I to speak to you as if there were no one else in the room?" He said, "Yes!" "One other thing," I went on, "This is bringing the Russian Revolution." We went into breakfast. He drew out the whole story from me, especially emphasizing anything that was dramatic. "By God! they're knocked out!"

he said, on hearing the losses. "No," I said, "They're not knocked out at all; they've simply got nothing to fight with." And I told him how the Third Caucasians had taken 7,000 prisoners in one night with the bayonet. "No! I know, I know," he said quickly, "Of course they're not knocked out. Now what do they want me to do for them?" This introduced the four requests of my friends of the Moscow munition committee, which he could take as coming from the people of Russia. I learned afterwards that he had tried to carry out all of them. The chief one, which was from Homyakov, was that he should make a public statement that we must do as much to arm the Russians as ourselves, and this he made more than once. Then he gave me a piquant instruction to go down and speak at those of our factories which had defaulted. He would himself arrange that I should address all the shop foremen, with the remiss management in the chair. "And tell them," he added, "how splendidly the Russians are fighting without the munitions which we promised and didn't send; and I'll come after you and back you up."

I think one of the finest qualities of Mr. Lloyd George was that he was absolute in his democracy. He talked to everyone as an equal. There was no question of authority; two keen minds were to see what they could make of the problem in question. I did go down to the factories. "Very pleasant," said the management from the chair, rather acidly as I finished, and then, as is always the custom in cutlery factories, they gave me a knife, but a silver one.

And now Sir Arthur Nicolson sent for me to the F.O. and told me I was dismissed, certainly for the best thing I had ever had the chance of doing. My post of official correspondent of the British Government on the Russian Front was abolished, and there would be no successor. "What will you do?" asked Sir Arthur. "Go back!" I said. "I have a letter from the commander of the Third Army asking me to come as soon as possible." The matter had to be referred to Sir

George Buchanan, who never failed to help a subordinate out. "He's your friend," said Sir Arthur comfortingly.

I have never learned the explanation of my dismissal. I have had my turn of dismissals, and these things don't usually happen with explanations. All of our little band of Englishmen in key posts in Russia–all personal friends, though of the most various antecedents and opinions–were in turn threatened with dismissal, and in the event none of us actually left. For one thing, all the rest cried out too hard to their respective chiefs, for we were a freemasonry of danger, understanding, and perhaps of achievement. Knox, who was the keystone of our military position, was at one time light-heartedly ordered to our front in France. Bruce Lockhart went for a time but came back. Of our Ambassador I will tell the story later. These statistics which I had brought back had been gained simply enough, they were given me by the Head of the Department concerned. I found a partial explanation later in the turn of events in Russia; it was just about this very time that the Empress was starting her great and successful fight against the Duma, and it was the Duma's requests that I had brought to England.

I went over to the War Office and offered my services to General Macdonogh, Director of Military Intelligence–my first introduction to that great master of his field. No one else had a standing invitation from a Russian field commander, and they were readily accepted. There could not be any salary, as I could not have a commission; and if I had had one, I couldn't have gone at all in this irregular way. "May I write for the *Daily Telegraph?*" I asked. "Certainly," said Macdonogh. I told its proprietor, Lord Burnham, I couldn't telegraph except in case of a Russian victory, which, by the way never came; but he offered me one thousand pounds a year, which was just double what I had received from the Government, and he gave me a splendid lunch to introduce me to my new "colleagues," who included that grand old veteran of journalism, T. P. O'Connor.

Before I left London my old friend and editor, St. Loe Strachey, of the *Spectator*, gathered together a private meeting of London editors, for me to tell them in confidence some things which they might have at the back of their heads when they were writing about Russia. One of those who came to this meeting was another splendid man with whom I later became great friends, Sir Reginald Hall, Director of Naval Intelligence, and he brought me a message from Mr. Balfour, who was then at the Admiralty, asking for a single sentence to put into a speech which he was just about to deliver. I suggested: "Men against metal."

When I got back to Irmánov, now in the Pinsk marshes, I sent him the little silver knife from the British munitions factory, asking for ten kopeks in return, which I duly received. "But that's all nonsense," said Irmánov, "when they say you mustn't give a knife to anyone for fear of quarreling with him." He added, "My wife gave a lovely sabre, and we've never quarreled in our lives."

## THE MARSH OF PETROGRAD

The city of St. Petersburg, now renamed **Petrograd**, had been built on an unwholesome marsh which, at this moment, when the ruin of the Russian Monarchy was coming to its culmination in the rear, was more noisome than the marshes of Pinsk.

I was told that I must come and fill a place at an Anglo-Russian dinner. My hired dress clothes fitted me very badly, and seeing one of the most pleasant of all my Duma friends, a kind of Edward Grey of Russia, Nicholas Lvov, I thought I would seek seclusion with him in his corner. A waiter touched me on the shoulder with the message, "Professor Maxim Kovlalevsky asks if you will come and sit next to him."

As I followed the waiter, I saw to my alarm that Professor Kovlalevsky was acting as chairman. Next to him was an empty place, which, no doubt, he wished to fill. "Let me introduce you first to your next neighbor!" said the professor, adding. "The President of the Council of Ministers"–that is to say the new Premier of Russia, Stürmer.

His was an astounding appointment. When I asked old Homyakov what he knew of Stürmer, he replied "Only that he is a robber" and that was pretty well all that most of the public did know about him. What we now know, as firmly and documentarily established, is that Stürmer was raised to this high office by Rasputin with the help of the Empress and was no more than a puppet, in mortal fear of the master who had put him there. Stürmer had been instructed to pose as a friend of the Duma and had opened with a "liberal" speech which carried no conviction whatever to anyone.

Now at this dinner, to celebrate friendship with England, there was naturally a good muster of Members of the Duma and also our true and faithful ally, the Foreign Minister, Sazonov, whom Stürmer was soon to get rid of, himself combining the Foreign Office with the Premiership. The Duma had greeted Stürmer with a cry of "Deeds, not words!" and this was the refrain of the speech of a visiting English M.P., Mr. Hemmerde, which with a great deal of relish I took care, as he spoke, to translate to my eminent neighbor. "Deeds, not words!" said the English M.P. "Hurrah! for the Imperial Duma!" "Very good, very good," said Stürmer.

Some anonymous verses, which were circulated about this time, gave a very good picture of this "marsh" of Petrograd–

## OUR MOODS

We do not take defeat amiss,
   And victory gives us no delight:
The source of all our cares is this:
   Can we get Vodka for tonight?

> The victories we can do without.
> No! Peace and quiet is our line,
> Intrigues and scandal, evenings out
> Trimmed up with women and with wine.
>
> We only want to know: next day
> What Ministers will be on view;
> Or who takes who to see the play;
> Or who at Cuba's sits next who.
>
> Has Vyrubova had to go? [1]
> Or can Kuvaka give you joy? [2]
> Or how the Germans knead their dough,
> Or why on earth there's Shakhovskoy? [3]
>
> And does Rasputin still prevail,
> Or do we need another Saint?
> And is Kshesinskaya quite well? [4]
> And how that feast at Shubin's went.
>
> If the Grand Duke took Dina home,
> What kind of luck Macdiddie's had—
> Oh if a Zeppelin would come
> And smash the whole of Petrograd!

In February, 1916, being still in Petrograd, I said to the Duma president, the doughty Rodzyanko, "We're always talking of fighting Germany to a finish. What is the finish? Wouldn't it be well to talk more about the conditions of peace?" Rodzyanko took this up, and we had a series of private discussions, dealing in turn with the claims of each of the little nations which we hoped to liberate from German control. Milyukov, who was then the real leader of the majority in the Duma, was in the Chair. Most of the other prominent Duma men were present, and Harold Williams and I were there from the British side. Much the most interesting of

[1] Friend of the Empress and of Rasputin.
[2] A new mineral water.
[3] A minister backed by Rasputin.
[4] A famous ballerina.

these meetings was devoted to the Czechs. They had what was apparently the most desperate position of all, half way between Berlin and Vienna. The spokesmen of the other little peoples had come to us as petitioners. Not so the Czechs! They marched into the room in considerable force, with what I thought was an excessive vigor. The Russians asked them to put their case. It seemed a very petty one. The Czech soldiers, as I have related, came over of themselves, often under fire. Instead of being employed in the Russian army, as they wished, they were sent to work, as far as I remember, for a very ill-organized tramway company. This was their principal grievance. We interrupted them several times, asking them to tell us more about Czechoslovakia; for instance, what was its proportion of the industry of Austro-Hungary? To every question they had a prompt, short, and convincing answer, and then they went back to their wretched tramway company and the ineptitude of its management. As I had been rather responsible for these meetings, I leaned across to them and said, "These gentlemen are very anxious to help your cause. Won't you tell us what you want them to do for you?" "Do for us?" they said, "Declare us one of the Allied Nations, and we'll do the rest for ourselves." If only there had been the same spirit in the Russians! One could see how great an impression the Czech answer made on them.

It was somewhat later on that I was received by the Tsar at his Headquarters, in the provincial city of Mogilev. The Third Army had sent up my name for the Soldier's Cross of St. George; the medal of the same order I had been given in the crash in Galicia. I was invited to attend the lunch of the Imperial mess, and my sponsor was that great gentleman, Sir John Hanbury Williams, who carried out with such honor and distinction the duties, at times difficult enough, of British military attaché to the Tsar himself.

We were all formed in a circle, and our charming little host came in, always anxious that everyone should be happy in his company. It was pretty to see how he exchanged chaff with the veteran Count Frederickz, who was keeping the anniversary of his personal service to the Sovereign; he had even served the present Emperor's grandfather, Alexander II. The Tsar always paid special attention to any new guest. "You are well decorated," he said kindly, fingering my cross and medal, both of which as he knew, could only come from the authorities in the field. He stood in front of me, happy in the life of the Front and almost jumping up and down to show how deep he had been in the muck. After lunch, he returned and had quite another little talk. "I must tell you, Sir," I said, "how deeply the great Russian retreat of last year (when they were practically threadbare of munitions) was admired in England." "I'm so glad you can tell me that," he said simply. "I was afraid you might be beginning to think we were a poor ally." How could one realize that one was talking to an Emperor, and how happy he would have been if he had not had to be one! I asked him if I might now be free to move about in other armies besides the Third, in which I had passed a year. "Of course," he said, "there will be no difficulty."

Armed with this authorization, given in the presence of our own British military representative, I went to an enemy of former days, the troublesome little official in charge of the issue of passes, whom Wiggins had so skilfully circumvented when I joined the Third Army. "I congratulate you!" said the little man. "How do you suggest that we should word the pass?" "Well," I said, "you might copy this one"; and showed him my credentials with the Third Army. Late that evening he sent me round, by a mounted trooper, a pass authorizing the Englishman Pares to visit hospitals in the rear. Fortunately there was now in Mogilev a senior officer of the Third Army who had been promoted to a post at Supreme Headquarters. To him I went and told him my trouble. "Don't go near that little ass again!" he said. "Get

into a train, and go up there! They all know about you."
That was the end of that particular difficulty.

One interesting feature of the second year of war was
an organized peace propaganda direct from the German
front to ours by means of war prisoners. Even German
N.C.O.'s during their examination made detailed speeches
on subjects which seemed quite above their understanding,
such as the relative financial situations of the two sides in
the war. This propaganda had no success at all. It seemed to
me later that it had been deliberately switched to the rear,
where it was only too successful.

## RUSSIAN AND BRITISH FRONTS COMPARED

In the spring of 1916, I knew there was to be a Russian offensive in the north near Lake Naroch. A great deal
had been done by now to arm the Russians, both by the
Russian munition committees and by the Allies, and I
wanted to see how much difference it had made. We had
enough for a good offensive—Ludendorf has himself confessed
that he was much surprised. We went forward for several
days, but there was not enough to go around everywhere,
and suddenly headquarters took away all our heavy guns and
planes for use elsewhere. Of course, the Germans saw this
at once and fell heavily on us.

We were in poor positions, easily commanded, especially
by a nasty hill which our soldiers called "Ferdinand's nose"
after the King of Bulgaria; the valley in front of it, they
called "The Valley of the Shadow of Death."

From a visit to another Division I came back to Baluyev,
the wise old general in charge of our offensive. A terrible
noise was going on: I wanted to go up, but he didn't know
where he could send me. Every Battalion in the front line
was reduced from a normal 1,000 to between 90 and 100.
Their field guns bombarded us at 800 yards; they used every

kind of weapon, including poison gas. At the end of each hour they stopped to see if there was still any resistance, and then gave us another hour–five in all. When they came up, on the testimony of each Russian battalion commander, their rifles were slung over their shoulders, for they knew they were coming into an empty place where life had been practically destroyed. The only bayonet charge was ours. The enemy didn't try to meet us with the bayonet, but retired and pounded us again with his guns. The Russians only went back a mile and a half. The Smolensk regiment, a very fine one with which I had been photoed a few days before, had only seven officers left out of 37. And still the men were singing the Easter psalm, "Christ has arisen from the dead, conquering death by death." And what other weapon had we to fight with?

An examining commission came up to us from Headquarters. They had much better have examined themselves. When they had gone, Baluyev's officers, wanting to comfort the poor old fellow, took us all to an open-air film in the garden. It came on upside down, and the corporal who was operating it humbly apologized; but this just suited Baluyev's mood. He grunted out in the darkness, "I command you to continue upside down!"

Again I was given all particulars and decided to take them to England. Mr. Lloyd George received me at once and sent me for a week to the British Front in France. "You've been more than a year with the Russians," he said. "Go and see what we've got that they haven't, and I'll get it for them." As I went up to the British Front, I was curiously reminded at each successive stage by the growing likeness to the Russian. The mood became more and more the same till it was actually identical; the same quiet talk, the same healthy jokes, the same knowledge of all the main things which needed to be known, and the same disregard of all rumors as "rear talk." There was one difference; I

have seen troops of each army in the trenches under shell-
fire at that difficult moment when their own guns could not
reply. Among the Russian soldiers there was a kind of ascetic
mood, as if they were only thinking, "I must be where my
brothers are being hit." The British seemed to me to be
mentally noting down each blow for reprisal as soon as
possible—"There's another! Don't forget that one!"

There was another difference in the extent of No Man's
Land. With us, it was generally several hundred yards broad,
and it all belonged to us, for the night fighting was all ours.
I can remember something like a kind of mass meeting of
Third Caucasian private soldiers there; these clever children liked the excitement of being in an "interesting" place,
where they might "catch a tongue"—that is, a German soldier.
On the British Front the distance was only a few yards, at
one point, eight; at Arras both sides were ensconced in different parts of the same house. In general, the contrast was
between town and country, particularly in the noise at
night.

I had been in the air with the Russians, and now I
went up with the British. The Russian machine, a New-
port, was so obsolete that it took 40 minutes to get up at all.
It carried no machine gun. The Russians could only try to
ram the enemy, which brought both down—and there were
no parachutes! The British machine flew straight up. On
the Russian Front you could not identify the front line except by some church or house that you knew; there was no
second line. In France, both sides of the Front were torn up
by trenches for miles, and to advance was simply to put one's
head in a pocket. I asked for our air maps of the German
entrenchments and was given them, and later I saw the
expression of surprise on the face of General Alexeyev, then
Chief of Staff of the Russian Army, when I laid them before
him. I was also promised in France fourteen British trench
helmets. In our army they had reduced head casualties from

30 to 33 per cent; the Russians, who had none, sometimes even took their spades into action for cover.

I lunched with the British Commander in Chief, Sir Douglas Haig. He asked me many questions, and the most interesting were on the political position in Russia. Brusilov was at this time breaking the Austrian Front in Russia and taking hosts of prisoners. Haig said he wished he could take as many. I ventured to suggest that this was perhaps only a political success, that those prisoners might be coming over of themselves, and of this I had full confirmation when I got back to Russia. "You'll have plenty to do at the peace," he said kindly.

In London I went to Colonel Hankey, Secretary of the War Cabinet; and after he had telephoned, he sent me straight on to Lloyd George. In our first conversation, Lloyd George had seemed to me nothing less than electric, putting me quick and diverse questions, travelling at once to first conclusions, then, so to speak, dashing back over the wires and trying something else. This time it was even more striking. I was put in an empty bedroom in the Norfolk Hotel, at that time the Ministry of Munitions. Suddenly Lloyd George dashed in, put a vital question, got my answer, and disappeared as rapidly. I waited on the chance of more, and the same thing happened again. It was as if he had got the world in general, lined up in relays, in those innumerable bedrooms, and was catechizing each informant in turn.

At Newcastle I received my trench helmets and my air maps. The helmets bore a startling label, "Property of His Britannic Majesty–War Goods." This I promptly detached, as I was going through neutral countries, full of German spies. This time I was carrying both British and Russian dispatches, which I tied together. I had no difficulty with all these goods till I reached the terminus in the Russian capital. I declared the trench helmets at once at the custom house, saying, "They're a present from the British Army to the Russian." "You must pay duty on them," they said. "All right. How much?" "We don't know; you can't have them now." For two weeks those officials kept me running about between one office and another. I think they must have been either German or pro-German and hoped I would stop worrying about my goods. But I stuck to it and got them out, and delivered them at Russian Headquarters. I was careful to keep one, and wore it everywhere on the front line. "What's that?" my Russian friends would ask. "Our trench helmets." "Why can't *we* have them?" "You'd better ask for them. That's why I'm wearing mine!" I said. It was only many months afterward that I saw on the Russian front a box labeled "English Trench Helmets."

I had predicted the Russian Revolution to our Government in the summer of 1915. A year later, on the channel boat crossing from France, I had fallen in with Protopopov; he was then leading a visit of the Duma to France and England. We met again in the Norwegian capital on our way back to Russia, and taking my arm, he walked me up and down the station, expatiating on his zeal for the alliance. At his next stop in Stockholm, he had a secret meeting with a German banker, which he later found it difficult to explain to his colleagues in the Duma. Arrived in Petrograd, he called on me to ask me to introduce him to Sir George Buchanan. This was a blind. I was feeling throughout the interview as if I had brought to the Embassy some vulgar tradesman calling for orders. Almost directly afterwards, he had turned his back on all his former associates and, by grace of Rasputin, had been appointed to the all-powerful post of Minister of the Interior. From this time onward, as the police reports themselves testified, revolution was a certainty. It was self-evident that the Tsar and his wife would have to go–they had no supporters even in their own family. Obviously the immediate successor to power was the Duma, in which I had so many close friends. What followed next would be their affair. My country was in alliance with the Tsar and his government in a world war. The right place for an Englishman at the moment was the front, and I went back there as quickly as possible.

## THE CARPATHIANS AGAIN

I was lying on an army cart going up a "corduroy" road, built by the army, that led to the top of the wooded Carpathians. We had always felt somehow, when we retreated, that we should someday again be fighting here, and this was part of the great gains of Brusilov's most ingenious offensive of 1916. I was translating into verse a long fable of Krylov, which I had committed to memory; the motion of the cart helped the rhythm, and I have since always associated that fable with the magnificent pines all around me, reaching a hundred feet high.

On the top was a broad open space called appropriately "Starry Ply" (*Stary Plai* in Ukranian); and here was our forward unit of the British Red Cross. We were close to the frontier between Austria and Hungary, and glorious views stretched on all sides. All the enemy inhabitants had gone; we had only the bears who lived in these forests.

In November, from the Division which stood in front of us, I got secret word of a coming offensive. I was told to sleep for an hour or two at a first aid point near the front, then I rode up to Divisional HQ, and all night we went up more mountains till we were again on the top. The Carpathians rise in parts to 8,000 feet; and to get here, the Russian infantry had had to storm the various heights without any serious artillery preparation. Here one could see to the farthest mountains bordering the Hungarian plain.

For once, we were in front of our timetable–an hour before dawn. Our troops were already massed in the valley in front of us. Ordinarily, we only surprised the enemy when we were so late that he had given us up. "We may as well start," said our Chief of Staff. "The fat majors will be running about asking for their coffee," said a young lieutenant. But unfortunately the surprise was entirely for ourselves. Our guns had started, but the troops in front of us telephoned that it was they who were being hit. "No you aren't," we said inconsequently, but presumably they knew best.

We were perched on a high peak, and all through the day we were straining our eyes on the valley beneath us; but what sank into my memory, was the distant mountains beyond. At one moment our observation post became the target, and we all had to scurry into our dug-out. "Did you pray to God?" said one of my comrades to me simply. At half-past five our two regiments in front of us, the Lidsky and the Novotroksky, were to go to the attack. We told the Lidsky that they had now two gaps in the enemy barbed wire in front of them, made by our artillery, and we told the Novotroksky they had one. The order was repeated formally at 5:25; and I could not help recalling the famous bumping races at Cambridge, with its "5,4,3,2,1" ringing out before the starting gun went. We had been quite right about the Lidsky. We watched them as they went up to the enemy trenches. It took a quarter of an hour. Then the Germans sent up a rocket to show that these trenches were now a target for their own guns; we had lost only 300 men. As to the Novotroksky, we were quite wrong; there was no gap, and a nest of machine guns was on the other side. The men wouldn't come back and lay down where they stood. Their loss was about 3,000 or three-quarters of the regiment.

Next day came a thick white fog, so compact that I went out and had a snow bath, quite unseen, about 20 yards off. The glorious view, of course, was wiped out. The enemy guns, which had taken their range in advance, were all day pounding our troops. The Molodetsky regiment had plowed its way through the enemy line in the fog; it was out-flanked and suffered great losses. Our field telephones had all been destroyed. Our observation post was shattered, and we crouched in our narrow dug-out where we had slept side by side.

As no one else knew German, I was asked to take over the questioning of a young enemy captain of the reserve. He was very obliging and told us all he could; he said the enemy had no second line, which was often the case on this front. At the end he asked a favor—might he be sent on that night to the nearest town! The Germans had lateral railways behind their front, but we had nothing of the kind, so I translated the question for our Chief of Staff to give the answer officially. "Tell him," said the Chief of Staff, "that he'll have to walk ten miles to the nearest railway station." Then the prisoner asked if he might share our officers' quarters, and I showed him our rat-hole.

The Novotroksky telephoned that all their stretcher bearers were down, and the next day I went down the mountain to bring up our own British Red Cross unit. The slope was very steep, and I could only just see my Cossack guide close in front of me, but as usual my horse looked after the job. Another Red Cross unit had already been sent up. I found our own in charge of a British surgeon with one untrained assistant, no drugs, no stretchers, and one tent, outside of which more than half his patients lay in the cold November mud. He patched up 400 in four days. Most of them must have reached the base hospital with gangrene. We reckoned that we repaired for the front line 40 per cent less than the Germans.

One night, in the lull which followed the last action, I took up to the front line the Head of our British Forward Red Cross Unit, Dr. Flavell, a very sound man who had seen mountain war service in the Vosges in France. I asked him afterwards to summarize his impressions. They were three.

First, the officers shared to the full in the hardships of the
men, and this was absolutely true. Second, life under these
conditions was impossible for more than a fortnight. I had
to tell him that a fortnight was the normal duration of front
line service, followed by a week in reserve, and then another
fortnight in the front line. Third, any man wounded in
stomach or legs was a lost man. Our road to the rear was
precipitous, and covered in day time by enemy machine guns.

Our Red Cross unit was very popular. It had far the
best drugs and far the best dentist, a charming young man
named T. from Welbeck Street in London, whose services
were enthusiastically sought from far around. Our people
were constantly visiting the Division and distributing valuable clothes and stores. In consequence they received a
pressing invitation to be feasted by the Divisional Staff.
T. was unfortunately one of those people to whom the
smallest drink of vodka was overpowering. Our hosts stood
round the party, calling "Drink to the bottom!"; and the
nurses surreptitiously passed their little glasses on to me to
dispose of, as I was immune to vodka except for indigestion.
Dinners of this kind involved numerous speeches and toasts,
and no one else in our unit talked Russian. I was hard-
pressed to keep up my end when someone whispered that
T. had succumbed. They had carried him to the stretcher-
bearers' quarters, where he lay snorting like a hog, and I
tried to hold the fort till we could get him under way. He
was carried to a cart. An austere nurse of our party stood
beside him, reviling the poor fellow for his innocent failure.
"Never shall we forget this day!" I went on, continuing my
speech, and gradually retreating towards the door. "But we
can't let you go like that," said the General. "Hornblowers
to the fore!" And as the horns echoed back from the hills
through that lonely little Carpathian valley, we made off
as best we might, with T. murmuring, "Jolly old fellows!"
This was how we had to keep up Anglo-Russian friendship.

# CHAPTER VII

## The Revolution
## (1917–1920)

### The Streets of Petrograd

I HAD a strange experience on New Year's Day, 1917. I think
George Borrow calls it "the black streak." I have had it
very rarely. At the new year, one instinctively surveys the
world in general and takes stock. The outlook was full of
hope. I knew Rasputin had just been killed. It was clear
that the Tsar and his mischievous wife were well on their
way out. Who came next? There was no alternative to a
Duma government full of my personal friends. Sir George
Buchanan would have the easiest time that an allied ambassador could desire. And what should I do now? Obviously,
keep out of all party questions as I had always done, and
set myself to serve as a personal link with England, above
all in matters of education, which were my natural field.
With the anxiety that naturally goes with such a survey, I
looked all around for difficulties. I thought of the Bolsheviks, with whom I had already had contact; all their leaders
were far away in exile, cut off from us by the conditions of
the war. And then, without any logic in fact, quite inconsequently, "the black streak" came over and covered me,

and it was no use arguing against it. Something catastrophic was to happen this year.

I dropped in one day on the Chief of Staff of the Division, Colonel Lipko. He was humming:

> Bad luck will right itself;
> Wilhelm will shoot himself!

He showed me a map of the enemy sections in front of us. All the key points were held by a thin line of Germans; the unimportant intervals were filled with masses of Austrians. He also told me that by the efforts of the Russian public, very heavily supplemented by the Allies, we were now equal with the Austrians in munitions and not far behind the Germans. This will serve to explain our optimism, and also the increased vigor of the German propaganda on our rear.

There was a pathetic incident at the feast of St. George. The General of the Division, a splendid tall man whom they called "The Eagle," addressing the Knights of the Order, said, "I somehow feel that we shall not be thanked for the dangers and privations which we have faced out here, but that they will somehow be held against us." We little knew at the time how prophetic these words were to prove.

Colonel Lipko had built a little leaky wooden hut for him and me, which he called "Hotel London." One night he came and sat on my bed. "Bernard Ivanovich," he said, "we've had a telegram. There's a new Commander in Chief –it's the Grand Duke Nicholas." This meant that the Tsar had resigned the post. "What do you think of it?" I asked. "Splendid!" he said. "And there's a new Cabinet too." He ran off the names. I could hardly believe my ears. They were all my personal friends, Lvov, Guchkov, Milyukov–even Kerensky. "And what do you think of that?" I said. "We've got honest men in power," he replied. "Now we shall win the war. We're to expect another telegram," he added. That was self-evident; it must be the abdication of Nicholas II; otherwise these men could never have come into office.

It was thus that we heard, in conquered Austrian territory, of a Russian Revolution. I can say very definitely that the first short period, a fortnight or more after the March Revolution, was one of optimism and of improved discipline. The time of no munitions was well over, and spring, we thought, would bring a victorious advance from our own side. We knew the Germans were outnumbered, and on our front there was often no second line of defense. A break through, as shown by Brusilov's success last summer, was far more easy with us than in France and could open up wide possibilities of a war of broad maneuver. But very soon it was clear that there was far more going on in our own rear than what we had been told. It was a wholesale break-down of the State, which had been coming for more than a year. With us, it is true, far away from Petrograd, the morale for a time was definitely better. It was when the first new drafts came up from the rear that one could guess from their sullen, challenging faces what was happening there. Before long, arrived some students and a spectacled lady who told us they had come up "to explain the revolution." It must be borne in mind that the army was like an enormous web and that at Headquarters far in the rear there were very few troops. These visitors were emissaries from the new Soviet in the capital and had no difficulty in getting through. They told us that peace was about to be signed in Stockholm, that the salute to officers was abolished, that there was soon going to be a land partition in the rear, and that the men had better get home in time for it. In a couple of months, there were 2,000,000 deserters. Troops remained in the front trenches till relieved, but then went off *en masse* and there was no stopping them, so that very soon the fighting practically ceased.

For me it was obvious that I should return at once to Petrograd and come face to face with the Revolution. After arranging for the retreat of our Red Cross unit, I joined Peter Keeble, the lively young head of our British motor column, and together we made a nightmare journey from Kiev to Petrograd. Keeble had brought a chicken which, with rationing, just lasted us out for the two days. Our compartment was several times rudely assaulted, and one berth reserved for us had been appropriated in advance, so I slept comfortably enough on the floor. From time to time, Keeble would open the door briskly on attempts to force a way in, and say "Angliisky offizier," which was always effective. In the corridor there were everywhere squatting sleepers, like a crop of mushrooms. When we passed through the Imperial village of Tsarskoe Selo, it looked so soiled and sordid that we could get a glimpse of the great extent of the change.

In Petrograd everything had gone drab. There were no cabs. Soldiers shuffled about without their belts, entirely out of hand. The streets were posted with every imaginable kind of placard–"After the Russian Revolution, the Russian Reformation." "The land of the happy peasantry,"–this turned out to mean Denmark. "United States of the World: original subscribers become life members!" Or simply, "Self-organization," an anonymous placard giving a mysterious address. In all sorts of odd corners there were little groups only just formed, which knew nothing of each other, but each imagined it was saving the country. As I was still in uniform, I used to amuse myself by walking up the Nevsky and saluting every officer I met, to see them cheer up for just a minute. At one point a man with a strong German accent was reviling England, with a little group listening rather indifferently. "Will you say that again, please?" I asked. "I'm an Englishman." The little crowd who were obviously our friends, said, "Now you're going to have

England's answer!" The Russians never fail to give you a good stage lead.

The streets would boil up from day to day with all sorts of queer little meetings. I used to notice that these small crowds would look round instinctively to see if the police were coming, though of course they well knew that the police had been abolished altogether for the part they had taken in firing on the people in the first days of the Revolution. You would find an ignorant soldier explaining to a few bystanders that "Annexia ought on no account to be allowed to come to the throne." The Soviet had come out for a "peace without annexations (annexii) and contributions (contributzii)"; but the speaker evidently thought that Annexia was an extra daughter of Nicholas II. Contributzia was thought by some to be a town which the British had seized. One village sent up word to the capital that it had removed the portrait of Nicholas II; could it be supplied with a portrait of Revolutzia? From time to time these little meetings became big, and then something would happen.

I found some of my Cadet friends very arrogant at this time. To my congratulations one young man replied, "A British *subject* congratulates a Russian *citizen*." All sorts of vague and inchoate planning was in progress; but it always seemed to me then, and it seems so now, that we ought to have marked our calendar, not by anything achieved but by what parts of the structure of the whole State were falling away from us. The last year of the monarchy, when Russia was really ruled by the Empress and Rasputin and their disreputable puppets, had been a gradual and complete demolition of this structure. Now the police were gone, and the army was going too.

## AT THE PETROGRAD SOVIET

As soon as I got back from the Front, which was a month after the Revolution, I went to the newly formed Soviet of

Petrograd, the first in the country, which gave a lead to all
the others and contained all the important men. Lenin was
sent through from Switzerland by arrangement with the
German General Staff, which sealed up his railway car so
that he should not engage in any activity while passing
through Germany, and he arrived in Petrograd on April 16,
just a month after the fall of the Russian Monarchy.

I found the Soviet in the old familiar Duma, once so
quiet and gentlemanly and now mobbed and dirty. It was
a vast, amorphous assembly, elected haphazard in haste and
with all the atmosphere of the street, though it had appropriated the hall of sessions of the old Duma. It was most
unwieldy; and even in one day it might adopt resolutions
which were quite incompatible.

It had recently pronounced in favor of "a peace without annexations and contributions," which was a purely
German formula, "and self-determination of peoples" which
was the watchword of the Allies; it had simply put these
two formulas together. I sought out the Secretary of the
Soviet, Sokolov, who stood between Rights and Lefts, and
asked him which of the two they meant. "Both," he said.
"Excuse me!" said I, "I'll put it another way. Is the restoration of Poland to the map of Europe an annexation? So far
it has been carved up between the three neighboring em-
pires. When we speak of no annexations, do we take for
granted the wicked old frontiers of the partitioning em-
pires?" "I suppose not," he said; he seemed hardly to have
thought the matter out. "I should have been surprised," I
said, "if free Russia had been only willing to do less for
the Poles than the old," for the reunion of Polish population had even been in the program of the Russian Monarchy. To this Sokolov agreed. "Then how will you get them
their natural frontiers?" I asked. "By plebiscite," he said.
"And who will hold the plebiscite?" I countered. "At present
these territories are all occupied by the enemy." "We shall

ask him to withdraw," said Sokolov, "and to let the people vote." "And if he won't?" I asked. "I suppose we shall have to go on fighting," said Sokolov. "In that case," I said, "I think we can shake hands, for we mean the same thing."

Then we went on to the question of the Czechs. "Do you know what they did?" I asked. "I should say it was the most striking form of plebiscite. Three whole regiments of Czechs came over to us wholesale, one of them under fire, because they wanted to go on fighting on our side. Those regiments have been struck out of the Austrian Army. If they go back to their country, they'll all be hanged as traitors. I don't see how we can avoid going on fighting for them." "Why didn't we hear more about all this?" said Sokolov. "I suppose," I replied, "that the military authorities preferred to regard this as a kind of military victory." At this point a soldier member of the Soviet interrupted, and confirmed me in the strongest way. At his place on the front, hundreds of Czechs had come over in the way I had described, and were simply counted as war prisoners. Sokolov was deeply impressed; he invited me to draw up a statement for the Soviet, and possibly later to address a meeting there.

He then raised a question of which I readily recognized the justice. The Soviet was pressing for a re-definition of the war aims of the allied countries. "Surely," he said, "the Russian Revolution has to be regarded as a *nouveau fait* of the first importance." It was a good deal more than a "new fact!" We had at that time in Petrograd two excellent representatives of British Labor, who have played distinguished parts in parliament, Will Thorne, later Father of the House of Commons, and James O'Grady, who was later Governor of New Zealand for our first Labor Government. I offered to bring Sokolov a statement on our attitude from these and other Britishers of distinction then in Petrograd. I got the statement and the signatures which I sought without difficulty, but unfortunately our office conditions at that hectic time were as irregular and as inadequate as pretty well everything else in Petrograd. We seemed to be moving at the rate of ten years in a day, and by the time our statement was in type, those with whom I had been dealing on the Russian side were all quarreling among themselves. That was the character of our life at that time. It was as if you were sliding down toward a precipice. You clutched at a tuft of grass, it gave in your hands, and you slid further down the steep slope.

## THE END OF GUCHKOV

Soon after reaching Petrograd, I also visited Guchkov, who was now Minister of the Revolution both for Army and Navy. I found him almost completely worn out. "We'll go into my bedroom," he said. "I'll lie down and you talk!" He had barely returned from a hurricane campaign of speeches all down the Front, nearly all of them successful when he made them, but leaving no effect the next day. He had had rheumatic fever. He suggested that I should go back to the Front and address the troops as an Englishman and an ally, and he supplied me with letters to the chief generals. General Kornilov, at this time Military Governor of Petrograd, came in to leave a report; this was the only time that I ever saw him.

In May, I was lunching at a favorite place on the Nevsky Prospekt when a big procession came past. This was the first attempt of the Bolsheviks to capture the capital. There was great resentment because they carried arms; the first mood after the revolution was one of universal brotherhood, as if the millennium were already reached. The demonstrators carried placards with the words "Down with Guchkov and Milyukov!" These were the two chief friends of England in the Cabinet; and later we learned that these watchwords were directly supplied by telegraph from Germany. But there gathered a far larger crowd, unarmed but determined. They were on their way to the Ministry to encourage it to more vigorous measures. An officer walking by the side called out, "Come along! This time it's for Russia." I discovered that I had two companions, a soldier and an elegant young lady on very high heels, who had linked up arm in arm with me on either side. We halted in front of the Mary Palace, and there were a number of speeches mostly from plain folk. Lenin was attacked as a German agent. "We've had one despot, and we don't want another," said one speaker.

Next day I again went to the vast War Ministry, where Guchkov camped with his simple family. Again he was resting on his bed, and he told me he could not get his colleagues in the very diverse Cabinet to back him up. I went next day again to see how he was, and to my surprise he was standing in his fur coat in the snow in front of the War Office, making one of the best speeches of his life. The great crowd was listening to him with instinctive respect. He was very plain and direct. He told them that if they could not learn how to organize order, it would be bound to end in a military despotism. When he finished, a young attaché explained that he was a sick man, and the crowd dispersed quietly.

The next night he told me he was resigning. His condition for staying on was a firm restoration of order at the Front, and his colleagues had not agreed to this. He went and faced the hostile Soviet. His speech there began with "Gentlemen"–not the customary "Comrades." He gave the record of his devoted life-work for the army; his audience listened intently throughout and at the end broke into a great spontaneous burst of applause. However, directly afterwards the Bolshevik Zinoviev was expounding defeatism from the tribune, and all that Guchkov had said was forgotten. He went down to the Front as a simple Cossack, and was the last man out in the retreat from our conquest of Chernovetz. With him the other principal challenger of the autocracy, Milyukov, also passed into history.

## Sir George Buchanan
### Spokesman of England

England was indeed fortunate in having Sir George Buchanan as her spokesman in Russia in this troublous time. His predecessor, Sir Arthur Nicolson, had a more precise intellect, but for the time of crisis something else was required. Buchanan was England in Russia. The Russians could see in him, shining bright through the storms, all that the best of England stood for—honor, frankness, a deeply understanding sympathy. He had wretched health for most of his stay in that unhealthy city, but that made no difference to his courage, his clarity, and his constancy of purpose. For a lesser man, the revolution would have changed everything; it left him the same, and as clearly recognizable as before for what he was. I remember how a leading Marxist said that he was a great figure in Russian history.

Sir George had a curious simplicity of speech which was sometimes even baffling. He said exactly what he meant; but at times it seemed almost as if something more was wanted, or even as if he might himself not see all the import of his own words; but that was not so. Two sayings of his I particularly remember. Quite near the beginning of the war, he said very simply, "I wish we did not ask them to do too much." That seemed a very ordinary thing to say, but it was the whole point of everything at that moment, as anyone would have recognized later. In those times, his French colleague was always battering at the door of the War Minister or the Tsar for some greater effort on the

Russian side; and the Tsar, who was the essence of chivalry, had no idea of what his own too ready orders involved. The other occasion was about half way through the ruin of the army in the summer of 1917. Sir George said, "Perhaps if we can keep them in line till the autumn, some day they'll be grateful to us at home!" And Hindenburg attributes it to the vigorous work of the British Embassy that the Russian break-up only came too late to save Germany.

Sir George Buchanan always defended those who served him. Once a hostile member of the Foreign Office wrote asking him to give me a scolding and henceforth to serve as a censor of any dispatch of mine to England. I first learned of the matter in a trench at the top of the Carpathians from a note in his own hand, telling me how he had already dealt with the matter. He had replied (1) That he could not give me a scolding because he agreed with what I had written; (2) That he was too busy to act as censor of what I wrote; (3) That as he lived in Russia, he could not be the best judge of what should be published in England, thereby throwing back all the responsibility for publication on the complainant.

The Ambassador asked me at one time in the summer of 1917 to translate the news to him, as his interpreter was on holiday. The regular papers had become very irregular; so I scraped up what I could find and looked through it on my way to the Embassy. "Shall I read this?" I asked. "It's a speech of the German Chancellor to the Reichstag." He was giving all the details of Russia's secret treaties with her Allies, which must have been part of the work of Sir George. I might have expected some expression of annoyance. He only said quietly, "They must have got it from here." At another time, the new Foreign Minister of the Provisional Government, who was always too optimistic, told Sir George that the government intended to attack the

Bolsheviks from behind his house; the Embassy stood on one side of the Trinity bridge and Lenin's headquarters were on the other, so that Sir George was actually living on the front line. They wanted him to move with his family for safety to the center of the town. "And what did you tell them, Sir?" I asked. "I said my wife and daughter want to see it." What a delightful answer! That was England–and next day, as we all expected, there was nothing to see.

Tramping over the sultry parade ground behind the Embassy, I came on the official committee elected by the Cossacks. I had met their spokesman on the platform of some of the public meetings which were in full spate at that time. They told me they wanted to go to the Embassy, and would I come and interpret for them?" Sir George received us at once. "Perhaps we've done the wrong thing in coming here," said the Cossacks. "We are just soldiers, and don't understand diplomacy. But we've heard all sorts of nasty things said against England. Now we Cossacks are friends of England, and we want to answer them; so we thought we'd come to you, and you'd tell us the right answers." "Thanks very much!" said Sir George quietly. "What are these things they say?" They reeled off a number of unpleasant items of German propaganda, with which I was already familiar. At each item, Sir George would say little more than a single sentence, plain and convincing. When they had got through their list, the Cossacks retired into a corner and conferred with some excitement. "And now," they said, "you must explain to him that the next question comes from the Cossacks, his friends." It was very simple. "If Russia makes a separate peace, what will happen?" Very quietly and almost casually Sir George replied, "Why, we shall win of course, but it will take a good deal longer." The effect was overwhelming; they all looked positively aghast. The Cossacks were bred on military loyalty; and now your ally, after you had deserted him, was going to win

without you. They returned again into their corner. "Now,"
they said, "tell him this! If Russia makes a separate peace,
the Cossacks won't." Sir George gently patted the leader's
shoulder. "Bravo Cossacks!" he said.

At my hotel, about a mile from the Embassy, I heard
one night machine-gun firing from that side. It was about
12:30 P.M. I shuffled on my uniform and went out. Fright-
ened shopkeepers were standing outside their doors, wanting to know what was on now. On the great open square
between the river and the Embassy all was now quiet. An
ambulance came along; I hailed it and asked for details. A
Bolshevik nest had been cleared out, they said, and it was
all over. I turned to go home, but by what instinct I don't
know, I tried the door of the Embassy. It was unlocked.
Two Russian soldiers were asleep inside. I went up almost
to my chief's bedroom door, told the soldiers what I thought
of them and went home. "You're not guarded, Sir," I said
to Sir George the next morning. From that time one of the
military attachés, all of whom knew some Russian, slept at
the Embassy, but none of those diplomats who were asleep
there on that night could conduct a business talk in the
language of the country!

One night about 9:30 P.M., I dropped in as usual for
a cup of tea to tell the Ambassador and his wife that the
town was quiet. "As far as I understand, I'm recalled," Sir
George said to me. I couldn't help it, and I said, "It's a
damned shame. There'll never be anyone like you here
again." Sir George had cabled the Foreign Office who apparently knew nothing about it. The Premier, Mr. Lloyd George,
had sent out the Labor leader, Arthur Henderson, with a
mandate to replace Buchanan. But Henderson, to his great
credit, had the modesty and wisdom not to use it.

Sir George left later after the Soviet Revolution; some
of us were afraid that he would leave his bones there. But
before he went, he did something for which I know no

parallel in the history of diplomacy. He advised the British
Cabinet to release Russia from her pledge of alliance; it was
the best chance of keeping her friendship, and the only
chance of saving the Liberal Provisional Government.
Though this advice was not taken, before he finally went
home, he issued a farewell message, recognizing that the
Russians had done all they could, which was the very best
point of departure for a resumption of relations in the future.

## KERENSKY

With the same questions as I had put to Sokolov at the
Soviet, I went on to Alexander Kerensky. This was my first
of a great many talks with him. It was the First of May
by our Western calendar; and the Russians were keeping it
for the first time as Labor Day without restraint and
apprehension. It looked like some great imaginary, brotherly,
international country where all the most diverse interests
and parties were insistent on being friends; for the fraternal
atmosphere of the first relief from Tsardom was not yet
gone. Long winding processions of all sorts of different
vocations–professional, industrial, military–were passing,
interlacing and saluting each other, as they passed.

Kerensky was ever so much more alert, informed and
understanding than Sokolov. He was always a particularly
honest politician, in whom the man is quite as visible as
the views. He took up the question of Sokolov, whether the
war aims of the Allies should not be re-written. This brought
us to the principle of self-determination, and Kerensky had
realized at once that this raised all sorts of other questions.
"I am for it," he said, "but I have told my colleagues that
we are cutting off the bough on which we are ourselves sitting." He was thinking of the infinitely diverse elements
that make up the Russian State. He put directly, though in

the most friendly way, the three awkward questions which I
had always to meet at that time, whether in conversation or
on the platform. What was the British attitude to self-
determination in Ireland, in Egypt and in India? I did not
pretend that any of these questions were really settled–only
that they were on the way to settlement–and that the direction which they were following was always towards national
freedom. I think I may fairly say that what I told Kerensky
then, has not been too imperfectly justified by the course
which British policy has followed since. This may be said
for Egypt and for Ireland. As to India, I put it that whenever there is really a united Indian opinion calling for our
withdrawal, there will be nothing left for us but to go.
Kerensky was not governed by phrases; his view was discriminating and statesmanlike; and he recognized, much better
than many others at that time, that there were other questions in the world besides self-determination.

At that moment, Kerensky was recognized all round as
"the coming man." His profession before the revolution was
that of a barrister, and he stood out as a brilliant defender
in political trials, which certainly offered plenty of danger
and little enough remuneration. Standing between the
liberals and the revolutionaries and regarded as the leader
of labor, he was always preaching the principles of liberty
as they are understood by the Anglo-Saxon democracies. It is
useless to blame him for not trying to be a dictator, for
dictatorship was exactly what he was out to defeat. In the
hectic days at the Duma during the overthrow of Tsardom,
by the testimony of political friends and opponents alike,
he was the only man who kept his head. He had the brilliant
idea, as soon as he knew the troops were joining the people,
to tell them to march to the Duma and put themselves under
its authority. The Soviet was unwilling that any of its leaders should join the new Government. Kerensky, though one
of its vice-presidents, as well as a Member of the Duma,

accepted office in the Cabinet as Minister of Justice, reported
this at once to the Soviet and carried it with him. By this
he established an essential and vital link between the two
contending authorities. He set himself, in the main very
successfully, the task of stopping an outbreak of savagery
against those connected with the old regime; that was really
the point of his abolition of the death sentence, which was
already retained only for martial law and political cases.
In his first speech to the Moscow Soviet he declared: "I will
not be the Marat of the Russian Revolution."

Kerensky was only in the early thirties. I never shared
the extravagant estimate of his abilities during his rise to
power, and still less–in fact not at all–the contumely heaped
upon him after his fall. He was trying all through to combine all patriotic elements in Russia, and he was entirely
opposed to the swamping of all her interests in a general
flood of world revolution. In that early period, immediately
following the fall of the Tsar, to dictate was impossible, even
for Lenin. The eight months odd of Kerensky's prominence
were equal to far more than eight years of ordinary history.
The State was practically in dissolution, and so was society.
With all this, Kerensky tried to continue to carry out Russia's debt of honor to her allies in the war, and that of
itself made his ultimate success quite impossible.


## CORPORAL FEIT AND HIS REGIMENT

Dropping in at our British propaganda office, which was
chiefly concerned in combating German propaganda, I met
a young corporal named Feit–a Lithuanian I think–who had
come to find some Englishman to speak in his regiment.
He said they were debating the rival claims of England and
Germany; and of course Germany held the master cards,
as she asked only for peace and we for more fighting. Before
I went with him, I supplied him with a copy of extracts from

the extravagantly militarist works of the German General Bernhardi, which had been translated into Russian. I knew well that what I should be talking to would be the irresistible urge to peace.

We arrived at some very dingy barracks. As far as I could see, Feit seemed to be in command. He put me in a side room, to wait there till he would send a soldier to me. "Then," he said, "you must be prepared to stand on a bench and answer any questions."

When I entered the place of meeting, the officers, who seemed to have been degraded to the ranks, sat among the men, looking very gloomy. Feit was on the bench concluding his speech. With an audacity I could hardly help admiring, he was using the extracts from Bernhardi, leaving it to be supposed that he had made them himself. After each passage, for instance on the beauty and necessity of war, he made a sarcastic comment. "Now comrades," he went on, "you'll say that's all very well, Feit. The Germans are bad, but the English aren't any better. Now, Feit, you go and study the English! No, comrades, I'll do much better than that. I'll put on this bench an English professor, and you can ask him any blooming question you like!"

Here was a splendid lead; and as often before and since, I was very grateful to the Russian stage instinct. I knew what questions were coming; I could almost visualize them on a little circular of German origin; I had had to meet them at pretty well every meeting and was ready with all my answers, whether good or bad. So as soon as I was sure we had got to the end of the list, I called out, "Now, comrades, more questions! You haven't asked me anything like enough." And all the questions which followed were of a totally different kind, naive and friendly.

Two years later, when in Siberia, I received a visit from Kolchak's legal officials. Feit was in Siberia too, and had been arrested by them as a suspect. He had appealed to me.

I told them how useful he had been to us in Petrograd, and they promised me that that should be held to his credit.

## "A Concert Meeting"

Among the entertainments of the early playtime of the Revolution were the "Concert Meetings." There were meetings of all kinds, but the "Concert Meeting" was something especially *recherché*. The Imperial Opera was impounded to play or sing appropriate tunes before each speaker; for an Englishman, of course, "Tipperary"; for a Frenchman, "The March of the Sambre and Meuse" out of the French Revolution. I remember a young French woman in a Jacobin cap, with two flags held over her, singing the Marseillaise with great determination. The fighting had really stopped, and there was no sign that the listless bourgeois audience understood her as she would have wished; so she leaned forward towards them, dropped her voice and pleaded: "Citoyens! Citoyens! Aux armes! Formez vos bataillons!"

I spoke in a vast circus, crowded to the full. On the platform were a group of sailors from the Black Sea Fleet of Kolchak, who were preaching discipline all over Russia (he was the only commander who could still maintain it). As I came on to the platform, I was demonstratively embraced by Alexinsky, leader of the Bolsheviks in the Second Duma and now turned Moderate. This was a recognition of what Harper and I had done, to see that the foreign press got a truthful account of the forcible dissolution of that Duma. We had, as usual, a selection of the most varied celebrities, each awaiting his turn; it reminded me of the last hours in a London music hall, when the "big stars" at last appeared. The turns had to be very short; in that vast building one could only hope to get through a couple of sentences, shouted at the top of one's voice.

There was the Serbian Minister, a little pleading figure. He said: "If I have to tell my country that no more help is coming from Russia, *I shall kill myself.*" And then he passed through the audience, with kind strangers begging him not to do it. He didn't!

And now Governor Francis, Ambassador of the United States, punctuating each word and translated by an interpreter: "I have cabled to my country that Russia will not stop fighting! (tell 'em *that*.) My government has replied putting a million dollars at the disposal of the Russian Red Cross! (tell 'em *that!*)."

And now it was my turn. "You say, we British are fighting for Capitalists. Don't insult us! We aren't fools. If anyone tells you that, just say one thing. Say that we sent to this war 2,000,000 volunteers."

And then the curtains of the Imperial Box parted, and there was Kerensky, the champion speaker of that turbulent time, in workman's costume and flanked on each side by a military aide. He called us to order and discipline and effort in the name of "Her Majesty, the Russian Revolution!" It was a great phrase. Kerensky had that eloquence which commands a great crowd, and he was never afraid of his audience, however unruly. To a mutinous regiment he said, "Is this a revolution or a riot of slaves?" But alas the "Persuader in Chief," as he was then called, had a hopeless task; for each of these thrilling summons to duty was forgotten with the next speaker.

## The League of Personal Example

After this Concert Meeting some young men came and asked me to tour Russia with them. They belonged to the moderate Marxists called Mensheviks, under the lead of the veteran teacher of Marxism in Russia, George Plekhanov. As I have mentioned, as soon as I grew up I had abandoned

allegiance to any party and have maintained that attitude
to all parties ever since. So when the Revolution seemed to
break everything up, I wandered among the different parties trying to find the border line which divided our friends
from those of Germany. Definitely the Mensheviks were on
our side; in fact at this time they were its most vigorous
advocates. They realized the obvious fact that if Germany
won the war the Russian Revolution was finished, and that
therefore they must now go on fighting with Russia's allies,
both for Russia and for her revolution. As a matter of fact,
the war was to go on for a year and a half; and Lenin and
the Bolsheviks took an enormous risk when they left the
Allied side to defeat Germany without them. Our appeal
was •convincing enough for the educated classes; but Lenin
had got the right word for the masses—namely that the poor
man had to fight the war and only the rich man would profit
by it.

It was because the Mensheviks were on our side, that
they invited me to come with them. Of course, we British
were always discussing these questions among ourselves.
General Knox, who was an extremely able military attaché,
mobilized his staff to speak in barracks and factories and
ask the Russians to go on fighting. In my view, when we
had once said that to them, we ought to find other reasons
not in our interest, but in theirs. Sir George got Knox and
me to debate the question in front of him, and took my view.
Before starting on my tour I asked him if I might put it to
Russian audiences that if it was really their interest to go
out of the war, we as their friends ought to accept that, and
that was the view that Buchanan took when he suggested
to the British Cabinet to release Russia from her pledge of
alliance.

Our travelling party took the audacious name of "The
League of Personal Example." We wore red and white arm-
lets. The War Office provided us with a special train. We

took any theatre, without paying for it. Our meetings were always crammed, but our success was only at face value; everyone cheered us, and then went away hoping the war would soon be over.

We were like a revivalist meeting where outstanding offenders of the past now preached morale and discipline. There was the wise and sagacious Vera Sazulich who, as almost a girl, had fired point-blank at the Governor of St. Petersburg. The sailor Lyashchenko wore a hat-ribbon saying in letters of gold, "Hero of freedom"; he had served ten years hard labor for the mutiny of the battleship Potemkin. We had a sergeant, a most respectable and domestic man, who, near the outbreak of the Revolution, had arrested the commander in chief, the Grand Duke Nicholas. Perhaps our brightest star was a young Lieutenant, Astákhov, the first officer to join the troops on the day of the great uprising in March. With him were a number of privates of the Volynsky Regiment of the Guard, which rose first. We had other soldiers who had escaped from German captivity and could tell what the Germans were like. Sharing my compartment' was a clever young follower of Plekhanov, who suggested to me questions which the Bolsheviks would find it difficult to answer. The leader of our party was the veteran, Leo Deutsch, one of the first so-called Narodniks, who went as missionaries of politics among the people in the 1870's.

We took one of the two largest theaters in Moscow,— of course for nothing, as we were the "League of Personal Example!" I was the only foreigner, but still in a Russian uniform. As an Englishman I was indeed on trial, and this helped me do my best; it was one of the very few of my speeches in which I felt that I had put over all that I had meant to say.

I spoke for an hour in Russian; we were speaking for the "Liberty Loan" to the Provisional Government and this was, so to speak, my profession of faith. I said first that if

I was really a friend of Russia, I had to forget that she was in alliance with us; if it were really best for her to leave this alliance, I ought to understand and wish it too. But was it? If the Germans won this war, what would become of the Russian Revolution? Was it the interest of Russia to leave the Western democracies and put herself at the mercy of Germany, who knew no mercy? Was it not to give the Kaiser a cheap triumph over his own Socialists? What did we English understand by "freedom"? Was it the law of the strongest, the freedom to do anything that one wanted, and would not that lead straight to a new dictatorship? Where was the point of just changing one's master–changing one's executioner? Freedom, if one thought it out, really meant one's respect for the freedom of others–the free association of numbers of individual independent wills. At the end, I dropped my voice and said: "Let's go together!" One need not, with a Russian audience, have any doubt of the response to a direct appeal. They all rose and stood up for a minute. Young Astákhov, as he was speaking for the Liberty Loan, took off the cross that he wore next to his body and handed it over; and as he did so, two gold watches were handed in simultaneously from the audience. Then we speakers went all through the packed theater, collecting for the Loan.

The comradeship of our travelling party constantly reminded me of a football team on tour. Supposing, after I had done my turn, someone shouted out something against England, any of my comrades who followed would get his teeth into the interrupter. The soldier members used to come along to me to discuss platform points. As we approached Kiev, our leader, Leo Deutsch, became very agitated. That was his native city, and he had last left it with the half-shaven head of a convict. He was now to march at our head into the public garden to the sound of the Marseillaise, but he complained, unjustly as it proved, that the wicked Bolsheviks had tried to prevent him from speaking by stealing the roof-plate of his mouth!

As always happened in those days, our party soon began to melt away. Deutsch embarked on a private program and found no work for the rest of us. Even Astákhov, to his great annoyance, was summoned back by his regiment, which had now gone Bolshevik and objected to his appeals for more fighting. In the end, only four of us were left, the little Menshevik, the mutinous sailor, the sergeant, and myself. The mutineer and the sergeant, who had most kindly attached themselves to me almost as if they were unpaid valets, said that we ought to be holding many more street meetings. Would I join in, if they got one up? We were in Poltava, and the place they chose, was beside the monument to Peter the Great's historic victory over Charles XII of Sweden in 1709. When I arrived, the mutineer was already in full flow of eloquence, claiming that Russia mustn't stop fighting till she had won the Straits! "He's just finishing," said the sergeant, "will you speak next?" But before I could begin, he stepped forward to introduce me. Pretty well every Russian has the gift of speech and can make great play with his imagination. "This is our English comrade," he said, "our professor comrade. You see he has got the Cross of St. George. Let me tell you how he won it," (of which, by the way, he knew absolutely nothing!). "We were all crouching in the trenches! Suddenly he rose, and we all followed him! He led us into the enemy lines. There he stood, dripping with blood!"—the little crowd stood listening to him with a mixture of incredulity and indifference.

We travelled on till I found myself alone in a goods wagon with some forty private soldiers who were returning from Kerensky's offensive. They were talking of the fallen Tsar and his wife; and it was so interesting that I wanted to hear it all and listened in the corner which they had kindly offered me. They didn't say an unkind word. The worst expression, about the deeply unpopular Empress, was "for her own pleasure"–clearly a reference to the common slander in reference to her intimacy with Rasputin, then almost universally believed in their ranks. The Tsar they regarded as simply futile. "I'll explain it all to you," said one, and there followed a typical, homely peasant version of Russian history. "You see, his father was a big strong man like one of us, full beard, loose trousers, and top boots; but when his son was born, he called out, "What's wrong with him? He's come out all wrong! Send for a doctor!" The doctor says, "Your Majesty, your son's an idiot. You'll have to have him shot!" And then the doctor got shot instead, so now they knew all about it!

I was on my way to the widow of my dear "Wiggins," to persuade her to come to Petrograd and perhaps to England. The countryside was full of soldiers who had deserted; the local peasant girls called out for a ride in my cart. I found Mrs. Zvegintsev and her two small children without any protection except for a fearless Czech schoolmaster. In the four days that I was there, she lost the last four hundred pounds of her income. Each night we heard the drunken roar of a village meeting near by. I sought the help of the administrator who was in charge for the Provisional Government, but he could give no comfort and felt none. "Every committee now," he said, "gives orders to the one above it. This is the kind of Government we have got!"

The Zvegintsevs had always been most generous and helpful to their peasants, and they on their side had nothing whatever against them. "We shall be very sorry when you have gone," they said. "You may not know, but we didn't often come back from your land without taking something from it. Now couldn't you ask the present government (with which they assumed that she had as much influence as before) to let all your land be given to no other peasants than us, and then you may keep as much as you like."

## THE VOLUNTEER REVOLUTIONARY ARMY

Why I was the only foreign member of the All-Russian Central Committee of the Volunteer Revolutionary Army, I never knew. Things just happened like that. The Russian mind is very international; and in this case some of the organizers were among those who had shown me about on the Front. My fellow members included both officers–all quite young–and men. The men explained to me that they were little interested in politics; they only wanted to be treated with the respect due to human beings. As I was an Englishman, they said, I should no doubt understand this.

This committee was the creation of a young colonel named Muraviev. He was a Left-Wing Social Revolutionary, the only party which after the Communist Revolution for a short time shared in the power with the Bolsheviks. He was a tall dreamy young man with high forehead and visionary blue eyes, and I liked him.

He had a fine idea. We must remember that as soon as the Tsar was down, it was ordinarily just the most intelligent of the revolutionaries who were keenest to go on fighting. Lenin and his Bolsheviks were the exceptions. Muraviev began enlisting volunteers, principally from the socialists, just when the common soldiers were deserting *en masse*. We did get as many as 50,000 recruits, and if luck had helped us, it wanted little for us to get far more than that. Any who had escaped from German prisoner camps would be ready to join us. We had some political units, socialist of course. We had also the women battalions of the famous Bochkareva; they carried poison, had 80 per cent casualties and once captured a German trench. All we English in Russia–we were all personal friends, whatever our job–were thinking all the while how many lives we should lose on the Western Front if Russia dropped out, so that we had a right to be interested in Muraviev's work.

He went off to Kornilov, then Commander in Chief, for his approval. Kornilov was a simple Cossack, risen from the ranks, and he gave it readily. He even invited Muraviev to set up a department at Headquarters. We had also been invited to act under the authority of the War Office in Petrograd. We debated the choice; I was for accepting both; we couldn't get recruits without a base in the capital; on the other hand, our association with Headquarters would help us to keep our men from becoming tools of the politics of a given general. If I remember rightly, this was the answer which Muraviev gave at Headquarters. But this time, he could not get through to Kornilov and was blocked by the Chief of Staff, who was a strong conservative.

Muraviev's instrument for successful recruiting was a revolutionary oath of a non-party kind. There was now no real authority in Russia. The Tsar was gone. The new Constituent Assembly had not yet been elected; nor could it be, without the necessary preparations. Thus we substituted the oath, as representing as well as possible the public conscience of the time. It was an oath which any reasonable and patriotic Russian could take, expressing loyalty to Russia and to the Revolution. We were going to plant in every unit of the Front little groups who would advocate our oath. Russians generally act in masses; probably a given unit would either reject the oath altogether or would take it wholesale. These last would be the only units which could be trusted to go on fighting. There was now a lull all along our Front, which for the Germans had become a kind of rest cure, and those who rejected the oath might as well be sent home. But the Chief of Staff would have nothing to do with our oath. He wanted only recruits, to handle as he pleased.

Muraviev, therefore, on his return had to confess failure. Our committee was already beginning to split into the rival forces which were to face each other in November, and Muraviev was bitterly attacked. Personally I did my best to stand up for him, but as a foreigner, I could not be at home in a Russian committee divided against itself; so I asked that my membership henceforth should be only consultative, and this was put on the minutes. I was anyhow going to England to beg munitions for our organization.

Before I went, I had a heart-to-heart talk with Muraviev. He earnestly assured me that if either the Provisional Government or the Soviet or his Party declared for a separate peace, he would part company with them. I had only got as far as Sweden when Kornilov's ill-considered march on the capital had split our committee endwise; and it was Muraviev who, in the "October" Revolution, led the Bolsheviks to the capture both of Petrograd and of Kiev. But he cannot have been comfortable with them, for he later tried to pass over to the Whites and was shot.

I was in Liverpool when I read of the Communist seizure of power on November 7, 1917. What I sent to the local newspaper was printed by the side of a dispatch of Harold Williams direct from Petrograd, and I noticed with satisfaction that we both said about the same thing.

All my work had to be begun over again. The Provisional Government, which the Communists had now overthrown by force, had stood for just those principles of constitutional rule which we recognized ourselves, and it owed its overthrow largely to its loyalty to us in the impossible task of keeping Russia in the War. The new rulers not only repudiated the many millions of pounds which we had spent on munitions for Russia but also confiscated every scrap of property of the numerous British families which had lived there for many generations.

It was especially in Liverpool that I had preached Russian friendship and inaugurated the university study of Russia. I felt I must face the music and give an account of my stewardship. I spoke in the Repertory Theater, almost

a university enterprise, which we owed to the genius of
Charles Reilly. I would not have a chairman and came on
alone. There was a respectful silence. I was speaking throughout on the defensive, slowly, carefully, and plainly. My plea
was that we in England had done not too much, but far
too little. The kindly Vice-Chancellor who had slipped in
somewhere at the back, told me afterwards "I was anxious
for you."

As we came out from the theater, the newsboys were
calling out the lynching of the Russian Commander-in-Chief,
General Dukhonin, to whom I intended to go as soon as I
returned to Russia. This was my personal friend, Wiggins's
Chief in the Third Army; I had been with him the first
time that, as Colonel, he led his regiment in action in
Galicia. On the immediate morrow of the Bolshevist triumph in Petrograd, Lenin on the long phone ordered him
to open direct negotiations across the lines for an armistice
and separate peace. Firm Liberal and firm friend of England, Dukhonin refused. Lenin deposed him straight off,
and in the presence of his successor, the Bolshevik, Lieutenant Krylenko, the soldiers, mad for peace, literally tore
him to pieces.

## Through Siberia in Civil War

For all my interests and hopes in politics, the two saddest years have been 1918 and 1938. In 1918, all hopes of
liberalism in Russia had failed; and as Russia was cut off
from Europe, all my work to build up the study of Russia
in England seemed bankrupt. Sir George Buchanan had
telegraphed for my return, but he was himself coming back
to England. I was sent out, but only got as far as Stockholm.
Our wise minister in Sweden, Sir Esmé Howard, afterwards
Ambassador in Washington, kept me there till the rest of
our Petrograd Embassy came through. We discussed the

whole situation. We were all friends, and we resolved to make our criticisms of the government policy to our chiefs when we got to England.

My report was to Mr. Balfour, who had succeeded Grey as Foreign Secretary. He was always uniformly kind to me. "Don't be afraid of coming to us," he said. "We know you come here not to criticize but to help." I put it to him that as we now had no ambassador in Russia to coordinate our policy, the representatives of our various departments at home were taking all sorts of different courses, and we were bound to lose any reputation for honesty. Mr. Balfour was keenly interested and set up a central Russian committee in London under Buchanan, but it never had any real authority.

We had lost Russia, but we were still at war with Germany. I sent in a memorandum to Sir George Macdonogh at the War Office on what would happen if the Germans, now masters in Moscow, ever got control of the Trans-Siberian Railway, which meant also of the resources of Siberia. My "memo" was approved by the British Chief of Staff, Sir Harry Wilson, and was sent on to President Wilson at Washington.

We had asked Admiral Kolchak, who had offered us his sword, to try to set up a new Eastern Front. Old friends of mine, Generals Knox and Blair, had been sent out with a mission to help him, and I joined them in January, 1919, with a curious commission, neither diplomatic nor military, which left me the greatest latitude. I was to give addresses in Russian to farmer audiences right through Siberia, and I may say that my chief object was to explain to the Russians what responsibilities we were not prepared to take on ourselves in their internal dissensions. Our cause was not that of the Tsar but of the Constituent Assembly, which on January 18th, 1918, had been dissolved by the Bolsheviks under the threat of machine guns after one single sitting of a day and a half. Though finally elected under Bolshevik rule, it was predominantly Social Revolutionary, and only about a fifth of its members were from the Bolsheviks. We might by our presence help the Russians to an opportunity of a free choice of their government, but we could not try to settle their choice; and this I explained in each of my addresses to the farmer audiences through-out the country.

It was a strange adventure. I was my own agent and carried my own posters, printed in Vladivostok, announcing "Lectures of B. I. Pares, Professor of London University" (the post to which I had been transferred from Liverpool while on War service). In each place I took the local theater without payment, and asked the Mayor or some other authority to collect representatives of all political views, from right to left. This was a most satisfactory way of scooping up all local information, for of course I was able to get them to debate in front of me. I gave three public lectures in each place. The first was on "The Allies' Debt to Russia" and was founded on my experiences on the Russian Front in the Great War. The second—rather inconsequently as it might seem—was a history of the British Labor Party. Far the ablest politician whom I met in Siberia was General Gondatti, formerly the Tsar's Governor General of the Amur and now out of office. He said to me after the second lecture, "Now I know everything you are going to say in your last," which was a frank discussion of all the Russian disagreements on a background of British public opinion. In Harbin, a center of the most old-fashioned conservatives, as I was coming out from my lecture, a lady just in front of me said, "I loathe all the Allies," and I could hardly help saying to her, "You know, I quite agree with you!" The whole fantastic enterprise was a huge impertinence.

I had been given what was called a "half-carriage" on the railway, with a Union Jack on it, and could hitch on without ticket to any train. All my food I got from the American store in Vladivostok, including a good part of the quince jam which they had not disposed of. For batman and bodyguard I had a fine Czech soldier, Jan Bubnik; an Englishman would have only been an embarrassment, and in the general breakdown of character I could not have depended on a Russian. We dismissed in succession five Russian conductors, for the most various but convincing reasons. We barricaded my end of the carriage; and at the other end Jan had both his revolver and mine, which I never learned to use. We made a rule that we should never both be out of the carriage together; if we had, we should have found it completely pillaged and gutted, windows broken and cushions torn out; but with these precautions we lost nothing whatever until poor Jan, who knew no English, finished our journey in advance of me at King's Cross Station in London and was not able to save my fur coat from an English thief! All along the Trans-Siberian there were robber bands which often attacked the trains, and we agreed that if our carriage were raided by more than four men we would surrender. Often we would see a wrecked train lying beside the line.

The Czechs were by far the most efficient of all the very various foreign forces then in Siberia, and at every station Jan found all that we wanted. As to the rest, they were not fighting and were easily demoralized. Each intruding nation was responsible for a different section of the line—and all were suspicious of each other. The Japs dominated the Far East; the Czechs held Irkutsk, where the Russian governor was a workman; the Italians, in utterly inadequate winter clothing, were in Krasnoyarsk; the French and British, with Poles, Serbs and others, were nearer the Front; the Americans were mostly engaged in relief work and, under a very capable chief, Mr. John F. Stevens, they controlled the railway. An old friend from the Great War, commanding the

Russian troops in Irkutsk, said to me, "Now I don't say this because you are English, but because we know each other. Your people are the only gentlemen here; you can tell it by the way they walk down the street; and if you knew what the rest were like, you'd be sorry for us." Even the Czechs certainly suffered in Russian opinion for doing too much.

## THE SIBERIAN CO-OPERATORS

In this way Jan and I trekked slowly from one end of Asia to the other, and at last arrived at Omsk, the capital of Kolchak, which I already knew and liked. I had not wanted to approach him till I had some idea of the country which he was handling. But Kolchak never really controlled Siberia; his ill-organized forces were like a foreign element in it. For the soundest thing in Siberia was the Co-operative movement, on typically English lines, which took no part in the civil war and was harassed by both conflicting sides alike.

At Vladivostok I got in touch with the Siberian Co-operators, and I had conferences with them all along the Trans-Siberian Railway. Sometimes I stopped in their hostels, which was very much like staying in a students' dormitory, only that the company was changing every day. The Co-operators were the salt of Siberia. Their movement was as much cultural as economic or commercial. Practically everyone belonged to it; in Chita, for instance, they were 100 per cent of the population. They ran the primary schools, half the newspapers (which were often printed on coarse brown paper) and three quarters of the magazines. They ran the cinemas, which were primarily educational. They ran practically all business which ran at all. In fact they were really Siberia.

I have always been sure that the ideal of the Russian peasant is practically the same as that of British Co-operation, though of course mainly agricultural. They did not like the

Bolsheviks. "We," they said, "are a pyramid standing on the village; Bolshevism is a pyramid upside down, trying to stand on its point!" Co-operation, in their view, could not be called either co-operation or operation if it consisted only in carrying out orders from the government. Later I understood that they were making a shrewd choice of government laws, to see which they would try to bring into effect. On the other hand, they kept entirely out of the civil war which was in progress. "We will do nothing," they said to me, "to prejudice our future reunion with our brother co-operators under the Soviets." Though they suffered from both sides, the hindrances to their excellent social work only made them more devoted to it.

In Novo-Nikolayevsk–now Novo-Sibirsk and capital of Siberia–where they had their headquarters, they invited me to a special big conference of their various organizations. Their great dream, said the chairman, was to open up communications with British Co-operation, which they regarded as the mother of the movement. Would I go to Holyoke house in Manchester, the British Headquarters, and convey an invitation for a strong delegation from England to visit Siberia? They would not have a penny to pay from the time that they landed. They should bring films illustrating the whole of public life in England, not only of industrial processes and agricultural improvements but of the manner of our elections, beginning with the agitators, the crowds on the streets, and the "bobbies" keeping order, and ending with the passing of our laws. They should take back to England corresponding films of Siberian life. The party should leave some of its members to take an active part in the Siberian organization (no doubt in marketing abroad), and it should take back with it Siberians to gain the same experience in England. I did convey the invitation at Holyoke House on my return, but by that time political events had made the dream impossible.

## SOCIAL RECONSTRUCTION

It was still Revolution and Civil War too; but while I was in Omsk, I made an approach to Kolchak's government which might have a value for the future. I wrote to its Foreign Minister to inquire whether England could be of any service in helping to rebuild the shattered public services of Siberia. To show clearly the difference between our attitude and the German, I purposely emphasized my assumption that this help would have to come not only from us, but from any other country which could best give it.

In reply, I was invited to attend a special meeting of the business Ministers of the Cabinet—Finance, Education, Ways of Communication, Trade, and Local Government. I asked first whether such help was desired, and each Minister in turn replied that it was indispensable. As to its character, I was supplied by each with all details of shortages. Two-thirds of it was engineering of all types; chemistry came next and public health organization was very important. The government set up a special commission to get to work on the matter, which we generally described as "social construction"; but events moved too fast, and not only the government, but Kolchak as well, disappeared before anything could be done. The Co-operators had told me of three German attempts to secure a financial hold over their work. In the end, the task was to be resolutely tackled by the right people to handle it, that is, by the Russians themselves, under the leadership of Stalin.

I reported to Kolchak the shooting of hostages by one of his generals, and he removed the offender from his post. But the great war was now over, and the big allied armies had gone home. We had no more need of an Eastern Front, and gradually those whom we had asked to set it up were left in the lurch by us, one after another. British units had orders to avoid fighting, and to their utter mortification, had often to give the first signal of retreat. This reacted at once on the Russians, and every inefficiency on their side reacted on us. I went up to Kolchak's front, but it was now quite fluid. His last commander in chief, General Dieterichs, very able but appointed far too late, had only a single aide-de-camp. As he told me, he needed no more, for his command had practically sunk to the dimensions of a single regiment.

While I was in Ekaterinburg, now Sverdlovsk, I several times passed the rather handsome mansion in which the Tsar and his family had been massacred. One morning when I woke up, I found that the house in which I was sleeping had been abandoned by its owner and that I was absolutely alone. I was giving three lectures here, and the last was still due. Jan came rushing in from the station and started shovelling all my things into my army sack; but I took him round to our British headquarters and we learned that the Bolsheviks were still about 30 miles off. I gave my lecture, and we left by one of the last trains. Kolchak's officers had been going off by themselves with their families, and appropriating locomotives for the purpose. The workmen were all on strike. But our good railway general, Archibald Jack, standing between two interpreters, took command and got everyone away. He kept three trains especially for the railway workers, and himself went in the last. At the rate of about one mile an hour, we toiled back to Omsk.

## THE KARA SEA EXPEDITION

The only question left was how to get home. I was already five sixths round the world, and I had had so much retreating in Russia that I greatly disliked the idea of going back the same way. One of my friends of earlier days, Stephen Vostrotin, a Siberian business man and Member of the Duma, had organized in these strange conditions a trade exchange with England. The first to sail from Europe to these remote parts had been an English sea captain, named Wiggins, who had suddenly, much to the surprise of the Tsar's authorities, appeared on his ship at the mouth of the huge Siberian river, Yenisey, which can be followed right up even into China, and Vostrotin had spent his honeymoon on Wiggins's last voyage. Since then, Vostrotin had made the same journey with Nansen. That great explorer reckoned that in seven years out of eight, it was possible to come from mid-Siberia all the way by water to England, either by the Yenisey or by the Obi. Omsk was on the Irtysh, a great tributary of the Obi. At Omsk the Irtysh itself was already half a mile broad, though still 2,000 miles from the mouth of the Obi in the Arctic Ocean; and there a ship of the Hudson's Bay Company was to meet our river expedition with machinery and other goods sorely needed in Siberia. By river we were to bring for exchange rich raw materials, plentiful enough in Siberia and badly needed in England. If I took this route, I, so to speak, stepped aside from the main line of the Bolsheviks' advance, and might be able to skid round them to safety and home. Vostrotin arranged for the passage of myself and Jan.

What decided me was a visit to the leaders of the expedition. In the general wreck of character which I had encountered everywhere in Siberia, the commander, Dmitry, seemed to me a man more likely than anyone else to arrive at the destination which he set himself. He was a middle-aged lieutenant of the naval reserve, trained in the vast river service of the Volga, a big comfortable-looking man, singularly gentle but singularly strong; he commanded by the sincerity and firmness of his purpose.

An army officer was to have commanded our small squad of extremely dubious troops, but he fought shy of the job; and at the last moment we were joined by a charming little naval second lieutenant. He was hardly more than a boy, full of youth and adventure, and he still wore some tennis shoes which he had bought in Cairo! His name to my surprise was Henry York, but he had no English connections. "How did you come by that name?" I asked. "It was a kind of muddle," he answered and after a pause, "It was an utter muddle." So I did not press my inquiries. I did not want Jan to be berthed with the Russian soldiers, and entered him as my "sputnik" or fellow traveller.

We had to wait for days before starting. We had been promised a large batch of war prisoners, to handle our cargo. We had no real right to them; the Great War was over, and they ought to have been sent home. In the end, Dmitry simply went up the river and fetched them. Before the start, a priest and a deacon came down to bless the vessel. The priest preached a quite apt little sermon. His subject was the story of how Jesus walked on the waters and later fed the five thousand. We were to walk the waters in order to feed Siberia with what she most needed—machinery.

And so we set out down the great broad river, and soon we passed northward from the prairie zone into the illimitable uncharted forest that runs through half Europe and nearly through Asia; once we landed and walked a little way into it, but we were warned that it was the easiest thing to get lost in it irretrievably. From the boat it looked like a vast park. I could not but be reminded of the stories of the old Varangers or Vikings who, like their descendant, Nansen, were from the ninth century the earliest explorers of the great river system of Russia; for myself I feel certain that they penetrated into these Siberian waters. Their conditions were just like our own; they were warriors and traders. There was only one road, the river, and it was only there that they could meet with opposition; so they became warriors whenever they had to fight their way through. Only I think they must have been more efficiently armed for the conditions of their time than we were. We had a Poole gun and two machine guns, which the priest had conscientiously blessed like the rest of the ship, but no one seemed to know how to fire them off; once, when someone took a pot shot at some passing wild geese, the sentry in charge cut and ran for shelter.

The goods that we carried were also curiously the same. The Vikings' list included furs, honey, wax, and slaves. We had the furs; Siberia was a land of milk and honey; butter was a principal part of our cargo; and there were the slaves too—the war prisoners to whom we had no right. In the old days, the slaves carried the goods to market; with us, they were to do all the loading. They lived on barges. We had four river tugs headed by Dmitry's little flagship, the Volga. Each tug hauled three barges, so that we formed quite an impressive convoy. Our fuel was timber, stacked at various points for us along the river, which we somehow seemed usually to reach at night. Then the gangway, which was next to my deck-cabin, would be let down, and the war prisoners would come aboard with the timber; when the gangway was taken up again, I could feel that nothing more was likely to happen that night.

At Tobolsk the pilots had disappeared, but Dmitry went with a cab and brought some more. Henry York kept firm discipline among his little platoon. At one time, the war prisoners quietly discussed with us whether they might not seize the ship; but, they added, they had no one who would know how to sail it. We had borrowed from them two cooks for the Volga. Both, curiously enough, were "soccer" internationals. One of them, Kaufmann, approached me with great respect to ask if I would get him a passage to England. I was rather glad to have a leg in that camp, but I wondered how long Kaufman might need my help, and when I might need his.

One day, when we had reached the river mouth, Kaufmann woke me up with the news that the English ship had indeed arrived. I asked them to take me home. "Certainly," said the English manager, "but I must warn you that our ship is not quite safe!" The alternative would have been an Arctic winter and certain capture. Kaufmann and his friend were also provided for. When we rounded the peninsula of Ya Mal, we were told that we were only about 1,000 miles from the North Pole. Of the three outlets to the Atlantic from the closed Kara Sea, according to Nansen, one or the other is open for six weeks, generally in the late summer. Our journey was a pioneer enterprise in those waters, which have since been explored with such success and profit by the Soviets.

My route from mid-Siberia to England, by water only, was not so crooked as it would appear on the ordinary misleading Mercator maps. Roughly, I followed longitude 72 degrees East as far as the Arctic Ocean; and after that we were simply kicking over the longitudes at short notice for the rest of the way. On the global map, our way was much straighter. Quite soon, passing north of Archangel, we came to the North Cape in Norway and then slid down the Norwegian coast, where the rocky mountains are at their highest. After Siberia and civil war, this homely, peaceful country was a wonderful *détente*. The ship's mandolin band was playing the last favorite air of my dead sister, "Till we meet again." At Tromsö, I transferred to a Monitor, the kind of boat that mounts a river, carrying guns. It is like a soup plate with no depth, and practically can't sink, but also can't steer. At Aalesund, our small crew landed to see a comic show; at the end Lieutenant Babington, in the name of the British Navy, handed to the comic man a large cauliflower, assuring him that our George Roby always expected this particular kind of tribute. There I boarded a Norwegian Coaster, and unfortunately the ship's cat of the Monitor, which had sat proudly in the bows going up the Northern Dvina, followed me and was later washed over into the North Sea. At Bergen, I had completed my journey round the world.

Mr. Lloyd George had told me always to come and report to him whenever I returned from Russia. I called on his brilliant secretary, Philip Kerr, later Marquess of Lothian, and told him I was going to be critical of our policy. "I'll put it up to him," he said; but Lloyd George kept delaying, and was evidently not anxious to see me. At this point, I had to go to King George V to be knighted. "I know your view," said the King, "and I agree with it. Have you seen the Prime Minister?" "No, Sir." "Will you see the Prime Minister?" "Yes, Sir." This was just the kind of situation that delighted my dear old mentor in diplomacy, Lord Sanderson, and we sat down and concocted a letter explaining that I had been commanded to seek an audience of the Prime Minister. A telegram came with "Prime Minister" on the envelope inviting me to lunch, but Mr. Lloyd George was not there. However, I was taken into his private room at the House of Commons to drink coffee with him. Winston Churchill, who was then War Minister, loomed at the back of the room. "What am I to do? What am I to do?" said the homely Lloyd George, as he asked so many others. "I couldn't say what the Prime Minister of England could do," I replied, "but whatever it is, do tell them in advance, and stick to it!" "I know, I know," said Lloyd George. Winston laughed. Continuity of policy was not the forte of Lloyd George.

## PEAK OF BOLSHY SUCCESS IN ENGLAND

I could never have thought that Bolshevist propaganda could have made so much way in our sober England as when I got back from Siberia in October, 1919; and certainly this was due not only to the unbalanced conditions of the time but to a misunderstanding; indeed I have never yet met a real English Bolshevik, as he would be in Russia.

The British intervention there had been a dead failure. There could never have been any unless we had been at war with Germany; and we have done exactly the same thing in the Second World War on a much larger scale, entering without scruple any country which was under German influence and clearing things up. In Russia, we were at least standing for our own principles of constitutional government; and educated Russia was in the main for us and invited our help; but all the same, we were trying with the aid of armed forces, to impose our principles on Russia, which was both unwarranted and futile, and it lost all sense when Germany was put out of the war on November 11, 1918. I was always against world revolution, that is, against the forcing of foreign ideas upon us. But I have now to recognize that that was just what I had myself been doing in Russia. I was now bent on fighting their justifiable counter-stroke, and here I was on much firmer ground, as the fighting was now in my own country.

Our own "capitalists" were at that time of little use in meeting the threat. As has now been conclusively proved, our greatest shield was the good sense of our own working population, but it was without any really objective information on the subject of Russia. Again we suffered from our imperative need of study.

Practically the whole British colony in Russia, which had been fairly rooted there for generations, now gradually trickled back home, ending with native Britishers who could not even speak English. They had all been stripped of all their possessions and expectations there, and any of them were prepared to bear their testimony; but British Labor was for the time so much bemused by the Russian experiment that it was very hard to find a platform for them to give it. My gallant little friend, Captain Francis McCullagh, one of the most daring and famous of our pre-war foreign correspondents, sent out of Siberia four Russian workmen,

from the Izhevsky Factory, which had risen to the sound
of the factory hooter to fight the Bolsheviks. The workers
formed a brigade which made its way through them to join
Kolchak, who definitely stood for the dissolved constituent
assembly. But these four men were mobbed at their meetings, especially under the direction of Miss Sylvia Pankhurst.
The danger reached its peak in the spring of 1920. After that,
I felt at my numerous meetings that the tide was receding;
but I have far better evidence than my own. That is the date
fixed both by my friend Jack Murphy, the only Anglo-Saxon
member of the Comintern, and likewise by the Head of
the Criminal Investigation Department at Scotland Yard.
By the autumn, I felt I could go back to my new work in
London University.

There was always the greatest difference between *ad hoc*
meetings, even organized under the shadow of St. Stephen
in Westminster, which were regularly raided by organized
groups of loud-voiced "communists" and those time-honored
standing centers of education which had been set up largely
by the working classes themselves. In such an audience at
Halifax in Yorkshire, an interrupter was brought up to the
platform to apologize to me. The audience, which had invited me and paid me, had no desire to be entertained instead with a side-show from a local man. One began to see
all the good that had come from the far-seeing and objective
work of Albert Mansbridge.

How I wished that my Bolshevik friends in Russia could
have been present at the tumultuous Final Tie for the English football Cup on April 28, 1923, at Wembley between
Bolton Wanderers, the old club of William Pickford, and
West Ham in the East End of London! The ground, now
open for the first time, was rushed, and the enormous crowd
covered the playing pitch. Mounted police were trying to
push the intruders off, for the game to begin. And then, the
greatest assemblage to be seen in England was singing to

the movements of a white-robed conductor, who used his whole body as a kind of baton–"Abide with Me, Fast falls the even tide," chosen no doubt as easy to sing, but certainly not an anthem of World Revolution; and when King George V arrived to watch one of his favorite sports, the national anthem was sung with such a volume of enthusiasm as it could seldom have aroused. No, decidedly we were of no use to world revolution, as was to be proved with even greater humor in the comedy of the General Strike of 1926.

Official British Labor for the most part confined itself to a very intelligible attack on our policy of intervention in Russia which in 1920 was now on its last legs. Jim Thomas, when I saw him, said at once, "Of course, I know that it's a dictatorship there." A Mr. William Good, apparently ignorant of Russian, returned from an escorted visit to laud everything Bolshevist. I challenged him to a debate; and when he refused, I publicly described his report as "reduced to its proper insignificance." My challenge was at once taken up by an organization called "Hands Off Russia," which enjoyed important labor support. They invited me to twelve debates, two in each of the six largest cities in the country. They would pay all expenses. Each side was to put up a resolution. Theirs would be against the Intervention. In accepting, I said that I should very likely vote for it, but my own resolution would be "that we hoped the principles of free speech and meeting might prevail in Russia and that we were opposed to the introduction of the contrary principles in England." They did not carry their proposal any further.

## WILLIAM GALLAGHER

Almost at the same time I received a more modest proposal for a debate from a small Party called The British Socialist Party, which later was one of the principal components of the British Communist Party. It came in an envelope adorned with a red flag. These people were the genuine article; the champion proposed, Mr. William Gallagher, had received special commendation from Lenin.

Everything connected with this debate is a happy memory. I was invited by my opponents to suggest a chairman and consulted one of our older judges, Mr. Justice Bray. He recommended a distinguished barrister, Mr. Stuart Bevan, now a judge, who was accepted without demur and did his job with unimpeachable fairness. We arranged that the two sides should divide the tickets of invitation between them. Gallagher's "second," Mr. Inkpin, tossed up with me and won; but I was given not only the first word but an extra one at the end. I was loudly interrupted, while reading a quotation, with shouts of "Liar!" I said it was not for me to say, but that the passage in question came from the works of Lenin. Gallagher, who was ever so much more eloquent than I could hope to be, intervened to say that he would go away himself unless his supporters heard me with patience. After the meeting, he brought up to me his greatest friend. "He's my friend," he said, "but he's your side." And the friend and I discussed William and his views in his presence.

If I had had any free money at the time, I should certainly have bailed Gallagher out when a little later he and Inkpin were imprisoned as under trial. I wrote to congratulate him when he was the only Communist elected to the House of Commons, and received a charming reply. I had a talk with him at the beginning of our alliance with Russia in the Second World War, at a mass meeting in Batterson Park, when he said to me, "Churchill is doing splendidly." I was to address a large audience in the same period at his native town, Paisley. The Lord Provost (Mayor) and the Chief Constable entertained me first to dinner. I told them Gallagher was my only friend in Paisley. "The most gentlemanly prisoner in the world!" said the Chief Constable. "You have only got to get him off the soap box." And while I was still chatting with them after the meeting, a message was brought up. "Could Mrs. and Miss Gallagher come to see you?" They said to me, "William told us we must come up and shake hands with you."

There has never been more than one communist M.P. at any one time until the election of 1945 among the 600 odd members of the House of Commons—now there were only two. Till then, the only one was William Gallagher. Won't it be clear, why I have no fear of a communist revolution in England?

# CHAPTER VIII

## 𝔗𝔥𝔢 𝔖𝔠𝔥𝔬𝔬𝔩 𝔬𝔣 𝔖𝔩𝔞𝔳𝔬𝔫𝔦𝔠 𝔖𝔱𝔲𝔡𝔦𝔢𝔰
## (1919–1939)

### BUILDING UP THE SCHOOL

WHEN you are brought up sharp against a brick wall, what do you do next? Give up? That is what so many star reporters did in 1907 when the so-called first Russian Revolution ceased to be sensational and fizzled out. Those who stayed on, set themselves to know more about Russia, and they were later ever so much more useful in their alliance and the Second World War. A task as serious as Russia is not to be tackled only as long as it continues to be exciting. In my apologia before Liverpool in the Repertory Theatre in November 1917, my defence for our concentration on Russian study there was that we had done not too much but far too little. And now, it was not enough to join in the defense of our own country against the natural counterstroke of the Russian Revolution. We had to make good our own foundation for a further advance. That is now, in 1947, the lesson which is being learnt so well in America after the disillusionment of the alliance in the Second World War.

For the present I had no hope of getting back to Russia. The Bolsheviks, when they entered Ekaterinburg, had found on the kiosks the posters of my lectures of the three preceding days with their not too complimentary headlines. In fact, in all the first period of their rule, anyone who had seen and loved the old Russia was practically debarred from a visa. Communications were almost entirely cut off, and we were left to the meagre and untrustworthy information of a few fortnight travellers who never learned Russian and brought back practically the same views as those with which they had started. But I had so many and such various avenues that I was able to keep up-to-date with all the main changes in that rapidly changing period.

I had always kept my anchor in England and it was now for me to turn to my other task of organizing the study of Russia there. There was no more important lesson from the war than that we must know far more about Russia. It was also clear to me from the start that the Versailles settlement, in which Russia took no part, could not possibly be final and that another World War was much more than likely. It will be clear now that I was getting ready for the next time.

During the First World War Thomas Masaryk, later President of the Czechoslovak Republic, was living in London as a proscript under sentence of death in his own country. He was an intimate friend of Robert Seton-Watson, of whom there is much more to tell, and Masaryk became the senior lecturer in a School of Slavonic Studies set up in 1915 at King's College, London. The Principal of that college, Dr. Ronald Burrows, whom I had known in childhood, was at that time the foremost champion in England of the principle now described as "area and language," or nation study especially to be applied to those countries of which our public opinion was most ignorant. So far, the School taught elementary Russian and had a program of public lectures, given mostly by distinguished foreigners who like Masaryk, had at that time taken shelter in England. During the last phases of the War, I was invited to transfer my work from

Liverpool University to that of London as Professor of Russian, but really of Russian History, and to build up a School of regular teaching.

Throughout this work my pillar of support was Seton-Watson. Though everyone knew about him, I had not met him until my return on leave from Russia in 1915. My first co-operation with him consisted in my agreeing at once to sign a memorandum of his on questions of population at issue between Italy and Serbia, on no better ground than that I knew him to be the first authority on the subject, not only in Britain, but perhaps in Europe. In the delightful untidy study in which he used to plot with his foreign friends, I persuaded him that his career ought now to take the form of academic work. All the more was he invaluable because Russia was under a cloud and out of reach; and during this abnormal period, though there was an admirable scholarly output from the Poles, it was the Czechs who in the matter of organization did most to replace the absent big brother. The facilities which they gave, both to Russian professors and students and equally as much to us in London, were beyond all recognition and thanks.

The story of the building up of the School is a full one and covers from 1919, when I began work in London, to 1939 when I handed over the directorship to my successor and passed again into war service; and the best way of telling it, will be to take the various chief problems and to give our answers to them.

The fundamental objective was to obtain general recognition for Slavonic studies, which had so far received practically none. As it was so well put by Professor Theodore Collier of Brown University, Rhode Island, our task was to bring an unknown and remote subject under the best standards which had been worked out for the known ones. I realized very quickly that the way to do this in London was to secure our own academic authority, and this was to be done by getting for us what other subjects had, an academic Board of Studies of our own. London University was at that time still in a kind of chaos. From its beginning, over a hundred years before, it had been till quite recently only an examining body, and the majority of our graduates had studied anywhere all over the world and had only taken their examination from London. We had, for instance, 1,000 students from India, and we examined at Capetown or Johannesburg. It was just now that London was really becoming also a teaching university.

From the start there had been in London various University Colleges whose students passed their examination in the London University, but these colleges might and did have a great variety of teaching standards. To remedy this grave anomaly, the University wisely established Boards of Study to control the teaching in the various subjects; and these Boards were at that time practically the direct advisors in their fields to the Senate, which was the supreme arbiter of everything. When I arrived, we were included, as an annoying and perhaps unpopular new item, in a colossal Board of Medieval and Modern languages. I asked the wise chairman of this Board, Professor J. G. Robertson, whether he wanted us and, as I knew he would, he said, "Certainly not!" "Then," I said, "will you ask for us to have a Board of our own?" And that he willingly did. Our example was followed by others; and there are now in London, six boards of language study—Oriental, Classical (these two were always distinct), English, Teutonic, Romance, and now Slavonic. This enabled us, within the ordinary framework of teaching in the university, to write our own regulations and make our own curriculum, which now had the authority of the University as a whole.

But we were distinctly different from the other language boards; for from the start we adopted the principle now known as "area and language," which I had already followed in Liverpool and which was also followed in Berlin at the Auslandshochschule, or School of Foreign Study. Its head, Dr. Anton Palme, was and is a greatly valued friend of mine. We both knew we were working against each other, but we exchanged all information, and we always talked over every question up to date whenever I passed through Berlin on my way to Russia. This friendship was again actively renewed as soon as the First Great War was over. Late in the Second World War, the principle of area and language was boldly adopted by the fighting services of the United States and brought into active and general use.

It goes without saying that this is the right direction for foreign studies. Governments approve it, for their diplomatic and consular services; armies and navies support it, for they need men who not only know a language but know about the countries themselves. Obviously it is equally the right training for employees in trade and in journalism.

This meant that we intended to teach not only language and literature, but history, geography, economics, and social sciences, as relating to the countries of our study. Above all, we needed the control of our own subject in the teaching of Russian history. At that time (1920) the Board of History was, in my view, academically the best in the university, under the chairmanship of a scholar of great range and vision, Professor Alfred Pollard. He had just now founded that admirable institution, the Institute of Historical Research, with which we wanted to be in the closest communion. I asked Pollard if he would also back our application for a board of studies of our own. I put it that we wanted among other things to extend the teaching of history to include our area. He replied that that area could not be covered without us. It was arranged that all our work in history should be subject to the revision of the Board of History, of which Seton-Watson, myself, and others were also members.

Now came the all-important question of management, which caused us more heart-searchings than any other. We were the only central school in England, with a staff ultimately of 12 to 15 teachers in our subjects, no other British University having more than two, and most of them one or none. Therefore we carried a national responsibility. This was recognized by the British Government, which gave us an annual grant of £2,000, later in various ways increased till it was more than doubled. All academic relations of countries in our area came at once to us; and foreign Ministries of Education, especially the Czechoslovak, Polish, and Yugoslav contributed in the most generous way to our resources. Under the existing conditions, I could not ask any contribution from Soviet Russia without submitting to obligations of propaganda which were quite inadmissible; and as the minor Slav countries were doing so much for us in their own fields of study, I had to do the best I could for the Russian side out of our British funds.

Now if we were to carry these national responsibilities, it was essential that our work and purposes should be in our own keeping. This is exactly what cannot ordinarily happen. In any British or American university, a Professor of Russian economics is a kind of accidental luxury; it only means that a tenant of a post in economics happens to be interested in the Russian field. A teacher of Russian literature is under the direction of the general head of the teaching in literature, who has no special knowledge of, or interest in Russia. The control of all our work is in the hands of a management no more interested in our studies than in any other field of education, and probably much less.

That was our position in King's College. Dr. Ronald Burrows, the energetic promoter of nation study, died before his time almost directly after my arrival. His successor, not being a specialist in our field, did not really have so much special interest in us. More than that, he took an oppo-

site view to ours as to the rightful future of the University
of London, which at that time was in danger of breaking up
into various separate institutions, and this would have made
it impossible for us to maintain our central, national position. King's College was a delightful place where none of us
ever quarreled, however much we disagreed, but its outlook
in the new regime was decidedly limited and parochial.
Consequently, all that we did outside the walls of the college seemed to be regarded as unduly ambitious and even
improper. Never was I invited into the presence of our
governing body until at last I was summoned for a scolding. I remember leaning against the mantelpiece in my
workroom and thinking, "This can be turned into victory."
I had secured before this the recognition of an advisory
committee of our own, with a personnel which may without
offense be described as of greater distinction than the governing body of the College. I was aware that the central authorities of the University, who appreciated our attitude in the
controversy about its unity, would be ready enough to take
us over if necessary. Therefore, after listening to my scolding
at the College, I replied, "Yes, I agree, we must be a great
nuisance to you. Wouldn't you prefer to do without us?"
Thanks to a new Principal of the College, who understood
us exactly, it all worked out as I had forecast, and we now
rose to the dignity of a central institution of the University,
with a governing body of our own, the choosing of which
was handed over to our advisory committee.

I suppose we were almost the only instance of a staff
which was able actually to select its own management, and
we made it at once everything that we wanted. Together
with the three formal highest authorities of the University,
it includes directly appointed representatives of the Foreign
Office, the Board of Trade, the War Office (for the training
of interpreters), the Board of Education, the London County
Council (which is the local authority for education), the

London Chamber of Commerce, the Associated Chambers of Commerce of Great Britain, Oxford, Cambridge and, inside the University, the heads of the major colleges (to make our language studies available to their students where desired), and especially two closely kindred schools, the Institute of Historical Research and the School of Oriental studies. Our Council also included the foremost scholars in Great Britain in our field. Our two successive chairmen, both of them nominees of the Foreign Office, Lord Treowen, and after him the Earl of Onslow, were indefatigable promoters of our work. I cannot describe what an enormous difference this made to our advance; I regarded it as a great victory obtained at a single stroke.

The question of staff, which was essential and fundamental, was of course governed by that of finance. Once I had experts in our 12 or 15 subjects; all I had to do with my morning correspondence, was to write the initials of the colleague who was to deal with the matter, and give him free passage. This was even more important with the training for the degree of Ph.D. It was impossible for any other university in England to choose, as we could do, from a variety of different experts in our field, the right supervisor for an intending candidate; and without any arrangement on the subject, the other British universities generally sent their students for this degree to us. We were also glad to be at the service of American students for such part of their studies as they found convenient, and we were just across the street from the British Museum; these Americans could of course present their theses in their home universities.

We made from the first a necessary and close distinction in the matter of language teaching, and we had different teachers for the two different kinds. Philology we regarded as a study in which language is itself the subject; and we had a fine lecturer in comparative Slavonic philology, Norman Jopson, who later became professor of all comparative philology at Cambridge. But in general, 19 out of 20 students had no need whatever of philology; for most of them, the subject in which they are interested is not philology but literature, history or economics, and language is for them, therefore, not a subject but a tool of study. In this too there can be a severe discipline, but it is a quite different one; this is really work which, in the case of German or French, would be done in a secondary or high school, and for this too we had a quite first rate master of his craft. We are proud to recall that we Slavonics, who in setting up teaching on area, appeared to be rebels against the old curriculum, were the actual Board of Studies which initiated the establishment of a seventh language board, exclusively for philology, of which Jopson was the gifted and active secretary.

In our language and literary course for the B.A. degree, we followed religiously the accepted standard, and I need not describe it except to say that we added a new subject, the study of the history of literary criticism. But for the teaching of area, we introduced a parallel and optional course, which was entirely our own creation. It will explain itself. 1. Translation and composition (simply to show familiarity with the language); 2. History; 3. Economic history; 4. Laws and institutions (these four subjects were compulsory both for the historian and for the economist). The historian then proceeded as follows: 5. a special period of history; 6. literature as an expression of the social history of the country; 7. a period of European history; 8. an essay. The economist completed his course as follows: 5. a subject of economics (copied from the program of the University of Moscow, agriculture, industry, trade, or finance; 6. economic geography; 7. general economic history and theory from 1800; 8. an essay. There is, of course, as much difference in Russia as in England between the student of literature and the student of economics. In these courses, every student had a very full program; but he was burdened with nothing that was not a natural part of it.

More simple and perhaps more practical was the course which we were able to set up for visitors to the University from any quarter who did not require, under our regulations, to pass the entrance examination and did not obtain a degree. In its place, they received from the University a so-called Academic Diploma, for a course of two years' study. Half of it was in the use of the language, one-quarter in the history of the country concerned, and the last quarter, at choice, in its literature or in its economics–the former for students in journalism, the latter for prospective employees in trade.

I should like to say here that the Ph.D. degree, introduced I believe *via* the United States, was to us of the first value. In subjects more generally known, the candidate has probably to discover some neglected question of secondary importance, as the whole field has been tramped over by others. In our case, nearly the whole field was new; and it would be quite easy to write straight off 40 subjects of the first importance, in which the student would prove to be for Anglo-Saxon scholarship the first pioneer.

It was an enormous advantage to us to be an integral part of a great University with some 13,000 internal and 13,000 external students. We never closed our doors, but linked up in every way with other colleges and institutions. Our economic teaching was all done in co-operation with the London School of Economics, which paid a substantial part of the salary of our teacher. Our closest kinship was with the sister school of Oriental Studies founded a little earlier than ours; it was they who had invented the Academic Diploma. Its Director, Sir Denison Ross, was a glorious colleague. Any disputable subject on our frontiers was treated in co-operation. Ross always represented our cause as well as his own on the Senate of the University. Our conditions were extraordinarily similar. We each had a lot of language teaching to do, because it was not to be obtained elsewhere. We were each very weak on the staple degree courses for the university; and for the "ordinary" or "pass" degree we never encouraged any student of ours to enter. On the other hand, the Ph.D. flourished in each of the schools. We were equally close to Pollard's fine Institute of Historical Research, which immensely strengthened the "area" side of our work. It would be a long story to tell how we ultimately obtained the realization of our dream in the matter of geographical location. We were next door to both these two colleges and the University Library, with a back door entrance to the British Museum.

London is a splendid base for an enterprise of this kind. London University has always been proud to call itself the poor man's university. Special provision is made for those who by day are working at salaried jobs; in fact, one large college is composed of evening students. The University demands exact information as to how many hours in the week are pledged to other work than study, and the student is then informed how far the period of his work for a degree must be extended. We always felt that people of this kind deserved all the help that we could give them. Then again, in contrast to the older universities, it was London's boast that anything that a man could do, could also be done by a woman. The sources from which students came to us were extremely various–sometimes even curious. A man of fifty volunteered for a degree course in Czechoslovak because his daily work was in a translation office. The foreigner in London could make free use of us. In particular, we had a number of refugees from Russia, who had lost everything in the revolution. It will be seen that we had quite a number of lame ducks, which made our work all the more human and interesting.

Then too, there was a very satisfactory arrangement, by which we could tap the larger colleges for students. By the Intercollegiate Lecture system, students of other colleges paid the School for any work which we did for them. This might bring us engineers, chemists, or others, who were far off from our field but wanted to include the Russian language in their tools of study. Generally, it required a certain spirit of adventure to launch into Slavonic study. Never in my experience did any who entered it finally give it up, but we had to tell them from the start of our difficulty in later finding posts for them.

We held annual conferences with teachers of Russian in the other British universities. We fixed the time by their convenience and we always had a goodly and spirited attendance. At first we thought that these meetings might outlive their usefulness when we had dealt with a few initial problems, such as the transliteration of the Russian alphabet into ours. But it turned out that the conference became busier and more interesting with every year. There were things which we could do in common far better than separately. We obtained a certain authority in approaching public bodies for support, or in dealing with the educational organs of the countries within our field of study.

We also built up a similar authority by what we called our "Members of the School." The invitation to join this body was always based exclusively on scholarship and published work, and it was always accepted. We invited as Corresponding Member the principal scholars in Slavonic countries or in similar schools to our own in France, Germany, and Italy. Our letter of invitation offered the services of our School to those of their students who might come to England, and we asked them to do the same for ours in their own countries. We had also a "school letter" giving an introduction to these foreign scholars; it was equally at the service of American teachers or students who passed through London on their way to their respective fields.

I remember in particular, one opportunity which made my mouth water. A sturdy and firm-footed, middle-aged lady, of that kind that act as nurses to absent-minded foreigners, brought to us about half of the staff of the famous Moscow Art Theatre, second to none in its all-round perfection of stage production. Poor folks! They did not like Bolshevism and so kept out of Russia; and foreign audiences could not understand them. We were told that they were thinking seriously of learning English and acting Russian plays in our language. This was a dream! Everything connected with such a venture must be A-1 in quality. First the teaching! We had the right man next door in University College, Professor Daniel Jones, a unique authority in phonetics; we had often been in contact with him, and he consented to hold a special class to teach English pronunciation to these desirable students, most of whom, to start with, would be trained elocutionists. Then came the question of English versions of Russian plays. These were very few in number, and there were still fewer that could be used as acting versions. If so, we must turn to our translators, of whom he had quite a fine panel, and they must do their work in close contact with the Russian artists. I had got as far as this, when their English nurse blew in to tell me that her wards had had a heated discussion, of the kind so dear to Russian artists, and had decided to give up England and go over to act their plays in France.

## "Scotus Viator"—The Flying Scotsman

I have been most happy in my "twins." I seem to have had one for each of my chief interests—"Wiggins" for Russia, Harold Williams for Anglo-Russian friendship, Samuel Harper for America, and the "Travelling Scot," Seton-Watson, for building up the School.

If anyone doubts what romance there can be in scholarship, he should study this extraordinary career. Seton, only child of a Scottish laird, was early left an orphan with spacious means and far-reaching perspectives. Winchester, probably the greatest school in the world for the training of character, has produced in long centuries a mould which gives worth and stability to the average boy; but the mould itself is a challenge to the children of vision, and Winchester has sent out many "scholar adventurers." Seton set himself to a study of modern Europe. In all things he had a strong, often a passionate bias; but he carried all the weapons and checks of scholarship, and with him scholarship was something like a Highlander's claymore. He would have loved and followed with Highland loyalty his fellow-countryman, John Macdonald Mackay.

Seton has been one of the finest and most intrepid of British pioneers in the field of foreign study. He began with Italy, but soon he passed on to Hungary, and since then he has been cutting his way through the tangled jungle of Danube and Balkan history. After long and keen study he produced in a year or two, a trilogy of major works on British foreign policy, especially as it concerns this area, from which over and over again major wars have sprung; and some day, if he lives, the whole of his field will be covered by first-class books. As a reviewer in the field of history he is, I think, the best I've ever known. He follows what Archie Coolidge of Harvard called "the topical review" –he is reviewing not merely the individual book but the whole topic, picking out what is new and original in that book on a given subject and confronting it with the best that he has learned from others. In spite of his strong prejudices, in which he recalls one of the most inspiring of historians, Michelet, to Seton may be applied in honor the admirable definition of Professor Theodore Collier, "Our task is to bring remote and unknown subjects under the best standards worked out for the known," and that is why he was justly elected a Fellow of the British Academy. It will be seen at once how essential were the genius and talents of Seton-Watson within the late cultivated pale of our historical field.

Rubs and conflicts–and we seemed sometimes almost to live on them–could only be welcomed in the vitalizing partnership with such a man. Most fortunately, before we ever met, we had arrived independently, not only at the same general objectives in our task, but also at a kinship on most of the major issues that face political thought and temper. His penetrating intellect was that of a brilliant and simple child. "Please sir," he would say, "brain wave!", and we would add new thought to thought with the same delight with which we might have been writing a comedy for amateur Christmas performance. In everything that he suggested, Seton was daring. My chief role in our routine collaboration was to induce him, out of sheer goodfellowship, to omit here and there a peculiarly aggressive epithet, but to achieve this I always had to propose some alternative with vigor in it.

When Seton first went to Hungary he was, I believe, received with the greatest enthusiasm. Hungarians are essentially a top-dog race; so, obviously, are the English and, still more so, the Scots, who very often rule over the English. In the vital middle years of the nineteenth century, English Whig Liberalism formed a very good model for Hungary, chafing at Austrian rule; and from the days of Palmerston, Hungarians have always been cordial to anyone who came from England. But Seton quickly saw through the Hungarian caricature of British parliamentarism. Despite the most classical of all ethnical falsifications, such an eye as Seton's could not fail to see that large numbers of Hungarians were not Hungarians at all, but subject Slavs; and with his discovery of the Slovaks, whom he later did so much to put on the map of Europe, Seton gradually became public enemy No. 2 in Hungary.

Public Enemy No. 1 of today is the Czech leader, Dr. Eduard Beneš, and Seton's studies naturally brought him closer to the Czechs who, quite unlike the Asiatic Magyars, are close kinsmen of the Slovaks. But he first became intimate with Benés's great teacher and predecessor, Thomas Masaryk, himself a Slovak, son of a coachman of the Austrian Emperor and later displacer of the Hapsburgs in the Imperial Castle in Prague. But Masaryk was first a philosopher and then a statesman, and the moral influence of his teaching was almost as great among the other Slav peoples of Austria. When two of Seton's South Slav friends came out to Russia in 1916 in a Yugoslav deputation, and I suggested to them that we should bring Seton himself out to Russia, they said, "That man must not cross the North Sea. To us he is God!"

I must not try to tell all Seton's story for him. It is piquant, inspiring in the highest degree, a great tale of a great adventure. When, in the Treaty of London, England traded away to Italy, still a neutral, population which should have gone to Serbia, an ally, Seton and Wickham Steed were almost the only Britishers who knew enough of the subject to offer a formidable protest. Seton later attacked Sir Edward Grey in what I thought a very intemperate article in the *English Review* and was called up into the army, from which at my request he was later liberated by Mr. Lloyd George. But all this while, he was the principal informant of our Intelligence Offices; and where he thought necessary, he anonymously attacked British policy in his fine little "New Europe," which swallowed up much of his private means, but was the standard-bearer both in England and America of the views for which he stood; and these views in the end, entered almost wholesale into the program of the Allies. Seton and Steed perhaps did more than anyone else to bring about the union of the Serbs, Croats, and Slovenes in the new Yugoslavia. When he returned to Slovakia after the war, the little schoolgirls were all lined up in white, and Seton and his wife were greeted with cannon! Fortunately both of them had a strong sense of humor. A statue

of Seton was put up, but later when the quarrels of Czechs
and Slovaks threatened to ruin his work, he asked that it
should be taken down; and it was thrown into the river before Slovakia threw herself into the arms of Hitler. What
a story!

## PRINCE DMITRY MIRSKY

I first met Dmitry Mirsky as an oriental-looking boy in
the country house of his father, who was that rarity, a Liberal
Minister of the Interior under the Tsars and by his good
sense, frankness, and courage may be said to have ushered
in that period which gave Russia a representative national
assembly. After the Revolution, I got Dmitry, now an émi-
gré, appointed as our lecturer in Russian literature and
literary criticism under the lively impression of a hot discussion in which he brilliantly countered my views. He certainly
did much more than his duty by us. Like several others of
us, he gave a public lecture once a week, and out of these
courses came firstclass textbooks of Russian Literature, and of
Modern Russian Literature, and an excellent study of Pushkin. Literary criticism is a very favorite subject in Russia,
and he set us a standard of it far above anything I have met
in our subject in England. He had a wonderful store of
live and varied knowledge, mobilized with perfect ease, a
marvelous memory and an English style of his own which
held me captive even when crossing a London street. He
made adventures of his own in the English language, daring
but always successful.

Mirsky had passionate enthusiasms which succeeded
each other. He had fought with the White Army, and at one
time he thought Maria Tsvetayeva one of the world's greatest poets. Then for a time he proclaimed himself an Eurasiat,
a supporter of that strange view that Russia forms a kind of
separate continent of her own. He was our irrepressible bad

boy. Nevill Forbes, prim Oxford scholar, read us a paper illustrating the life of ancient Kiev from the old heroic ballads. Mirsky interjected the criticism that there was no historical evidence for the authenticity of the heroic ballads before the seventeenth century, when they were first written down. This was very unfair. They had been and still are transmitted orally–one even came into being under the Bolsheviks–but it seemed to knock the bottom out of poor Forbes' paper.

Mirsky in the end went communist. As soon as I felt this change was likely to be permanent, I told him it would not make any difference in his position in the school. I thought he would be happier in Russia. He took this up in a letter to me from France during a long vacation. He was going onto a Soviet passport, and would I ask the British Home Office for leave for him to stay in England? I wrote that I would do so; but the Home Office would certainly require from me a pledge on his behalf that while in England he would not work for the overthrow of our own system of government by violence. To this he did not reply, but on his return he told me he could not give this pledge, so I left his relations with our Home Office to himself. While still with us, he attacked me violently in the press as a "mouth piece" of reaction. I took his political views as temperamental and did not reply.

At the end of the next session he went off to Russia, but it seems he arrived there just in time to come in for the elimination of the Trotskyites. We met in Moscow in 1935, on the stairs, so to speak, I coming in and he going out, and had a pleasant chat. At my next visit I found his quarters were sealed up; he was evidently in prison. I heard of him later as exiled to Siberia and conducting a provincial paper there, and again later that he had died in conditions of starvation. It was a thousand pities that his shining intellect should be lost.

## OTHER BRIGHT STARS OF THE SCHOOL

We had plenty of other highlights in the School. By the nature of things, with only communist views smiled upon in Russia, we had the pick of the emigrants, which, on the arts side, meant the flower of Russian scholarship. I found drudging at language teaching in London, Alexander Meyendorff, a European scholar, lecturer in peasant land law at Petersburg University and a vice-president of the Third Duma.

Meyendorff had had intellectually an unkind and lonely life. He was the one liberal-minded baron of distinction in the Baltics; most of them were stock reactionaries. When the Letts were practically excluded from the Duma by the crippling of the franchise in 1907, they told him they felt they would still be adequately represented by his presence. He could not even be sure whether he was a Russian or a German, for he had in him good blood from both races. In the Duma, as he told me before the Revolution, he could not sleep before making a speech; he seemed always to be asking himself whether his opponents might not be right. Yet in the debate of 1910, on the Bill which grievously curtailed the liberties of Finland, he made one of the best speeches in his life; and when the voting of all the clauses was taken on end, he stood up at his seat in the middle of the house, with his hands in his pockets, in undemonstrative opposition, which was the most telling protest against the whole Bill. He was, in fact, almost a martyr to objectivity. He was to have been Ambassador of the short-lived Provisional Government in London. We brought him up to a Readership in Russian Laws and Institutions, an appointment which we made the occasion for a great revel of the School. On the various academic bodies on which it was now his duty to sit, he was in himself a glorious reminder of the dignity and achievement of the old Russian scholarship.

Then there were our two bright and shining lights of language study, Jopson and Boyanus. I reckon that philologists may be divided into the live and the dead. Jopson is the livest that I have known. His enthusiasm might take him into the Spreewald, near Berlin, to hide somewhere to find out whether the vanishing Wends still talked their dying Slavic tongue when they thought they were alone. He had a wonderful broken-down car, which he drove, bending over the wheel, just as if he were correcting Language papers! I reckoned that the odds were 10 per cent that nothing would happen, 35 per cent that Jopson would be killed, and 55 per cent that he would kill someone else! Jopson was one of the most gifted and, if need be, humorous of translators. His one trouble was only that, packed with knowledge as he was, he could not sit down and put some of it on paper, so it was very hard, with scarcely any published work to show, to get him raised to a professorship. But no one who knew anything about the subject could be in any doubt of his brilliance; and almost the moment we had done this, Cambridge snatched him from us as professor of all comparative philology. In both wars, he served as the resourceful head of the Department of Uncommon Languages in the national censorship. And there he showed a courage which is not always seen in expert scholars when they pass under the stifling blanket of official subservience.

It was delightful when we were able to harness together in the language work of the School our own Jopson with Boyanus from Russia. Boyanus was the maker of by far the best Russian-English and English-Russian dictionaries.[1] In Russia he was professor of English philology and phonetics, and director of radio teaching of language. He was married to an Englishwoman, herself a distinguished scholar of

[1] Originally by Boyanus and Miller. The Bolsheviks, after their manner, dropped the name of Boyanus after he came to England.

phonetics; and he came to us, not as an emigrant, but with full permission of the Soviet government. We simply put him in reverse, to teach Russian to English students.

With his help we set up a fascinating class in idiom–in my view, the highest form of purely linguistic teaching. The class was composed of our language teachers and those of their students whom they recommended as worthy of such company. But in this class there was complete equality and no chairman. The task was to take this or that Russian idiom and find the closest English equivalent. Even "close" was not enough; in lively competition, we could generally find an almost exactly corresponding term in English; the judgment was by acclamation.

Thus for instance, "Bros'te" in Russian means literally "Throw"–but the real meaning is "Shut up!" Someone would suggest "Drop it," which got honorable commendation; but someone else, perhaps the junior of us all, would say "Chuck it!" and then we would all clap. Boyanus had once been a theatrical producer, and he sometimes used to illustrate the shades of difference by changes of face, gesture, and inflection.

When Hitler came into power, he spoilt all the work of Russian study in Germany (and how he was paid out for that!) Till then, under the lead of Professor Otto Hoetzsch, they were in front of us. Hoetzsch was himself thrown out, and wrote me an S.O.S. on behalf of two of his assistants, and we found room for both of them, Sergius Yakubson and Leo Loewenson. For our librarian we chose Yakubson, and Loewenson stood by and helped in various ways. Yakubson was a great strength to us. He was what I call "an attacking librarian," one who does not leave the initiative to the public but takes it himself. Poor Yakubson left Russia because he was not a Bolshevik; he was turned out of Germany because he was a Jew; he was marked for internment in England in the Second World War because he was regarded as a German alien; but he ultimately found a haven in the Library of Congress as a specialist on Russian affairs in the Congress, with recognition there of the valuable services which he rendered.

Other stars were meteors who only passed through our School. Roman Dyboski, foremost scholar of English literature in Poland, then in his prime despite his amazing adventures and privations as a war prisoner in Russia, was lent to us for a year and a term by the University of Cracow. Encyclopedic in knowledge, voracious of work, he seemed able to simplify the thorniest questions for foreign listeners. We were much entertained too by the Czech, Frantisék Chudoba, with his mischievous smile, who would put up the most unorthodox interpretations of the English Classics and then confirm them from unanswerable proofs. Our Polish scholars were always first class; we had none better than Waclaw Borowy of Warsaw. With us, all the Slavs worked together in the common cause of our studies, but we were not without those "incidents" which are proper to anything Slavic. Poor battered Vladimir King, deranged by the Russian revolution, hit Mirsky in the face, of all places in the sanctity of the reading room of the British Museum, to which our students had been given special rights of access. A crooked Polish scholar had to be deported for forging the signature of Seton-Watson to placate a landlord insisting on rent.

In this exhilarating atmosphere, the School owed its stability and progress to no one so much as to its Secretary, Dorothy Galton. She came to us almost as an invalid; my only general instruction to her was never to come to work when she did not feel up to it; but her virile intelligence and her absolute devotion helped her to shoulder labors which sometimes seemed almost insupportable. In the Second World War she was dividing the week between Oxford and London and organizing our work in both places. Out of all this devotion grew rare administrative gifts: a discriminating knowledge of all the values in this wide field of study, of the various personnel and organizations, and a clear judgment of how they could best be utilized. It was only a highly gratifying recognition of these qualities, when the Rockefeller Foundation selected her as the best expert in England on the subject, to visit the chief centres of these studies in America, and to report on the wisest directions to be followed in organizing collaboration in this field between the principal agencies in the two countries.

## THE *Slavonic Review*

In June, 1922, we founded our *Slavonic Review;* later, to include the non-Slavonic countries of Eastern Europe, such as Hungary and Finland, we extended the title to *"Slavonic and East European."* A witty critic of our ambitions in King's College suggested the omission of the word 'East'!

It was a gorgeous opportunity. The smaller countries, apart from their not very convincing propaganda, had no mouthpiece in English–and for their scholarship, none at all. In Russia, the restrictions of the press to Communist views left none to the better half of Russian scholarship in arts and to such historical material. All the while, we were salvaging materials which should on no account be lost and would be keenly sought after whenever Russia should again recognize freedom of press. We held reserves for the future use of Russian libraries; but they were all destroyed by a single German bomb that wrecked the store-rooms of the King's Printers, Eyre and Spottiswoode.

We published three numbers a year, one in each university term, each of about 250 pages. It was a delightful task, not really spoiled by the furious editorial fights over the make-up of each number. We had the whole Slavonic world at our disposal, a world that is so specially near to nature with an infinite variety of materials of all kinds, and the only question was what to exclude; so that there was no doubt about being able to maintain the highest standard. Seton had a good share of that attitude which, in my view, wrecked the Versailles settlement, the arithmetic which counts each nation as one, whether great or small. The first question is, what is a nation; Scotland, as she is not independent, presumably is not one; but one wobbly Rumanian, who has to do exactly what outside pressure demands, counts by this reckoning for 10 or more Americans! We could never have squeezed Russia into the size of Slovakia; but there was no real need for me to be anxious, for in practice, the Russian side took good care of itself, if only by the wealth and quality of its resources. And in so many other matters we were absolutely agreed.

After a while, we began regularly with literature–if possible with a really good verse translation of a whole block of Slavonic poetry. Of course, one has no right to expect of any verse translations better than good second class. There is *one* English translation from Pushkin which Pushkin might himself have acknowledged. It is of the most inspired poem that he wrote, *The Prophet,* reproduced in its full inspiration by Maurice Baring.[1] But later, when we also had American help, we did some kind of justice to world poets not otherwise accessible, the Russian Pushkin or, equally magnificent, the Pole, Mickiewicz.

As I had charge of this section, this involved for me a very pleasant correspondence. Our best source of supply was the splendid school of Slavic verse translation built up in the University of California by that fine scholar and most lovable colleague, George R. Noyes. He had the sternest standards for himself as for others, and at the same time a perfect selflessness. Those are the qualities which really build up a school. For a given task, he would associate with himself a

---

[1] Reprinted in the *Slavonic Review*, Vol. XII, No. 34, p. 1.

student, to whom he always gave the chief credit. I too shared in this association with him though at very long range, from London to California, so that we always had to start operations months in advance and every letter had to be answered immediately on its receipt. This co-operation was much easier than it might seem. We could easily put on a single sheet of paper, with the references, our various questions and suggestions. That brilliant verse translator in our field, Professor Watson Kirkconnell, of McMaster University in Ontario, long before I came to know him personally, used to allow me this same pleasant form of literary duet. Our British end was chiefly held up by, Oliver Elton, who was giving all these late years to Slavonic verse translation; but there were also others who did very good work. Avraham Yarmolinsky, the scholarly keeper of Slavic books in the public library of New York, let us reprint the masterly version of Blok's tremendous poem "The Twelve" by himself and his gifted wife, Babette Deutsch. One enterprise which we found particularly interesting was the production of a really good English version of that great Hungarian classic, "The Life of Man" by Madach, which with a certain latitude might be described as a Hungarian "Faust."

On the prose side, the enterprising Jopson found us all sorts of little pieces, grave or gay, which included even a fair representation of Albanian literature. Of the others, I liked best the Polish prose romances and the Serbian tales of adventure. In this section, we all agreed to put a premium on the smaller nations, as there seemed to be no other way in which their literatures could become known to the Anglo-Saxon world. We always asked our foreign contributors of articles to let us do the translation. We had our own standards, and we thought no one should translate out of his own language, but only into it.

In our choice of articles we always, so to say, preferred a piece of meat to a hash. We published few general surveys, and those only of small unknown literatures, but many special studies, always by someone who had specialized in them. We were very glad to announce his existence to our public and often it did really help him. For that reason we liked to introduce some quite unknown aspirant to honor, preferably just at the time when he had completed a Ph.D. degree, but certainly not just a piece of it. It was as if we said: "Here's something new to you! Here's So and So! He's working at so and so! Watch him!" With this way of choosing our articles, I found our *Review* invaluable in my own teaching. To take a problem which was inherent in Russian thought and was constantly confronting one–who and what were the Slavophils?–I would say to my student: "Read the article on Ivan Kireyevsky by Henry Lanz of Stanford and you will know."

I can try to give an idea of the ground which we covered by naming some of the articles which we published, mainly on the Russian side:

"The English Rediscovery of Russia," by Inna Lybimenco, the principal explorer of the archives concerned
"The Liberal Movement in Russia," by Rodichev
two brilliant sketches of Professors Klyuchevsky and Vinogradov by one of their most brilliant pupils, Basil Maklakov, and one of the charming literary biographer Gershenson
a financial study, by the ex-Premier and Finance Minister, Count Kokovtsev
one on Lord Carnock (Sir Arthur Nicolson) by his colleague Lord Onslow
sketches of Dmowski (by Kozicki) and of Pilsudski (by Polyakov)
several able military articles by General Golovin
portraits of Lenin (one by Maurice Dobb) and two articles by Peter Struve on his contacts with him

a sound study of the Agrarian Revolution of 1917 by a
Ph.D. student from Australia, Lancelot A. Owen, and
a remarkably sagacious article by a young Russian,
Prince A. Lobanov-Rostovsky, now professor at Michi-
gan, entitled "Russian at the Crossroads"

Kolchak, by his Chief of Staff, Admiral Smirnov

"Russia's Crisis in the Far East" by the Siberian Duma
member, Vostrotin

"The Communist League of Youth," a most sympathetic
sketch by the socialist writer, Kuskova

"State Planning in Russia" by one who took part in it,
Jacob Miller

two studies of collective farming by Sir John Maynard and
Sir John Russell

Professor Chernavin's prison experiences in Solovyetsk

Yaroslavsky's speeches and instructions in the campaign
against religion

Soviet Law, by Dr. Freund

"The Last Words" of Radek and Bukharin in their trials;
and, as already mentioned, Russian documents in the
British museum by the famous scholar of revolutionary
history, Vladimir Burtsev.

We printed documents, and latterly we had published in
each number some twelve pages of Soviet legislation, in accurate translation, without any kind of comment–only the reference and the date. These were nothing less than invaluable.
If only they could have been read at the time when we published them in England and–still more desirable–in America,
far fewer people would be ten or even twenty years late in
their knowledge of what was going on in Soviet Russia. We
had also a Russian Chronicle. This could not be so completely satisfactory; we had a wide choice of sources, but the
best was the news gleaned from a very thorough survey of
the Soviet press in Paris under the wise and wholly objective

direction of Paul B. Anderson of the American YMCA, who has a profound understanding of things Russian, visible and invisible. Our section of reviews, I must say at once, was never properly organized and was only redeemed by the contributions of the brilliant Seton. The obituaries were better, but alas! how many I had to write myself! In all, we published fifty-two numbers which, with obvious gaps, amounted to a small Slavonic encyclopedia.

## THE *Review* ON RUSSIAN RELIGION

As at least some kind of substitute for direct intercourse, the *Review* did help us to keep in contact with certain sides of life in Soviet Russia; in particular, with one which was a stumbling-block to any real understanding with the Anglo-Saxon world.

After the all-out frontal attack, which culminated in the religious trials of Easter 1923 and the martyrdom of Monsignor Budkiewicz, the Bolsheviks themselves realized that only indirect attack would have any success. They did smash church organization for all forms of religious belief, and they did successfully stop the training of clergy. That is why, with a number of friends and with the active support of Dr. Lang, Archbishop of Canterbury, we countered on the only ground left to us, with the maintenance of the one free college of Russian theological training and study, the House of St. Sergius, in Paris, which task we shared with the American YMCA, splendidly represented by Paul Anderson.

Sergius Bulgakov, son of a priest, was originally a leading Communist thinker and Professor of Economics in Moscow University. He had an extraordinary conversion to Christianity, which was in detail singularly like that of St. Paul. Under the Bolsheviks he became a priest. He remained one of the finest of all Russian thinkers; when he was expelled from Russia, he became Professor of Dogmatic Theology in the House of St. Sergius, of which he was the chief inspiration. I asked him to write for me a forecast of the future of religion in Russia. This he had already done in a theological essay on Judas Iscariot. He had seen both sides of the story, and he was absolutely fair to both. He dismissed all attempts to defend the purity of the history of the churches. In the Communist faith he saw first a passionate missionary zeal to make the world better for those who can do little for themselves, the children, the cripples, the aged and infirm, and in this he saw the same purpose that we understand under the motto of the Kingdom of God on earth. These ideas he had outlined in the epilogue to his treatise, under the title, "Judas or Saul," which gave us one of the most inspiring articles that we published.[1]

Another gem came to us in a different way. Professor Misheyev, when flying from Bolshevist Russia, was sheltered, like so many others, by the independent peasantry in the province of Archangel. They had in their village one of those "tellers," often an old woman, who recited from memory the heroic ballads, reputed to come from the old Russia of the Kiev period. It is a striking sign of the unity of the country that these ballads born in South Russia, have been best preserved far away in the extreme north. Misheyev was taken to hear an old peasant lady of eighty give some of these ballads, which were only committed to paper in the seventeenth century. She recited several of them, and then paused for a few moments in an impressive silence. Then, beginning again with a short quatrain of peasant wisdom, she went on with a new heroic ballad of the twentieth century, which she had herself made under Bolshevist rule. It preserved the crude realism of the original ballads, together with their traditional characters: the Virgin Mary, who was identical with Mother Earth, the Archangel Michael, St. George, patron of Russia, the typical peasant hero Ilya Muro-

[1] *Slavonic Review*, Vol. IX, No. 27, p. 525, March, 1931.

mets, the typical townbred son of challenge and of venture, Vaska Buslayev. The new ballad told how religion came back to Russia. We translated it with its rough and various rhythm into Saxon English. After publishing it in our *Review* we sent the original to the House of St. Sergius to be put in its archives. The Metropolitan, writing to thank us, said, "This tells us that the old source is not dried up." [1]

## Archibald Cary Coolidge

In 1924 I was invited to teach for a semester at Berkeley in the lovely climate of California under the happy leadership of George Noyes. He had turned his faculty into a little family, where colleagues and their wives were all on Christian names. Berkeley had got its eyes on the Pacific and the countries beyond, and with a strong competitor close by in an equally vigorous school at Stanford, California was getting ready for the time when the lights should be turned on in that far part of the world. This, of course, was to happen at Pearl Harbor in 1941.

I was hoping to knit up close relations with American scholars. Our common interest was self-evident. In the same language, English, we were studying the same countries, and any piece of good work was as valuable on one side of the Atlantic as on the other. Also close relations between us would help us all-round, especially if we wanted to approach the Russian authorities to open their door, which stood barred against our students.

Of course, my first visit after landing in America was to Harvard, which had the pre-eminence in these studies, chiefly through the scholarship and personality of Archibald Coolidge, who was Professor of History and then Director (and indeed creator) of the Widener library. So far I only knew him by reputation, and I found in him one of the most

[1] *Slavonic Review*, Vol. XIII, No. 38, p. 251.

lovable characters and generous colleagues that I have known. He was the most modest of great scholars. At the dinner with which he welcomed me at the Harvard Club, with its delightful wainscoting and magnificent grate, he put his brilliant pupil, Robert Howard Lord, in the chair; and when a question on Russia was addressed to him, he would refer it to me saying, "Professor Pares probably knows more about this," which was generally quite untrue. Next day Coolidge, Lord and I established full connections. I offered house-room in our *Review* to American scholars till they should have one of their own; and on Coolidge's recommendation all the prominent Americans scholars in this field accepted our offer. "Archie's word goes," they said.

Coolidge was the gentlest of teachers. When he showed me any of the best American work in our subjects, he never explained its merits, but left it to me to find them out for myself. It was so with Leo Wiener's useful anthology of historical Russian literature, and with William Langer's scholarly book notes in Coolidge's periodical "Foreign Affairs," which were such a vast improvement on our own.

On my way back to England, I was invited to take part in the hectic midsummer discussions of everything in heaven and earth at the Institute of Williamstown, and we had no less than thirteen meetings on Russia alone. Here was Sidney B. Fay, who took the opposite view to mine on the responsibilities of various governments for the First World War; he put far less of them on Germany and much more on Russia. Fay, sportsman that he was, invited me to put my views to the students of his seminar; and Coolidge, thinking I might need support on the opponent's ground, took a train from Boston to reinforce me by his presence. We had one other question to settle. We needed to bring into line for the Anglo-Saxon world, as far as possible, the transliteration of the Russian alphabet; and in an afternoon walk we easily came to an agreement. It was Coolidge who had devised the system for the Library of Congress, and each of us had only to make one small concession.

Coolidge nominated three Russian scholars to act as "contributing editors" in America for our *Review;* they asked for the word "contributing" because necessarily the choice of material and the make-up had to be left to one side of the ocean or the other. He himself wrote the short introductory statement in our next number inaugurating the co-operation.[1] In 1940, in the Second World War, when conditions made all publication very difficult in England, we simply transferred our *Review* for the time being to Harvard, where it was chivalrously continued under Coolidge's successor, the late Professor Samuel H. Cross.

Coolidge was himself on the fringe of diplomacy. He went four times round the world. I think he did more than anyone else to introduce into the United States the serious and organized study of unknown countries, and it was probably due to his life work that at the treaty-making in Versailles, the British representatives found themselves bound to recognize with respect the high standard of the American delegation, in which Coolidge took part.

[1] December, 1929, Vol. III, No. 8.

# CHAPTER IX

## The New Russia
### (1920–1939)

### HIDE AND SEEK

### Shulgin's Daring Journey [1]

BASIL SHULGIN always appealed to me, though I did not share his views. As a convinced and highly intelligent young monarchist, he might have felt rather lonely in the very revolutionary Duma of 1907, but, being a sportsman he relished this piquant experience. From the tribune, he told the Lefts that he enjoyed making acquaintance with them, and then humorously asked: "But you don't happen to have a bomb in your pocket?" He was called to order by the over-serious Liberal president.

Shulgin, as the best of the Rights, played an important part in 1915, in bringing together all the reforming parties in the so-called "Progressive Block," which for the first time gave the Duma a stable majority. His mind and manner reminded me very much of a young Arthur Balfour. He wrote far the most lively and objective account of the months preceding the revolution, giving a wonderfully graphic picture of its four hectic days, when the House was invaded by the Soviet and the Duma members slept anywhere on a bench

[1] Shulgin published his account of this journey in the *Slavonic Review*, Vol. VI, No. 18, p. 505, March, 1928.

or a chair. He was absolutely fair to political opponents; and he has given us the best account of Kerensky at his best, at that time when everyone else felt the ground giving way under him. Shulgin was sent with Guchkov to get the abdication of Nicholas II. His presence alone would be a convincing proof that there was no alternative, and it is his account of that historic scene that will always stand. With Shulgin, difference of opinions made no difference to friendship. He once wrote to me that he particularly enjoyed having in me a friend in an opposite camp.

Shulgin fought with the "Whites" and had to go into exile. As one of the ablest of the emigrants he was invited, with a very few others, to meet a man named Yakushev who had come out of Russia to report on underground work there against the Bolsheviks. Shulgin was greatly impressed by Yakushev. This man spoke with a courage and hope which seemed new to the emigrant leaders. This was the time of the retreat of communism during the NEP. The work was going very well he said, and if any of his hosts cared to come and see for themselves, he thought they would share his opinion. He would offer a fifty-fifty chance of a safe return.

Shulgin had a son who had got lost somewhere in Russia, and he accepted this offer. He was instructed to come through the "windows," that is, with one of the bands of smugglers who made their way across at some point of that interminable land frontier. Though it would not be fair to describe him as a Jew-baiter, he had had political conflicts with the Jews, and with a stroke of his natural humor he decided to grow a little beard and disguise himself as a Jew.

It was an exciting enterprise. His guides negotiated the risky journey through the forest with great skill and brought him successfully to his native Kiev in December, 1925. They lodged him in a quiet suburb, and someone came and stood outside when he could go abroad safely. At one time he was chased and nearly caught, but with care he could see all he wanted to see. He had sharp eyes, and made good use of them. Changing his disguise to that of a small Soviet Commissary, he was taken on to Moscow, and then for a flying visit to Leningrad.

In Moscow, he was told there seemed a chance of finding his son; and he was given that rare thing, a sleeping car ticket, for a train journey. In Russia trains often stop without any particular reason. At such a halt between two stations an irregular passenger entered the carriage. Shulgin was alone. The new arrival sat down opposite him and took out of his pocket one of Shulgin's own books, which he began to read. After a while, he hailed Shulgin by name, and engaged him in a fascinating conversation which covered all the questions of the greatest interest. At another unscheduled halt, the strange intruder disappeared.

It was now high time for Shulgin to get away. But first, the organizers of his journey had some long and earnest talks with him at their conspirative headquarters. "Had they guarded him satisfactorily?" they asked. "Wonderfully," he said. "Did he trust them?" "Absolutely." "Would he help them?" "Of course, but how?" "Could he put them in contact with centres of the 'Whites' abroad?" "Yes." "Could he collect money for them? They were sadly short of it." "Certainly, he would try." "And would he write a book on his visit?" "Well, he hadn't thought of that—wouldn't it compromise them?" "Oh no, not at all—he could send it first to their secret address, and they would cut out anything risky."

It was at this point that I came into the matter. The book was duly written and translated; it was very clever. The title was "Three Capitals," (Kiev, Moscow, and Leningrad), and Shulgin wrote to me asking if I could find an English publisher. Anything from Shulgin would be fresh and charming reading, and Jonathan Cape accepted gladly. At this point there was a delay, and then came a note from Shulgin asking me to call the whole thing off. It turned out that his journey, from start to finish, had been organized and carried

out by the Bolsheviks themselves. His book had been revised
in OGPU, and they had even offered him a royalty!

Yakushev had indeed originally been an anti-Soviet underground agent in Russia, and had made contacts with the
"Whites" abroad on a previous journey. There, in Germany,
an incautious letter from an emigrant to him had been inter-
cepted by the communists; and on his return he was arrested
and ordered, under the strongest possible compulsion, to continue his foreign trips in the interests of the "Reds." He only
consented to do this because he regarded the emigrants as
having betrayed him, and he would not give away the names
of any of his fellow-workers in Russia. Now the whole story
came out, and "the windows" were closed. It seems to have
been touch and go whether Shulgin would be allowed to
come back; but the organizers maintained with good reason
that they had made quite a good enough job of it in the
interest of their present employers.

### "Whom the Gods Love"—

Acting as External Examiner in Russian for the Honors
Degree at Cambridge, I concurred readily in granting a first
class to Gareth Vaughan Jones. He was a distant kinsman,
but the delightful charm of this bright and lovable Welsh boy
brought him much nearer to me than that. He never looked
anything like his full age; he had a quick, keen, clever mind
and was entirely open and simple in manner. One was full
of hope for his future.

When he had finished at Cambridge, Gareth came to
work with me at our London School for a Ph.D. on the history of the Russian Press, but he was also engaged by Mr.
Lloyd George to write for him what they called "briefs" on
current opinion in Europe, as ascertained from press materials. Gareth had many other languages besides Russian.
These "briefs" came back to him with Lloyd George's mark-

ings, which were simple but original. Gareth travelled with Hitler and Goebbels on their plane during the German election of 1931; he did not think Goebbels looked very Aryan. Lloyd George was as fond of him as I was, and would say on his return from such a trip, "We must open a fresh bottle of champagne for Gareth."

This brilliant boy made two outstanding journeys to Russia, where he was at first very acceptable. He would carry on him as much condensed food as he could and simply go roving. It was impossible not to like him; one of his many attractions was his singing of Welsh songs. When talking to young men of his own age in Russia, he would ask the usual questions and get the regulation answers. Then he would smile, and the Russian boys would also smile, and a real conversation would follow. They would sometimes touch his clothes with surprise, and ask if it was really possible to get such things in starving England. The most important paper in Wales gave him a commission to travel, interview, and write as he pleased at its expense.

Once after his return from Russia, I was entertaining to tea at the School Mr. Ivy Lee, publicity agent for the Rockefellers. Mr. Lee had also just returned from Russia, but I thought it unlikely that he would have seen as much as Gareth, so I asked Gareth to meet him. When we were alone again, Mr. Lee asked me, how much I thought Mr. Llyod George gave to Gareth; I guessed about £400 a year. "What nonsense!" said Mr. Lee. Soon afterwards Gareth was at the end of the 'phone. "Mr. Lee has offered me a thousand a year," he said. His American earnings he spent for the most part in helping to buy a house for his parents, who were devoted to their only son.

Gareth never forgot those who helped him; I always had news of his last enterprise. In this way, I learned that Russia was now closed to him. He had run into a local famine, and on his return to Moscow he had been outspoken on the way the authorities had handled it. But Russia was everything to him. As for me, I saw in him the best successor to my own work.

Gareth tried to make his way in through "the back door" by way of Mongolia. The Chinese authorities warned him that they could not guarantee his safety, and he held them absolved. He was captured by bandits, who demanded a high ransom. Gareth, we heard, delighted them with his Welsh singing. But the Japanese were in hot pursuit of them. Hurried along at a hectic pace, Gareth in the end found that he could ride no longer, and so—on the spur of the moment as it appears [1]—the bandits shot him. He was one day short of his thirtieth birthday; I learned of his death from a newspaper poster, while passing from one station to another in London. With those bright gifts of heart and mind, and with a judgment which was at once quick and just, how invaluable he would have been to us later!

## LIGHTS HALF SEEN

Both for Harper and for myself, though we were now working apart, the uprooting of all we had done with the dissolution of the first two Dumas was nothing to the revolution. Now all the landmarks were gone without exception: all the foundations were dissolved or covered by one great waste of water. A clear sheet, in which at first only destruction seemed evident.

It looked as if all the seams of character were loosened. Happy anyone who could be sure of his neighbor. One of the

---

[1] That the end must almost certainly have come this way, was confirmed to me in 1945 by Mr. Owen Lattimore. This distinguished Far Eastern scholar and traveller was close to the scene of the tragedy later, and knowing the languages and habits of these parts, was able to give me a much clearer picture of Gareth's end. The bandits were continually chased by Japanese troops from place to place, which often deprived them of access to their favorite enjoyment, opium, and at such times their actions were very summary.

finest of Russian scholars, who had stayed on to serve in Russia, meeting me in a London hotel said: "And now I don't know how I'm going to meet my son" (who had joined the emigration), and as we changed seats more than once even there, to get away from inquisitive neighbors, he said: "I'm used to this!" In Russia, I was told, when a train stopped, all conversation automatically stopped too.

The backwash of the Russian dispersion covered all the world from Europe, through America to China. In those days I used to seek out anything familiar, my old school for instance, and took comfort to find it was still there. In Canada or the States one was comforted too in finding such a large part of the world in which the names were in English.

As to relief of Russian distress, the task seemed hopeless. The whole of what was called society, including the professional classes, had been reduced to beggary, so that they could not help each other; and in the days of Anglo-Russian friendship every house had been open to me! This top layer of Russian society, which had so easily been uprooted, once it was detached, seemed something very frail and weak. One thing it still had, and that was dignity. The women, pretty well everywhere, were better than the men, and especially the old ladies. There was Harold Williams' aged mother-in-law, now over ninety, who had stayed on in Russia after all the rest of the family and came out with a better understanding and a firmer faith in her country than all the rest. When Harold's coffin was twined in the old national colors, and escorted by nearly the whole Russian colony in London to the cemetery, the old lady sat on alone there after all had departed: "Why couldn't it have been me?" she said. These old high-bred Russian families had often kept their English governess as a sort of eldest daughter long after the children had grown up; and it was now that the English Miss could show her mettle. The names over a milliner's shop in London read: "Varya and Miss Green." Countess Heyden was still Varya and Miss Green, her old governess, was still Miss Green.

As to Russia itself, it seemed like an infinite wilderness of scenes in patches with no cohesion and no end.

My dear old friend Andrew Shingarev lay dying in his bed in the prison hospital in Petrograd, where he had been bayoneted by hooligans on the day of the forcible dispersion of the long awaited Constituent Assembly. His only crime was that he was a Liberal; and watching him as he grew in stature in the last three Dumas I believed I might some day see in him a Prime Minister of a Liberal Russia. He was the author of a widely successful system of public health; at every budget of the Dumas he was the unfailing champion of the peasantry. The last book he was reading was the *Tale of Two Cities* by Dickens. He had written that if he had to start public life again, he would follow the same good course. Lenin himself, I am told, deplored the shame of his death.

It was little Mr. H. V. Kaeling, wiry British trade unionist, trained lithographer and sportsman (he might have been another William Pickford) who told me the details of Shingarev's end. Engaged by the Tsar's Ministry of Education before the revolution, he learned Russian perfectly from his workmen and peasant friends. It was in the peasants' country homes that he found health and character. When pay and food stopped, he escaped on skis to Finland. Enticed back, he was thrown into prison and went through the usual midnight police examinations. Kaeling took a pride in answering the endless questions with spirit, and when a sympathetic questioner (there would usually be one in Russia) asked him how he did it, he exploded the company by answering cheerily: "Oh that's all right I've been married for sixteen years!"

Then there was the equally wiry little war correspondent Francis McCullagh. Captured by the Bolsheviks in Siberia, he concealed his military identity as Capt. McCullagh of the Worcestershire Regt. and claiming his rights as a well known pre-war reporter in Russia, actually interviewed the assassin of the Tsar, who, of all things, had been pensioned off as a life insurance agent! He too went through the ordeal of the midnight questioning: his shorthand had been almost completely deciphered by the Cheka. After the communist retreat of 1921, having rendered some journalistic service to Trotsky, he was allowed to return, only just in time for the preparations for the great campaign against religion of 1922-3. McCullagh was a keen Catholic. He took a shorthand report of the trial of the Catholic clergy, recording their firm refusal to cease teaching children under eighteen; and when Lieut. Krylenko, the public prosecutor, obtained the death sentence for Monsignor Budkiewicz, which was carried out on Good Friday 1923, McCullagh carried all his evidence safely out of Russia. The indignation in all civilized countries (it was not long after the Soviet's conclusion of trade treaties) was enough to break off the intended trial, on the same count, of the Russian Patriarch Tikhon in the following week. The Patriarch was set free; but his health was broken. In this strange world of contradictions it was another friend of mine, a nephew of the great Russian prophet of Anarchism, Bakunin, with his wife conducting a surgery on communist principles of equality, who in spite of official discouragement cared for the Patriarch till his death. When they urged him to rest, he would reply, "There will be time enough to rest. The night will be long! The night will be dark"!

An old English friend, visiting a group of Christians in Moscow, tried to comfort them by saying that their ordeal must soon be over. "No," they said, "we have not yet suffered enough." In the State prison of Solovetsk in the Arctics, a number of exiled bishops, returning to the apostolic vocation of fishermen, joined every morning in the Eucharist. We managed to get through some food supplies even there.

I had lived with Russia so close and so long that it could not be otherwise now; and every now and then something new recalled something old and things or parts of things seemed to join on together again and to present some wider kind of perspective. No personal griefs or losses could be allowed to disturb the picture. I had to look at Shingarev and the rest as friends who had gone down in the war. It was the only way. The old top layer was gone for good. On the other hand, it was always quite clear that Russia would last much longer than any of the changing phases of communist experiment. In this sense, it was very literally true that the things that were seen were temporal and the things that were unseen were eternal.

The two things which had most of the eternal about them were Russian religion and the Russian people. And the two went always together; for, as I have said, in Russia it is impossible to get away from the other world; in this sense the attempt to drive the instinct of faith from the Russian mind–always from the first a misunderstanding–was foredoomed to failure. It was quite truly a confusion between Christ and Anti-Christ: that was the sense of the new Heroic Legend of the old peasant woman of Archangel, brought back by Professor Misheyev: "The State had got wrong with the community and it had dragged the Church along with it." Both had to be put back right with the community. How could the barren gospel of Pobedonostsev, still less the rule of the foul Rasputin over the Church, be taken to be what they claimed to represent? The Church was being purged, and thus brought back to the people. What should have been its social program was now on the other side; indeed, as Bulgakov wrote in his "Judas or Saul," "This will of the communists to a better world will not be held by God to shame." He wrote to me from a concentration camp in Russia: "With all this some of the priests falter; but those who endure in prison and poverty are tempered and illumined to great beauty, and anyhow there are martyrs to speak for Russia before the throne of God."

How would it all end? Here was a determined group of a few keen thinkers, rigid in their austerity yet capable of every kind of pliability in practice, trying to implant their new lesson as they first saw it. And each of the great drives was followed by a steady drift of the public away from what they taught. I was waiting for a synthesis when they would discover how much of their program they could realize and the public would recognize how much it could accept.

The peasants were throughout more intelligible to me, as they had always been. They were doing just about what would have been expected, going their own way and fending off intrusion as far as they could. They were an ocean in which Bolshevik propaganda seemed to drown; so did the early state farms of Lenin, incompetently manned and unintelligent of their surroundings. Once it was clear that the new rulers did not stand for peasant property, there was a ring of peasant risings all around Moscow. My Robert Smith, born and bred of British parents in Russia, who when I first met him in 1912 could hardly pronounce his own name in English, a thin tubercular scholar sent from Moscow University to the Crimean Riviera–when the German troops came through there, felt in his British bones that this was no place for him and trekked in 1918 clean through Russia from end to end, to Archangel; and his only difficulty was to persuade the friendly peasants that he was not an advance agent of some Bolshevik punitive expedition, come to confiscate their grain. All our friends lost their estates; but peasants hearing they were short of food would bring supplies all the way to Moscow; and they would entertain members of the family revisiting the old home with the greatest friendliness, only explaining "Now it's we are the owners." This is the picture that we got from Anton Karlgren, a Danish professor who like Harper and myself had visited rural Russia year by year before the revolution and now gave us the first view of the peasants' victory, won at the cost of five millions who had

starved in the great famines of 1921-1922. The communist
hand relaxed its hold, because the communist plans did not
work. In the seven years that followed there was a long drawn
rest from the pressure while the country recovered in its own
old way. This was the period of the so-called Kulaks, which
simply meant competent and thrifty farmers now allowed
once more to hire labor and use machinery. They were the
masters of the situation and were in a position to block the
supplies of the starving towns. Through all this period access
was much easier. I was well informed, and it seemed as if
common sense was winning of itself. I was enabled to regain
some contact with the cooperators of Siberia, who might have
been taken as representatives of the whole peasant mass. They
had enough freedom to go their own way, to succeed in
persuading some of their exiled colleagues in England to return. It was a most fascinating spectacle. On the one side all
the resources of power; on the other human nature defend-
ing itself as best it could. This was the time when it was said
in Russia that the corpse was proving stronger than the
surgeon.

From this time onward the best of our news came
through American reporters. England had recognized the
Soviet Government in 1924 but was engaged in constant
wrangle over breach of engagements and the use of trading
facilities for Communist propaganda. America had yet to give
recognition, and it was as if the American pressman had
therefore more to offer. But to settle down, go where one
pleased and get to know Russia was still almost impossible.
No one came as near to it as Albert Rhys Williams who did
manage to stray about for long periods among the Soviet
villagers. Walter Duranty filled the gap in Moscow as best
he could. William Chamberlain, in his twelve arduous years
of study, passed beyond journalism and produced a valuable
history of the Revolution. But we had still to wait for one
who could confront the present with the past til the return

of Samuel Harper, whose *Civic Training in Russia* is the
high mark of American scholarship in this period. Later we
were to profit very directly from the experience of young
American technicians who shared in the actual work of the
Five Year Plan. Unique among American contributions was
the work of Maurice Hindus, whose brilliantly poignant pictures of the life of his own village under Communist rule
made the Russian peasant accessible and even audible to us.

## THE BRITISH GENERAL STRIKE

In September 1925, the British Trades Union Council
held its annual Congress at Scarborough in Yorkshire. The
most important of the guests received as "fraternal delegates"
was Comrade Tomsky, head of the Soviet Trades Unions. A
prolonged coal dispute of the British miners was in progress,
and the miners called urgently for support of the T.U.C.
We can hardly be wrong in crediting to Tomsky's advice the
program adopted at Scarborough. The T.U.C. claimed the
allegiance of all manual workers for any move which it might
make.

Having so long known the Prime Minister, Mr. Baldwin,
I called on him. He was comparatively free and ready for a
talk on Russia, but I had only one thing to say to him–that
the T.U.C. program exactly followed the tactics by which the
Bolsheviks had won through in Russia, when they took as
their motto "All Power to the Soviets!" It would simultaneously immobilize all activities throughout the country, and
the T.U.C. would thereby come into power, which of course
would mean a deprival of equal citizenship for everyone
else. As "Punch" put it, in a proposed new version of the
refrain of "Rule, Britannia!"–

> Serve, Britannia! Serve the T.U.C.
> And Britons never, never, never shall be free.

The test came in May, 1926, when the T.U.C. called a general strike. We all went to bed on a Sunday night, knowing of the T.U.C. threat and ultimatum; we did not know very much of the Government's preparations for defense. Anticipating a complete hold-up of traffic, I had come in from my house ten miles away, so that, if necessary, I could walk to my work at King's College in the Strand.

It seems that pretty well everyone else was thinking just the same thing. On that Monday, when the streets ought presumably to have been empty but for the followers of the T.U.C. I saw one of the most wonderful and inspiring sights of my life. Everyone, like myself, was instinctively walking to his work. The streets were thronged with cars all moving into the center; almost any car would give you a lift. Practically all our 2,000 students arrived duly at King's College; of the large staff of teachers I think only two could not get there. Our Engineering Department was at once mobilized to help replace the strikers on the tubes (subways), and so well did they do their job that those whom they replaced began to doubt whether they would be wanted back. One of our boys went to Waterloo terminus as a porter. In front of him was an old gentleman, burdened with heavy luggage. "Don't you want a porter, Sir?" asked our boy. The old gentleman turned around and said indignantly, "I *am* a porter!"

The whole episode was like the very best of the war; all its spirit and humor, and none of the killing. The community instinct returned at once, and there was a conquering atmosphere of good temper. A street block in one of the poorer parts in the East End was opened up, not by police or troops, but by the Rugby Football scrum, brought up from Mr. Baldwin's old university, Cambridge, who amid general amusement, with no other weapon than their hefty weight, pushed their way through. My brother, Lance, in charge of a brewery in South Wales, was completely surrounded by a whole population of miners on strike. They sent in a deputation to tell him, he would be allowed to go on brewing if he put on each of his lorries, the permit notice of the T.U.C. He told them quite quietly that he couldn't possibly do that. There was a pause. He knew very well that the last thing the strikers would stop would be the brewing of beer. It is related that the deputation came out from the brewery wiping their mouths and saying, "It's all right, beer is food." With British chivalry, they continued to supply him with coal throughout the strike.

It was the victory of the ordinary citizen who, by simply going on with his work, made any class or party triumph impossible. On the other side, the strike order had been very loyally obeyed, and the strikers were waiting for further instructions. But none came. The next step must be to violence, and none were less anxious to embark on that challenge than the sober and law-abiding Labor leaders themselves. Their objective was quite different; it was to get a majority in parliament by our traditional methods and come into power that way. The whole event was out of date in England; for in a class sense, Labor had already "arrived." The one side in the dispute was as bourgeois as the other. Consequently, the loyal strikers were left stranded. There was nothing for them to do; and the way they filled in the time, was the most humorous comment on the whole performance. In several big towns, they played impromptu football matches against the police, who were also not too heavily burdened with extra work. No games were ever more correct or polite. In Plymouth, where the strikers won by two goals to one, the chief constable's wife was invited to kick off!

Mr. Baldwin and his government carefully refrained from all provocation; indeed, that was the Premier's strength throughout, and it was the reason why in this time of confusion, he was three times elected by the population to his high office. But he had a very firm grip on the situation. Troops

.were there, and every one knew it. The radio was entirely in government hands, and even in spite of its limitations, it was successful in replacing the practically complete absence of the press. At least all the main facts were known, and false rumors were stifled at birth. The final scene, which by a special stroke of wisdom was relayed to the public, was the best anticlimax of all. The Chairman of the T.U.C. visited the Premier and simply called off the strike, and the Premier simply shook hands. They did no more than follow the ritual of the improvised football matches.

When Herbert Smith, sturdy Yorkshire miner, had led an early labor deputation to Moscow, Lenin said to him, "You must have a heavy civil war." Mr. Smith seems to have greatly resented a foreign dictation of our "civil war." Mr. Purcell, who led another deputation, was told by the foreign commissary, Chicherin, that the Soviet Government refused police protection to one of the British interpreters, Mr. Mc-Donell, who as once a British consul in the Caucasus, knew Russian and quite a lot about Russia. Mr. Purcell replied "If Mr. McDonell goes back, we all go back." It's no use saying that kind of thing to British Trade Unionists.

So here was the civil war, right enough, but it was in the wrong place, not in England, but in Moscow. The British General Strike had come at the very peak of the bitter fight between Trotsky, the advocate of "permanent revolution," and Stalin, the champion of a policy of construction and national defense, and above all of common sense; and our strike played a very important part in this duel. Radek, the brilliant columnist of *Pravda,* wrote that the fiasco in England was worse than a bomb. The arch-revolutionary Zinoviev lost his place at the head of the Third International. Trotsky has claimed to have found in the British Strike, ammunition for his charge against Stalin of betraying the revolution. But it was Stalin who won through.

## An Incident in New York

In 1929, just after the expulsion of Trotsky from Russia, I was in New York, having come over to renew the American connections of our School, and in an incident of my visit I saw another index of the transition which was going on in Moscow.

A trade deputation had come over from Russia; their program being presumably to get credits and, if possible, the recognition of the Soviet Government. They were entertained at dinner by the Council of Foreign Affairs, and a personal friend took me with him as his guest.

After the dinner the Head of the Soviet State Bank, Mr. Scheinmann, was asked to address us. He spoke in French and did not raise any controversial question. We were then invited to put questions to him, and his Russian interpreter would translate the answers. In the interpreter's answer to one question, I noticed the omission of an important word. I leaned across the table and, addressing Mr. Scheinmann in Russian, I asked, "Did you not say 'partly'?" He replied "Yes." The chairman then invited me to put questions straight to Mr. Scheinmann in Russian. I was a guest, and not anxious to intrude, so I only put one question to him. "I know," I said, "that you have stopped confiscating property, and also that every business deal of yours is fully carried out. I only want to ask, do you think you will ever confiscate again?" "We are two different economic systems," said Mr. Scheinmann, "There might come a break, and then we might confiscate again." "And who is to settle when there is to be a break?" asked one of the Americans present, when I had translated Mr. Scheinmann's answer. The fact is, Mr. Scheinmann had been much too plainspoken, and the interpreter looked almost confounded. Mr. Scheinmann had given in New York what was perhaps still the already vanishing answer in Moscow. I note this because 1929 is the first year of almost unchallenged control by Stalin, with his reversion to a policy of common sense. Mr. Scheinmann lost his job, and, though we often met later, he bore me no ill-will; indeed, in the humbler post of Head of the "Intourist" agency in London, he even kindly rendered me several valuable services.

## GETTING BACK TO RUSSIA

I would like it to be understood that all this time I had been hanging on to Russia, in spite of the clouds that obscured her to us, in view of possible future friendship and co-operation. Except in the early troubled years after my return from Siberia, when all trustworthy communications were broken. I had managed to keep the closest watch on the shifting policies and periods. Friends living in Russia had told me that the Chronicle in our *Review* was a very faithful reflection of these changes. It was later the foundation of my Penguin *Russia*.

In February, 1930, came the "liquidation" of a million families of prosperous farmers; all their possessions were confiscated; they were put into carts and bundled off to the timber camps; their offense was thrift. This was the first time that events in Russia ever robbed me of sleep; the whole poignant story is to be found in its true colors in the brilliant pages of Maurice Hindus's *Broken Earth* and *Red Bread;* the author revisited his own old native village when it was under the harrow.

It was now that I made my first serious attempt to get back; at least Trotsky and world revolution were, in the main, things of the past. My application was received with the greatest courtesy by Intourist in London, and forwarded to Moscow. The form which I had to fill out revealed all my past villainies. "What parts of Russia have you visited?" "More than 40 provinces." "From what place did you leave the country?" "From Obi Bay in the Arctic Ocean." "With what papers?" "Papers of the British Government." Both the officials and I were smiling as I wrote all this down. I received a message with polite regrets that the *visa* had been refused.

From 1933, the date of Hitler's accession to power in Germany, it was impossible not to see the plain and sensible outlines of Stalin's statesmanship, designed to meet the new menace of Hitler's openly declared intention to invade and conquer Russia. The new trend of legislation was all the more striking because the immediately preceding period, with the culmination of the pressure of the first five year plan, taken all round, was the roughest in all Stalin's administration. The imminence of the new danger, not only from Germany but also from Japan, was first reflected significantly enough in a remission of arrears for taxation for the Russian population on the Far Eastern frontier (December 11, 1933), which was later extended to the whole country (February 27, 1933). Rationing was abolished on March 26, 1934; the profit motive received substantial encouragement. The articles of association of the collective farms were called in, and local initiative was much extended (February 18, 1935). The family, and later the past of Russia, were fully restored to honor. Discipline was fully re-established in the schools, and on the insistence of the Government, propaganda was replaced by objective study in 1934. It was perfectly clear that Stalin, having now got his heavy plant and arrived at the production of consumers' goods, was seeking the full support of the peasantry for national defense.

With this, it was equally clear, went a bid for the cooperation of the Western democracies against the common fascist menace. 1933 had also been the year in which Russia successfully renewed relations with the United States (November 16, 1933). The years 1932 and 1935 were marked first by a pact of non aggression and then by an alliance with bourgeois France; the year 1934, by Russia's entry into the

League of Nations, was now led by France and Britain. It was obvious which way the wind was blowing, both in home and in foreign policy. In 1935, knowing that our *Review* reached official circles in Russia, I opened our April number with an article on "New Trends in Eastern Policies." The critical sentence spoke of "the recklessness of conducting an internal warfare on the mass of the population between two foreign wars." [1] I have never met Stalin, and I judge him far less by what he says than by what he does, but I was perfectly certain that I was here expressing his thought.

This was the chance that I was waiting for. As Director of the Central School of Russian study in England, of course I ought to go back as soon as they would have me; but now they themselves needed our friendship and, as always in any European conflict, I wanted to see their country and mine on the same side. I could therefore go now on my own terms, keeping in full my independence and all my existing Russian friendships. The same British interest, which had first sent me to Russia, made it imperative for me to take this chance. The Russian approach was now not to a given class in our country, but to our good, sound England as a whole, which under a wise conservative Premier had stood the shock of world revolution better than any other country in the world.

## WITH THE RUSSIAN EMIGRANTS IN PARIS

No loss of independence! No loss of friendships! Then clearly the first thing to do, was to go over to my numerous emigrant friends in Paris, where at this time, following the vagaries of the exchange, most of them were congregated. Paris was now a museum of all the old-time parties in the Duma. The one man who could get them all together for a common purpose, was my old friend, Guchkov. He asked

[1] *Slavonic Review*, Vol. XIII, p. 546.

me if I would give a report on British opinion on Russia.
"No," I said, "I will open a discussion, and there is a question I want to put." I discussed the significance of Hitler's
accession to power in Germany. Then I put my question,
which to most of them must have seemed a sour one: "Which
would you prefer, that Hitler should conquer Russia or that
the Soviet Government should defeat him?" "You have put
us a very difficult question," they said. "Yes, I know that,"
I replied, "but what is the answer?" "Oh, there are several
different answers," they replied. "This question splits us
clean through." "Then may I hear the different answers?"
I said–for that was just what I wanted to get out of this
meeting. From the debate that followed, it seemed clear
to me that all those for whose political judgment I had any
respect were for the victory of the Soviets, but the average
higher ex-officer of the Tsar was for Hitler. An acid test
had come for Russian patriotism.

## WITH THE SOVIET AMBASSADOR

The next thing was to go and see the Soviet Ambassador, Mr. Ivan Maisky. His immediate predecessor, still in a
period of world revolution, had been Sokolnikov, the principal Russian signator of the Treaty of Brest-Litovsk, by
which Russia, to whose help we had come with the best of
our ability, left us in the last war. It was an insult to send
him to the King of England, who, I believe, left him to be
received by the Prince of Wales. He was later to be effectively eliminated by a Soviet law court.

Maisky, as one could see at once, had come to London
with a very different purpose, not to teach us revolution,
but to regain the friendship of our country. He had lived
with us in the times of the Tsar as a bookbinder. He had
excellent English, and an admirable understanding of English ways and instincts, especially those which are least often

put into words. More than that, I am certain that he himself had a real liking for our people. I don't think I could have known, when I went to him, that I was entering on one of the most valued and appreciated friendships of my life.

"Let's see," he said quietly. "You were with Kolchak"–there was no particular emphasis in his voice. "Lots of things have happened since then," and I reflected that it was a new set of men who were now charged with the representation of Russia. "I think it can be done," he said. And it was he alone who did it, though the very intelligible delay lasted into my next term's work, and I had to postpone my journey till Christmas of 1935.

## A FRIENDLY AMBUSCADE

And next the emigrants again. I was invited to dinner by the widow of my dear Harold Williams, and I was looking forward to a quiet evening spent in memories of my friend. But when I reached the house, I found that I was faced with many of the most irreconcilable Russian emigrants in London. Among the least formidable to me was the well-known "White" general, Deníkin, now with a white beard, who was over in England on a visit. I had not met him before, but I took to him at once.

Evidently most of them were very worried at the thought that I was about to return to Russia. They were too polite to say all that they were thinking, but I was confronted with a succession of hints, to which it was not difficult to supply the meaning. Would I be poisoned? Was I a traitor? Should I be easily fooled? At last I got tired of it, and talking straight to the General, who I felt would give me a straight answer, I asked, "Which are your apprehensions–are they physical, are they moral, or are they intellectual?" This provoked a smile. "We were thinking," said Mrs. Williams, "that perhaps the Bolsheviks would wipe your spectacles for you,"

which meant that they would take me in. "Well," I said,
"that's intellectual," and I thought it the least un-
complimentary of their suggestions; "I don't think I've got
much of an intellect; but I've got a very good nose," and I
proceeded to mention as many as I could of the most un-
savory blackguards of the old regime. "Now I happened to
know all these gentlemen," I said, "and when I met them,
my nose suggested it would be wise to keep a little farther
off." "As long as the nose is in order," said the old General,
"the thing's all right." There were still complaints; and in
the end I felt compelled to say, "The Russian people is
there, not here."

## BACK IN MOSCOW: FIRST IMPRESSIONS

Others of my friends gave me similar warnings. For myself, I felt sure the Russians would either keep me out or
treat me in the handsomest way. I went, before all things,
to reopen connections for the School, and our Secretary,
Miss Galton, came with me at her own expense. She had
been in the U.S.S.R. before and was an excellent introduction, as her father was still President of the old Fabian Club
of Socialists, and this helped to open all doors to us.

I have described this visit in a tiny little book called,
*Moscow Admits a Critic.* The moment we came out of the
Moscow terminus on to the street, any remains of the old
views of the emigrants, on which Europe had lived for the
last 15 years, dropped from one's shoulders like a worn-out
cloak. No country had moved so rapidly or had changed so
often and so substantially as Russia, and yet the most
fundamental thing in the atmosphere was that it was still
the old Russia—the Russia of that great and cordial family,
the Russian people, who had always been its real attraction.

Moscow looked almost surprisingly the same; and the
new buildings of the second five-year Plan, more durable than

those of the first, did not seem to break the old charm; the quaint, many-colored bulbs of Basil the Blessed looked bright and various as ever; they were not out of harmony with the gorgeous marbles of the brand-new subway; the group of railway stations in the north, built before the . Revolution in the old Russian style of house architecture, did not look out of date. The red stars at the peaks of the buildings in the Kremlin did not clash with the rest. At one point, I thought I noticed a broadened street in the old city; our Intourist guide could not confirm my impression, but our driver, an old Muscovite, did. The asphalted streets and squares were new, but they gave a new grace to the great spaces.

Everywhere there was a holiday mood, as in London— it was Christmas time and Christmas trees were again on sale. The consumers' goods, at which the Plans had aimed, had at last arrived. Stalin's big, streamlined sentences, by which he talked to the public, in white letters on red cloth, were posted up everywhere. "Now, Comrades," they said, "life is better, brighter." Whole Russian families roved the streets together and filled the stores. The Park of Culture and Rest was full of pleasure and gaiety, especially for children. The tiniest had a little fortress of their own, inaccessible to grown-ups. It was worth while reading the posters of the new "Fronts," directing all efforts of the community, for instance, to the war against bugs; the Russian people were always being called to march forward together in some new enterprise.

## AT THE SOVIET FOREIGN OFFICE

I rather deliberately avoided anything which might give the appearance that I had come back as a penitent, nor did I wish to launch into an attempt to see all the celebrities; Stalin, at that time, was not a member of the Soviet

Government, though he was its master through his absolute control over the ruling party, and he still remained
almost unapproachable.

I asked our Ambassador, Lord Chilston, to send me to
Litvinov, at that time Foreign Commissary. Few of our
Britishers in Russia went near the Embassy, which was closely
watched. At his Christmas-Eve party, Lord Chilston, as he
put it, introduced me to his British Colony in Moscow; I
think there were about eleven persons, all associated with
the old regime; before I left, I knew of some forty others,
quite different, especially young technicians in the Soviet
State Service.

Mr. Litvinov, though not well, kindly came down to the
Foreign Office to receive me. I laid before him only a signed
mandate from the chairman of our yearly conference of
teachers of Russian in Britain, asking me to negotiate for
facilities for our students to come to Russia. This, of course,
involved an equal latitude for Russian students to come to
England. "But won't they be arrested?" asked Mr. Litvinov.
Fortunately, I was able to tell him that I had been in advance to the British Home Office; there I had suggested an
academic committee of our own to preclude any misuse of
our facilities for political purposes, and this suggestion had
met with a friendly reception. I had no need to ask whether
the Russian Government would exercise control over our
students in Russia.

We also wanted to invite Soviet scholars, like those in
other Slavic countries, to accept honorary membership of the
London School. "But you've got the emigrants," said Mr.
Litvinov. "Certainly," I said. "As a British University, we
invite scholars without regard to their political views, and
we want of course to have yours." Mr. Litvinov thought the
Soviet scholars would not wish to accept. The matter was
left there; but I was passed on to his assistant, Mr. Nehmann.
With him I had a promising talk, and later I was given a

fine banquet at the House of Reception of the Foreign Commissariat, lasting some three hours, during which we continued our discussion.

"The emigrants," said Mr. Nehmann, "were set a time limit to return and did not come back, so that we have to regard them as enemies." I ventured to say that a time limit was the last thing I should have thought of. "Do you happen to know," I said, "that Guchkov is now dying of cancer in Paris?" "No," he said, "we didn't know that, and Guchkov was *someone*." "Well," I said, "I am thinking not of Guchkov's generation, but of the young Russians abroad, many of whom, I know, would like to come back and take a part in the work of construction which you are now carrying on in Russia." Mr. Nehmann in reply mentioned favorably the application of a young man very closely connected with a former Minister of the Tsar–it is true, one of the best that the Tsar ever had.

I also told him of my visit to Paris at Easter and the sharp division of opinion which it revealed on the subject of loyalty to Russia. "It is not my business," I said, "but yours and theirs; but you have a bridge to the patriotic section of the emigration, should you wish to use it!" I was later thanked by emigrant Liberals for the line I had taken.

I asked if they could not set up in Moscow a hostel for British, American, and some Russian Students, with admission to the colleges relevant to their studies, and, if possible, with contact with student organizations in the university. As things were, the exchange was a fatal bar for a student's purse. It stood at an almost legendary figure. When I reached Moscow in December, 1935, one would have had to pay in the ordinary shops 2s. 7d. for a value of 3d. (65 cents for 6). In foreign currency one could buy things at a reasonable price. On January 1, 1936, this last facility was abolished; and the ordinary exchange, by a stroke of the pen, became 9d. for

4d. (19 cents for 9). The rouble was not quoted outside Russia, and inside the country a Socialist State could make it whatever it liked.

In providing for such visitors to the country as it would allow to enter, the Government had made special arrangements by which the matter was put outside the exchange; travellers by Intourist were really guests of the country and were entertained throughout, including railway journeys, much under cost price. I asked for a similar provision which might be called Instudent. It would apply to far fewer persons, and would be far more valuable in its effects on foreign opinion; but if it was to have any value, it would be absolutely necessary that the students should be able to settle down to regular and prolonged study in Russia. Otherwise there could never be any more Wallaces or Williamses or Barings. Mr. Nehmann said, "We are not at all satisfied with our foreign observers. I am not thinking of their good will toward us; but they don't take any real trouble to get to know about us and to understand us." Much the same thing was said by Mr. Litvinov to the American Ambassador, Mr. Joseph E. Davies.[1] I urged that if foreign knowledge of Russia was to be left to short-time tourists, it was hopeless to expect that the Soviet Union could be properly understood abroad.

Sam Harper, who had gone back to Russia long before I did, backed my idea at his next visit, and in 1937, Professors Cross and Simmons of Harvard allowed me also to mention their names in support of it. The progress of the idea through the various channels reminded me closely of the old regime. I had to get the support of four different departments of the Soviet Government. These were V.O.K.S., Intourist, and the Foreign and Education Commis-

[1] "We do not like being just looked at, gullibly talked of, preferring to be studied and, of course, to be properly understood."—*Mission to Moscow*, p. 365.

sariats. I got them all. The actual decision depended on a fifth, the Committee of Higher Education in the Commissariat of Education. As I was leaving Moscow in 1937, its chairman rang me up to say that this was a very promising scheme, and that we should have a definite answer soon. We have never had it yet, and till we do, this question blocks the progress of Slavic studies in Britain and America.

In the Second World War, I saw Mr. Litvinov in Washington, just before he left his Embassy in America. He discussed with me American ignorance of things Russian. I asked him what he could expect, till Russians could come freely to America and our students could study freely in Russia. No friendship between peoples can be based upon seclusion and suspicion.

## V. O. K. S.

The institution which gave me most help in the matter of the hostel is called V.O.K.S. These four letters represent the All-Union Society for Cultural Relations. (*Vsesoyuznoe Obshehestvo Kulturnykh Snoshenii*). As I understood it, V.O.K.S., which is of course a creation of the Soviet Government, is there to give foreign educationists more extensive help than Intourist can arrange for them, but within the limits allowed at the time by the other Soviet authorities, especially those of police. As far as they are concerned, the authoritives of V.O.K.S., who have been picked for that purpose, are sincerely keen and anxious to do as much as is allowed. My program of 1935-1936 was made with their help.

"I am one of the old intelligentsia," said the chief official. (And that was just what he was.) "We won't bother you with the ordinary program. Let's just sit down and find out what you'd like to see!" Even of more help to me in my various visits was Mrs. Lydia Kislova, who worked out for me the details of my program. My suggestions were special to me and some of them were unusual, but V.O.K.S. enabled me to realize the whole program to my full satisfaction. Further, they always sent a guide with a car to take me to the place in question. These guides, often apparently well-educated persons out of the old regime, who had been admirably trained for their task of interpretation, especially in foreign languages, were nothing but a help to me. V.O.K.S. also told me that if I wanted a car, I could ring one up from the garage; and this was significant of the progress made; for in 1931 V.O.K.S. itself, I was told, had only one car!

There was much of Russian consideration, and sometimes of Russian humor, in these services. We were shown so many plays and operas, always finely staged, that we asked for a respite, as their lateness impinged on the next day's program. For the most part, they dated from the old regime. The first play shown me was Griboyedov's classical social comedy, crowded with epigram, which I had translated into English verse under the title "The Mischief of Being Clever"; Meyerhold had so enlarged and embellished the production that it lasted far into the night. Almost the first theater to which I was taken, was the one in which I had faced the Bolshevik heckling on the platform in the summer of 1917. I mentioned this detail to my guide, but I imagine she may have been instructed that bygones were bygones, for she only said, "Never mind!"

The past of Russia was again held in high honor. Three times a Tsar was shown on the stage, and each time as an object of respect or sympathy. One of these was actually John the Terrible, the special interest lying in his discovery of a natural daughter. What might not one have expected in the dramatic treatment of "The Terrible" after a Russian Revolution? Another was John's weak son, Fedor, the typical last of a dynasty; and when he threw himself on the ground and asked, "Oh, God, why did you make me

Tsar of Russia?", how could one help thinking with sympathy of Nicholas II? But there was also his formidable great-grandfather Nicholas I, the very concentration of the autocracy, and his appearance in the pageantry of a Court Ball had even been specially inserted in Chaikovsky's opera "The Queen of Spades" in Meyerhold's new post-revolutionary version. The insertion was vigorously applauded. I asked my host, the British Ambassador, whether Meyerhold might not get into trouble for this; but the Ambassador was familiar with current life in Moscow, and dismissed my fears summarily. The new regime by this time felt quite strong enough to pay honor to the old.

And the new regime could show new theatrical achievements which would have thoroughly scared the old. Each of the lesser national elements in the vast and various array of Soviet population–the Georgians, the Jews, and the rest –had now its own special theater with plays in its own language. But the most charming of all these novelties was the theater planned only for children, who came not in classes, but in groups of friends, to see dramas which never "played down" to them, but were within full reach of their intelligent appreciation and enjoyment. The attention was so keen that it created its own discipline; but the outburst of delighted chatter as the curtain fell was in itself confirmation enough both of the wisdom of the choice of plays and of the intelligence of the little spectators.

## THE SOCIAL SERVICES

We had told them at V.O.K.S. at the outset that we were especially interested in the social services of the Soviet Union. These, together with the settlement of the racial question, exactly the opposite to that of the old regime, were their "strongest suits." I had long since made up my mind that Russia was far more permanent than the first fantastic vagaries of the Communist experiment, and I was convinced that only those of the new ideas would take root, which were grounded on the old instincts of the Russian people. Certainly, in the case of the social services, there was a pre-existing foundation in the excellent though restricted work of the liberal Zemstva (or county councils), which carried out in a missionary spirit all that the suspicious government of the Tsars did not prevent them from doing; and this had created a corps of devoted social workers, ready for the generous initiative of the new regime. But what an enormous difference in scope and in effect!

Take only the care of infants! A writer far back in the London *Times* had said that the food supply of Britain depended in part on Russian infant mortality. The Government was then exporting for profit grain that was sorely needed at home. The Zemstvo work was devoted in the first place to keeping Russian children alive, so that its first care was for efficient midwifery. But all that was a drop in the bucket; and now Russia had gone at one great bound from the last place, as I really believe, to the first. One may inquire what this means for the future of the country. The Slav peoples are very prolific, but the inhuman waste did not allow this to take its proper effect in Russia. What will be the population in another fifty years?

In the earliest days of the new experiment, the Soviet Government was only in a position to show to its selected group of uninformed and unintelligent visitors what it would wish to do. Now the long planned apparatus was there. The child is cared for, from before its birth, and the mother too. Child care always lay within the broad and human spirit of the Russian people; now it was an organized reality, the first of all the solicitudes of the State. A pretty little feature of it was the institution known as "Mother and Child," whole suites were provided at the main railway terminals, where a working mother, on her travels, could leave her child in the happiest and healthiest surroundings till she had found a job in the new city. The

Russian genius found a motherly pleasure in surrounding the new child life with an atmosphere of health and beauty.

Education begins after the crêche at three. The Kindergarten (3-8) is already under the commissariat of Public Instruction. From eight starts the regular educational system, already an accomplished fact for all in European Russia, with a marvelous achievement in the backward Asiatic areas, where in some parts it started from less than one per cent and has reached to seventy-two, in itself a terrible index of our British failure in the backwoods of India. This was achieved in Soviet Russia far less by compulsion, for the Russian child was always keen for knowledge, than by a social censorship of shame, in which the children themselves carried the flag; and education in no way stops short at what used to be called the "half-literacy" of the old regime, but pushes forward, stride on stride, and most of all in the Red Army, always demanding rather intelligence than accomplishment. Again a revolution in itself, and wholly for good! And in the center of the educational curriculum stand, not the dead languages of English Public Schools, but the instinctive favorite subjects of the Russian child, sometimes frowned upon and hedged off under the old regime, nature study or biology.

The chief memory of a visit to the new Russia is of the young, and it is an inspiring and exhilarating memory. One of my four trips before the last war, when I had with me a party of English schoolmasters and schoolboys, was spent exclusively among them. In all that I can remember of the old capital, which has so often changed its name and character, the raw and misty Leningrad, the happiest experience was a feast of the little Pioneers in their palace, once that of the last Dowager Empress who, I am sure, would not have begrudged them their pleasure. The children now have their own initiative which gives a new freshness to the life of the old worn city. It takes the form of improvised entertainments of all kinds, in which performers and audience share alike in the enjoyment of doing something together. That was always the Russian's instinct. He was never happier than when he was sharing a task, or a pleasure, or both with someone else; but now it is organized, and one experiences what that means if one listens to the happy chorus singing or watches the little boy or girl monitors as they move about, conscious of their responsibility, to see that none of those who have elected them shall be left out of the common enjoyment. This is another of the ways in which the new Russia has awakened to a new life, the innate instincts of the old, and out of them created a new world. a new community. The Russian always loved a pageant. Formerly these were sometimes provided for him, now every one has a hand in it. The Russian always took to a new sport, now it is a whole community that is at play. It is "the release of energy," the chief achievement of the Revolution.

And with care for the child goes care for the old, the infirm, the cripple. There is a complete system of social insurance, including what may be called vocational damage from debilitating occupations. All this is under the name of economic security; and the Russian now knows, almost automatically, that none can be left entirely stranded without the instant care of his Mother Russia. That is where English Liberalism of the Manchester type stopped short, and that is perhaps the chief cause of the collapse of the historic Liberal party in England. And one may ask oneself, which is the more practical benefit to the citizen, political democracy, which does not yet exist in Russia, or this ubiquitous care of the State for its people.

## Anti-Religion

Turn from the social services, one of the "strongest suits" of the Soviet Regime, to the weakest, the attack on all reli-

gion. It is the weakest because it is purely negative; all that
is positive is on the other side.

To start with, you can't drive out belief by force; indeed, it may be the most unreasonable form of faith that
is hardest to extirpate. Both the major commanders of the
attack have had to find this out. As we now know, Lunachar-
sky, who as Commissary of Education led it from 1917 to
1928, was always doubtful of its wisdom; and in 1928 he confessed "Religion is like a nail; the harder you hit it, the
deeper you drive it into the wood." Yaroslavsky, President
of the Godless, who took over from him, in his instructions
to his followers in 1937, makes a wholesale confession of
failure. And beyond that, if you wish to make this attempt,
don't choose to make it in Russia, where all the greatest
spokesmen of the spirit of the people, Tolstoy, Dostoyevsky,
Turgenev, have been instinctively religious. I well remember the intolerant atheist intellectual of pre-Revolution days,
who was shocked that in the freedom of Sunday meetings
in Hyde Park in London one could find some so ignorant
as still to be discussing religion; but that is as like Tolstoy,
as the phrase-quoting Intellectual of that time was like
Klyuchevsky.

For all who have no Russian, this subject was still a
closed book in 1935. Neither Intourist nor V.O.K.S. could
be asked to do anything to open it. If on demand a church
was shown, it would be one comparatively deserted when
all are at work–Sunday was abolished by the six-day week.
We saw a woman praying on the steps of a closed church,
another at her prayers in the early morning in the fields.
Sir John Russell, who in his journeys every three years entered one cottage after another, found icons or religious
pictures in nearly all of them; for the closing of churches
turns the cottage into a chapel. I found the same on collective
farms, and the attempt of a guide to explain that they were
only there as a decoration broke down, because I happened

to know Russian and had heard the housewife's sturdy profession of faith. One did not go about asking anyone if he were a Christian. I learned a good deal from a Christian workingman with whom I had some ties of memory. Most parents, he said, were religious, and most children followed their parents. In the recent census, far more were still religious than admitted it (and the census figures were withdrawn because so many did.) It had to be left to the next war to bring out these realities; then they came out clearly enough, as in the remarkable picture of the young Red Army poet, Simonov—

> You know, I am sure that this, this is our country;
>    Not the townhouse where life went so easily by,
> But these hamlets so plain which our grandfathers traversed,
>    With plain Russian crosses to mark where they lie.

I found ordinarily that, in spite of the restricting conditions, I could still get what I wanted from the officials themselves. I asked to see Yaroslavsky, but he was too busy to see me. But if one inquired courteously the reasons for this or that policy, one always got an excellent index of the measure of conviction behind it. The national ownership of the means of production was defended with real enthusiasm. The explanation of the attack on religion was little more than a prescribed formula.

I wandered unescorted for over two hours through the Anti-Religious Museum in the old Monastery of the Passion, since destroyed, where one side of the passage walls showed the presumed religious view of the world, and the other that of science. There was a definite breakdown on the latter side, when the scientific theory of the soul confined itself to a diagram of the nervous system—without any answer to the question what set the nervous system going. I heard one of the new school lessons of anti-religion which, in a last desperate effort, the atheist crusaders had substituted for no religious teaching. Anti-religion is something which can't be taught without throwing suspicion on the sincerity of the teacher. This one, a highly educated lady, concluded an excellently reasoned sketch of the history and the decline of the old Roman Empire with the quite inapposite exclamation that it was an Englishman, Charles Darwin, who had broken the yoke of religion. This was apparently a compliment to her visitor, as she bowed to me–and she later explained that she had had to get in this part of the curriculum before the end of the session.

No! Here the victory is with the other side. Again unescorted, and in the company of that wonderful lady, Muriel Paget, who did so much for wounded Russians and stranded old Englishwomen, I saw the strength of religion in one of the great church festivals.[1]

The most striking of all differences between the old Russia and the new lies in the vigorous braced-up faces of all; and this stern expression of purpose stood out fully as much in the great Christmas congregation in the spacious pro-Cathedral. The road to it was thronged with a vast crowd that reminded me of our Saturday crowds at a League football match. I had the same reminder inside the church; I instinctively recalled the pressure of our English Cup Finals. A Russian church contains no seating accommodation; and here we were all packed so tight that it was only by constant appeals that the deacons could make their way through to collect the necessary offertories, without which the parish would not have been able to lease the church building from the State. One received a striking correction of the reports of casual, short-time visitors to the Soviet Union, of whom probably very few attended a great church service, that religion was now confined to the old. That was what the government tried to bring about, when it

[1] My Penguin *Russia*, p. 175.

cut off all public instruction for the young, but Yaroslavsky, President of the Godless, had declared this to be an illusion. Here one saw whole families together; and all of them, before leaving the church, made their way through to the front to kiss the cross in token of loyalty while religion itself was under challenge. On raised seats sat the elders of the congregation, responsible for the upkeep of the parish. The music was more beautiful and inspiring than before the Revolution; when one church was closed by the government, the best singers of its choir went to reinforce another. I can echo the words of Sergius Bulgakov: "And in our persecuted churches you will find a fervor of devotion which I should be happy to see in the churches of western Europe!" Outside, another great crowd was waiting a full two hours for a later repetition of the service.

## JUSTICE

It is not generally recognized that Russian justice was not instinctively cruel. The first law code dating from the eleventh century, was markedly more humane than the Byzantine, from which it was copied, especially in the punishments prescribed and in its recognition of rights of women. It is still almost unknown that the death sentence for ordinary murder was abolished under Elizabeth (1741-1762). The use of torture followed later. Capital punishment was retained only under martial law or for political offenses; that was the real weak point in the system, and at times some or other form of martial law was almost universal. For this reason, in the latter days of the monarchy, which are still described in Russia as "the time of peace," public condemnation of capital punishment was perhaps sharper there than in any other country in Europe.

Ordinary justice in Russia, before the Revolution, was lax and humane. Even then the prison was called the House

of Correction. Not much use was made of solitary confinement, and it was in prison that an ordinary peasant or
worker learned the first rules of health. This humane attitude toward ordinary non-political offenses is more emphasized than ever under the new regime, and confinement is
treated on principle as a means of correction.

A judge with whom I talked even dared to contrast the
Soviet "correction" of criminals with "capitalist vengeance."
So I asked him whether the concentration camps had been
closed, which seemed to stop his boast. In a talk with a
Young Communist, I asked what proportion of the community had not yet accepted the new regime, and he gave
the figure of two millions; this, I believe, corresponded to
that of the prisoners in these camps at that time.

I have witnessed two trials under ordinary Soviet law.
In each case the atmosphere of the court seemed almost
casual. The judge was trained, but his two assessors only
partially. He took a leading, but not unfair, part in the
trial, himself examined the accused in full, while giving all
latitude to the barristers on each side. In a case of ordinary
murder, he invited a full explanation from the accused,
who made a long and surprisingly frank statement. There
was none of the sternness and precision of an English law
court.

There is, of course, one enormous reservation which
no one can ever shirk or forget. What most strikes us as
clashing with our deepest instincts is that the terrors of Russian justice are specially reserved for freedom of political
opinion. Of that, the ordinary visitor sees nothing.

An incident in one of my visits showed how radically
things had changed in Russia. If there was one man whose
permanent departure I was ready to welcome it was Zinoviev, bully and coward, tyrant of Leningrad, responsible for
an unlimited number of judicial murders of ordinary middle
class citizens. Never could I have pictured myself as back

in Moscow when Zinoviev was executed for treason. Buying a newspaper as I came out of my hotel, I read simply: "The sentence has been carried out."

## Bolshevo–The "Strays" Reclaimed

This glance at the system of Soviet justice would have been very incomplete without our visit to Bolshevo. This visit was the most important item on the V.O.K.S. program. Bolshevo is an institution which we should in England call a Reformatory. Here were to be found the former waifs and strays of that desolating period when children, already often sent roving by the loss of their guardians through war, famine, and epidemics, were also torn from the custody of their parents under a pretentious plea of adoption by the State which, if only for economic reasons, could then do little for them.

We were shown over Bolshevo by a young man, who had been the sixth to be admitted there, and was now on the administration. He described to us how he lost his parents and, looking me in the eyes, he went on, "I, what is called, stole." For this he had to go through years of correction to recover his rights of citizenship.

By this time (1936) Bolshevo was a large and vigorous community, where many of the original entrants had now remained from choice. It was certainly a real center of civilization, with its own schools of painting, music, and drama; it seemed that the strictest care was taken in details to make it a real home; for instance, it was the habit to house all the members of the dramatic society in a given apartment-house to make it easy for them to rehearse their plays. All were still under a discipline if they remained in Bolshevo, but it was intelligent and its watchword was the word "social." It did not seem to me unduly intrusive. I would say that the whole atmosphere was that of a deeply

human school of character building, and certainly the life
and spirit of this institution suggested happiness rather than
correction. There can be no doubt that many of these young
folk have already rendered sterling service to the creed of
the "community" professed by their leaders.

## A Meeting of Railway Workers

I had asked to attend a worker's meeting, and I was
taken to one at which a young and rather tired official tried
to explain the difference between socialism and communism.
It has long since been established in the Soviet Union that
whereas Socialism has already been achieved, communism
is still only a goal for the future.

I sat among the workmen. The young speaker was ineffective and pedantic; his speech for the most part consisted of a string of quotations from Marx, Engels, Lenin,
and Stalin. The workmen were evidently not satisfied. They
showed a vigor which one could not have seen before the
Revolution in the presence of government officials. To challenge an official view, was then to ask for trouble. But in
those days, the officials were like a race apart; now they are
of the same cloth as the people, and that is a very big difference.

These workmen, throughout the speech, were pelting
the speaker with little bits of paper, containing questions,
which were picked up and opened by the businesslike chairman. The questions were very pertinent, and might have
been put at any meeting of workers in Sheffield or Pittsburgh.

At this we should not have felt any surprise, if we had
been adequately informed. It is of course true that a political meeting of workmen to demand the resignation of Stalin
could not be held in Russia, though that very question was
raised and voted on in the numerous Central Committee

of the Communist Party in 1929. But the workmen not only may, but are expected to meet regularly to discuss another subject which is probably nearer to them–namely the task which has been assigned to their factory by the State Plan, and to say whether it is feasible or what modifications are required to make it so. This is a peculiar kind of democracy which will not be found in Sheffield or Pittsburgh, where the decision rests with the employer. There is no employer in the Soviet Union except the State, as represented by its appointed authorities. They take the fullest account of the workmen's representations, and sometimes the assignment in question travels up and down more than once between planners and workers before a definite adjustment is reached.

Here were some of the questions raised at this meeting: "When we get Communism shall we still get paid for overtime?" There was no doubt where the wishes of the audience lay. "Under Communism shall we still have marriage?" The speaker seemed to me to be uncomfortable. I think he felt he had to say yes, so he explained that parents were anyhow generally fond of their children and this would very likely keep them together. This was long before the present divorce law, which goes far beyond England and America in enacting a progressive tax for every new divorce. The question which interested me most was this: "Is it really possible to equalize different people's abilities?" To this question, Stalin's answer is a decisive, "No."

## A Young Communist Leader

V.O.K.S. also arranged for me a most fascinating talk with a typical young leader of the Communist League of Youth. He was in his early thirties. We sat facing each other across a small table. I was particularly struck by the sincerity of this young man and his pride in his subject. He looked me straight in the eyes throughout, not as an enemy, but as a friend. He was not only very cordial, but was very fair and objective in the outline which he gave me of this most important organization, which builds up the reserve of the ruling Party.

I asked him first what was its objective. He replied, "It is educational with a bias," which was exactly true. "What is the bias?" I asked. "We tell them, for instance, that religion is a myth," he said. I interposed, "If God had been the same thing as slavery, we could have agreed with you" (this was a reference to their anti-religious propaganda). He in no way resented this interruption. Then he went on, "We tell them that drunkenness degrades a man." "And what do you do about it?" "We warn him; if needed, we warn him again; and then we expel him from the League!" There is no question at all that this is a very serious punishment, for the League consists of the key leaders among the young and anyone expelled is deprived both of privilege, opportunity, and of honor.

He explained that the League had had two great schoolings; the first, in the civil war, and the second in the Five Year Plan; and the second schooling was far the most thorough. One may say that both these victories, the military and the civil, were chiefly won by the devotion of the young. He xplained further the wonderful expansion of initiative, enterprise, and adventure which had come to the young, through the Revolution; thus again Sir John Maynard is verified in his view that the "release of energy" is the principal achievement of the Revolution. I could understand this better when my young friend gave me the ages of his chief contemporaries and named the posts which they held. Nowhere was this fascinating scope of initiative more attractive than in the long-neglected regions of central Asia, which now form autonomous republics. Among those backward peoples the work of the League has much less to do with politics than with culture and civilization; the medical side of it alone is a colossal field, hardly touched before the Revolution. One has to realize in full that one result of the boycott of Russia by Europe was to throw the Russians back on to their own country and to replace the school of world revolution with a new school of young administrators.

I should like, if she will pardon me, to take as a shining example of this aspect of the Communist Revolution a young Soviet friend. Masha Scott is already well known to the American public–as the heroine of her husband's book "Beyond the Urals," as the subject of a special study by Pearl Buck, and as a spokesman of her country at many meetings. She was born a peasant in my favorite province of Tver, now Kalinin. She was one of seven sisters, all of whom, but for the Revolution, would have probably remained working on the land, possibly illiterate: their ages are probably almost all within the thirties. The eldest is now a professor of ancient history, another is a qualified chemist, another holds a medical post, another is an engineer. The brother has been decorated for his part in the defense of Leningrad. Lately the mother was specially honored by the Soviet government as mother of seven daughters, and is entitled to travel free anywhere in the Soviet Union for a year at the government's expense. I have constantly dropped in on the Scotts and their two small daughters, because there I could have the rare feeling of being in the real Soviet Russia. There was no question of communism. Masha has no taste in that direction; for a good Soviet Russian it is a standard to which one hopes some day to live up, and it means devotion to the community. Meanwhile she is absolutely true to her country as it now is, and has defended it with infinite spirit and good humour at many a New York meeting.

At the end of the talk my V.O.K.S. companion put a friendly question: "How were these matters being dealt with in England?" Feeling the responsibility of giving a reply for my country, I thought carefully for a minute, and my answer is one which I would give at any time. "If you are thinking of the grafting of Socialism on a Capitalist world, that began, in legislation too, in my country long before it began in yours. It is going a different way and slower, but if you think that nothing has been done, you will make a great mistake." He did not challenge my answer, which he took simply as my reply to his question. I do definitely oppose their conventional theory that they alone are social- ist and that every one else is pure capitalist.

I must leave no doubt at all that the new Russia is far less accessible to us than the old; also, as I keep on insisting, that till this is radically altered, there cannot be any general confidence between their country and others. In the old days, as now, it was only the Government and its police that were prohibitive. Then, as now, Russians appreciated the difficulty in getting through to them and were all the more grateful to those who did so; and, of course, there is no other people that is naturally more hospitable or more communicative. But the Tsar's police, though almost as suspicious, were far less efficient; and once past the standing barriers, the way was comparatively open. Now it is far harder. In practice, this obstacle, to any inquirer who has not the language, is fatal. One who has it, cannot be in Russia without learning something at every step.

## COLLECTIVE FARMS

On the collective farms which I saw on my various visits before the last war, I was first struck by the almost grandi- ose dimensions of these new enterprises, in comparison with the bleak and dingy aspects of the old Russian village. Certainly civilization had come down to the country, and the village was now playing its part in the whole life of the State. There was a new order and neatness. Everywhere the co-operative stores, with a supply which would have made an old-time peasant open his eyes. Everywhere the hospital, sometimes with two doctors; everywhere the school, the club, the newspaper. The radio alone is in itself a revolution in a remote Russian village; so is the provision for public lectures. But there was a reminder of the "Fairy Villages," staged in Crimea for Catherine the Great by her principal statesman, Potemkin, in the precision with which everything was shown; these villages looked more like institutions and less like communities. From this precision it was sometimes possible to escape, and I did get some plain talks with peasants.

At one moment this "precision" became absurd. Only two out of my very many guides were anything but helpful; but in 1939, one of them tried to take complete command of our English party. As we had a doctor with us, I took him into the new hospital, but she came after me and turned me out; no talks were to take place except in her presence and with her as the interpreter. Some of the party had asked to see how the people lived. She, so to speak, put this on her schedule, "No. 7; how the people live?" When she got to No. 7, we were taken into an office, not an ordinary cottage, where a family was seated, eating eggs and drinking tea. Later, at the great central Agricultural Exhibition, I saw an exhibit from this particular farm, and there was a picture with exactly the same scene. I think it was the same family; was it the same eggs? All this staging and secrecy is silly and defeats its own purpose.

I was chiefly interested in the effects of the fairly radical revision of the regulations in 1935, which left a substantially greater freedom of initiative to the peasants themselves. The original attempt to force on them "State farms" or, as they were sometimes called "grain factories," in which the worker was hardly more than a wage earner, had in general proved a failure. If I have rightly gauged the peasant's own ideal, it is a combination of personal property with close co-operation with his neighbors; that is what was almost certain to come out of his long corporate history. Before the Revolution, as soon as Stolypin had given satisfaction to the peasant's simple desire for property, co-operative farming of an up-to-date kind sprang up everywhere on lines not unlike those of the creameries in Ireland or in parts of England. And now that they had got back to something more like these conditions, work was going forward with enthusiasm.

It seemed clear that this was so from 1935. When did it begin? Talking with one of the keenest workers, a sturdy, old peasant lady from central agricultural Russia, I rather wickedly hazarded an allusion to 1931. "1931?" she said with vigor. "That was revolt." Both government and peasantry were free to admit that in that year there was a state of war between the two. This brings to my mind a comment of the wisest eye-witness of all the changes of the revolutionary period. The radical alterations of 1934-1936, he said, were not merely acts of grace or even of understanding on the part of Stalin, who had the sense to see that this was the way to national support, but also genuine victories of the peasantry. By now, there could be no doubt of the collective spirit with which they threw themselves into their work.

If this was only just in time for the coming war, still it was in time. I had always been looking for a synthesis, when the government had found out how much of its program it could achieve, and the population had found how much it could accept. If the collectivization of Stalin had not been achieved before the war, there would have been wholesale hoarding of food, as in the First World War; and the whole supply being concentrated before all things on the army, it would have broken down as it did then, which proved to be the immediate cause of the Revolution.

And there was something else which had a lively influence on the war. Stalin's pre-war modifications had given back considerable latitude to peasant property in livestock. But the main feature of his collectivization, the brigade system for plowing, sowing, and reaping under chosen leaders, was retained and it was the best possible preparation for the highly organized guerilla warfare which was to follow.

## A Railway "Incident"

'Istoria' (a story) or 'Incindent' are words used to describe those charming, little muddles which make up so much of the attraction of everyday Russian life.

Scene: the train from the frontier to Moscow.

*Each of us has received his "platzkarte," or place ticket which gives him sleeping space for the night.*

### Scene I: In the Corridor.

*Conductor:* Are you interested in a little bit of tea?

*Professor:* Thanks very much. Now please, one of our English passengers is a sick man. Have you such a thing as a night vessel?

*Conductor:* A night vessel?

*Professor:* Yes, a pot.

*Conductor:* No, but we've got a doctor.

*Professor:* He doesn't want a doctor, he wants a pot.

*Conductor:* Well anyhow, the doctor's no good. He's very young.

### Scene II: The English Ladies' Compartment.

*G. an elderly and highly respectable man.* This is impossible! I'm a married man! I've never been put in with ladies before. (*Plunges for the door and slams it on Professor's thumb; parks himself in an empty berth.*) The English ladies smile.

### Scene III: In the Corridor.

(*Enter a Russian civilian, probably a local physician. He is an elderly, mild-looking man, who might have stepped straight out of a tale of Chekhov. He disappears into the carriage where G. has parked himself. A rough growl is heard from G. Hurried exit of the local physician, who says*) I can stand in the corridor.

*Professor:* Not all night, I hope! May I look at your ticket? (*It is for the seat which G. has appropriated*) I'll go and get your seat for you.

*Passenger:* I can stand in the corridor.

*Professor:* No you shan't. (*To G.*) That's his seat! You know we'll get into trouble with this. (*Manages to persuade G. to come out*)

*To Passenger:* Now, sir, your seat is free.

*Passenger:* I can stand in the corridor.

*Professor:* Conductor, come and help! This man's too good for this world. He won't take his own seat. (*Gently pushed by Conductor and Professor, Passenger yields to pressure and goes in, still with an air of apology.*)

### SCENE IV: THE LADIES' COMPARTMENT.

*Conductor:* Someone has got to have that empty place. We must put a Red Army soldier here. (*The ladies regard this with rather less complacency.*) And we've got you your pot. (*This fortunately said in Russian.*)

(*Conductor now discusses the whole incident with Professor and Train-doctor; each takes the other side, as Russians seem to like doing. Conductor emphasizes the obligations of Russian hospitality, and Professor, the social duties to one's neighbors. Ultimately, a pleasant young man, deputy of the leader of the English party, in deference to the ladies, agrees to occupy the empty berth.*)

*Conductor, Train-doctor and Professor join hands:* It's settled! It's settled! It's settled!

(*And so we all go to sleep, feeling somehow that life begins in Russia.*)

## AGAIN THE EVE OF WAR

In August of 1939, it seemed clear that we were in for a new war. Again to me the most pressing interest was that Russia should be with us and not against us. A moment's thought, and we can see that it makes all the difference.

That month I spent in Russia with a distinguished English party under a delightful leader, Sir John Russell, Director of the Experimental Station of Agriculture at

Rothamsted. Sir John had been visiting the Soviet Union for some time past. Not for a long time had he heard anything about world revolution there. Nearly every cottage which he entered, and they must have been very many, contained its icons, often by the side of a picture of Lenin. He found still, as in the past, a great antipathy between country and town, and also a superfluity of workers for a given job, as compared with England.

As we passed through Smolensk, that sturdy frontier town, I had a glorious view of the magnificent walls built by Boris Godunov, which he called "the precious necklace of Russia"; the early dawn was tinging them a deep red. In the seventeenth century, they stood the test of a long siege by King Sigismund of Poland; they were only partially damaged by Marshal Ney on his retreat in 1812; they were soon to be battered by the artillery of Hitler, which reduced this most picturesque city to ruins.

For the third time I went down the Volga. There I completed my cycle of public addresses all round the world, either in English or in Russian, by two little lectures which I gave to our party; the first was on the citadel of Nizhny-Novgorod (now renamed after Maxim Gorky); the second was on the boat near Simbirsk, the home town of Protopopov, of Kerensky, and of Lenin; this linked up reasonably with the last of my Siberian tour at Ekaterinburg in 1919. On the boat, I noticed that the Russian passengers, as they had never done before, talked quite freely to me about the ominous political situation.

Sir John had especially asked that we should go to Sarátov; there seemed to be a difficulty about it, but in the end we were somehow landed there through a temporary delay of the river service. There we were lodged in an old-fashioned hotel which had often entertained the Russian gentry and also, no doubt, Stolypin, who first made his name as Governor here in the stormy months of 1905. An old waiter still lingered on from those times. He told me that things were decidedly easier now: "One can live! One can eat!"

I carried away a very definite and new impression of the Volga, as now under Soviet rule. This great river of the Russian people was now in the people's hands. Instead of the flabby remains of the old gentry class, the initiative was now with a new generation of keen administrators who seemed to know their jobs and were happy in doing them to the best of their ability. Enormous improvements were in progress. World Revolution seemed a distant memory.

Our voyage stopped at Stalingrad, a vast, new industrial city on the site of an old county town. On August 11, I walked across the square to a local cinema and saw a most amusing movie, which satirized the forcible German occupation of Ukraine in 1918. Bread and salt are offered ironically to the German invaders, but are followed with such insults that the offerer is driven out, to become the head of a local guerilla. A German military band, conducted by a fat and greasy Prussian band master, blares its loudest, while cattle and fowls are shepherded on to trains bound for Germany. I am told that this movie continued to be shown throughout the duration of the Russo-German Pact.

It was clear that preparations for the coming of war had made a deep dent in the budget improvement of recent years. Much of my very best information was derived from young British and American technicians, working regularly in the Soviet service. Even before the time of Peter the Great, Russia was always dependent to a certain extent on foreign technicians. It was understood that she would dispense with these whenever she developed technicians of her own. She certainly had not reached this stage before the First World War. The first sign of it, as far as I know, came in 1937, for the five year plans had served as a great school. In that year, the British and Americans were facing for home. The Russians could now replace them, as was later to become evident in the Second World War; but apart from that, so much of Soviet industry was now being militarized that the government did not welcome the presence of foreign engineers in its factories.

In Moscow, we found that our own dreary and abortive negotiations for a common front against Hitler were still dragging along. After Russia's exclusion from the conference at Munich, both government and public greatly relished the advent of rival suitors from England and from Germany; I am told that they lodged them in two houses next to each other. V.O.K.S., which, be it remembered, is an official institution–entertained our party with the poignant movie "Professor Mamlock." A Jewish surgeon, the best in Berlin, was hounded by the Nazis and ultimately shot by machine guns, while he was making an eloquent appeal against the senseless destruction of all the highest cultural values of the past in Germany. Our hosts did not wish us to miss a word, and told the whole story in English. This was on August 15th. On the 17th the highest officials of V.O.K.S. dined with us publicly in the National Hotel and made speeches, undoubtedly sincere, in Russian before the waiters on friendship with England. On the 18th they took us out to see a very striking demonstration of Soviet air power, at which the whole of Moscow seemed to have gathered; I do not remember ever having seen so many cars. The display included both civil and military aviation. We saw a great shower of varicolored parachutes in the air together, a short and sharp engagement, and finally a glimpse of a vast bomber which hurried past us and disappeared. The propaganda of the loud speakers was all anti-fascist. Our party was included in the cinema picture to be shown all over Russia.

That night we left Moscow, and next day we passed the Polish frontier–this was the line fixed by the Treaty of Riga in 1921, which has now become so famous. I had lived in these villages in the winter of 1915 with the Russian Army.

The population was the same on both sides–White Russian; here the Poles, as Marshall Pilsudski had himself avowed to me, were not more than 20 per cent–really much less. It is always an experience to pass a land frontier, and here it seemed particularly artificial. I brought the party out to the corridor, to watch the crossing. On each side was a high wooden pulpit on which stood a soldier with leveled rifle –the first a Russian, the second, a Pole. We stopped in a field on the actual line. Here a Russian soldier walked along the train, to see if anyone was hanging on under a carriage. A Polish soldier knelt with raised rifle, to shoot anyone who might jump out.

In Berlin I spent the Sunday (August the 20th) chiefly at the Zoo, watching the workers from the east end take holiday with their families. It was a fine day, and the elephants were giving an excellent performance, but the faces of all seemed to wear a strained look, which we had not noticed in Russia. Almost directly after our arrival in London, came the news of the signature of the Russo-German Pact, by which Russia contracted herself out of the coming war and thereby made it inevitable and immediate.

## IVAN MAISKY

I have the most sincere admiration for the way Maisky carried out his very difficult task of recovering the goodwill of England, and I was throughout in the greatest sympathy with his task. He had against him all the antipathies aroused in us by the world revolutionary theory which, as he knew and recognized, I also shared. The difference, in my case, was that I recognized and shared his purpose from the start, and admired the understanding with which he worked for its success. In the period of appeasement in British policy, his position to a lesser man would have been intolerable. Russia was regarded as in disgrace, accepted only on suffer-

ance and expected to do nothing which would spoil the
tempers of Hitler and Mussolini. Yet Maisky throughout kept
his cool head and suffered no loss in dignity. He very well
knew throughout this period that if England as a whole–
the England not of the chanceries and the drawing rooms,
but of the great cities and the streets–had been called upon
to choose between Russia and Germany, it would have chosen
Russia; Hitler himself did everything to make this inevitable; but Maisky, as he always recognized, was accredited
not to the people of England but to its government. He
stood his ground, bided his time, and in the end won out
to the full by the sheer logic of events.

Maisky had that outstanding intelligence which of itself senses at once the limits within which two men of different loyalties can work confidently together. I saw him frequently and, without ever being really ruffled, he allowed
me to say to him the plainest things in the plainest words,
provided they were always said in friendship for his country. At first, "country" was not often a word he used, for it
had not been in fashion in the international period; later,
it was "the Soviet Fatherland," but also "Russia."

Let me take some of our conversations! I could tell him
freely of talks which I had had with representative emigrants, to illustrate that on some subjects their views were
the same as his. I always thought it right to make quite plain
my view that the treatment of religion in Russia was a
fundamental obstacle to British friendship. I think he must
have known that through that period I was vice-chairman
of the British committee of the Russian Church Aid Fund.
Maisky, whether on this or on other subjects, never talked
propaganda, but rather as an English fellow-disputant might
have done; as he loyally put them, the views of his government consequently sounded far more convincing. I asked
him once whether it was not evident that Jesus Christ was
what in Russia was called a proletarian (not, as absurd So-

viet posters pictured him, an agent of "capital"). Maisky
made no difficulty in accepting this and carried the discussion on to ground where we could both agree, namely the
extravagant misuse of religion as a weapon of the Tsar's
government. He told me how, when he was a schoolboy at
Omsk, the chaplain, a sleek careerist of a type which I recognized, obtained through the confessional the names of boys
who talked politics, and gave them to the police, with the
result that these boys were punished.[1] "But surely," I asked,
"this was not religion, but a gross caricature of it. Could not
the reality be distinguished from the perversion?"

At the time when England was being flooded with news
of the great purges and executions of 1936-1938, I told the
Ambassador I felt they were doing a great deal to spoil his
patient work for our friendship. He showed no annoyance,
and countered legitimately with a reminder that in Russia
there was no capital punishment for ordinary murder. I
admitted this at once, but I went on: "What surprises us,
is that you should keep it only for the people with whom
you disagree." I added, "The reason why I regret anything
that interferes with the friendship of our two countries is
that I think the integrity of the territory of the Soviet Union
is a matter of concern to the British Commonwealth." He
replied at once, in the simplest way, "And I think the integrity of the territory of the British Commonwealth is a matter
of concern to the Soviet Union!" He proceeded, "You and
we have got pretty well as much as we can manage, and they
(the Axis) want to take something from each of us." "Yes,"
I said, "we are for the *status quo.*" "You weren't always for
the *status quo,*" said Maisky smiling.

Mr. Maisky always regarded me as a conservative. I did
not complain, though I keep rigorously out of parties; but
weren't our British Liberals really also conservative? I took

[1] The story is told in Maisky's book *"Before the Storm"* (Eng. Ed.,
p. 154).

refuge in the pretty Russian phrase, "the eternal conservatism of England," which, by the way, very much pleased
Mr. Baldwin, when I told him of it; and hasn't it carried us
through our most dangerous crises, particularly that of
World Revolution propaganda?

Never did anything that Mr. Maisky told me fail to be
confirmed by the following events. After Munich, he said
to me, "I can't think that England is degenerate." I didn't
like listening to this, but I liked to hear him say it, and
I am convinced that he was really fond of our country. I
asked, "What will you do now?" "Well," he said, "we shall
wait to see whether you stick to this policy,"–(that is, of
persistent appeasement). "And how long will you wait, do
you think?" "Perhaps six months or so." "And if we stick
to it?" "We shall lock our own doors and see to our own
defense," which is an exact definition of the purpose of the
Pact of Non-Aggression with Germany on August 22,
1939.

After the Pact, I went to him again. "This is not an
alliance," he said, "whether political, military, or economic,"
and it certainly was not. "Then how much help will Germany get from you on the economic side?" A great splash
was being made in Germany over the economic treaty of
the same date. "Much less than you get from America," said
Mr. Maisky.

After the treaty which divided Poland between Russia
and Germany, I asked Mr. Maisky whether Russia felt herself responsible for the German gains of territory. "No," he
said. This was important; for if she had done so, we should
practically have had to go to war with her, because of our
pledge to Poland. I noticed how Russia, of herself, withdrew from the initial line of military demarcation, which
ran right through Warsaw, to a line nearly identical with
that recommended both to Poland and to Russia by Lord
Curzon in 1920.

On October 6, 1939, Hitler appealed for peace on the basis of his conquest of Poland as an accomplished fact, and Molotov backed up this appeal in Russia. Maisky explained this to me by saying Russia was, above all things, against an extension of the war–which was only consistent with her whole policy since Hitler's appearance. What she needed urgently, was peace. Maisky explained that Russia would prefer a negotiated peace to a vindictive one, which would follow the triumph of either side, and would bring more wars. Then it looked like a stalemate, and he recognized that this, at best, would only be an adjournment.

In the later months of 1940, Hitler, like Napoleon, having failed in a direct invasion of England, was preparing to realize his original object, the invasion of Russia, and was therefore moving steadily eastward. Every step of his on the map made this more clear. He was sweeping the little countries into his net under the name of "the New Order." On November 12th, Molotov came, to talk with him in Berlin.

I was extremely anxious about this question and, relying on Mr. Maisky's unvaried kindness in the past, I took my courage in both hands and asked to see him in the first days of June, 1941. Asking him to excuse my bluntness, I said, "I think there is a point to which Russia can't retreat without losing her regime." (I purposely emphasized the regime.) Mr. Maisky did not quite relish my frankness, but he did not discourage me. "I think," I said, "that if you allow the Germans to come into Russia, to do their production and transport on the spot, your regime is finished." Mr. Maisky showed no annoyance, nor did he evade the question; he simply looked straight at the ground. I concluded that if the demand had been made, it had not yet received a final answer.

On Friday, June 20th, being more and more anxious on the subject, I asked to see him again. He was just starting out of town, but he invited me to come. As I waited in the great lounge of the Soviet Embassy, a side door opened and some of the staff came out. "Eto bor'ba" (That means fighting) said one, evidently with no dissatisfaction. A minute or two later Mr. Maisky came out smiling, and at his invitation I repeated my former question. He took my arm, and as we walked to the door, he said, "You'll see we're going to be masters in our own house."

A day and a half later, Hitler had invaded Russia. The day that began with his invasion ended with Mr. Churchill's speech in the House of Commons, putting England in alliance with Russia. I told Mr. Maisky I thought he had done more than anyone else to bring about this alliance. He replied, "I don't think diplomatists do very much. In my opinion a good diplomatist is one who reduces the unfavorable factors to 40 per cent and makes 100 per cent of the good ones!" That, I think, is exactly what Mr. Maisky had done, and nothing gave me more satisfaction than the real ovation which he received on his next public appearance.

Before I started for America in December, 1942, I took his advice, as I took that of some English friends, as to what points I should particularly try to bring home to the American public. "I wish you could get it out of their heads," he said, "that we want to make a revolution there." And then, somewhat even to my own surprise, he added, "I think you can explain to them the question of religion in Russia"–one on which I had left my attitude in no doubt with him. But here again he was correct in forecasting the future; for that obstacle too was soon to disappear. Before he left London to resume work in Moscow, he wrote to me in America a letter which I shall always keep among those which I value highest. It ran as follows:

12th September, 1943

Dear Sir Bernard,

On leaving this country for good, to take up my new duties at the Foreign Commissariat in Moscow, I would like to say good-bye and to thank you for all that you have done for the cause of rapprochement between our two peoples, for your friendly attitude to me, and your important work in getting the Russian people understood by the British people. I appreciate very much the translation you did of Krylov's Fables, which I find excellent.

I send you every good wish for success in the future.

Yours sincerely,

I. Maisky.

No matter what may be the variations in M. Maisky's official positions in subsequent fluctuations of Soviet policy, he did a great work for his country at one of the most critical times in its history and will be remembered as a true friend of ours, convincing because he himself was convinced.

# CHAPTER X

## In the Second World War

### "Bird" for "Bird"

I FIRST learned that we were at war through a false air-raid warning, a quarter of an hour after our declaration. I was in bed in London, resting from several recent night journeys in my last Russian tour, and from the task of mobilizing our School for war service. We all ran, as we were, to the ground floor for shelter.

My flat was one of the two top ones on a staircase of ten. We were at the gates of Battersea Park, a very beautiful one, which the poor of Battersea rightly regard as their own. Half a mile across lay the biggest power station in London, the local gas works, and other targets, such as a railway line and a bridge. Few of us knew our next door neighbors, but now we all made friends and found out how much we had missed. As my lease was just expiring, I was able to transfer to the ground floor. And just as well! For later there was a shell hole in the roof just above my pillow in my old flat.

A new Intelligence Department was just being set up, to take part in the study of current events in foreign countries, and our School took charge of the east of Europe,

364

with Seton Watson for the Danube and Balkans, William Rose for Poland, now become very important, and myself for Russia. Rose, who was soon to take over the Directorship of the School from me, was unique as an expert on Poland. It was not merely that he had a Doctor's Degree from the University of Cracow. A man of supreme integrity and fairness, he had an unequalled influence, gladly welcomed, over leading men of the sorely tried nation. He could calm them, as no one else whom I have known. We also put at the disposal of the new department the services of others of our staff at the cost of London University. As Russian press news came through to us very slowly, we set two of our staff, Yakubson and Turin, to listen in to the Moscow radio; and as the Soviet radio can only give views approved by its government, this was of the greatest use to us. Meanwhile, we not only continued our language teaching in London, which was now needed more than ever, but we organized it also in Oxford, in co-operation with the lecturer in Russian there, Professor Konovalov.

*Pravda,* which was my daily study for those critical months, was, of course, no secret document, but a newspaper like any other, read all over Russia and obtainable abroad, but it was also a most authoritative index of Soviet policy. It gave the lead to other papers in Russia, which received every evening by radio a dictated statement giving the general direction for their next day's leading articles. From this point of vantage, I had a most entertaining view of the Soviet interpretation of the pact with Germany which puzzled so many observers at the time. The Germans tried hard to present it as an alliance, and the Soviets, each time, dashed such hopes and brought it back into line with the real aim of Russian policy–keeping Russia out of the war. The Germans sent an impressive economic deputation into Russia, but the last thing the Soviets were likely to do was to give them free passage. The only satisfaction which they gave to their new "friends" was in words alone. The whole Russian Press was notified at one stroke to print recriminations against England. The theme chosen was the British Intervention of twenty years before, of which every event was now commemorated. No mention was made of the simultaneous German intervention of that time. Also, the name of the leader of the British Intervenion was invariably omitted. This was Mr. Churchill. The Russians had studied his recent insistence on taking account of Russia, and knew he might be useful to them later on.

So things went on till the vast German conquests of the spring of 1940 and the speedy fall of France. Then came another lightning change and the whole Russian press was switched on to a new tack. British war news was moved into the first place. Both sides, it now appeared, were "imperialists." Britain was not yet beaten; and it was certainly not in Russia's interest that she should be, for now there was no doubt but that Russia came next on Hitler's list.

It may be imagined how invaluable it was to me, that I was able to go at any time to Mr. Maisky to ask a straight question and to get a straight answer, invariably confirmed by the sequel. For instance, to know that Russia in no way identified herself with the German settlement of Poland proper, or that Russia had no wish to see Germany anywhere near the Black Sea. The results of these talks, I invariably reported to my colleagues. I regard as my principal service in this period, my memoranda conveying warnings that certain suggestions of British policy must automatically bring us into war with Russia, for instance, any bombing of Baku while Russia was still neutral, or the arrival of a British contingent on the Finnish front in the Russo-Finnish War of 1939-1940. Most important of all was a memorandum on the Curzon Line, as the most reasonable frontier between Russia and Poland, drawn up with the help of that fine Russian scholar, Humphrey Sumner, when in September, 1939, the Red Army crossed the existing Polish frontier. Our view was from the first taken by the British Government, and has since been confirmed by the final results.

My view could not be popular–with Russia under very intelligible suspicion, and later with an exiled Polish Government settled in England. So far I had had the fullest support and approval from my colleagues; but on an evening in March, 1940, I received a sudden and unexpected visit from my Chief asking for reductions in my department (much of which was paid for by the University of London), and asking whether I would dispense with Humphrey Sumner. That, I said was quite impossible, so I was told that I must go myself. Proposals of other economies, or even that I would myself work without salary were rejected. I believe I know from whom my dismissal came, the spokesman of appeasement of Hitler was still in power–and I must add that later on the most honorable amends were made to me.

I recalled that, after all, it was only like what had happened to me in World War I, when I brought to England the particulars of the Russian shortage and casualties and the requests of the leaders of the Russian public. So I simply sought other war service.

Meanwhile, with a tinge of malice, I set about writing my Penguin *Russia*. I had been given the "bird" (which is English for dismissal) and I replied to one bird with another! The first edition of 50,000 was exhausted in a week or two. Other editions followed, carrying the sales before I left England, to a quarter of a million. I had a little bit of fun over the second edition. The Educational Supplement of the *Times* had reviewed the first. It thought that "Mr. Bernard Pares" had done a creditable piece of work. This could not have pleased the editor of the *Times,* who had been one of the foremost "appeasers." So, the next week, his Literary Supplement, in a savage review, said that it was "pathetic" to find "Sir Bernard Pares" writing such things. This reviewer had evidently had little time to read the book; and it was not difficult to give him the answers to his criticisms by simple references to the page numbers. This I did in a short note, inserted in the second edition, on the reviews of the first. Far the most helpful, I said, was the *Times;* for everyone would now have to read the book to find out which was right, "Mr. Bernard" or "Sir Bernard"; and this, no doubt, was why the first 50,000 had been sold out so quickly.

There has always been a special flavor in my relations with Penguins, whether British or American. My friend, Ian Ballantine, of New York is scarcely more than 30. The Lane family in England are a little bit older. It was a sister and three brothers, one of whom, I grieve to say, was killed on dangerous war service. The brilliant Allen Lane had discovered a new public. I had a letter from a group of older publishers inquiring whether my *"Russia"* had been subsidized by the British Government—the least likely thing in the world. If not, they said, they couldn't understand how at sixpence it was an economic proposition; they were thinking of trying something of the same kind themselves at one shilling. The Penguins, up to the war, cost sixpence; for ninepence they printed my Russian Fables of Krylov, with the Russian text facing my English, and their own compositors transposed it almost without mistake from the old Russian spelling into the new. I once told Allen Lane that I proposed to ask leave to address the Publishers' Association and to move a vote of thanks to Penguins, for helping to sell their own costlier hardcover books by the same authors. This is what actually happened to me too; but I didn't need Allen Lane to tell me that I should certainly have been kicked out of the room.

## IN THE LONDON BLITZ

It was at the gates of Battersea Park that I went through the London Blitz. In spite of all that we lost in life and property, there was never any experience for which our country had more reason to be grateful. The years of appeasement had been very distressing; any of us who knew anything about Europe, were well aware that our name stank there. Even through the first year of the war, the "phoney" year, we were still very limp. We were suddenly raised to "the finest hour" in our history, with our finest war leader at our head. At once all class distinctions disappeared. The old lady on our ground floor flat, now next to my own, had been there for over thirty years, and I for nearly ten, but we had hardly ever spoken. Now she guested us with tea and cakes whenever there was a raid. We sat strung out in a row facing the wall in her narrow passage, the various house servants with the rest, and read in turn anything cheerful, for instance Dickens' *Pickwick*. One of us–our local Nazi, as I used to think of him, almost bellowed into the wall facing him; but how well I remember the beautifully modulated voices of a veteran solicitor and a school head mistress! The nastiest moment was when we heard the bombs actually descending. Even some who were very brave couldn't help an instinctive shiver. They never got the four targets just across the park. One string of bombs was only a hundred yards off from getting all four of them.

Of course, the river Thames was an admirable guide for them. 140 yards off from us on the other side, a land mine knocked out twenty houses and made twenty more uninhabitable. The number of victims was surprisingly few. We were always glad when we heard our big naval guns in the park break out in reply. Then the enemy always went back or high up, and anyhow was no longer heard. I don't remember more than one actual dive, and that might have been one of our own planes. There was a daring German dive-bomber who crashed the chapel of Buckingham Palace, and it was the silliest thing to do. It put our King on the same level as the long-suffering poor of East London, who had often to meet the first attack, and there was a special tang in the song of those days, "The King is still in London." One

morning, after a heavy night raid, my old lady said to me,
"When you left me last night, I thought I would have my
bath. I was just stepping into it when the siren went again,
and, I said: 'To hell with Hitler, I will have my bath.' " The
nice old thing was so pleased at having used a swear word.
London, and indeed England, was like a besieged city, and
we were all one, braced to all sacrifices. It was indeed our
"finest hour"; and when it was over and we were gradually
coming down to earth again, there was truly even a lurking
feeling that we ought to have some more to keep us up to
the mark.

## THROUGH BRITAIN FOR THE ALLIANCE

And then, in a day and a night, on the famous 22nd of
June, 1941, came the first of our two great salvations, Hitler's
invasion of Russia (the second was, of course, Pearl Harbor),
without which we could not have hoped for anything more
than a stalemate, ruinous for all, if even for that; and with
this came the end of my own unemployment. I have already
told how I tracked the new great turn on its way, when relating my talks with Mr. Maisky. Even before this, I was invited
to see the high official whom I regarded as really responsible
for my recent dismissal. I sat down some distance off and only
drew nearer to him when he progressively drew nearer to me.
He told me I had been right all through; and before leaving,
I wrote his name in the second edition of my Penguin. I
thought it was a diplomatic, but very handsome apology. On
the invasion of Russia, the *Times* swung over me and landed
almost beyond on the other side. The Literary Supplement
wrote and asked me to write for them, which I did with
pleasure.

From the Ministry of Information I received a request
for "Speakers' Notes on Russia" for those who handled the
regular news meetings all over the country. In reply, I sug-

gested that it would be much better if I met the speakers themselves for discussion. This led to a series of "seminars" in all the twelve districts of the country. These discussions usually lasted two hours and covered all the chief questions relating to Russia. They always interested me. In Glasgow, an eminent Scottish divine found a kinship between features of Communism and of Calvinism. I remember another incident of a visit to Glasgow. I arrived at night in rain and blackout, and couldn't see the next person to me. There was no transport, and I asked the nearest shadow the way to a rather distant hotel. The shadow took my arm and also one of my suitcases, and we went more than a mile together. When I could see the man, I found he was a "down-and-out." It would have been the easiest thing for him to slip away with my suitcase. The Glasgow people told me proudly that this could not have happened in Edinburgh. In a crowded meeting at Edinburgh, where the air is "clearer and keener," I was properly heckled. One questioner asked, "Would the Ministry of Information have sent you to tell us all this a year ago?" I said, "No," and was told by the spokesman of the Ministry that I had given the right answer.

The new attitude of our public toward Russia was an immediate and complete change, equivalent in kind to a revolution. This will be understood at once. At Nuneaton in the Midlands, which had had a battering something like that of Coventry, the Mayor opened the meeting with the words, "We all know who has given us a quiet night." The Russians had brought us immediate relief from the Blitz, and that was something which every man in the street realized. At Coventry, I spoke among the ruins, as usual, with all parties represented on the platform. The Bishop, one of our finest, alluded to an after-dinner remark by a high-placed conservative which had been much quoted, to the effect that it might be a good thing if the Russians and Germans killed each other off. "Is it possible," asked the Bishop, "that that should have

been said in England? How incredibly mean!" In a spacious
chapel in Northampton, in the same district, the Mayor, as
strictly nonparty, was again in the chair with an all-round
platform. "Why didn't we know more about Russia?" he
said, no doubt thinking of their magnificent resistance to the
invaders. "We must have light"; and then the audience, or
I might almost say the congregation, was called on to sing the
hymn, "Let There Be Light!" That was the "lead" for my
speech! In another big town, I was called in by a very high-
placed conservative (he had never been sympathetic to my
views) to ask me to set right with the Russians a peculiarly
tactless and much quoted remark by a close friend of his own.
Birmingham, as I was forewarned, was still critical. That was
the home city of Neville Chamberlain.

I went all round the country speaking on Russia for a
year and a half–literally from Inverness to Cornwall. I think
the largest town which I did not visit was Norwich. Nearly
everywhere the attitude was fundamentally the same, but it
was very interesting to observe the distinctive local differences in kind. Lancashire, with a great spate of meetings, was
all out for Russia; in the more isolated industrial communities in the folds of the Pennine Hills, I was more than once
surprised to find serious students of really informing books
on this much abused subject. The north, round Newcastle,
was equally keen and enthusiastic. After all, it was not only
the Russian fighting that attracted us. We were ourselves,
in our own chosen way, now living collectively, as was in-
escapable in the conditions of a besieged city, and the community principle was at the root of the Russian resistance.
Wales, again, as usual, had a spirit of her own. That is a nation of poets. The best thing for a speaker to do in Wales
is to ask the audience to sing a hymn first. They so much
enjoy it. Their hymns are their best music, and they are far
the best part-singers in the country. This helps what might
be called the "uplift." They have a special Welsh word for
it. At Cardiff, the real capital of Wales, the chairman said,

"I'll put them in the right mood." This might have seemed alarming elsewhere, but that was exactly what he did, and he put me in right on the top of it.

The south of England is generally the slowest to think, and the southwest still lags somewhat behind the rest; but now it was the south and east coasts that were nearest to invasion. At Hastings, as they told me, I was speaking five minutes by air from the colony. Brighton always has the stage instinct, and here we had one of the largest and best organized meetings of all, preceded by a beautiful selection of Russian music, wonderfully rendered; I came away even forgetting to put on my jacket again, with all its treasures. Canterbury Cathedral stood gloriously intact, with ruin all round it. The famous Dean of Canterbury, Dr. Hewlett Johnson, who has written so enthusiastically of Russia that I cannot always agree with him, had in civil life been an engineer. In preparation for a great raid, he had devised a system of ladders, to deal immediately with the incendiaries; and when the threat became a reality, he was there in his vestments on the street, successfully directing the defense. Everything all round was reduced to ruin.

It may be said at once without any kind of exaggeration, that everywhere the Blitz was medicine; the measure of the danger was the measure of the spirit to meet it. Within a short space of time, I spoke in Harrogate and in Hull, both in that same fine county of Yorkshire and only some fifty or sixty miles apart. At that time, we were having a simultaneous levy for warships. Harrogate, which was so far untouched, is a rest cure for the rich, with medicinal waters and great hydros; only here did I find actual traces of indifference and even of defeatism. Hull is largely a city of the poor, and had been grievously battered. Harrogate, I am told, did not reach their quota of contribution; Hull more than doubled it.

At Portsmouth, on the south coast, which was constantly raided—I had three raids in my day and a half there, and spoke through one. My host had developed a quiet technique;

of day raids no notice was taken; night raids were spent under a large iron table where we could all lie side by side. At Southampton the raids, just then, were even more frequent. Almost the whole center of the town had been gutted; when people parted company, the ordinary greeting was "Good luck!" At Bootle, a separate borough in Lancashire, which is practically the line of the Liverpool sea-going docks, only one third of the houses had so far been left habitable. I visited the Rotary Club, always a standby of sound convervatism, and the spirit of help and sacrifices reminded me peculiarly of Russia. Lowestoft, on the east coast, consists of one endless street, running by the sea; no one stayed there who was not needed. Each night my old host and his wife sent their maid servants into the country for safety and managed for themselves. The meeting was set for seven-thirty, "because nine-thirty is Jerry's time." And "Jerry" could blow in here unbeknown at any time and at any point. Little ships lay close in to shore by day, to rest from their night work of watching out for the sound waves. Many of them had been damaged.

I had no serious difficulties, except in London. Here there was a collection of those who had a maximum of party prejudices, as leaders of the various political organizations; each of them had his own party views on Russia, which for them had become a party question, and was not ready to welcome other views. Curiously enough, I found most difficulty with British Labor.

## THROUGH AMERICA FOR THE ALLIANCE

From now on, my right place of work was America. A far vaster and more various country than my own, with its large and diverse racial groups, much more remote from things Russian, and for that reason much more backward in knowledge of them. Yet in the long run, America was certainly more important than any other country to the alliance and to the peace. Being now in favor again, I went on badgering the Ministry of Information until it sent me there, at first for three months, and I am here still. The Ministry had a branch service in the United States, with an old and firm friend in charge of our speakers in Professor W. J. Hinton, who had had to witness my fantastic oratorical ventures in Siberia. On the American side, there was in New York an ideal lecture agency under the direction of another of my best friends, that distinguished public man, Dr. Stephen P. Duggan, attached to the Carnegie Institute, who had guided all my steps in my journeys of 1924 and 1929.

I was ordered to repair to a lonely bay in Scotland. There I saw perhaps the most beautiful and certainly the largest ship I had ever seen; the perfect form of its structure disguised its vast proportions. It was the Queen Elizabeth. On board was an equally wonderful company. A veritable feast for a first-class journalist, for everyone had a story and a purpose; we had men of all nations and all callings–diplomatists, soldiers, sailors, wounded and war prisoners. In mid-winter of 1942 we raced across the Atlantic eluding all submarines by sheer pace, swirling about from north to south and back, and finishing the voyage almost on record time. It was a tense experience, and it was only when we knew we were half a day from shore that someone tentatively and listlessly strummed on the lounge piano.

Sam Harper had at last given me word to come. I got two of his short, concise letters, full of fact and suggestion, after I reached New York. We were to do a radio duet on the Chicago Round Table, and how I looked forward to playing partner with him again! Before I could reach him, he was unexpectedly found dying in his bed; he had been in excellent form the previous evening. I spent three memorable days with his devoted brother, Paul. We had always been pressing Sam to write his memoirs, and we had no real idea how much of them was complete. It was all done to the very end, and all in type and readable, and with this there were short, invaluable notes for the coming peace settlement. Sam never did anything by halves. I saw all his students; every one of them was in full stride in his work, and each knew exactly at what he was aiming.

I was piloted right round America from afar, with telegrams where necessary, by two most able young secretaries, Eunice Lisowski of Dr. Duggan's and Katharine Aikins of Hinton's organization. They worked closely together, and the result was perfect, so that I had no cares except my lectures. Certainly, as Harper had forewarned me, the conditions of winter travel were heavy; but except for the inevitable night journeys I hardly had to notice them. My worst experience was a delayed crossing of the Bay of Fundy in a snow blizzard and a night journey in a sleepless freight train, where I talked all night with a stray wanderer who insisted that I go and see his family at Medicine Hat in Alberta.

In general, through all my journeys, I was simply surrounded by kindness of the most practical kind. This is no phrase of recognition, but the simple expression of a sincere gratitude. The two best examples of hospitality that I know are the Russian and the American, in many ways very much alike, and both are far more *effective*–that is the right word– than the British. We do our best, but we have never taken too much trouble to organize hospitality. Those of my countrymen who have enjoyed Russian and American hospitality hardly know how to return either. My recollection of American hospitality is that I would mention my lack of something and that it was almost put straight into my hands. There was a sincere respect for what we had gone through in England, and I can't think there can ever have been a happier time for an Englishman to spend in America.

I started by going straight through Canada to the Pacific, speaking in each chief town on the road. At Saskatoon we had 40° of frost, but at Vancouver I came out in February into a kind of spring. British Canada has still very much left of the mid-Victorian atmosphere. I was filled with admiration, almost amounting to awe, at its loyalty to the mother country. They have achieved what seemed impossible, in realizing all our ordeals and dangers without having experienced them themselves, and at once feeling, thinking, and acting in accordance. In the United States the people had given us full measure of credit; they had a touch of envy of our trials and had even conjured up imaginary air-raids, to get as near to our experience as possible. From Canada I passed down the Pacific Coast, staying with my old friends and colleagues at Berkeley; I was housed in the Student's Union, and a charming young boy kept me up half the night, distressed at heart by the faintness of the hope for an ideal world. The winter of 1943-1944, I spent by arrangement in the Middle-West as a guest of the University of Wisconsin in Madison. Every time I went back there, I felt I was going home. I lived in the Students' Memorial Union and they would always be coming round me to ask questions about Russia. But the best part of my time was spent in going over and over again into Chicago, to speak at meetings. I felt that the local reputation for isolation had certainly another side to it, and indeed I was never seriously troubled by the views of the *Chicago Tribune*. I don't know that the Mid-Westerners took them much more seriously than I did. And certainly, I found several little clubs or other centers which derived a special enthusiasm from their reaction against the lack of knowledge all round them. As I went further West from Chicago, I became more and more fond of the Middle-West in general. I think there is an excellent core of public opinion in those parts. The farmer's mind is a good one. There are not many faddists about, and there is no serious opposition to meet. So far, there had been no reason why those sound and sensible people should have been expected to know anything about Russia. Now, they knew they had to and they never failed to give me a fair chance of telling them what I knew.

I found a very lively center of interest in Cleveland and its surroundings. This city can be proud of one of the best organized public libraries in the world, with a long tradition of wise and imaginative direction. I would call it "an attacking library," which does not just wait for the readers to come to it but takes active steps to challenge their attention. We had tried in our own little way to make it a model for our School library in London. Cleveland has to meet a domestic challenge of its own; only 15 per cent of its people are Anglo-Saxon, and one-third are Slavs. There is in one quarter a vigorous branch library which is mainly Slav. The spacious and stately Union Club is a center for keen discussions of world interests, always kept in motion by Dr. Brooks Emeny and his Council of Foreign Affairs. One felt the intellectual keenness and had a peculiar pleasure in going there.

In Wall Street, New York, and its surroundings, I found quite a special interest in Russia. The bogie of Communism frightens the inheritor of an income earned by someone else; but it has no terrors for the vigorous Captain of Industry, with his eye on the future rather than on the past. That is why Mr. Eric Johnston's tour in Russia was such a great success. Through my friend, Major Ormerod, I was invited to a whole series of business luncheons, to speak of the work of construction carried on in Russia, which has really been much the most important feature of her public life, also of the far greater possibilities of developments of the same kind which seemed likely to open up after the war.

In general, I have always been refreshed by an American audience; they come prepared to enjoy themselves, the intimate bond which they establish with the speaker, the alertness, humor, and good nature of the questions. How can one fail to respond to an audience when they write of you as at Rocky Ford, Colorado?–

## FROM *THE ROCKY FORD GAZETTE*

### April 10, 1945.

Sir Bernard Pares (pronounced like the three bears) "whooshed" in precisely on the stroke of 8:00 o'clock last night. Then when the final question was answered, he announced "that was all" and "whooshed" out of the auditorium without giving anyone an opportunity to delay his return to the hotel with private questions for another 30 minutes.

Sir Bernard is no rostrum speaker. He sat on tables with his feet propped on the front pew of the church. He marched up and down the aisles if he hadn't heard a question. He stood up, then leaned palms down on a table to get a better look at the eyes of the front-row listeners. By the time he had spoken only a few sentences the entire audience felt as if he had been in their midst many times, and was a very close friend.

I would say, in a word, that the chief difference between wartime opinion in England and America was that in America they had not been bombed. We too, in the last war, had a very small proportion of our casualties in our homeland. I think that all other distinctions relate to this difference. Had they the experience, they would, I feel sure, be just the same, for there is a certain, specific, individual pride in the American which would produce the same reaction as with us. But bombing is not one of those things which are easy to imagine, and the rear remains the rear. And in this case, the rear was huge and very various.

## My Impressions of America

This time I have been in America for nearly five years; my visits of 1924 and 1929 each lasted several months, with extensive travel. This time, I have lived for considerable periods in Ithaca, New York, Toronto, Syracuse, Seattle, Kansas City, and I spent the winter of 1943-1944 in Madison,

Wisconsin. I have been often on the move, and frequently in New York and Washington, D. C. Now that I've settled here (I still have my British passport) I should like to write my impressions of this great country. They are impressions only, and not an analysis.

My first impression is of its greatness and abundance, and I find both inspiring. I can well understand that it should have so long been contented with itself, and how truly it has seemed to so many indeed like a new world; far from all of the cares and worries of the old. I like to sit in Washington Square–Greenwich Village is my favorite part of New York– and hear the various languages that are spoken there. These people come from the most widely separated countries, but I think there is one thing common to all of them which shows itself in a certain American pride and contentment. I believe that nearly all are better off here than in the countries from which they come. I feel the same stimulus, myself, the stimulus of the potential, something which has no limits, like the freshness of a new birth. My favorite part of the country is the Middle West, or to be more exact, the "Further Middle West," before one reaches the Desert and the real West, the country with the vast spaces which is still in a stage of exploration. It is far more like Russia than it knows, and so are its people. So often it is the intervention of governments that is responsible for misunderstanding between peoples.

America seems to me like a great sprawling young giant, not one nation but many, and they meet here in what has so often been called a melting pot, which is creating a new young life of its own. The environment is all spontaneous, something that makes quickly and simply for friendship, for acceptance by one's neighbors till one should show that he does not deserve it.

That is what makes America so different from my own country, and one is constantly reminded of our limitations;

but the Englishman rejoices in this scope, and that is why he is also at home in Russia. This lies behind all our games and all our imperial wanderings. In the short lived peace of Amiens (1880-1881) Charles James Fox, regarded at home as too great an admirer of Napoleon and of France, visited the Paris Exhibition. Napoleon who was short of stature, standing by a globe, pointed a finger at England and remarked how tiny it was. "Yes," said Fox, who was counted the second fattest man in England, "that is where the English are born, and that is where they hope to die; but in the course of their lives they embrace the whole world with their activities," and the big man with his broad arms embraced the whole world. Isn't that why so many of us gave a start to the history of this country?

But it is just the size and the youth of America that make life here different from life in England. It is not one country but many, and I think they don't get joined together. The great sprawling giant has not yet learned the use of all his limbs. I do not see how there could be such a compact public opinion in America as there is with us. It is like a number of different communities, that do not yet know each other. With us, pretty well everyone at one time or another has to come to London. We know all about each other, or if we do not we can find out by asking, which saves a lot of time and trouble.

One thing that surprises and confuses me is the precious and jealous particularism of the different states. The more so as their divisions are so artificial. It passes into all sorts of peculiarities of law: behavior has to be different in different parts. Even in one state one may be legally married, and in another not. This, together with the great distances, seems to me to create a certain indefiniteness, which leaves room for all sorts of misunderstandings, a vagueness which one does not fight but evades or rather by-passes. One bows to the local conditions and goes his own way. Personal relations also, are naturally more fleeting. It would be harder here than in England to fully "conquer one's fate,"–to realize in full detail a settled purpose; one might have to change to another purpose, just as promising and just as good, and there is always plenty of choice, so that the change comes easy. This gives a certain elasticity in which we English are lacking. The misunderstandings may remain forever unexplained. Friendship, so cordial at the outset, seems to leave so much to chance. In some cases, this environment of indefiniteness seems to me to produce a certain social nervousness, which with us is for the most part left to women.

All this makes little difference to ordinary life, which is generally so much more free of worry than with us. But it is in the organization at the top that one notices the absence of our compactness something like a kind of looseness of the joints. Take, what strikes as a standing anomaly, the fact that what is with us London is here divided between Washington and New York. The government official with us comes out from his day's work into London and is conscious of it all around him and also of what it thinks of him. Here the principal national officials have all been segragated into one place where the pulse of the nation, so far as it is one, is not so perceptible. And they are all dependent for their jobs on what is happening in the great hinterland behind them. As to the divisions between the two main political parties, it seems to us unintelligible. Except for family or other loyalty, we cannot see what is to settle the choice at a time of election. Also the great party machines seem like something remote and inaccessible to the man in the street, with a separate language of their own, as they certainly are not in England. We do not understand what settles the major issue, why this leads to that. It is something like the same with the Press. It seems almost to go on separate from the life of the people with laws of its own–much more like playing a game than it is with us.

We must not make the ordinary mistake which almost any country makes about another, to demand a consistency not to be expected of any great mass of human beings. But here, owing to what looks like a certain imperfection of articulation, we find it hard to see how the public mind can reconcile its "opposites." It is difficult to understand the contrast between how life is lived and the principles which it seems to accept; on the one side, the hard road of competitive individualism, on the other, the naive generalities which the idealist declares to be absolute in their application, such as no "power politics" and no "spheres of influence," both of which are here as they are everywhere else. In isolation, that is, without the experience of common friction, it was no doubt easier to lay down these general laws and to claim for them a sort of "platform acceptance."

Of one thing I can judge more closely, as in all my visits here, the milieu in which I have moved has been that of the universities. In 1924, it seemed to me that they were much less a part of the whole nation than they are now, they did their good work with far less account of the public and of its praise, and this seemed to give them a certain general remoteness or even pedantry. In 1929, they had a considerably wider fringe of public interest and support. Now, they seem to be a normal and vigorous part of the life of the country, with a much stronger hold on its interest and conscience. Over the whole period of my contact with them, they have had much further to go than with us, but they are going much faster.

## AMERICA ON THE WORLD THRESHOLD

The present is a momentous stage in the development of American history, and no well wisher of this country should desire to see sudden and ill-considered change. America must find her way. Yet her present situation calls for all sorts of adaptation, which in some respects may almost amount to a transformation. The old happy isolation, which together with the ever successful advance over an almost empty continent made so much of the charm of this New World, is no longer possible unless America is to break with the rest of us. What was right then, may have to be reconsidered now in the light of an entirely new situation, and in this new era of the atomic bomb the first steps may even be decisive.

Michelet has written that the advent of every new national *infantry* marks a new chapter in the civilization of the world. This will hold good in history successively for the infantries of Spain, France, and Germany. The present is the advent of two national infantries which so far have never played so great a part outside their own borders. They are the Russian and the American; and at present they are locked together in a joint grip on Berlin. We English depend on the result, and it is very natural that fine British internationalists such as Sir Norman Angel and Sir Alfred Zimmern have decided, like myself, to stay on here indefinitely; for it is quite possible that Great Britain out of the very full experience of her past, especially when that past seems almost to be repeating itself on this side of the Atlantic, has something to contribute.

At present, we have in America the inevitable relaxation after an intense struggle, a search for the familiar past of our own country. We English, not then reduced to temporary exhaustion went just the same way after the First World War, and I think it is not a bad guess to take it that America is now about where we were then; but the return to the vanished past proved impossible. Present-day America will now find nothing to lean upon in present-day Europe. There, as everywhere outside Russia, is going on a fight for freedom (who knows if it may not come in Russia itself); but "free enterprise," as at present understood in America, is not one of the combatants in this fight, which is between communism and a democratic socialism. America has to equip herself to meet the new situation, and it is not likely that the old luxuries of an existence apart can be maintained. If American policy is to have an impact to correspond to American military strength the direction at home will be rather to concentration than away from it. The giant will have to pull himself together.

It might be said that while America was unlikely to take any action, American criticisms were not taken too seriously abroad, for instance with us in England, and rather were good-humouredly dismissed. But now all professions of principle are vulnerable, and departures in practice become a matter of concern. Molotov has been playing on this theme throughout the whole work of the U.N.

Above all, in my view, there must be a realization that one world does not mean an Anglo-Saxon world. Our ways and thoughts, our institutions are very peculiar to ourselves and very difficult to transplant elsewhere.

We British, in our comparative isolation under Victoria, had almost come to think that we were a law to the rest of the world. Nothing was a greater barrier to our finding good will in other countries.

> For since she helped in licking Nap the Fust
> And pricked a bubble just about to bust,
> With Rooshy, Prooshy, Austry all assistin,
> There ain't a face but what she's shook her fist in.

So wrote James Russell Lowell of us, and again

> We own the ocean tu, John
>    You mustn't think it hard
> If we don't think with you, John
>    It's just your own back yard
> Old Uncle S, Sez he, I guess,
>    If that be so, sez he,
> The fencing stuff will cost enough
>    To bust up friend J.B.
>    Ez well as you and me.

The "fencing stuff" is of course the armament, and it is apt
to be expensive. That is why the warning is no longer for us,
but chiefly both for America and Russia.

Then there are changes which would now seem to become imperative here. I think the public will have to know
more clearly which of the great parties it wishes to place in
power: at present it votes at the same time for Wallace and
Bilbo. Or again, nothing was more reasonable than that when
there was a natural discount on *all* foreign commitments; it
should have been possible for a *minority* of the Senate, where
the hinterland of the country is given an artificial preponder-
ance, to cancel any foreign engagement. With the U.N. sitting
in New York, how can one ask that any decision at last arrived at there should be subject to annulment by a *minority*
of any national assembly? Ways will be found out of all these
difficulties. Some solutions have already been canvassed and
even practised; but the pointer towards change is very
evident.

As far as my own field is concerned, there is one need
that is more conspicuous than any other. Clearly the fate of
the world depends on the relations of America and Russia.
What Russia does, will depend on her; but for America the
first need is a really informed public opinion on Russia. It
is too obvious to anyone who knows much about the subject
that at present there is nothing of the kind. I have spent my
life in this field; and over here, I sometimes feel utterly bewildered by the hopeless aberrations to right and to left–at
present predominantly to right, and I find the general picture utterly foreign to all that I know about the actual facts.
A shrewd American judge has asked for a definition of Communism. Webster's Collegiate Dictionary makes Socialist a
"synonym of collectivist, nihilist, *communist,* anarchist, bolshevik; these groups are agreed in distrusting capitalist control of industry." All that one can say about the man who
wrote this particular section is that he was an ignoramus

for he bunches together a whole number of quite different things, whose differences are just now being fought out
all over Europe. Would it not be as well, also, to define what
exactly is meant by "Un-American activities?" To be critical
of the opposite exaggeration, one finds often a simple refusal
to face any fact which is unfavorable to the Soviet Union. I
should like to ask, for instance, whether anyone has ever read
of a debate and a vote at the meetings of the Supreme Congress of Soviets under the very pretentious "Stalin" constitution?

### The American's Knowledge of Russia

In England, in 1918, a Prime Minister's Committee declared our knowledge of Russia to be "abysmal"; there was
only one professor of the subject, who happened to be myself. It is abysmal here now. I don't see how this can be
blamed too sharply. Till the United States resolved on active
participation in world affairs, how could one expect of the
citizen of Iowa or Colorado any such knowledge as he would
have of the affairs of his own country? I have said that these
remote states are my favorite part of America, and certainly
there was none where my task was easier. I had only to be
fair and keep my temper, as my audiences always did. There
is the core of a very sound public opinion in the Middle
West. The farmer's mind is a good mind; there are not many
faddists about. It is a clear field and there is practically no
expert opposition. I did not ever see any particular reflection
of the views of the *Chicago Tribune*. Efficiently as it is run
as a newspaper enterprise, I don't think that its particular
attitude on politics was taken too seriously. The general attitude of my audiences seemed something like this:–We don't
know much about these questions; we are completely confused by conflicting views; tell us what you know, and we
will form our own judgment. From now on, both Iowa and

Colorado are well aware that they have got to know about these things.

But, in the general ignorance, it is just to these conflicting views that the public is at present a prey. The giant is being led by the nose. One very disturbing feature, unknown in England, is the presence of so many ethnic groups–say for instance in Cleveland or Milwaukee. Each has its own bias, that of the country from which it came. That these ethnic groups should act as valuable cultural ties with the countries from which they came, is all to the good; but it would be fatal if they were allowed to dictate American policy toward their countries of origin, and that is what some of them are organized to do. Many of these people left their own countries because they were entirely dissatisfied with things as they were there; for instance because their own views were not followed. And they are therefore not the best judges of our relations with them.

Much the closest organized are the Poles, and they have behind them the Catholic Church. The duel between Russia and Poland began not with Versailles and the Treaty of Riga in 1921, when most Americans began to look seriously at Russia, but go as far back as the tenth century when Poland became Catholic in 966 A.D. and Russia Orthodox in 989, and it has gone on almost without interruption ever since. Now it happens that I took up the cause of Poland, that is, the domination of Polish population by Russia, forty years ago in 1907, as will be seen from my association with Roman Dmowski, described earlier in this book; But I was never for the domination of Russian peasants by Polish landlords, which was the result of Pilsudski's march into Russia when Russia was down and out; nor did I ever think it could be permanent without a joint British and American army on the spot to back it–and not even then. I am pretty well aware which are Poles and which are Russians in these parts; for I had a unique experience when I was pushed through the whole of the disputed area with the Russian Army in the First World War; and, in fact, it was Marshal Pilsudki himself who told me that he had just come back from a district on his new frontier where the Polish population was 20 per cent of the total. I was still in favor of Poland getting Lvov to the east of the Curzon line. I have no particular love either for Russian or for Polish statistics, but never have I seen a more complete distortion of facts than in the figures presented to the American public during the presidential election of 1944: I could give many examples. From a Polish point of view, therefore, it was very desirable that my voice should not be heard.

The Poles got to work on me as soon as I landed in America. At my first meeting, in New York, hardly a public one but a gathering of my colleagues in Slavic Studies, someone asked me whether I thought Russia would restore the Riga frontier of 1921, and I said "No." This was sufficient to prompt a plea to Dr. Duggan that he should not sponsor my lectures. Later the Poles, who did not challenge me at my many meetings, made a habit of protesting to the nearest British consul. My maintenance was then on the charge of the British Government, but the Poles were equally dependent on British and American funds. In the end, I had a message from our Embassy which made me ask to see our Ambassador. He quite reassured me, but to ease the position and maintain my independence, I myself decided to go on to my own resources, and at the same time on to the American quota. (October 1944).

That the Poles after their terribly harrowing experience should react in this way toward Russia is only intelligible; but there is another feature of the anti-Russian journalism in America which is much more puzzling. Of the regular spokesmen of this view who are constantly appearing and reappearing as authorities on the radio and in the press, almost a majority are recognizable as former spokesmen of world revolution. Mr. Louis Fischer, when he visited me in London in the earlier years of Communism, was certainly a fellow traveller. Mr. Max Eastman was the author of a pamphlet on "The End of Socialism" in Russia (a ridiculous thesis, it seems to me), which he attributed entirely to Stalin. I understand he has since made something like a recantation, and Mr. Eugene Lyons is another penitent. But these are the old Trotskyites whose fury against Stalin is due precisely to that for which I am grateful to him. Of course, anyone who knows anything about the subject is aware that Trotsky stood for "permanent revolution" and Stalin for "socialism (he does not say communism) in one country," a policy which made possible our alliance in the Second World War. Though I do not suggest that they have thought of this, it is clear enough that the best way back to World Revolution would be a third World War with the atomic bomb between America and Russia. But to shift on to Stalin the old menace of his bitterest enemy Trotsky seems to me unpardonable and a travesty of all the facts.

Mr. William Henry Chamberlin is different. He is a recognized American scholar on Russia, and I do not cease to recommend the valuable historical work which caused him such labor and privations in his twelve difficult years there. Only I cannot understand what he is doing now. With some others he founded a scholarly journal *The Russian Review* at Boston, and it is doing very good work. I was invited to associate myself with it, but later read a furious all-round diatribe by Mr. Chamberlin against Russia for all the Hearst newspapers, with no kind of discrimination or perspective and sometimes literally screaming in capital letters. I withdrew my name from the *Review* suggesting that Mr. Chamberlin should choose between leadership in Russian studies and this kind of journalism. Whether my letter had anything to do with it or not, Mr. Chamberlin in the next number made his choice and has resigned his editorship of *The Rus-*

*sian Review.* It was an honest choice; but I wish it had been the opposite, for there are all too few of us who know the subject as well as he does; if they will put first the informing and not the inflaming of the public, and I cannot help feeling, that as a scholar, he must sometimes find it hard to forget a great deal of what he knows.

What is really wanted is Americans who know Russia. But what is the use of hoping for that if the Soviet government keeps out of Russia nearly all who will not praise it. Mr. Chamberlin, as I understand him, is one of the many professional journalists whom they have alienated. This Soviet attitude has to be faced by us; but we also have to face any counter criticisms with which it may seek to justify itself here. I fully expect Mr. Molotov, among his many ingenious arguments of this kind, designed to make us look at home, to ask where we are to find the true voice of American democracy—whether in the four elections of Franklin Roosevelt or in the eighty to ninety-odd per cent of the press which consistently opposed him. On the Russian side, the position is quite plain; the Press is official and always speaks only for the government; but he may claim that the American Press has to prove itself a faithful mirror of public opinion.

Here, the unpopular course, as far as the Press is concerned, is to say anything in favor of the Soviet government. The *Reader's Digest* decided to distribute to some 13 million readers the negligible judgments of Mr. William L. White, who had no knowledge of Russian and only a five weeks escorted journey through Russia. Mr. Raymond E. Davies, who must have fifty times more knowledge of Russia than Mr. White and was sometimes with him during this trip, wrote a telling reply, friendly and conclusive, but it appeared only in *Soviet Russia,* which can hardly have one hundredth of Mr. White's readers. Consequently, it is Mr. White who goes in America; and I've even received an anonymous postcard asking how I dared to challenge his judgments. Mr. Max

Eastman wrote a furious attack on Stalin in the *Reader's Digest,* to which I sent a very moderate reply, but it was returned to me unpublished. In England, I understand that Mr. Herbert Morrison before his regrettable illness was taking up vigorously the question of the fairness of the newspaper chains and indeed a royal commission was appointed in March 1947. But far better than any government action is the reaction of a really informed public which can come only with more knowledge. Here, at present, there seem to be no standards, and that is a fatal weakness. When we had Lord Macauley in England, the man who published rubbish might receive such a caustic public chastisement in one of Macaulay's famous essays as to make him wish he had never written. We have no such scourge for rubbish about Russia.

Gilbert Chesterton, among his charming platitudes disguised as paradoxes, used to say that no newspaper could give you the news of the day, because you would not buy it. The newspaper would tell you that Jones has poisoned his wife; the real news of the day is that thousands of other couples are getting on quite well without any thought of assassination, but no one will give you a nickel to read that. It is headlines that sell a paper, and often they do not even correspond to the text which follows them. A distinguished American editor was asked whether "Peace" was a headline. He replied "Once!" It is a grim answer. Yet Peace is at this time the insistent demand of every country; and that both the press editor and the press proprietor know. For all that, press profits are not to be won by a simple repetition that all is well, or even that things are going right. On the contrary, from that point of view, there is a heavy premium on saying that they are going wrong. It is that way that the big money is to be made.

In the days when real news was worked for on the spot by resident foreign correspondents and when professional editors, for the most part honest men, were wholly responsible for what they published, freedom of the press was a principle of the first importance which carried its own explanation. It is different when "freedom of the press" really represents "freedom of the purse," that is, of the controlling proprietor who chooses what he will pass on to the public. News about one's own country can usually be checked; news on foreign countries more often can not. Who expects the citizen of Iowa to detect the misrepresentations whether of Russian or Polish racial statistics? (And generally he has only seen the second!) There is something to be said for the principle that those officially responsible for the fate of their country should have a voice in saying what latitude should be given to misrepresentations about another country; and in time of war this is always, at least partially, admitted in the shape of a national censorship. Still better is that social censorship by which the editor himself excludes extravagant views that are bound to cause unnecessary offense.

The world was empty after Hitler. So was the Press. So was the Alliance. "Nature abhors a vacuum." So does the Press. In time of peace the Press carries an increased responsibility. Is it imperative that the vacuum should be filled with a new enmity? If Press interests suggest that it should, national interests imperatively demand that it should not. May we not fairly ask professional writers on foreign countries to take account of this? For those who will not, I can only suggest that if their efforts lead to a third world war, they should lead the first battalion into action, armed with their pens!

## RUSSIAN STUDIES IN AMERICA NOW

Whether we are going to be friends or enemies with Russia, we shall be at a permanent disadvantage until we know more about her. The rulers of Russia are in the same position with regard to us, but however much the Russian people are kept in ignorance, they themselves do know all they need. The only question is whether they understand all they know. Stalin's understanding, to judge from his public statements, is excellent; but there are others in the Politburo and he is not there for ever. Molotov seems to me peculiarly uncomprehending. As we all know, Russia is less ready for war than we are; then why does he not begin to help us to make peace? I wonder if he at all realizes how much good will his tactics have lost for his country since 1945?

With us it is quite different. Our action must rest on public opinion, and in the long run that is our greatest strength. The bald contradiction is the glaring contrast between American military power and the knowledge which can direct its use in the national policy. That means a race between study and prejudice, with the atomic bomb in waiting in the background.

There can be no doubt at all that this has been completely understood by the directors of American education. The great Foundations, that beneficent feature of American public life which does such credit to capitalism, have done very much for Russian studies, helping to establish new schools and promoting individual research of every kind. The Rockefeller Foundation has enabled the American Council of Learned Societies, which is listed among the various world academies, to conduct a comprehensive scheme for the translation of important Russian books. The best Russian-English dictionary, no longer available in its Moscow edition, has been photostated and reproduced here. Favored by such help, new Departments of Russian study are springing up all over the country. From Pearl Harbor to October 1946, that is under five years, the number of American colleges offering Russian has risen from 19 to

112. The greatest advance of all was made when the Army and Navy authorities declared for the principle known as "area and language," which means the study not only of the language but of the country, with its history, economics, literature, laws and institutions, and public life. We have been struggling for this in England since the First World War, and had attained it in Russian studies; but in the United States it was at once applied all round. Even when the Army and Navy classes stopped, the general advance continued faster than ever. The teaching of the language could and should be entrusted to native Russians; of these there are plenty, and they have well repaid their debt to American hospitality. But the teaching of the public life of Russia, its history and economics up to date, if it is to be unbiased and objective, cannot be entrusted to them alone. Any new burst of activity such as I have described was bound to be confronted at the outset by a deplorable shortage of American teachers, and there is no incident in this all-round development that I think more important than the opening at Columbia University in October, 1946, of a special Institute of Russian Studies. This is due to the munificence of the Rockefeller Foundation, and it was the last act in the great work of President Nicholas Murray Butler for the two causes to which he had devoted his life, those of study and world peace. This Institute has, in my estimation, united in one place a good half of the very top rung of American scholars on Russia, who can therefore be available simultaneously to the same students. This is the necessary first step to the creation of that supply of American teachers which can make these studies flourish all over the country.

I have been privileged to take a part in this work. The reader will find our English solutions of just the same problems in my account of the School of Slavonic Studies in London of which I was Director between the two world wars, and all our experience has been at the service of the leaders of the same movement here. The Schools of London and Columbia are united in close co-operation.

My own experience in American universities in these years has consisted in giving a jog here or there to the movement, and this helps me to speak with knowledge and conviction of its vitality. Of the keenness of the students there cannot be the slightest doubt; and I expect here the same result that I have found in England, namely, that no one who takes up these studies ever entirely drops them. One notices in some places a pardonable feature of extreme youth,–the idea that with pace and pressure the whole thing can be done very quickly. One is asked to dash through all Russian history in a month, after which the same students can pass on to the study, say, of ancient literature. In such places I have sat in my office for appointed weekly hours, waiting for students who wanted to know more, but in vain; and if my part was the only part and consisted only in standing up before a class and talking to it, no serious achievement is to be expected.

It was different with that extraordinary assemblage of picked students from all parts, including even some professors, which gathered under the brilliant organization of Professor Ernest Simmons at the Summer Schools of 1943 and 1944 in Cornell; and this venture has now been repeated in many other places. I am specially familiar with that at Syracuse. But I have found something even more completely satisfying in my regular session's work at Sarah Lawrence College, Bronxville, to which I am now attached. I do not myself think that lecturing alone can be called real teaching without the addition of tutorial work with each individual student. That is the principle on which the program at Sarah Lawrence has long been based, so that I fell into a milieu in which everything, including expert library service, was ready to hand. We have had a long fight over this question in England; the tragic duel between

Mackay and Muir at Liverpool University was a part of its history. With the system which in Oxford is called "tutorial" and at Sarah Lawrence "conferences," the bulk of the work is individual. At Sarah Lawrence, we are a class, a team, and we go all through Russian history from the beginning together. We meet each of the great controversial questions at its origin and follow its story through. But each student, like the member of an orchestra, also undertakes on behalf of all some important aspect of Russian history and in a special paper communicates the results of the study to the rest. One can imagine how much can be done by each student with fifteen hours of reading a week and each has a special weekly conference with me. I have never had teaching which rewarded me more, and I am myself surprised at how much my students have added to my work.

In general, then, America has made a very good beginning, and we are ready with our side of the work. It remains to be seen, if there is to be any true and intelligent friendship between the two countries, if our contact is to be not with the Russian government but with the Russian people, that the jealous masters of the Kremlin should open their doors and let us get through to it. Otherwise how can we think that they really wish for our confidence or for our friendship?

I have an even stronger reason for my attachment to Sarah Lawrence College: in fact, I do not see how it could have happened anywhere else. This was real education. We teachers were responsible for following all the thoughts and interests of our students, and this we did in our weekly conferences; on this depended our joint direction of their studies. "Go and be an uncle to all these girls," said our brilliant young President, and it was an easy task, congenial to all concerned.

One of the brightest of my delightful class, Anne Norton, daughter of the well-known publisher, had not long ago lost her dearly-loved father; and she asked me simply if I would take his place. My Annie had a second sense. She was asking for just what I could best do, and she was offering me what I most deeply lacked. I think it was one of the prettiest things ever done to me. I agreed at once with great gratitude. So we have adopted each other as father and daughter or daddy and dochka, and we found that it was as if the kinship had been there all along.

I have mentioned earlier in this book that over thirty years ago my own home life had ceased, and it had never been replaced till now. I am very proud of my five children. When I have to spell my name on the phone, which is nearly always, I use their initials: P for Peter, A for Andrew, R for Richard, E for Elisabeth, and S for Susan: this is a coincidence, and Susan was originally Ursula. All five, when once the tension in the home was removed, have grown up to be a great satisfaction to me. Richard, a child of vision and genius, Scholar at Winchester and Balliol and Fellow of All Souls', went high as a volunteer in the Board of Trade during the war, and is now Professor of History in the University of Edinburgh. Elisabeth is on the staff of the Royal Institute of International Affairs and has done useful work for the Foreign Office. Ursula, a child of peculiar charm and brilliancy, was at the head of a room in the Ministry of Information, which had to find answers to the lies of Goebbels. Peter was chased round the world by Hitler, as British Consul in various places which he took, and cultivated a shrewd instinct of leaving at short notice. Andrew, a special pet and pal, was with the guns in France and Germany from "D" Day onward, and was officially responsible for clearing up the filthy Nazi camp of Belsen.

But, by the nature of the settlement made so long ago, it was all too little that I ever saw of my daughters in the period which really mattered most and both are now happily married. So it will be understood how grateful I was for my Annie's lovely offer. It has filled me with deep happiness and contentment which double my strength for my work, and it is to her that I dedicate this book.

What followed was very amusing. At the time when Annie made her offer, I was anything but a desirable object. Up to now, I had myself been surprised at my wonderful health. Till now, my dear boy, Peter, then at the British Embassy in Washington, had seen to my every need; but he was now transferred, as both he and I had hoped, to diplomatic service in Germany. My endless journeys between New York and Washington ceased to have the same point. I had sunk to a very low ebb. I was suffering from a throat complaint which seems common in New York; a thoughtless warning from a doctor sent me to a specialist who declared it to be unfounded; I was doing the best year of teaching I had ever done, but my lectures were interrupted by a rasping cough.

Annie was a leading spirit in the class, and they were all mobilized to salvage me. One of them offered me a room to rest in whenever I was tired. We had in the class a boy, Hans Rogger, the best student I ever had, as outstanding in character as in intellect. I was so far certainly the one shabby figure on the campus, and he went through my wardrobe with great delicacy, and brought me back to respectability. In all this, as in their study, my class were of one mind, and I have never seen their like.

## "But by Jingo if We Do"–

When I was a little boy of ten, the music halls and streets of London were ringing with the following song: the singer was a big, burly man with a booming voice known as the "Great MacDermott" and recognized as "The Statesman of the Music Halls." He sang:

> We don't want to fight, but by Jingo if we do,
> We've got the ships, we've got the men, we've got the
> money too

> We've licked the Bear before, and we'll lick the Bear
> again,
> The Russians shall not have Constantinople.

This is the historical origin of the word Jingo, as used to describe an inflamed national patriotism. Meanwhile, the British fleet and the Russian army stood locked in hostile contact just outside Constantinople, not as they are today locked in a would-be friendly co-operation at Berlin, but with guns trained for action.

Russia had just won decisively in a war provoked by brutal atrocities, practiced by the Turks on the Slav and Christian subjects of the Sultan–impaling was one of their favorite amusements. This had aroused in Russia nothing short of a national and religious crusade, which could not be mistaken for any scheme of dynastic aggression. Turgenev wrote perhaps the most charming of his novels *On the Eve* on this subject, following the flaming course of a young but fragile Bulgarian patriot through Russia, everywhere stirring to life the strong ties of a common race and a common faith. Dostoyevsky, ex-convict, reprieved on his day of execution as a "revolutionary," was fervently calling for the restoration of the Orthodox Cross on the Cathedral of Saint Sofia. Cherniayev, famous Empire builder in Central Asia, and Rodichev, the flower of Russian liberals, were alike volunteers with the Army of plucky little Serbia, which had taken the field in the cause of its kinsfolk. But the contention of Disraeli was that Russia must nowhere emerge upon the sea at any point between England and India.

This was the claim of Disraeli and "The Great MacDermott," to be repeated today by Mr. Churchill and Mr. Bevin. The British Liberals thought very differently from Disraeli and "The Great MacDermott." They followed with ardent enthusiasm the Midlothian campaign of Gladstone. The Turks, he maintained, had no national claim on

Constantinople; they were an "armed camp," only there as conquerors and should be expelled from Europe "bag and baggage."

The tension was relieved by an invitation from Bismarck, at that time the leading statesman in Europe. He offered to act as "an honest broker." Not the bones of a single Pomeranian grenadier, he said, should ever whiten in a dispute over Constantinople. All the great powers carried their dispute to Berlin. There, ultimately, the already concluded peace treaty between Russia and Turkey was cut in pieces and replaced by an international settlement. Bulgaria had been liberated from Turkey exclusively by Russian arms. The Treaty of Berlin cut it in half. Also, it set up a European guarantee of the new Bulgarian frontier directed against any Russian aggression, and in the end the new Bulgarian State was given a German sovereign, as had previously been done to Rumania on her liberation from Turkey. To Austria, who had taken no part in the war, Europe awarded a military occupation of Slavic Bosnia and Herzegovina.

This was a signal landmark in the long history of encirclement of Russia. From 1801, England had been committed to this policy, namely a preventive block on the issue of Russia from her land-locked frontiers: a policy which has later been given the name of a "cordon sanitaire." So Russia had won the war, but lost the peace, and she never forgot it. Two years later, by an overwhelming Liberal victory in England, Disraeli, the champion of the Treaty of Berlin, was finally swept from office.

These events really set me on the road to my own studies. When I was able to begin them I was from the outset convinced that it was useless to seek friendship of Russia on the principle that we British might be wherever we liked in the world, India, Burma or Egypt, but that Russia must always be kept from getting out to the sea. I thought this a monstrous proposition. But I also thought it a doctrine doomed to failure. Sea power and sea predominance were not to be won by the simple possession of harbors and the construction of a navy. Twice in modern history this has been made convincingly clear; first, in the long life and death struggle between England and Napoleon, and in the Second World War, what was it that made possible our retention of India, the victorious African march of Montgomery and the invasion of Normandy?

England had renounced this policy in the period which led up to the First World War, or there could have been no alliance; and meanwhile, "the Pomeranian Grenadier" had established himself pretty firmly at Constantinople, for in 1913 the command of the garrison of the city had been entrusted to a general sent from Germany, Liman von Sanders. On December 2, 1916, on the eve of the Russian Revolution, England and France officially agreed to the Tsar's acquisition of Constantinople after a joint victory in the war. Russia went out of the war after the Revolution and Russian policy of those days, with Trotsky's general threat of World Revolution, had chiefly itself to thank for the revival of the "cordon sanitaire." Since then, we have again been Allies in a common victory. On the day of writing this (May 7, 1947) I read that Mr. Bevin, while claiming international control of the Dardanelles, refuses to admit it for the Suez Canal. The old, old story; freedom of the seas, yes –see Atlantic Charter–but for us and not for you. And this time Britain hasn't the men or the money, and have we even the ships?

From this summary, which is also the main theme of this book, my view of the present sharp crisis in Anglo-Soviet-American relations and of the so-called "Truman doctrine" will have been anticipated. The question of the Dardanelles is a geographical one, not ideological. If it had been ideological, I should have expected American support to have gone to such sturdy exponents of Democracy as Holland, Norway, Czechoslovakia, or Finland who could do something for themselves and would be worthy partners in its defense. Turkey had already been driven by the Allied peoples of the Balkans in the wars of 1912-1913 from all but the European bank of the Dardanelles and has transferred her capital elsewhere. She retains only a military stranglehold on Russia's natural gateway. The new policy can only be recognized in Moscow as hostility to Russia as Russia.

In November 1940, Russia was in peaceful relations with Germany through a pact of non-aggression which was later broken by Germany in June 1941. We now learn several details of a negotiation between the two in Berlin during a courtesy visit of Molotov on November 12. Hitler, so we are told by some of his closest collaborators before their execution in Nuremberg, opened the discussion by declaring that the time had come to divide up the British Empire.[1] Molotov dissented from this view. Hitler proposed a deal to let Russia through to the seas, but only at the Persian gulf. Molotov, on the other hand, expressed an annoying interest, not only in the opening of the Dardanelles to Russia but even in that of the Sound, which the Germans declared to be intolerable. Hitler, so his fellow-workers tell us, proceeded without delay to fix May 15, 1941, for his invasion of Russia, a date which he changed later. The invasion brought the alliance of Russia with England.

Mr. Firlinger, the able Czechoslovak ambassador in Russia, and later Prime Minister of his country, told Mr. Edgar Snow: "For Russia victory means the opening up of gates which for centuries have barred it from free access to the rest of Europe." He thinks Russia will see to it that no force arises again to impose a barrier. No one knows more or understands more about Russia than the Czechs. Also to no

[1] See *Foreign Affairs* for October, 1946, "Light on Nazi Foreign Policy," by DeWitt C. Poole, pp. 130-154.

country is it more important that Europe should not be divided between East and West. They are necessarily inseparable from both. In my view, and I know them very well, no country can do more than theirs to serve the cause of Democracy as we understand it, far more than the Greek monarchy or the Turkish army.

The "Truman Doctrine," as I understand it, arose, very appropriately, in doctors' caps and gowns at Fulton, Missouri, when Mr. Churchill, after his crushing defeat in England, campaigned in this country for a rescue of the British Colonial Empire by the United States. As this plea was clearly enough geographical, it aroused no enthusiasm in Washington, and in his second speech in New York, he did some clipping of his wings. On that very day, the new British Prime Minister announced our frank and unqualified offer of independence to India, whose possession used to be the basis of our quarrel with Russia. I do not see that since then the Truman Doctrine has changed in character. Mr. Churchill has been quoted as having said: "The President seems to have come into line with us," that is, presumably, not with the England of Gladstone but with that of Disraeli and "The Great MacDermott." "But by Jingo if we do!" And America has the ships, the men, and the money required. The fantastic picture of an American democracy trembling before the logic of Communism has been boosted to the utmost, to make us forget that the challenge is geographical. For Russia it is not the beginning of the building of peace, but the first crucial step towards conflict, in which the geographical factors would all be in favor of Russia.

## GERMANY AND RUSSIA

But even this crucial question is not the most important of all. A greater one, and for us even more vital, is waiting for us just round the corner, and just as imperatively demands knowledge, consideration, and settlement before it is too late. That is the question of the future of Germany, and especially of the future relations of Germany with Russia, with which I began and end this book.

Germany remains in defeat the largest and most forcible national block in Europe, situated in its very center. Could there have been a Europe without it, or can there be now? In 1918, we made the enormous mistake of counting her out for generations, as reduced to a status of helots, working for the rest of us. Have we already forgotten with what extraordinary rapidity she was again up and at our throats? Forms of state may disappear; the material for them, in its substance, and quality, remains.

Again, though in a changed form, the question which has been before us all through, the question which decided the future in 1878 at Berlin, confronts us as before. And it has caught our triumphant and confused coalition napping as it did in 1918. Every widening of the breach between the Allies of yesterday does more to bring back Germany as a major factor into the middle of the picture. One has only to appeal to the testimony of each of the major spokesmen of the present "peace-making"—to Molotov on September 18, 1946, to Bevin speaking in the House of Commons, on October 22, 1946, and above all to Byrnes at Stuttgart on September 6, 1946.

Prime Minister Smuts of South Africa, speaking at Aberdeen on September 16, 1946, said that "the Germans must be reintegrated into our Western system, otherwise they are lost, and a dangerous vacuum will be created in Europe."

It is less than ever possible to peer into the future, but some things are plain enough. It is as clear as before that if Germany and Russia were united—that is to say, German industry and technicians with Russian agriculture, raw resources and now a new industry—they would be unbeatable.

Nor can Germany in the long run be kept disunited against her will. Previous attempts of the so-called "Concert of Europe" to split even such little countries as Rumania in 1855 or Bulgaria in 1878 failed as soon as the Concert itself split up and the little people were left to themselves.

Nor can Germany be occupied for ever; have we forgotten the irrestitible pressure on Congress to fetch the boys home as soon as the actual fighting was over? Germany would assuredly lean towards the side that stands for her reunion; that, at present, is Russia.

We have to face this issue and recognize the clash of interests. Facing Russia always means standing up to her; there is nothing else that the Russians respect. There is a great deal in our favor. It must first be clearly recognized that "free enterprise," as it is now interpreted here, in present-day America, has nothing to lean on in present-day Europe. There, the contest that is going on is one between Communism on the one side and on the other a socialist democracy fighting for freedom. Mr. Webster will have to recast his definition into something intelligible. No country that has been through the Nazi hell, especially the sturdier of the democracies, will for a long time lose its sense of what James Russell Lowell called "the worth of being free." And who knows whether that lesson may not yet have its value for Russia? The Russian and German peoples are not sympathetic to each other, and infinitely less so since the atrocities of the Nazi invasion.

The huge German people is singularly malleable to any national purpose. Their rapid comeback on us in the Second World War is a warning which perhaps means more for Russia even than for us. But these people are first-class workers, and they will go where they can find work. We learn [1] that at present there is a flourishing two-way traffic, in spite of all regulations, between the British zone of Germany and

[1] Margaret Peacocke in *British Magazine* for September, 1946.

the Russian: "Working hands" pass from the British to the Russian, and "mouths to feed" pass from the Russian to the British.

But democracy can only win with its own weapons, and not by borrowing those of the other side: by facing the argument and not by flying from it; by welcoming free speech and free self-criticisms and not by stifling them. And, so far, it is the lesson of two World Wars that democracy can stand the test. In both these wars it was the totalitarian state that best organized all its resources, and when it failed to achieve a swift victory, it was the first to come to the end of them. It is through the reserves of its strength that democracy can always come out the eventual winner. And this has a meaning as much moral as material. If it is to meet fearlessly any challenge which faces it, democracy cannot be limited by any definitions of past achievement but must be free to show the life that is in it, by calling upon all its rich potentialities for further development.

### AND NOW?

This book, as it stands up to this point, was sent to the printer before July 15. The vital months, through which its appearance has been delayed by printing and other difficulties, have seemed almost to bring the world to the verge of another war. I do not myself think that that catastrophe is now close upon us. Every instinct of the peoples of the world cries out against it, nowhere more than in Russia, and that must be well known to those on both sides of the line between East and West who are daring to step closest to the breaking point. Nor is Russia, at least, in any condition to fight for years to come. This interval was granted to us, as it was to Sodom and Gomorrah, before they met the fate of Hiroshima. Russia, in these years of maneuver since the fighting stopped, has wasted untold reserves of world good will. We on our side have an infinity of simple fact to learn and, above all, to digest and understand. Let us, at least, be grateful for this respite and make all use of it in time.

Thanksgiving recess 1947.

# Appendix

*All my life, I have been singing, rhyming and translating, and I append some examples, as part of a personal portrait.*

### TO G. L. P.

*My brother Lance and I always kept up a taunting birthday correspondence in verse. Each addressed the other as Dig (dogs). The following, written in the spring of 1916, from the Russian Front, was the last of my many so-called "Dogsy songs," to the tune of "John Anderson, My Jo John."*—

> My Digulet, my dog Dig,
> Across the Farnham grass,
> While tender fauns sit up to gaze
> The changing fieldsmen pass.
> The old leg-breaks come curling in;
> Does Beggar [1] care a fig?
> He hits you out to kingdom come,
> My dogulet, my Dig.
>
> My Digulet, my dog Dig,
> The goalposts fade in gloom;
> The infants of the Oxfordshire [2]
> Foresee the coming doom,

[1] R. B. Eggar, the hard-hitting captain of a neighboring village cricket team.

[2] The Oxfordshire Light Infantry Regiment, our stoutest football antagonists.

408

And crushing past their broken ranks,
    Comes through in fighting rig
The hero of my football days,
    My dogulet, my Dig.

My Digulet, my dog Dig,
    The second half wears through,
And Irman [1] calls, and up we start,
    And making straight for you;
And all are out to do their best,
    Our Nelson leads the jig;
We feel the breath of spring again,
    My dogulet, my Dig.

My Digulet, my dog, Dig,
    Years come and years depart,
And life and death draw closer yet
    The bond of blood and heart;
When victory peeps above the clouds
    And hopes and hearts and big,
I feel my partner by my side,
    My dogulet, my Dig.


TO E. E. B. ACROSS THE YEARS
1885-1935

Those sunlit days seem still so near,
    Alive with inspiration;
Your songs were coming year by year
    And each a new creation.
All round your puckish fancy played
    And filled our world with beauty,
And at the back one thought that stayed—
    The constant call to duty.

We could not know how stark and drear
    The years that lay before us,
What time we learned your wisdom here
    And sang your songs in chorus; [2]
Yet well we faced, by you well-schooled,
    That stern examination:

---

[1] Irman was General Irmaánov, commanding the famous Third Caucasian Corps. He is described in this book as "The Happy Warrior."
[2] The Upper Sixth Form of 1885 at Harrow.

With one that wrote,[1] and some that ruled,
    And one that led the nation.[2]

Your words come back like minute-bells
    In hours that claim decision,
With all the charm that in them dwells
    Of chivalry and vision.
They lift us still to "work and will" [3]
    From all that's poor and narrow;
Be sure, old friend, there is no end
    To all you taught to Harrow.

### TO GEORGE MC CAULEY TREVELYAN, O.M.[4]

(On his appointment as Master of Trinity College, Cambridge)

When I was at a school you know—
It's really rather long ago—
Two men there were who shaped our thought;
'Twas public spirit that they taught.

The first went where you now reside,[5]
And I again was at his side;
The second on the well-loved hill [6]
Stayed teaching you and others still.

And now a Freshman I would be—
In G O C. if that's still free [7]
So will you please put down my name?
I know you'll teach me just the same.

### WHEEDLING WARDLING

(One of my many family songs with its own tune.)

*Mr. Ward, tailor, was so extreme in his enthusiasm for the Liberal cause that apparently he never enforced payment from his clients of this persuasion. Conservatives were less likely to patronize him.*

Wheedling wardling, weedy Ward
To me in confidential tone

[1] John Galsworthy.
[2] Stanley Baldwin, three times Prime Minister.
[3] A quotation from Bowen.
[4] Our greatest living historian.
[5] Dr. Butler, Headmaster of Harrow, and later Master of Trinity.
[6] Mr. E. E. Bowen.
[7] My old rooms at G. Old Court, Trinity.

Declares that all his father's hoard
　　Right soon will be his own.
Wheedling wardling, weedy Ward,
Wheedling wardling, weedy Ward,
Thy father's hoard for thee is stored,
　　Thou greedy, weedy Wardling.

Whistling wardling, wistful Ward
About the shop with pleasure pries;
The stock, the stores he there explores,
　　Delight his eager eyes.
Whistling wardling, wistful Ward,
Whistling wardling, wistful Ward,
What dreams of joy thy senses cloy,
　　Thou blissful, wistful wardling!

Worldling wardling, whirling Ward,
Launch out on pleasures gay and free!
Thy father gives the shop he leaves,
　　Thou worthy heir, to thee.
Worldling wardling, whirling Ward,
Worldling wardling, whirling Ward,
Launch out and steer on gay career,
　　Uncurling, whirling wardling!

Warbling wardling, waltzing Ward
Unlocks in haste his father's tills—
Some notes are there, but these are rare;
　　The rest are Liberal's bills!
Wandering wardling, wan-faced Ward,
Wandering wardling, wan-faced Ward,
From that fell day he pines away,
　　**An ailing, wailing wardling.**

Wheedling wardling, tweedy-weedy Ward
Too speedy-weedy, greedy-weedy wardling.


ON THE FRONTIER WALL
*by*
Viktor von Scheffel—
Tune by Franz Abt

A Roman stood while all men slept
　　The frontier wall protecting;
Far from the fort his watch he kept,
　　To East his gaze directing.

What hostile shape moves o'er the stream?
    What sound comes softly nearer?
No note from some Horatian theme,
    But strains that chill the hearer—
Ho, hammer, hammer hard, athwack-awack-awack.
Upon thy shivering shirtless back!
    Thou naughty rogue! Thou naughty rogue!

He erst had woed a German maid,
    A Chattine chieftain's daughter,
In leathern jerkin, garb of trade,
    At forest tryst had sought her.
Now comes the vengeance, one, two, three!
    They scale the mound before him;
With yell like wildcats just set free,
    Their clubs come crashing o'er him.
Ho, hammer, hammer-hard, &c.

He drew his sword, his pilum tried
    As proven soldier wielded;
But vain were Roman wrath and pride;
    His strength to numbers yielded.
They bound him fast, and like a sack,
    They hailed him homeward hieing,
And when the cohort found his track,
    The distant pines were sighing,
Ho, hammer, hammer-hard, &c.

The Chattine parish Council see
    'Neath oak primeval seated,
Till Odin's feast of Yuletide be
    With blood of foe completed.
E'en now he feels how barbarous jaws
    Will champ the cold collation,
When fair-haired sweetheart pleads his cause
    With tears of indignation,
Ho, hammer, hammer-hard, &c.

Now all the tribe were deeply moved
    To see how each loved other;
"Unloose we straight her choice approved!
    We take him for our brother.
Her home be his! Be she his bride!
    Revenge henceforth be scouted!"
And over all the country-side
    As nuptial song they shouted,
Ho, hammer, hammer-hard, &c.

Ho, hammer, hammer-hard, athwack-awack-awack
Upon thy shivering shirtless back!
　　　Thou naughty rogue! thou naughty rogue!


### THE SHORTEST CRUSADE
*by*
Viktor von Scheffel
Tune by Franz Abt
(Favorite war cry of the Liverpool University Girls' Hockey Team)

Hildebrand and his son Hadubrand, Hadubrand
Rode in fine fury for Holy Land, Holy Land.
　　　Due out of Venice next morning.

Hildebrand and his son Hadubrand, Hadubrand
Soon lost their way on the lonely strand, lonely strand!
　　　There they sat flouting and scorning.

Hildebrand and his son Hadubrand, Hadubrand
Found a small pub called the Four-in-Hand, Four-in-Hand,
　　　Pub with good liquor from Burton.

Hildebrand and his son Hadubrand, Hadubrand
Came back next day from that lonely strand, lonely strand;
　　　Each had a hat and a shirt on.


### THE NIGHT RAID OF THE RODENSTEIN
*by*
Viktor von Scheffel
Tune by Franz Abt

Then Rodenstein cried: "Yo ho ho!
　　　My roaring host, stand by!
To Swilford Magna let us go
　　　To drink the parson dry.
Come out there! come out, you lazy lout there!
　　　And say for sake of heaven,
Oh can't I get a drop of drink
　　　At half past eleven.

That grave and godly clergyman
　　　Came growling to the door.
With bell and circle, book and ban
　　　He bade the sprites give o'er;

"Get out there! get out, ye lazy louts there!
　　And perish unforgiven
Or ere ye get a drop of drink
　　At half past eleven."

The Chief he chuckled, then replied:
　　"Sir Priest, a way I see;
A ghost to whom your door's denied,
　　Can turn your cellar key.
No Sir! With wine inside, not so, Sir!
　　Hurrah! We've all got by;
His cellar holds a decent stock;
　　We'll drink the beggar dry."

Poor pious soul, despair! despair!
　　Ill fiends thy powers deride.
In vain he shouted down the stair
　　Till vaulted roof replied:
"Ye swine there! a-swilling wine of mine there!
　　Ye greedy swine, for shame!
Oh leave me still a living wage,
　　As priests have right to claim!"

The clock struck four. From all the host
　　A hollow roar did swell:
"Sir Parson, now we've pledged our toast!
　　Sir Parson, now farewell
Out there! out from rousing bout there!
　　Thou Reverend Sir, goodbye!
We haven't left a drop of drink;
　　We've drunk the beggar dry."

That parson cried "Oh thanks! oh thanks!
　　You've left no drop for me?
Then I myself must join your ranks;
　　Field Chaplain there I'll be.
Out there! out to rousing bout there!
　　Sir Knight, I give you cheer;
For now you've had my wine, they'll want
　　Another parson here."


### DER SANG IST VERSCHOLLEN

The wine tastes no longer, the song seems to die;
　　All dazed and bemused round I roam.

The houses are tossing, the wind blows them high;
  The waves are a tossing with foam.

The clouds are all falling, the stars tumble down,
  The clouds have been swilling all night.
I stand like a rock, like the world's corner stone,
  Like a King in my freedom and right.

How swiftly the streets and the squares all go by!
  I knock at each door as they go;
I'm a wandering student, a poor devil I,
  Who'll shield me from weather and woe?

A girl on a balcony beckons afar,
  Her hair in the wind streaming bright;
I swing myself up, and I strike my guitar,
  Her eyes, how they shine through the night!

And she kisses and hugs me, I cannot tell why,
  I ne'er saw the damsel before.
I'm a wandering student, a poor devil I,
  Yet she hugs and she kisses me more.


### THE TOFF IN TOOLEY
(A literal translation of the *König in Thule* of Goethe, by Dr. John
Sampson, Librarian of the University of Liverpool.

*(This beautiful German lyric of Goethe defied translation. Samp-*
*son and I tried hard to do it—first separately and then together.*
*Then Sampson took it away and made one simple change—he*
*turned the German king into an English costermonger (peddler).*
*Here is the result, which is, I think, a great piece of English litera-*
*ture.)*

There was a Toff in Tooley,
  A gallous gent and brave,
To whom his dying Joolie
  A hansome tankard gave.

'Twas arf his soul, you twigged it?
  'E prized it, pore ole chap,
And ever, as 'e swigged it,
  'Is eyes turned on the tap.

But 'ere 'e kicked the bucket,
  Beset by kinsmen smug,

'E worned the blighters, "Chuck it!
    'Ands off that bloody mug!

"Not yet I've quit the tiller,
        So ax the boys to meet
And at my seaside villa
        I'll stand the crowd a treat."

Up stood the game old party;
        The beano'd gone off well;
'E downed his tiddly arty
        And 'urled the mug to 'ell.

'E saw the pot a sinkin,
        A-rinkin round the sea!
'Is old mince pies was blinkin,
        And never more drank 'e.


### LAZY LAD

*This Welsh song, discovered by the Celtic scholar, Glyn Davies,
for the Liverpool University songbook, is an essay in word spinning,
the same phrase reappearing in different connections. Under his
direction, I "Englished" it as follows:*

I went one day to my father's house,
        To get some Scouse,
        To my father's house.
I went one day to my father's house
        To get some Scouse
                For dinner!

My father said: "You shall have no food.
        For you're no good,
        You shall have no food."
My father said: "You shall have no food,
        For you're no good,
                You sinner!"

My fond mamma said: "Oh Dad, that's bad!
        You see that lad!
        Oh Dad, tha's bad!"
My fond mamma said: "Oh Dad, that's bad!
        You see that lad
                Grows thinner!"
*(With more on the same pattern)*

## TO A CHIEFTAIN

### (To John Macdonald Mackay)

*This salute, at his departure, was expressed in a tribute by John Sampson in Romany, which under his supervision I translated as follows:*

Seer and leader, midst the rest
Who are here to hymn thy praise
Be my tribute too expressed,—
Wandering tongue of upland ways.

Thine the dream, the vision thine
Which the blind were not to see;
Thine the eye that could divine
Realms that waited victory.

Learning's fair and sunlit ground
Thou couldst survey, where the free
Muster here on earth to found
Mansions for eternity! [1]

This thy dream! The vision blest
Dimly from the plain we see;
Who will win the shining crest?
Who will lead to victory?

Thou the clansmen didst array;
'Twas thy pibroch fired us there.
'Twas thy claymore carved a way
Through the legions of despair.

True to each that shared thy hope,
Raising, heartening, all thy clan.
Chief, on every battle slope,
Thou wert ever in the van. [2]

Now beneath the evening skies
Fall'n the strongholds, one by one;
Now against each high emprise
Write upon my tablets: "Done!"

Not to thee we bid farewells,
Leading still thy faithful few;
In thy work thy spirit dwells
Till thy largest dream came true.

[1] This verse is Oliver Elton's rendering.
[2] This verse is Elton's and mine.

DEGREE DAY AT LIVERPOOL UNIVERSITY
INTROIT

(Tunes: "Lohengrin" and "Widdecombe Fair")

March Derby march![1] On Stanley on!
You be our Chancellor, Dale be our Don!

Lord D., Lord D. get out your best gown!
Just the right men for our Doctor's degree
Have come up to see us in Liverpool town,
There's Rosebery,[2] Cromer,[3] John Morley,[4] John Burns [5]
Sir Archibald Geikie and all.

They'll pass no exam, for you'll spare them all fuss;
Just the right men for our Doctor's degree!
We hope that you'll be just as easy with us
As with Rosebery, Cromer, John Morley, John Burns,
Sir Archibald Geikie and all.

It soon will be quite a respectable roll—
Just the right men for our Doctor's degree!
For the Liverpool Varsity loves to take toll,
(*Here follow the names of all previous recipients, with a number of non-recipients popular with the students*)
With Rosebery, Cromer, John Morley, John Burns,
Sir Archibald Geikie and all.

*The students, packed in the two opposite galleries, shouted across to each other:*)
("How Came Archie Bald?" "By Degrees")


JOHN BURNS' BODY

John Burns' body was a waving of a flag;
John Burns' body was a leading of a rag;
John Burns' body the police were keen to lag;
As he went marching along, John, John.

John Burns' body broke the House of Commons' door;
John Burns' body took the House of Commons' floor;

[1] The Earl of Derby, Chancellor of the University
[2] Former Prime Minister
[3] Former British Commissioner in Egypt
[4] Famous Liberal British Statesman
[5] Famous Labor Leader

John Burns' body was the pillar of the poor;
    As he went marching along, John, John.

John Burns' body in the Abbey we will lay—
John Burns' body, when John Burns has gone away;
But John Burns' body takes a Doctor's gown today,
    As he goes marching along, John, John.

### ON THE TONG-TING-HOU
*(Made up for my children: own tune)*

The moon was shining bright upon the Tong-ting-hou,
        And the junk slid through
        With the sing-song crew,
And the lilies all were lapping in the creeks and on the shallows,
And the bells went dong-ding, dong-ding, dong-ding, too.
        On the Tong-ting-hou,
        On the Tong-ting-hou.
Oh, the moon was shining bright upon the Tong-ting-hou,
Oh the moon was on the waters of the Tonga-tinga-Tong-ting-hou.

The fluffy little islets on the Tong-ting-hou
        Were so clear to view
        In the deep, dark blue,
And the geese were splashing white amidst the foam and in the
    night
And all the bells went dong-ding-dong-ding, dong-ding, too.
        On the Tong-ting-hou,
        On the Tong-ting-hou.
Oh, the moon was shining bright upon the Tong-ting-hou.
Oh the moon was on the waters of the Tonga-tinga, Tong-ting-hou.

Go to sleep and lie at rest on the Tong-ting-hou,
        On the broad, calm breast
        Of the Tong-ting-hou.
In a high ecstatic doze, while the fishes bite your toes,
And the bells go dong-ding, dong-ding, dong-ding, dong-ding, dong-
    ding too!
        To the dream be true,
        Till the night pass through!
        On the Tong-ting-hou,
        On the Tong-ting-hou
Oh the moon was shining bright upon the Tong-ting-hou,
Oh the moon was on the waters of the Tonga-tinga Tong-ting-hou.

SONG OF THE THIRD RUSSIAN ARMY

Tidings from the Tsar of Germans,
　　Tidings to the Russian Tsar!
I will come and break your Russia,
　　And in Russia I will live.

Moody was the Russian Tsar,
　　As he paced the Moscow street;
Be not moody, Russian Tsar!
　　Russia he shall never have!

Gather, Gather Russian hosts!
　　William shall our captive be.
Cross the far Carpathian mountains!
　　March through all the German towns!


"WIGGINS"
*(To Alexander Zvegintsev in the Pinsk Marshes, Autumn, 1915)*
*Dear Wiggins was killed in his big plane very soon afterwards.*

Dear Wiggins, I thought,
When thinking of naught,
If we are to portray
Our life day by day,
This is the way that we ought.

The air hangs heavy; the spongy ground
Spreads ooze and vapour and mist around;
Each German attack with the bayonet repelled,
And so we stand to the ground we held
　　From Dvinsk to Minsk,
　　From Minsk to Pinsk
　　From Pinck via Svinsk [1]
　　To Vladímir Volynsk.

We squelch and splutter and can't get on;
The sluts of Slutsk look slushy and wan;
The Jew stands scratching his greasy skull;
The moony muzhík is heavy and dull,
　　From Dvinsk, etc.


[1] "Svinsk" (Swine-town) is an imaginary place through which all roads in this slushy region seemed to run. All the other names are of real towns.

No beer, no spirits to cheer dull care!
A bag of potatoes our only fare;
If you'll get rheumatics, then I'll get the gout,
And we'll see who's the better at sticking it out
  From Dvinsk, etc.

We sit here and grunt till the Germans shunt;
They jolly well wish they were out of the hunt.
If ever inclined to visit our front,
You'll find the best way is to start—in a punt
   From Dvinsk to Minsk
   From Minsk to Pinsk
   From Pinsk via Svinsk
   To Vladímir Volynsk.

### TO G. L. P.
*(From the Russian Front 1916)*

There was a man who lived at home
  And brewed aggressive beer.
The Germans shouted o'er the foam;
  "He charges much too dear!"

To ship the dumper's cheaper wares,
  The German fleet was planned,
Which they, to wreck the House of Pares,
  At Overcliff [1] would land.

The Tsar of Russia cried in haste;
  "This man shall not be downed;
For I remember how he paced
  The Kremlin's sacred ground."

At this the legions of the Tsar
  Went forth to meet the foe—
How many of these troops there are,
  I don't exactly know.

The Cossack galloped fierce and free;
  The Kalmyk waved a gun;
The bounds of ancient Germany
  Were overborne and won.

And wheresoere the conquerors went,
  The vats were all abolished,

---

[1] At Gravesend

The brewers to Siberia sent,
And German beer abolished.

----

And when the English lads advance
Through William's broken line,
And when the gallant boys of France
Have cleared Alsace and Rhine,

When Schwarz-weiss-roth has lost Schwarz-gelb [1]
And Prussia's ranks retreat
Till somewhere, close about the Elbe,
The allied armies meet,
Oh then, be sure, in all their hosts,
No lager shall be known;
The conquering hosts shall pledge their toasts
IN SHRIMP [2], and SHRIMP alone.

And this, the sovereign decree
That ends the giant tussle:
Let every pub in Europe be
A new "tied house" for RUSSELL.[3]

### TO AN AEROPLANE
(Anagram sent to E. V. Lucas of *Punch,* Master of Anagrams)

. . . of the clouds, thou . . . along,
Nor . . . for aught that . . . on thy flight.
No . . . are left but the hum of thy song,
Thou . . . of terrors, so frail, so strong,
That . . . for genius and feeds on light.
Now put him away in his . . . Goodnight!
. . . me these rhymes, if you find them inane,
But fill in the . . . before you complain!

*(The last line, with an additional "light," was supplied by a friend
of Mr. Lucas.)*

Anagram sent to Mr. Lucas,
*In answer to an inquiry as to the authorship of the first.*

Ye . . . of the Runic seer
Who wove the loom of sword and . . .

----

[1] The colors of Germany and Austria: black-white-red and black-yellow.

[2] Prophetic of the next war—hence thee awful rhyme.

[3] Russell's Brewery "SHRIMP BRAND." A "tied house" sells only one brand of beer.

Who firmly grips, nor roughly tears,
'Tis he that . . . my prickly. . . .
Then . . . no trouble! . . . me true!
My hidden name will leap to view!


### ANONYMOUS RUSSIAN VERSES

*On the appointment of Stürmer as Foreign Minister. In 1916
Stürmer replaced Sazonov, ironically called "Lord," as devoted to
England and the Alliance. Paléologue is the despondent French
Ambassador. The German names at the end are those of Ministers
or favorites of various reactionary Russian sovereigns. Nashchókin
was the greatest of Russian Liberal statesmen.*

Fresh comes Stürmer from the Palace
   In his diplomatic role.
Deutschland, Deutschland über Alles!
   Russland, Russland, lebe wohl!

Friend of Russia's bold freemasons,
   Cursing Petrograd and all,
See how Lord Sazonov hastens
   To his Finnish waterfall.

"Stürmer, Stürmer, very shocking!"
   Mutters Grey in far Hyde Park.
"He may say he is Nashchókin;
   I suspect he'll be Bismarck.

"Not for nought he looks a villain,
   Fur as red as fox—the pup!
And exactly like friend William,
   His moustachios twisted up."

As he dines with dames of fashion,
   "Ah, the future's full of fog,"
Ruminates in deep depression
   Our poor Monsieur Paléologue.

"Seems as if our work is undone;
   New appointments—very strange."
So Buchanan writes to London
   On the Ministerial change.

"Shall we run upon the shallows?
   Does it sound our friendship's knell?

Deutschland, Deutschland über Alles!
England, England, fare thee well!"

. . . . .

And when ends our warfare Punic,
Nesselrode, Kotzebue,
Biren, Ostermann and Munich,
Just as if they lived anew,

In their graves will shake with malice,
And above the bells will toll:
Deutschland, Deutschland über Alles!
Russland, Russland, lebe wohl!

### "PRETTY POLLY SEES TO IT"

*(On A. D. Protopopov; circulated in manuscript in 1916 on the*
*eve of the Revolution)*

#### ANONYMOUS

Premier Trepov keeps a bird,
Pretty politician,
Listening to every word
Of the Opposition.
Who says he agrees to it,
Who says he'll oppose it,—
Pretty Polly sees to it,
Pretty Polly knows it.

Times are so inferior,
Everyone grows thinner;
That concerns Interior—[1]
What we'll get for dinner.
Who has beef with peas to it,
Who goes short and shows it,—
Pretty Polly sees to it,
Pretty Polly knows it.

Too much for our puny forms,
Posing as dictator;
Profiteering uniforms
Pays a good deal better.[2]

[1] The food supply had recently been transferred from the Minister
of Agriculture to the Minister of the Interior, Protopopov.
[2] Protopopov had a cloth factory.

Make the man say please to it!
Make him pay; he owes it.
Pretty Polly sees to it,
Pretty Polly knows it.

You have full facilities
In our strange conditions,
Trader with abilities
Less than your ambitions
Show the pie! He'll freeze to it;
That's how you'll dispose it.
Pretty Polly sees to it,
Pretty Polly knows it.

What's our State authority,
Though there's plenty of it?
Much superiority,
Precious little profit.
Grisha [1] bends his knees to it;
Annie [2] asks: "How goes it?"
Pretty Polly sees to it,
Pretty Polly knows it.

Sow as you know how! And then
Crops will come, and pay too,
Keep your secret! Now and then
Bow the other way too.
Then, some sharp decrees to it,[3]
That will soon disclose it.
Pretty Polly sees to it,
Pretty Polly knows it.


TO SIR GEORGE BUCHANAN

*British Ambassador at the Revolution*
(Petrograd 1917)

*"Si fractus illabatur orbis,
Impavidum ferient ruinae"*
—Horace

[1] Gregory Rasputin.
[2] Anna Vyrubova, a go-between of the Empress and Rasputin.
[3] A decree dissolving the Duma was expected at any moment.

Nicholas sat on his golden throne;
An autocrat always should rule alone;
Nick couldn't autocrat, not for his life,
So he left all the power in the hands of his wife.
Sir George Buchanan, you'll please report
The kind regards of St. James's Court;
So one goes up and the other goes down
Till we all go tripping to London town.

The fair Alexandra, she didn't rule well;
She soon fell under a terrible spell,
And gave up the throne with never a sigh
To a roving monk [1] with a rollicking eye.
Sir George Buchanan, the King presents
His most perfunctory compliments;
So one goes up and the other goes down
Till we all go tripping to London town.

That riotous monk he ruled instead
Till a fortunate bullet went slick through his head;
Oh then King Demos rose in his might
To set up the order of truth and right.
Sir George Buchanan you'll please to say,
The King congratulates all the way.
So one goes up and the other goes down
Till we all go tripping to London town.

That poor King Demos very soon saw
He didn't know much about order and law,
So he found a young lawyer, with plenty of grit,
And asked him to sit on that throne—for a bit;
Sir George Buchanan said "Kerry,[2] my boy
King George could never such power enjoy";
So one goes up and the other goes down
Till we all go tripping to London town.

The day of settlement comes. We see
The frontline trench at the Embassy.
Midst showers of bullets, midst clouds of talk
Sir George Buchanan, he takes his walk—
If ever we felt our hearts in doubt,
We looked at you, and we saw it out,

[1] Rasputin was married and was never a monk, but he has often
been called one.
[2] Kerensky

For it's only as winners, and not tails down,
That we'll all go tripping to London town!

I think they'll agree, whoever you ask,
Sir George had a pretty impossible task,
But he easily sailed through this racket and rout—
By telling them just what he thought throughout;
And that is the reason, in all this stew,
Sir George Buchanan alone came through,
Though one went up and the other went down,
Till we all went tripping to London town.


### YOUNG LION'S EDUCATION

*Ivan Krylov, the most famous of Russian fabulists, died in 1844,
yet his fables are sometimes an uncannily exact description of later
events. This one, on the New Russia of 1917, I translated for Sir
George Buchanan in the summer of that year.*

God to the Lion gave the son for whom he pined.
    With animals you have acquaintance, maybe:
They're not at all like us! With us, a one-year baby
Is foolish, weak and small—both king's and common kind.
      A year-old lion, as one knows,
      Has long since left his swaddling clothes.
So at the year the king kept turning in his mind
How best ensure, his son shall not remain a dullhead
      And keep the royal fame unsullied,
That when the boy shall reign as he himself has done,
His people may not blame the father for the son.

Then whom is he to ask, or hire, or else compel
To teach the lad to know his kingly duties well?
      Entrust him to the fox?[1] The fox is clever
      But then, he loves to lie like ever!
To deal with liars, oh, the trouble that it brings;
And that, the lion thought, is not an art for kings.
      Perhaps the mole?[2] We're frequently assured
      What first-rate order in his house one finds;
He never moves a step until the ground's explored,
      And every grain that's served upon his board

[1] I think I knew the fox
[2] Milykov

Himself he cleans, himself he grinds.[1]
In short, report declares,
The mole's a mighty beast for miniature affairs.
But stay! Beneath his nose his eyes are sharp, 'tis said;
But can he see a yard ahead?
The moly system's good, but not for you and me;
And lion's realm is more than mole-hill, you'll agree!
Then why not try the pard?[2] The pard is bold and strong;
The pard can teach you tactics all day long.
But as to politics—on that he's not so clear;
Of civic rights he's not the least idea.
What kind of lessons then, can Leopard give in ruling?
A king must statesman be, and judge, and warrior too.
And fighting's really all the pard can do!
The children of the King are not for Leopard's schooling.
In short, then, all the beasts, and even the elephant [2]
Who in the woods that name for wisdom held
Which Plato bore of old,
All to the Lion seemed possessed of wits but scant
And most profoundly ignorant.


Well luckily or not—at present you must guess,
Acquainted with the King's distress,
King Eagle,[3]
Who had always shown
Great friendship for the neighbour throne,
Resolved to do his friend a service truly regal
And asked himself to educate the boy.
The Lion nearly jumped for joy;
And was there better luck, before or since,
Than this, to get a King as tutor for your prince?
With outfit new Young Lion starts
For foreign parts,
In good King Eagle's school
To learn to rule.
A year, two years go by. From all that pass that way,
There's not a word but praise; "He's wiser every day;
No scholar learned so fast"; 'tis so the birds all say.


At last the lad has served his final year.
The Lion sends to fetch him here.
The boy returns; the King bids all the beasts appear;

[1] General Kornilov.
[2] The S.R.'s, the peasants' revolutionary Party.
[3] Germany, Karl Marx.

When all have taken up their places,
His child he kisses and embraces
And thus addresses him: "Beloved son,
'Tis you must rule when I have done;
I'm facing for the grave; your life has just begun.
I'd gladly bid you reign instead of me;
But tell us first, that all may hear and see,
What various knowledge you have gained,
And how your subjects' weal, you think can be attained."
"Papa," replied the boy, "I've studied, thanks to you,
What none among you ever knew,
And from the eagle to the quail,
How best each breed of bird you'll raise,
Their favourite food, their various ways,
The eggs that each one lays,
And all that each requires—on not one point I'll fail.
Please read what this certificate attests! [1]
'Tis not for nought the birds all cry.
I'd fetch the stars from out the sky;
Then, if 'tis your intent that I this realm should sway,
I'll start and make my subjects straight away
Build nests!"

The Lion groaned, and all the beasts the same;
The Council hung their heads for shame.
Now, to the aged King, too late 'twas plain,
The studies of his son were vain
And scant the wisdom in his words,
That small's the need to know the customs of the birds
For him whom nature set the beasts to regulate,
And this the highest lore that monarch can command,
To understand
Your native land
And all that makes your country great.

### A PROPHECY

*(These remarkable verses were written by the brilliant young
Russian poet, Michael Lermontov, in 1831. They are an exact picture of Russia in 1918.)*

A year shall come, our blackest year of all,
In which the crown of Russia's Tsars shall fall;
The mob shall change its old, confiding mood,
And death and blood shall be our daily food.

[1] Membership ticket of the Communist Party

Law overthrown no more shall guard the lives
Of guiltless children and of tender wives;
Then stinking corpses shall send forth disease
To stalk throughout our wretched villages.
Men waving kerchiefs as they call you out;
Our land shall then lie parching in the drought.
Red flames shall glow upon our streams that hour,
And then shall stand revealed the Man of Power;
And thou shalt know him, and shalt understand
For whom he holds the dagger in his hand;
And this is woe to thee! Thy tears, thy plaint
For him that day shall make but merriment;
And all in him is ghastly, all is gloom,
Even to the sable cloak and lofty plume.

## WOG

*(Wog was my little daughter of 12, who was to come as an aero-
plane, with a company of little sister planes, to get me out of any
difficulty. I was in mid-Siberia, wondering how to get back to England by passing somehow around Bolshevik Russia.)*

Last night in Omsk, beloved Wog,
    I felt inclined to roam;
As I returned, a large black dog
    Accompanied me home.
The open prairie to relieve,
    There's scarce a dozen trees,
But from the river bank at eve
    Comes quite a pleasant breeze.

I looked! Across the boundless plain
    Came something through the air;
I stopped to gaze, and gaze again,
    And wondered what was there.
It seemed an India-rubber thing
    That flopped, and wheeled about,
And as it hung upon the wing,
    It's legs came kicking out.

In careless mood it lightly hurled
    A bomb upon the town;
The strongest building in the world
    Was sure to tumble down.

Said I: Why there's my Wog at play.
  Why, bless my soul, I'm right!
For there, about a mile away,
  Were ten more Wogs in sight.

They circled through the cloudless sky,
  Then swept straight down on me;
They caught me up and bore me high
  Above the polar sea.
The icebergs gleamed beneath our flight,
  The bears gave sullen roar,
We swooped—upon the Pole to light—
  Then journeyed on once more.

At last the cliffs of England's coast
  Along the horizon lay,
And all the attendant Woggie host
  Ranged round in close array.
It was a dream, my Wog was there
  To help her Daddy through;
But though some dreams dissolve in air,
Yet loving thoughts go everywhere,
  And some kind dreams come true.

**S. W.**

*In the visiting book at Seton-Watson's Scottish retreat in the Island of Skye.*

Scot and Saxon sallied forth:
Scot went South, and Saxon North.
The charm which drew them was the same:
The selfsame tutor taught the game.[1]
Scot and Saxon stand together
In Balkan or Siberian weather!

*Dedication to Seton-Watson
of my "Fall of the Russian Monarchy"*

---

[1] German penetration

## SCOTO VIATORI
## COMES VIAE

REPORT OF A DEBATE ON THE SENATE OF LIVERPOOL UNIVERSITY ON THE
EXTENSION OR CURTAILMENT OF THE INTERVAL BETWEEN LECTURES

> Released at last from Postgate's clutch
> The student cries; Too much! Too much!
> But when our Lehmann takes the floor,
> The student shouts and screams for more.
> But Watkinson, who's far from terse,
> Must lie beneath a special curse;
> His students crave for "smoke—or worse." [1]

(Posted in the Senior Common-Room, at King's College, London
in 1934)

On Walter Matthews, Dean of King's College, 1918-1932, Dean of
Exetor, 1931-1934, and Dean of St. Paul's from 1934

> With wisdom that holds and enthralls,
> With humor that charms, never galls,
> The Church always HATH USE [2]
> For masters like Matthews
> And maketh him Dean of St. Pauls.
>
> For years it was here that were seen
> That face and that mind so serene,
> And so let King's College
> Rejoice in the knowledge
> 'Twas here that he learnt how to Dean.

[1] With bated breath, we all asked what was "worse."
[2] Grin and bear it, or else find a substitute rhyme?

THE COUNTIES OF ENGLAND [1]
## To G. M. Trevelyan

*"La pianta uomo cresce forte in Inghilterra"*
*adattato da Vittorio Alfieri*
*ed. illustrato nelle opere di Giorgio Treveliano*

There's not a stretch of English soil
    Whose past is mean and poor,
And every county brings its spoil
    To enrich the varied store.

| | |
|---|---|
| The knightliest deeds a bard could sing | Tintagel |
|     Our ancient Cornwall saw; | |
| In Berks arose the Etheling | Wantage |
|     Who taught our England law; | |
| On Cheshire stream the Peaceful King | Chester |
|     Six kinglets held in awe. | |
| On Sussex height in Senlac fight | Hastings |
|     The bastard wins the day | |
| In Cumberland, the Scotsman's plight | Burgh on Sands |
|     Did royal death allay. | |
| Our Monmouth lad all fears defied | Monmouth |
|     And gave the Frenchman sport; | |
| Northamptonshire, what royal pride | Fotheringhay |
|     Thy fatal days cut short; | Naseby |
| In Middlesex, by Thames's side | Hampton |
|     The Dutchman held his court. | |

| | |
|---|---|
| In Durham Saints and Bishops taught | Cuthbert & Bede |
|     How best to live and die, | |
| And still to words with wisdom fraught | Lightfoot & |
|     The Durham chimes reply. | Westcott |

| | |
|---|---|
| An Earl of Leicester, for a time, | Leicester |
|     His sovereign Lord could sway; | |
| But Suffolk butcher, in his prime, | Ipswich |
|     In exile pined away; | |
| Not long did Essex plunderer hold | St. Osyth's |
|     The guerdon of his guile, | |
| And Yorkshire Earl, though rough and bold, | Wentworth |
|     Not long controlled our Isle. | |
| By feats of arms, a squire of Hunts | Huntingdon |
|     Expires as England's Lord; | |
| But bitter disappointment fronts | Eastnor & |
|     Statesmen of Hereford; | Brampton Bryan |

[1] Modelled on the "Armada" of Trevelyan's great-uncle Lord Macaulay. The reader is invited to see how many of the names he can guess.

The Wiltshire Commoner in vain                 Old Sarum
    Deserves an Empire's thanks
And Jew of Bucks must share his reign           Hughenden
    With Grand Old Man of Lancs;                 Liverpool

---

We link with Devon sea-dog's name              Tavistock
    The freedom of the wave;
A gentleman of Kent can claim                   Westerham
    Dominion for his grave,
And still undimmed the Eastern fame             Market Drayton
    A lad from Salop gave;
A Worcester statesman came to hew               Daylesford
    His conquest into shape;
A Hertford stripling's fancy flew               Bishop's Stortford
    From Cairo to the Cape.
In Oxford glades, with victory blest,           Woodstock
    The general sought repose;
But Norfolk sailor sank to rest                 Burnham Thorpe
    Before his conquered foes.

---

The Warwick poacher could descry                Stratford on Avon
    The mysteries of man;
The Lincoln scholar's searching eye             Woolthorpe
    Could Nature's secrets scan.
Plain were the mysteries of heaven              Cambridge
    To Cambridge poet's mind;
To Bedford cobbler's faith was given            Elstow
    The mission of our kind.
By Stafford critic's side were found            Lichfield
    A noble lettered band;
In Somerset an instinct sound                   Glastonbury
    The English novel planned;
And poet gathered poets round                   Rydal
    His home in Westmoreland.
Notts baron, rebel of romance,                  Newstead
    Rode high on passion's tide;
A lady miniatured in Hants                      Chawton & Steventon
    The pleasant country side.
A Welshman in a Surrey vale                     Mickleham & Dorking
    The world of whims portrayed,
And Dorset yeoman told the tale                 Dorchester
    Of rustic man and maid.

---

Her Geordie on Northumberland                   Newcastle
    Bestowed the gift of steam;

The spinning loom a wise man planned    Wirksworth
   Beside a Derby stream.
The homes of England! O'er the seas
   The world resounds their fame
And Belvoir's lordly terraces    Home of the Duke of
   Re-echo Rutland's name.    Rutland, tho not in
The sports of England! 'Tis their due    Rutland
   That foreign lands acclaim;
Still fresh in loyal Gloucester's view    Thornbury
   The Doctor's Jovian frame.[1]
The vigour of our island free
   Has girdled all the earth;
Where, save in wondrous Italy,
   Has so much life had birth?

### TO BASIL PARES

I want to write some lines of verse on
A singularly pleasing person;
And I must say, there's not another
Whom I'd prefer to have as brother.

Once, in the worst of Flanders' weather
He stitched the wounded Blues [2] together;
And now he sits and grants them pensions
Of quite inordinate dimensions.

He's got a lot of lively children,
Whose frolics sometimes are bewilderin';
I won't attempt to strike a balance
Of all their tricks and all their talents.

And now that winds and skies will soften,
I hope to see his face more often,
And that is for a simple reason:
That Spring has brought my Woking season.

### FOR ALL EVENTS

*(To a young wife expecting her first baby. She had chosen "Peter"
as the name for a boy; and her husband, who was more fanciful,
had selected "Idothea" if it was a girl. I had promised to contribute
an ode, but the occasion lagged. "Peter" arrived on the day of her
receipt of these verses.)*

You'll say there could be nothing sweeter
Than the angelic face of Peter.

[1] Dr. W. G. Grace, the most famous of English cricketers.
[2] The Royal Horse Guards.

He isn't quite as big as we are—
No more, of course, is Idothea.

The mystery of Alpha-Beta
Will be five minutes' work for Peter—
The kings of England down to G.R.
Will all be learnt by Idothea.

Alas! the one regret of Peter
Is this—that he may never meet her;
Unless—and who can tell us whether—
They both of them arrive together!
Perhaps they will—on a two-seater!

BEASTS IN COUNCIL

*by*

IVAN KRYLOV (d. 1844)

*(On the Munich Conference of September 29, 1938)*

Whatever rules you may devise,
Once put them in the hands of men that have no conscience,
    The part which most to them applies
They're sure to find some trick for turning into nonsense.

Wolf asked King Lion for the charge of all the sheep.
    By Fox's friendship and address [1]
    A work was spoken to the Lioness,[2]
But, as the wolf's good name is doubtful, more or less,
That no one should complain, court favour went too cheap,
    They planned that subjects 'neath the Lion's sway
        Should duly meet one day,
    When all and sundry they would ask
In what the wolf they'd praise, in what would take to task.
They summon all the beasts; the question is preferred,
And each, by rank, is asked, till every voice is heard;
    Against the wolf there's not a word.
So Wolf is put in charge of all the sheep dominion.

    But what were all the sheep [3] about?
    For lots of sheep were summoned too, no doubt.

[1] Mussolini was especially thanked by Mr. Chamberlain for his part in arranging the meeting

[2] ? Lady Astor.

[3] The Czechs, whose fate was decided at Munich, were not invited to the conference

> Well, no; they quite forgot, and left them out:—
> The very first to ask for their opinion!


### TO PETER PARES

*(First and last British Consul in Bratislava, Slovakia, until driven out at short notice by Hitler in 1939. An imaginary visitor to the Consulate speaks:)*

> Sir, I am of the British nation
> And Consuls are for consultation;
> But yours is such a restless town,
> I simply cannot settle down.
>
> I see, when walking down the street,
> A scowl on every face I meet;
> In fact, as I was coming here,
> A bullet whistled past my ear.
>
> However, some kind friend I met
> Remarked to me, "You needn't fret!
> In all your troubles, all your cares,
> You simply go to—Peter Pares."


### BROWN-BEARDED BEVAN

*(Brown-Bearded Bevan is an imaginary servitor of my niece, Dinah; he always starts with a muddle and in the end proves really useful. There is a whole library in verse on his bungles and successes. In 1944 she had just sent him to suggest ideas in Washington.)*

> Bevan said: "I've won the war.
> And that is what I came here for;
> So now I'll try to 'win the peace.'
> But troubles, troubles never cease.
> I, with my usual circumspection,
> Note there's a national election.
> So now I'll travel day by day,
> And in my cozy, furry way
> With bearded charm and counsel wise
> Compose all discords that arise;
> Hold meetings too in every town
> And calm the angry passions down."
>
> In Milwaukee
> Talkee, talkee.

Down to zero! Rather pawky!
Don't forget to leave your door-key!

Through Iowa,
Slower, slower!
Temperature getting lower!

Minnesota,
I'm a voter.
Please to put me on your rota!
I'll be sure to do my quota!
Then go on to North Dakota

Wandering onward throgh Nebraska;
If you like that girl, then ask her—
Bevan, Bevan, fie, oh fie!
Please restrain that roving eye!
I respect your exhortation!
Just a moment's aberration!
Dinah is my delectation.

Raise the banner
In Montana!
Then come back to Indiana:
I'm devoted to Diana.

In the gloaming
Through Wyoming
Westward roaming,
Oh, how free!
No embargo
On this cargo
From Chicago
To the Sea!


ST. HELENA

*The ode of P. J. de Beranger on the death of Napoleon in 1821.*

———

Wandering in exile, far from comrades all,
I found a Spanish ship which homeward plied;
Mean wreckage of a noble empire's fall,
On India's shores I had sought my grief to hide.
Six years have sped; the past forgotten be!
On dancing waves the day its radiance throws—
France, yet again, poor soldier, thou shalt see;
There waits a son thy dying eyes to close.

Hark! St. Helena! 'Tis the pilot's cry!
    'Tis there my hero's bitter days are past!
Good shipmates, here all thoughts of hate must die
    Join me to curse the jail that holds him fast.
Nought can I do to set my hero free;
    Now not e'en death a path to victory shows,
France, yet again, poor soldier, thou shalt see;
    There waits a son thy dying eyes to close.

Say does he sleep, resistless cannon ball
    That erst ten thrones at one fell crash laid low!
Can he not rise in terror o'er them all,
    Bear them to earth, and die in glory so?
Ah, from yon rock e'en hope itself must flee;
    No more the eagle heaven's own secret knows—
France, yet again, poor soldier, thou shalt see;
    There waits a son thy dying eyes to close.

If some strange ship is signaled from their shore,
    "Can it be he?" they cry in vain alarm?
Is he come back to claim his world once more?
    Haste we to bid two million soldiers arm!
While, racked with pain, perchance that moment he
    Bids France adieu and flies from all his woes—
France, yet again, poor soldier, thou shalt see
    There waits a son thy dying eyes to close.

Victory flagged to follow him so fast.
    She lagged behind; he would not linger yet.
Then twice betrayed, great-hearted to the last,
    Ah, but his path with serpents was beset!
No laurel wreath but needs must poisoned be;
    Death is the mead that victory bestows,—
France, yet again, poor soldier, thou shalt see;
    There waits a son thy dying eyes to close.

By genius great, and great by native worth,
    Thought he in sceptered pride to loftier seem?
Far, far above the kings of all the earth,
    There on his lonely reef he reigns supreme,
Twixt a world dying and a world to be,
    Like a vast beacon there his glory shows—
France, yet again, poor soldier, thou shalt see
    There waits a son thy dying eyes to close.

Good shipmates, say! what is it meets the sight?
   'Tis the black flag, I tremble as I gaze.
What? He to die? Glory, thou art widowed quite!
   Around me weep his foes of former days,
Far from yon rock in silence let us flee,
   In the dull west, the day's last radiance goes—
France, yet again, poor soldier, thou shalt see:
   There waits a son thy dying eyes to close.

### NAPOLEON

*(Pushkin's great ode on Napoleon, 1821, translated for the Pushkin centenary in Russia in 1937)*

The marvelous destiny is spent.
   He is gone. The great man is no more.
Sunk in the gloom of banishment,
   Napoleon's age of storm is o'er.
He is gone, the sovereign dethroned;
   Gone, Victory's most favoured son;
And for the man the world disowned
   Now has posterity begun.

Thou who in blood didst write the name
   Which long, full long, will fill our minds,
Sleep in the shadow of thy fame
   Amidst thy waste of waves and winds—
A most magnificent of graves.
   Where rest thine ashes in their urn,
No more the hate of nations raves,
   The immortal fires of glory burn.

So late o'er our dishonoured lands
   Thy ravening eagles held their course;
So late the kingdoms on all hands
   Went down beneath thy fatal force.
Alert to thy capricious mood,
   The rustling standards boded ill,
And thou upon a world subdued
   Didst lay the bondage of thy will.

When in the dawn of hope at last
   The world from slavery awoke
And when the idol of his past
   The Gaul threw down with furious stroke,
When on the place of riot lay
   The royal dead of ancient name,

And the inevitable day,
    The great, glad day of freedom came,—

Thou, while the raging people stormed,
    Thine own amazing part couldst find
And, in the noblest hopes it formed,
    Couldst feel contempt for all mankind.
Thy daring spirit could assure thee
    Of thy strange lot, with all its harm;
The dream of boundless power could lure thee,
    Even with its disenchanted charm.

The people to new vigour stirred
    Was stemmed in its tumultuous course;
The new-born freedom at thy word
    Fell straightway dumb and lost its force;
Amidst thy slaves thou couldst allay
    Thy thirst of endless power unchecked,
Didst lead their legions to the fray,
    Their glittering chains with laurels decked.

And France, to glory now a prize,
    No more those noble hopes would claim,
And fixed her fascinated eyes
    Upon her own resplendent shame.
To bounteous feast their swords were led;
    At thy approach all crashed in doom;
Europe was falling; o'er her head
    Was borne the slumber of the tomb.

'Twas done! In majesty of shame
    We saw the Titan o'er her stride.
Tilsit! at that opprobrious name
    No more need pale the Russian's pride;
Tilsit the arrogant hero crowned
    With his last glory: but the chill
Of rest, the irk of peace profound
    Stirred Fortune's child to venture still.

Vain dreams! Thy marvelous mind to ply
    And goad to doom, who found the art?
Throned in thy daring thoughts so high,
    Couldst thou not read a Russian heart?
Unwarned of that great-hearted fire,
    Thou still couldst idly calculate
That peace we wait at thy desire
    And learnest Russia all too late.

Russia, our queen of war, take heart!
    Again thine ancient rights reclaim!
Bright sun of Austerlitz, depart!
    Rise, our great Moscow, rise in flame!
Gone are times of bitterness;
    Our tarnished honour still we save;
Russia, thy glorious Moscow bless;
    War! War! Our pledge is to the grave.


With hands benumbed that grasp the prize,
    Still clutching fast his iron crown,
He sees the gulf before his eyes
    And reels and reels and so goes down.
The hosts of Europe are in flight,
    And all around the bloodstained snows
Proclaim the ruin of their might,
    And thaws with them all trace of foes.


Then all the world flamed up in wrath;
    Europe at last threw off her yoke;
And straight upon the tyrant's path
    The curse of all the nations broke.
The people's vengeful hand upraised
    The giant sees across his track
And every wrong is now appraised,
    And every injury paid back.


Redeemed are all his tyrannies,
    The wounds his feats of war have left,
By exile under foreign skies,
    Of freedom, life and joy bereft;
And to the sultry prison isle
    Comes some day one of northern race
And there in words that reconcile
    A tribute on that rock shall trace,—


Where, ever gazing o'er the sea,
    He called to mind the clash of arms,
The icy midnight misery,
    The sky of France with all its charms,—
Where sometimes in his wilderness,
    Forgetting war and fame and throne,
He mused alone in deep distress
    On that sweet infant of his own.

Yes, cover with deservèd shame
 That poor-souled creature who this day
Shall trouble with his stupid blame
 The uncrowned spirit passed away.
Praise him! For he our people showed
 How high the lot which ours should be,
And from his prison gloom bestowed
 The gift of lasting liberty.

### VERSES

*(Written, for a reminder, in 1898 on the eve of my first journey to
Russia)*

"All my fresh springs shall be in thee."

Awake! thou flame within my heart
 That I still more may be
That which I now am scarce in part,—
 Which yet is all of me.

I have no life, but that I live
 By thee and thee alone,
That so whate'er I have or give
 May always be thine own.

Long years of toil and conflict sore
 And living joys gone by,
The far strange country travelled o'er
 By one who once was I:—

With these, the thousand flowers to cull
 By paths where I must go:
The thousand faces beautiful
 Which I someday may know:—

All that the past has stored in vain,
 All that these blind eyes see,
And what still waits of joy or pain,
For both alike shall count for gain,—
 Can only live by thee.

I feel it still, the heavenly flame,
 For work, for toil, for strife;
It puts my parleying heart to shame,
 That glorious flame of life.

And though this flesh its glow receive,
    'Tis burning pure and bright
To shine when He, by whom we live,
    Shall say: Let there be Light!

We made it not, no earthly powers
    That heavenly source supply;
Breathed from a soul more strong than ours,
    It lives when flesh must die.

And if it shine more pure, more bright,
    From weakening flesh more free,
So, by God's gift, we earn our right
    To immortality.

# INDEX OF NAMES

445